Language, Cognition, and the Brain

Insights From Sign Language Research

Language, Cognition, and the Brain

Insights From Sign Language Research

Karen Emmorey
The Salk Institute for Biological Studies

LEA LAWRENCE ERLBAUM ASSOCIATES, PUBLISHERS
2002   Mahwah, New Jersey   London

Lawrence Erlbaum Associates, Inc., Publishers
10 Industrial Avenue
Mahwah, NJ 07430

Cover design by Kathryn Houghtaling Lacey

Library of Congress Cataloging-in-Publication Data

Emmorey, Karen.
   Language, cognition, and the brain : insights from sign language research /
Karen Emmorey.
      p.   cm.
   Includes bibliographical references and indexes.
   ISBN 0-8058-3398-6 (cloth : alk. paper) — ISBN 0-8058-3399-4 (pbk. : alk. paper)
   1. Sign language.   2. Language acquisition.   3. Biolinguistics.   I. Title.

P117 .E46   2001
419—dc21   2001031551
                                                                   CIP

Books published by Lawrence Erlbaum Associates are printed on acid-free paper,
and their bindings are chosen for strength and durability.

Printed in the United States of America
10   9   8   7   6   5   4   3   2   1

For Jon, Kay, and Tom Linker

Contents

Preface

The aim of this book is to illustrate what can be learned about human language, cognition, and the brain by studying signed languages and the Deaf people who use them. The book brings together and summarizes new and recent research and is written for the general reader who has an interest in sign language, linguistics, cognitive psychology, or behavioral neuroscience. The introductory chapter (chap. 1) lays out and debunks common misconceptions about sign language that are still present today. This chapter also describes the "homesign to pidgin to creole" progression that characterizes the emergence of sign languages and highlights what the study of signed languages reveals about the nature of language genesis and the processes that give rise to the birth of a language. The second part of chapter 1 characterizes the composition of the deaf population in the United States and the culture of Deaf people who are the primary users of American Sign Language (ASL).

Chapter 2 summarizes recent major findings concerning the structure of ASL from the sublexical (phonological) level to the level of discourse. The chapter outlines aspects of signed language structure that parallel those found in spoken languages and highlights linguistic variation attributable to the visuospatial modality. These studies help us to understand what aspects of linguistic structure are universal to human language and what aspects are influenced by the aural–oral or the visual–gestural modalities of linguistic perception and production. In addition, this chapter provides the linguistic background for the remainder of the book.

Chapter 3 focuses on the unique functions of space in signed languages and characterizes ASL "classifier" constructions that are used to indicate motion and spatial location. We investigate both the locative and non-locative functions of signing space in order to understand the interface between spatial concepts, abstract conceptual structure, and linguistic expression.

Chapter 4 explores how the modality in which a language is expressed affects the psychological mechanisms required to decode the linguistic signal, from perception to word recognition to sentence processing. The second part of the chapter focuses on issues concerning sign language production. We examine how signers monitor their signing ("ums" and "uhs" in ASL), whispering and shouting in sign, sign errors or "slips of the hand," and we ask (and answer) the question: Do signers gesture?

Chapter 5 addresses several questions: Do Deaf children learn to sign in the same way that hearing children learn to speak? How does language modality affect the nature of the language acquisition process? What is the relation between gesture and sign during development? Is there "motherese" in sign language? This chapter traces the acquisition of ASL from manual babbling in infancy, to the acquisition of syntax and morphology in early childhood, to narrative and conversational development.

Chapter 6 examines how late language acquisition affects grammatical knowledge, language processing, cognitive abilities, and the neural organization for language. With respect to language processing, we tease apart those aspects of the processing system that require early linguistic input to function efficiently and those aspects of the processing system that are more robust and remain relatively unaffected by late acquisition. We further explore whether and how late language acquisition affects non-linguistic cognitive processes, such as working memory and the ability to understand false beliefs (theory of mind). This chapter also discusses the contribution of the child to the language acquisition process, summarizing recent research concerning deaf children who have little or no consistent language input.

Chapter 7 explores what the study of sign language can tell us about the architecture of working memory. Working memory is traditionally divided into two major domains: verbal and visuospatial. This distinction reflects a fundamental division in human information processing. However, there is an ambiguity in how this division is defined. On the one hand, it could be defined in terms of sensory modality—auditory representations versus visual representations. On the other hand, it could be defined in terms of language—linguistic representations versus nonlinguistic depictive representations. This ambiguity raises questions about the nature of representations in working memory and the architecture of the system itself, for example, what role does sensory modality play in shaping working memory? What role does linguistic structure play? This chapter attempts to answer these questions and reviews recent experiments on working memory for sign language.

Chapter 8 presents studies indicating that the habitual use of a visuospatial language such as ASL has an impact on nonlinguistic aspects of cognition. Three domains of visuospatial cognition are discussed: motion processing, face processing, and mental imagery. Within each of these domains, there is strong evidence that experience with sign language enhances specific cognitive processes. These findings have important implications for the relationship between language and thought and for the modularity of mind hypothesis.

Finally, chapter 9 illuminates the nature of hemispheric specialization for sign language and related cognitive systems, examines *within* hemisphere organization for sign language, and addresses central issues concerning neural re-organization and plasticity. The chapter summarizes results from lesion studies, from brain-imaging studies (fMRI, ERP, and PET), and from studies using standard hemifield techniques. Research in this field is rapidly advancing, and this chapter provides a state-of-the-art summary of our current understanding of the brain systems that underlie the comprehension and production of sign language. The implications of this research for the nature of neural plasticity and the determinants of brain organization are discussed in depth.

The primary goal of this book is ambitious: to further our understanding of human language and its cognitive and neural underpinnings. Each chapter focuses on what the study of signed languages can reveal about central issues within a given linguistic or cognitive domain. Because of the breadth of topics covered in this book, a list of two to four references is provided at the end of each chapter as suggestions for further reading. It is hoped that the ideas and research presented here provide a springboard for further research that takes advantage of the unique insights that can be gained from the study of signed languages.

ACKNOWLEDGMENTS

This book has benefited from the insights and inspirations of several people. I owe a particular debt of gratitude to Edward Klima, who read each chapter draft as it came off the printer. Ed thought deeply about the many issues raised and provided insightful, reasoned, and constructive comments throughout. Pim Levelt also read the entire manuscript, and his comments and suggestions improved the focus, clarity, and theoretical import of the book. Dan Slobin has inspired me with his enthusiasm for the book from the very beginning. I would also like to thank the following colleagues for providing critical feedback and helpful comments on individual chapters of the book: Ursula Bellugi, Diane Brentari, David Corina, Karen Dobkins, Elisabeth Engberg-Pedersen, Susan Fischer, Greg Hickok, Judy Kegl, Diane Lillo-Martin, Rachel Mayberry, Stephen McCullough, Irit Meir, Richard Meier, Jill Morford, Carol Neidle, Carol Padden, Laura Petitto, Ethan Remmel, Wendy Sandler, Ann Senghas, Dan Slobin, Margaret Wilson, and Inge Zwitserlood. Of course, none of these people should be held accountable for my failure to heed their advice or for any remaining errors or misleading statements.

Graphics and illustrations are an integral and essential aspect of each chapter, and I would like to thank the following people for their skill and expertise in creating illustrations for this book: Lucio Cervantes, Kenny Hill, Yen Ma, Stephen McCullough, and Jonas Schurz-Torboli. I also thank the sign language models for their cooperation in creating the sign language illustrations and experimental stimuli. I also would like to thank Ursula Bellugi for permission to reproduce several line drawings from her collection of ASL illustrations.

I hope that the research and issues discussed in this book will inspire new ideas and investigations that explore the nature of language, cognition, and the brain by studying signed languages and Deaf people. Such investigations should be conducted in collaboration with members of the Deaf community as researchers and consultants. Without critical input from Deaf people, the research reviewed here would not have been possible. My own research, as well as the writing of this book, have benefited tremendously from the input of the following Deaf colleagues: Donald Baer, Kevin Clark, Brenda Falgier, Bonita Ewan, Melissa Herzig, Petra Horn-Rose, Amy Hoshina, Shane Marsh, Stephen McCullough, Freda Norman, Cindy O'Grady-Batch, Carol Padden, Kathy Say, Jonas Schurz-Torboli, and George Zein.

Finally, I would like to gratefully acknowledge the support of the National Science Foundation (Linguistics program) and the National Institutes of Health for the financial support that made it possible for me to write this book and conduct my own research reviewed here. The following grants supported this work: SBR-9510963 and SBR-9809002, from the National Science Foundation (awarded to Karen Emmorey); R01 HD13249, from the National Institute of Child Health and Development (awarded to Karen Emmorey); P50 DC03189 (awarded to Antonio Damasio), and R01 DC00146 (awarded to Ursula Bellugi), from the National Institute of Deafness and Communicative Disorders.

—*Karen Emmorey*

Notation Conventions

Conventions for the transcription of sign language have evolved over the years, but as yet there is no consensus regarding how to notate signs. One reason for the lack of consensus is that notation is not simply a way to provide a written form for signs; adoption of a particular notation system or symbol involves theoretical assumptions. The problem of adopting a universally agreed-upon notation system is not unique to researchers who work with signed languages. The International Phonetic Alphabet has undergone revision with a fair amount of disagreement and controversy (see Ladefoged, 1990). Below are the notational conventions and symbols that are commonly used by sign language researchers and are also used in this book:

APPLE

Words in capital letters represent English glosses (the nearest equivalent translation) for ASL signs.

JOT-DOWN

Multiword glosses connected by hyphens are used when more than one English word is required to translate a single sign.

GIVE[durational]

A bracketed word following a sign indicates a change in meaning associated with grammatical morphology, for exam-

	ple, the durational inflection in this example.
DANCE^{+++}	The verb is repeated.
<u>L</u>EFT	Underlining the first letter indicates an initialized sign (this sign is made with an L handshape).
B-A-C-K	Dashes between letters indicate a finger-spelled sign.
$\overline{\quad}^{t}$ BOY, GIRL PUSH	A line above a sign or sign sequence indicates the scope of the facial expression or other nonmanual behavior named above the line. In this example, "t" indicates topic marking.
rh-q	Rhetorical question.
DAD$_a$ VISIT$_a$	Letter subscripts (a–d) indicate a location in signing space that is associated with a noun or verb. This association can be made by articulating the sign toward a location or by gazing toward that location when articulating the sign.
$_b$HATE$_a$	The first subscript indicates the initial spatial location of the verb, and the second subscript indicates the location toward which the verb moves.
Lisa$_i$ . . . she$_i$	Subscripts i–k indicate coreference.
PRO$_{1st}$	A first person pronouns ("I").
hs	Handshape.
CL:5	A classifier construction produced with a 5 handshape.
2h	The sign is made with two hands.

CL:KNEEL-ON-SURFACE   A classifier construction followed by its English gloss (a description of the form of the classifier construction may follow in brackets).

/shh/   Back slashes indicate a nonsign gesture.

*   Indicates an ill-formed sign or sentence.

Chapter 1

Introduction

Once signed languages are recognized as natural human languages, a world of exploration opens up. Signed languages provide a powerful tool for investigating the nature of human language and language processing, the relation between cognition and language, and the neural organization for language. The value of signed languages lies in their modality. Specifically, for perception, signed languages depend on high-level vision and motion-processing systems, and for production, they require the integration of motor systems involving the hands and face. These facts raise many questions: What impact does this different biological base have for grammatical systems? For online language processing? For the acquisition of language? How does it affect nonlinguistic cognitive structures and processing? Are the same neural systems involved? These are some of the questions that this book addresses. The answers provide insight into what constrains grammatical form (chap. 2), language processing (chap. 4), linguistic working memory (chap. 7), and hemispheric specialization for language (chap. 9). As we see throughout the volume, the study of signed languages allows researchers to address questions about the nature of linguistic and cognitive systems that could not otherwise be easily addressed.

Before we begin, however, it is important to quickly debunk several common myths and misconceptions about sign language.

Myth Number 1: There is a universal sign language. No sign language is shared by deaf people of the world. There are many distinct sign languages that have evolved independently of each other. Just as spoken languages differ in their lexicon, in the types of grammatical rules they contain and in historical relationships, signed languages also differ along

1

these parameters. For example, despite the fact that American Sign Language (ASL) and British Sign Language are surrounded by the same spoken language, they are mutually unintelligible. Sign languages are most often named for the country or area in which they are used (e.g., Mexican Sign Language, Swedish Sign Language, Taiwanese Sign Language). The exact number of sign languages in the world is not known. The signed languages that will concern us in this book are not "secondary" sign languages, such as the sign system used by Trappist monks or the sign language used by hearing Australian Aborigines during mourning (when silence is required; Kendon, 1984). These systems differ from the primary signed languages of Deaf[1] communities in ways that suggest strong links to an associated spoken language.

Myth Number 2: Sign languages are made up of pictorial gestures and are similar to mime. As will become apparent in chapter 2, sign languages have an intricate compositional structure in which smaller units (such as words) are combined to create higher level structures (such as sentences), and this compositional structure is found at all linguistic levels (phonology, morphology, syntax, and discourse). It may seem odd to use the term *phonology* here because there is no sound in sign language; however, it turns out that sign languages exhibit systematic variations in form that are unrelated to meaning distinctions. That is, there is a componential level of structure below the level of the morpheme (the smallest meaningful unit) that is akin to phonological structure in spoken languages (see chap. 2). Such complex and hierarchical levels of structure are not present in pantomime. Pantomime differs from a linguistic system of signs in other important and systematic ways as well. For example, pantomime is always transparent and iconic, but signs can be opaque and arbitrary. The space in which signs are articulated is much more restricted than that available for pantomime—pantomime can involve movement of the entire body, whereas signing is constrained to a space extending from just below the waist to the top of the head. As discussed in chapter 9, the ability to pantomime and the ability to sign can be differentially affected by brain damage, indicating nonidentical neural systems are involved.

Myth Number 3: Sign languages are based on oral languages. American Sign Language has been mistakenly thought to be "English on the hands." However, ASL has an independent grammar that is quite different from the grammar of English (see chap. 2). For example, ASL allows much freer word order compared to English. English contains tense markers (e.g., *-ed* to express past tense), but ASL (like many languages) does not have tense

---

[1]Following convention, throughout this book I use lowercase *deaf* to refer to audiological status, and I use uppercase *Deaf* when the use of sign language and/or membership in the Deaf community is at issue.

markers that are part of the morphology of a word; rather tense is often expressed lexically (e.g., by adverbs such as "yesterday"). There are no indigenous signed languages that are simply a transformation of a spoken language to the hands. There are invented systems used in educational settings that manually code spoken language, but they are not acquired in the same manner as natural signed languages, and they do not arise spontaneously.

One might ask, "If sign languages are not based on spoken languages, then where did they come from?" However, this question is as difficult to answer as the question, "Where did language come from?" We know very little about the very first spoken or signed languages of the world, but research is beginning to uncover the historical relationships between sign languages, as has been done for spoken languages (e.g., McKee & Kennedy, 2000; Woodward, 2000). For example, the origin of American Sign Language can be traced to the existence of a large community of Deaf people in France in the 18th century (Lane, 1984; Woodward, 1978). These people attended the first public school for the deaf, and the sign language that arose within this community is still used today in France. In 1817, Laurent Clerc, a Deaf teacher from this French school, along with Thomas Gallaudet, established the first public school for the deaf in the United States. Clerc introduced French Sign Language into the school, and the gestural systems and indigenous signs of the American children attending this school mixed with French Sign Language to create a new form that was no longer recognizable as French Sign Language. ASL still retains a historical resemblance to French Sign Language, but both are now distinct languages.

Myth Number 4: Sign languages cannot convey the same subtleties and complex meanings that spoken languages can. On the contrary, sign languages are equipped with the same expressive power that is inherent in spoken languages. Sign languages can express complicated and intricate concepts with the same degree of explicitness and eloquence as spoken languages. The linguistic structuring that permits such expressive power is described in chapter 2, and examples of ASL literature and poetry are listed at the end of that chapter. This particular myth apparently stems from the misconception that there are "primitive" languages. This label is often applied to oppressed peoples. For example, it was used by turn-of-the-century Westerners to describe African languages (see Baynton, 1996).

There are two main objectives of this introductory chapter. First, I want to highlight a domain in which sign language research has recently had an important impact, namely, our understanding of the forces that drive language genesis. This research is tremendously exciting because it begins to answer basic questions about the nature of language origins (e.g., Does language creation occur gradually or abruptly?) and the critical role that children play in language change (e.g., What are the contributions of the child vs. the adult in the evolution of language?). Second, we examine the nature of the Deaf community in the United States. The research described throughout this book is primarily concerned with the members of this community, and, as we will see, the very nature of the Deaf population provides a unique opportunity to investigate the critical period hypothesis for language acquisition (chap. 6) and the effects of auditory deprivation versus linguistic experience on spatial cognition (chap. 8). It is also important to set ASL within a sociolinguistic context by characterizing language variation within the Deaf community and by contrasting ASL with other sign systems. Although research on other sign languages is presented throughout this book, the primary focus is on American Sign Language for two reasons: (1) The majority of research has been conducted with this language and (2) Focusing on a single language provides a coherent thread within the book. Nonetheless, we begin, not with American Sign Language, but with a new sign language that is emerging in Nicaragua. This project touches on issues that we will examine throughout the book, for example, the critical period for language acquisition, the gestural roots of sign languages, and the nature of linguistic structure in human languages.

DOCUMENTING THE BIRTH OF A LANGUAGE: THE NICARAGUAN SIGN LANGUAGE PROJECT

In 1979, the Sandinistas overthrew the Somoza government of Nicaragua and shortly thereafter began to establish educational reforms and public schools throughout the country. In Managua, a primary school for special education was opened to deaf children from all over the country (Polich, 1998). Prior to entering this school, deaf children had been generally kept isolated within their families (there was a great stigma attached to being deaf), and there was no interaction among these isolated deaf individuals. Kegl, Senghas, Coppola, and colleagues have been investigating what happened when these previously isolated children and adolescents came together and began to interact with each other (Kegl, 1994; Kegl & Iwata, 1989; Kegl, A. Senghas, & Coppola, 1999; A. Senghas, 1994, 1995a, 1995b, 2000; A. Senghas & Coppola, 2001; A. Senghas, Coppola, Newport, & Supalla, 1997; R. Senghas & Kegl, 1994). What these authors report is that even though the school initially advocated an oral (rather than a signing) approach to education, the children nonetheless immediately began gesturing and signing with each other on the playground, on the buses, and in class (behind the teacher's back). A language had evidently begun to emerge where none had previously existed.

Kegl, Senghas, and Coppola (1999) argued that the first step in this process was *home sign*, called *mimicas* by the Nicaraguans. Home sign is an idiosyncratic gesture system that is the sole means of communication between an isolated deaf person and his or her hearing family (see chap. 6). The home signs of isolated deaf Nicaraguans tend to be action based (i.e., pantomime like) rather than expressing names for things, and single gestures cover a range of concepts (e.g., "beard" for man, brother, father, etc.; Kegl & McWhorter, 1997; Morford & Kegl, 2000). Notions such as colors, emotions, or tense tend not to be encoded, and family members can usually list the small repertoire of gestures under the command of the home signer. Home signers also do not use multiple signs in a relational way that resemble syntactic organization. Thus, Kegl and McWhorter (1997) concluded "older Nicaraguan home signers, while possibly developing conventionality in their home sign systems, do not end up spontaneously generating a language" (p. 32). For a language to emerge, a community of users is necessary, and this is what the Managua school provided. Over 400 deaf children came together within a few short years after the school opened.

As previously isolated deaf individuals began to interact with one another, a form of intercommunication arose—a "pidgin" between home sign systems. This pidgin form constituted an intermediate stage between home sign and the emergence of a full-fledged sign language. Evidence for a distinction between this intermediate home sign pidgin and the full blown Nicaraguan Sign Language comes from comparing the signing of individuals who entered the signing community at different years in the community's history. A. Senghas (1995a, 1995b) and Kegl, Senghas, and Coppola (1999) compared narrative samples from individuals who entered the Deaf community either prior to 1983 or after 1983 and who were younger than age 10 when they entered (i.e., before the critical period for language learning; see chap. 6). This grouping compares the first generation of signers within the community (the pidgin signers) with a second generation of signers who were exposed to this pidgin as children. The linguistic distinctions between these two groups of signers (and isolated Nicaraguan home signers) are listed in Appendix B. Briefly, the generation of signers who came to Managua in the mid-to-late 1980s are more fluent, express more information in less time, and exhibit more grammatical complexity. These linguistic distinctions indicate that the second generation of signers acquired a much richer linguistic system than those who entered the community earlier (in the late 1970s or early 1980s). But how did this linguistic change come about? Was the evolution of Nicaraguan Sign Language into a full-blown language a gradual process or was there an abrupt discontinuity between the early pidgin form and what is now called Nicaraguan Sign Language? The data from A. Senghas (1995a, 1995b) and Kegl, Senghas, and Coppola (1999) argue for the latter hypothesis.

Specifically, A. Senghas directly compared *year of entry* (before or after 1983) and *age of entry* into the signing environment: young (birth–6½ years old), medium (6½–10 years old), and old (10½–30 years old). The year of entry results are those presented in Appendix B; that is, signers who entered the community earlier use a less complex pidgin form, whereas more complex signing is observed for those who entered the Deaf community after 1983. In addition, A. Senghas found that the chronological age at which a deaf person entered the signing community had a strong effect on fluency and on the ability to command more complex structures. Specifically, the younger group signed more rapidly, produced more arguments per verb, used spatial agreement to mark verb arguments (see chap. 2), and used more object classifiers (see chap. 3). Furthermore, the more recently the two younger groups entered the community, the more complex their language, but for the oldest group, the year of entry had little effect on the fluency or grammatical complexity of their language. This last finding provides evidence that there is a critical period for optimal language learning (see chap. 6) and, perhaps more importantly, that the changes in Nicaraguan Sign Language were being driven by the youngest children—not by adult members of the community. It is striking that the signing of a 7-year-old Deaf child exceeds the complexity and fluency of a 30-year-old Deaf adult who entered the community 20 years earlier—but this is in fact what Kegl, A. Senghas, and colleagues observed.

These findings indicate that Nicaraguan Sign Language arose abruptly when very young children began to restructure and regularize the highly variable and arguably impoverished sign pidgin. Why children, but not adults, have this capacity is discussed in more detail in chapter 6. The basic explanation stems from several factors: Children appear to be predisposed to find certain types of structure within their linguistic input, they have a limited memory capacity that acts as a noise filter, and the neurological substrate for language learning is still malleable and capable of change. The findings also show that the period of language emergence is extremely rapid—within a generation. Although the pidgin form is still used today by signers who were adolescents when they came to Managua in the early 1980s, this pidgin could easily disappear when these older signers are no longer in the community. The gift that Kegl and colleagues have given us is a record of a language as it is born, before the traces of its birth disappear with history.

Finally, it is worth noting that this type of research project could not be carried out with a spoken language simply because the circumstances that give rise to the emergence of a signed language do not exist for hearing people. Nonetheless, the type of language genesis and evolution observed in Nicaragua is not unique to signed languages and is found in spoken languages as the process of *creolization* (Bickerton, 1981; Kegl & Iwata,

1989). Spoken language pidgins arise when distinct languages come into contact via trade or domination. Pidgins, such as Tok Pisin, used in Papua, New Guinea, have relatively small vocabularies, limited morphology, and simple rule systems. It is important to note that the pidgin in Nicaragua arose, not from contact between already existing languages, but from contact between idiosyncratic home sign systems (Kegl, Senghas, & Coppola, 1999). However, pidgin languages are not anyone's native language, either spoken or signed. When a pidgin is adopted by a community and children begin to learn it as a first language, the pidgin becomes a creole language. For example, Haitian Creole is used by the descendants of slaves who arrived on plantations speaking many different African languages. These early arrivals first created a pidgin to communicate, which then became a creole when it was acquired by their children as a first language. Creole languages exhibit more complex word structure with a larger array of grammatical rules, compared to pidgins. For spoken languages, the study of the evolution of a pidgin into a full-blown language is quite difficult because evidence of the pidgin form quickly disappears—only historical records are left. The Nicaraguan case is unprecedented because researchers have been able to observe the creolization process firsthand.

THE AMERICAN DEAF COMMUNITY AND SOCIOLINGUISTIC CONTEXT

Approximately 2 million people in the United States are deaf and cannot hear or understand speech even with amplification; however, only about 300,000 people make up the Deaf community (Schein, 1989; Schein & Stewart, 1995). Members of the American Deaf community not only use ASL as their primary and preferred language, they also cherish it as a part of their identity (just as American Indians value Navajo or Cherokee as part of their individual and cultural identity). People who are deafened later in life seldom use sign language, and some deaf people educated in an oral environment also may not use ASL. Members of the Deaf community do not see themselves as disabled, preferring to be called "Deaf," rather than "hearing impaired" (Padden & Humphries, 1988). Deaf people form a community by virtue of shared values, interests, customs, and social goals, and Deaf culture is unique in its world view, artistic expression, and humor. Deaf people seek each other out and join together in many social, political, and athletic organizations both locally and nationally (as well as internationally). For excellent discussions of Deaf culture and the Deaf community see *A Journey Into the DEAF-WORLD* (Lane, Hoffmeister, & Bahan, 1996) and *Deaf in America: Voices From a Culture* (Padden & Humphries, 1988).

8

Although most Deaf people use ASL as their primary language in adult-hood, they vary widely as to when they were first exposed to the language. Deaf children born to Deaf signing parents are the exception; these children acquire sign language in a manner parallel to hearing children acquiring a spoken language (see chap. 5). However, only about 10% of Deaf children have Deaf parents (Schein & Delk, 1974), and thus over 90% of Deaf children are born to parents who do not know sign language.[2] Therefore, these children may have no effective language exposure in infancy and early childhood. A second reason sign language is often acquired late in childhood by many Deaf children is that, until recently, the majority of elementary schools prohibited signing in classrooms and discouraged hearing parents from signing (Lane et al., 1996). Deaf children with hearing parents typically acquire sign language when they enter a residential school and become immersed with other Deaf children and adults. ASL is not formally taught in these schools; rather, ASL is the everyday language of the children. Age of exposure to language often occurs around 4 to 6 years when many Deaf children enter residential schools; however, if the parents first send their child to a school that successfully suppresses signing, then age of exposure may not occur until much later. The educational and genetic factors of deafness thus create situations in which primary language acquisition begins at different ages, ranging from birth to quite late in childhood. The effects of such delayed exposure to language are discussed in chapter 6.

Much of the research described in this volume has been conducted with native ASL signers; that is, Deaf (and sometimes hearing) people with Deaf signing parents who acquired ASL as their first language from birth. For example, the linguistic analyses of ASL described in chapter 2 and chapter 3 were developed either by linguists working with native Deaf consultants or by linguists who are native signers themselves. The language processing experiments discussed in chapter 4 and chapter 6 generally distinguish between native and nonnative signers (i.e., those who learned ASL later in childhood), as do the memory and spatial cognition experiments discussed in chapter 7 and chapter 8. Finally, in chapter 9, some of the studies with aphasic signing patients were conducted with early signers (people exposed to ASL in early childhood), but all of the neural imaging studies were conducted with native signers. Understanding the sign language background of Deaf subjects is critical to interpreting results be-

---

[2]Lane et al. (1996) argue that the use of capitalized Deaf for children reflects that fact that if a child with little or no hearing is given the opportunity, he or she would naturally acquire a signed language and would be a member of Deaf culture. Similarly, Navajo children or Black children are called Navajo or Black as soon as they are born, even though they have not yet been exposed to Navajo or Black culture. As with adults, I use *deaf* when deafness itself is the critical issue and *Deaf* to emphasize sign language acquisition or use.

cause most spoken language psycholinguistic and neurolinguistic studies are conducted with native, rather than nonnative, speakers. Nonnative speakers and signers have language processing abilities that may be distinct from those of native speakers and signers, and the underlying neural systems for language appear to be different (see chap. 6). In general, experimental results from sign language studies can only be reasonably compared with results from spoken language studies when native signers participate.

Dialects, Accents, and Registers

Speakers in different geographic regions or from different social groups show systematic variations in language use, and these groups are said to speak different dialects of the same language. The same phenomenon occurs for signed languages (see papers in Lucas, 1989, 1996). For example, ASL signers from the Northeast and Southern regions of the United States often use different signs for the same object (compare British and American dialectal differences in word use: *gas/petrol, elevator/lift*). Southern signers also produce the two-handed form of signs more often than non-Southerners (see E. Shroyer & S. Shroyer, 1984, for examples of dialect variation across the United States). The Deaf African-American community in the United States also has its own dialect of ASL. Certain signs (e.g., FLIRT, SCHOOL) have Black forms that originate from the time when schools for the deaf were racially segregated (Aramburo, 1989; Woodward, 1976). These signs are used most often when Black Deaf individuals interact with each other and form part of the culture of the African-American Deaf community. Both regional and Black signing dialects also differ phonologically, but these systematic differences in pronunciation have been less studied.

For spoken languages, gender can also be a salient sociolinguistic variable influencing word choice and speech style (e.g., R. Lakoff, 1975; Tannen, 1990). Gender differences may also exist for signing (Nowell, 1989), but very little research has been conducted in this area for ASL. However, Irish Sign Language presents a fascinating example of gender distinctions arising from the social and educational environment of Deaf people. For over 100 years, the Dublin Deaf community maintained distinct sign vocabularies associated with men and women (LeMaster, 1990, 1997; LeMaster & Dwyer, 1991). In this community, the vocabularies of men and women were so distinct as to impair communication on everyday topics; men and women had completely different signs for ordinary concepts like *Monday, cat,* or *night* (LeMaster, 1997). These gender-differentiated vocabularies emerged from two residential schools that were segregated by gender: Saint Mary's School for Deaf Girls and Saint Joseph's

School for Deaf Boys. There was very little contact between the schools from the mid-1800s to the mid-1900s, and thus, during that time, Deaf girls and boys grew up signing in very different ways. After graduating from high school, Deaf men and women interacted with each other and also married. When this happened, women generally adopted the male signs for communication with men and mixed groups, but retained some of the female signs for use with other women or when they did not want men to know what they were talking about (LeMaster, 1997). Today, Irish Sign Language predominantly consists of male signs with a few remaining female signs, but there are no longer such strong differences between male and female dialects, and young signers are often unaware of the historical origins of gender-marked signs.

In addition to regional and social dialects, different "situational dialects" or language registers can be found for users of ASL. For example, the signing style used for formal lectures differs from that used for informal conversations or narratives (Zimmer, 1989). Formal ASL is slower paced, uses a larger signing space, tends to use two-handed variants of signs, and shows less co-articulation. In contrast, for casual or informal signing, signs that are made near the face may be produced lower down, one-handed signs predominate, and signs are co-articulated such that they "overlap." Shouting and whispering are also registers that exhibit lexical and phonological changes, and they are described in chapter 4.

The Alphabet Jungle: ASL, PSE, MCE, SEE, TC

ASL should be distinguished from invented signed systems used with deaf children in educational settings and from contact signing that may occur with nonnative hearing (and sometimes Deaf) signers. Most Deaf Americans are bilingual in ASL and English, although they may be more comfortable writing English than speaking it. When Deaf signers come into contact with hearing English speakers who have a limited knowledge of ASL, they may use *contact sign*, the kind of signing that results from contact between ASL and English, previously called *Pidgin Sign English* or PSE (Lucas & Valli, 1992). Lucas and Valli (1992) argued that contact signing is too complex to be called a pidgin, and it does not originate from the same sociolinguistic circumstances that give rise to a pidgin (see earlier discussion of pidgins and Nicaraguan Sign Language). Contact signing incorporates features of both English and ASL, for example, fingerspelling the articles *a* or *the*, and then producing an ASL sign or mouthing an English word while producing an ASL sign. The study of contact signing has interesting implications for what code switching means for Deaf bilinguals (see

Kuntze, 2000) and for the nature of bilingualism. For our purposes, however, we are concerned with ASL, as distinct from contact signing.

ASL is also quite distinct from *Manually Coded English* (MCE) which is a cover term for sign systems developed in the 1970s to represent the morphology and syntax of English, such as *Signing Exact English* or SEE (Gustason, Pfetzing, & Zawolkow, 1980). MCE was invented by educators (many fluent in ASL) as a means to make English accessible to Deaf children. The basic vocabulary of MCE consists of lexical items borrowed from ASL, but often the native handshape is replaced with a handshape from the manual alphabet in order to represent the first letter of the English word. The inventors of MCE created specific signs to represent the bound morphology of English, that is, suffixes like *-ing* or *-ed* that carry grammatical information. Signs are produced following English word order and are inflected according to the rules of English syntax. Manually Coded English contrasts sharply with the naturally emerging Nicaraguan Sign Language, for example, SEE was created by a committee of individuals, whereas NSL was created by a community. MCE also appears to present certain processing difficulties because of the linear nature of prefixes and suffixes, which are quite rare in natural signed languages (see chaps. 2 and 4). MCE is often used in classrooms that support Total Communication (TC) or simcom (simultaneous communication). The idea is that the same information should be presented in both speech and sign. However, it turns out to be quite difficult to produce a sign for each English morpheme while speaking at a normal rate, and the bound morpheme signs are most often omitted (Marmor & Petitto, 1979). MCE comes closer to representing English orthography than spoken English (Ramsey, 1989).

In the next chapter, we examine the linguistic similarities between natural signed languages and spoken languages, and we also uncover some of the typological variations that distinguish signed from spoken languages. This exploration sets the stage for the remainder of the book and also illustrates how the comparison of signed and spoken languages can provide a window into the nature of human language itself.

SUGGESTIONS FOR FURTHER READING

Lane, H., Hoffmeister, R., & Bahan, B. (1996). *A journey into the DEAF-WORLD*. San Diego, CA: DawnSignPress.

This book addresses issues such as the nature of Deaf culture and Deaf communities in the United States and abroad, bilingualism, educational policies, Deaf empowerment and oppression, and the history of Deaf people. Throughout the book, the authors enliven and clarify issues by including experiences from the everyday lives of Deaf people.

Lucas, C. (Ed.). (1989). *The sociolinguistics of the deaf community*. San Diego, CA: Academic Press.

The papers in this volume present research on the nature of language contact between Deaf and hearing people, social dialects and registers in ASL, and language use in Deaf communities. Other volumes in this series edited by Lucas are *Multicultural Aspects of Sociolinguistics in Deaf Communities* (1996; Gallaudet University Press) and *Pinky Extension and Eye Gaze: Language Use in Deaf Communities* (1998; Gallaudet University Press). Finally, the volume *Sociolinguistic Variation in American Sign Language* by Lucas, Bayley, and Valli is due to be published by Gallaudet University Press in late 2001. This volume presents a thorough description of phonological, lexical, morphological, and syntactic variation in ASL.

Chapter 2

The Structure of American Sign Language: Linguistic Universals and Modality Effects

The linguistic analysis of spoken languages can be traced back to Panini's phonological analysis of Sanskrit sometime in the 6th century B.C. In contrast, the formal investigation of the linguistic structure of signed languages dates back a mere 40 years, to the publication of Stokoe's paper, "Sign Language Structure: An Outline of the Visual Communication Systems of the American Deaf," in 1960.[1] The study of spoken languages thus rests on centuries of research, whereas the investigation of sign language structure is truly in its infancy. Although linguists studying sign languages have taken advantage of established analyses of spoken languages to explain many aspects of sign language structure, they have found that not all linguistic phenomena are easily accounted for by such analyses.

One goal of this chapter is to furnish a brief sketch of what we know about the structure of American Sign Language, which will provide crucial background for the following chapters. A second goal is to highlight what the study of sign language structure can tell us about the nature of human language. For example, it is only by investigating the linguistic structure of signed languages that claims regarding the universal properties of human language can be truly validated or disconfirmed. Further, any assertions that certain linguistic principles arise from properties of the speech articulators or from the auditory nature of speech perception can only be tested by examining languages with radically different production and

---

[1]A linguistic analysis of Sign Language of the Netherlands appeared in Tervoort (1953). However, this dissertation did not have the same impact on the linguistic study of sign language as Stokoe's (1960) paper.

perception systems (Coulter & Anderson, 1993). The study of signed languages provides a means to independently confirm (or refute) the adequacy of linguistic theories that have been proposed solely on the basis of spoken language data. Toward this end, the review presented here focuses on some unexpected similarities and some important distinctions that have been found between signed and spoken languages.

THE STRUCTURE OF SIGNS: MORPHOLOGY AND THE LEXICON

Like words in all human languages, but unlike gestures, signs belong to lexical categories or basic form classes such as noun, verb, modal verb, adjective, adverb, pronoun, and determiner. Sign languages have a lexicon of sign forms and a system for creating new signs in which meaningful elements (*morphemes*) are combined. However, sign languages differ from spoken languages in the type of combinatorial process that most often creates morphologically complex words. For spoken languages, complex words are most often formed by adding prefixes or suffixes to a word stem. In sign languages, these forms most often result from nonconcatenative processes in which a sign stem is nested within various movement contours and planes in space (Fischer, 1973; Klima & Bellugi, 1979). For example, Fig. 2.1 provides illustrations of the ASL verb GIVE with various movement patterns that indicate different temporal aspects. In chapter 4, we consider a processing explanation for why sign languages prefer nonconcatenative combinatorial processes and why spoken languages prefer affixation (specifically suffixation; Cutler, Hawkins, & Gilligan, 1985).

Word Formation and Morphological Rules

For both spoken and signed languages, morphological rules are governed by constraints on their combination and on their application to particular forms. For example, Fig. 2.1, A–C illustrates the citation form of the verb GIVE (2.1A), plus two aspectual inflections GIVE[durational] ("give continually," 2.1B) and GIVE[exhaustive] ("give to each," 2.1C). In the form of GIVE shown in Fig. 2.1D, the durational inflection applies after the exhaustive inflection to yield a form meaning "give to each in turn, over a long time." Such a verb could be used to describe someone at Halloween giving out candy to children, again and again, throughout the evening. In contrast, if the durational inflection applies prior to the exhaustive, as in Fig. 2.1E, the meaning of the verb is "give continuously to each in turn," which could be used to describe a teacher passing out several papers to

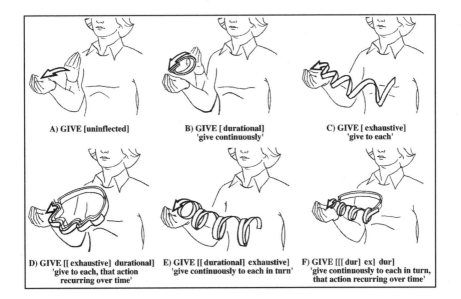

A) GIVE [uninflected]

B) GIVE [durational]
'give continuously'

C) GIVE [exhaustive]
'give to each'

D) GIVE [[exhaustive] durational]
'give to each, that action
recurring over time'

E) GIVE [[durational] exhaustive]
'give continuously to each in turn'

F) GIVE [[[dur] ex] dur]
'give continuously to each in turn,
that action recurring over time'

FIG. 2.1.   Examples of aspectual morphology in American Sign Language.
The durational inflection indicates an action occurs for a long time. The ex-
haustive inflection means roughly "to each and all." Illustrations copyright
© Ursula Bellugi, The Salk Institute.

each student in a class. Finally, the durational inflection can apply recursively, before and after the exhaustive, as in Fig. 2.1F. A verb inflected in
this way could be used to describe a teacher passing out several papers to
each student, and this action occurs throughout the day (e.g., for each
class). Thus, lexical meaning is dependent upon how morphological inflections are applied to the verb (see chap. 6 for evidence that late learners
of language are not sensitive to the recursive and embedding possibilities
of morphological systems).

Creating new word forms by compounding is very common across languages of the world, and this process occurs in ASL as well (see Fig. 2.8).
Another common morphological process derives nouns from verbs (or
vice versa). English can form nouns from verbs by adding a suffix (e.g., en-
joy–enjoyment) or by changing the word stress (rebél–rébel; convíct–cónvict).
ASL can derive nouns from verbs by changing the movement pattern
(Supalla & Newport, 1978).[2] The movement of the noun reduplicates (re-
peats) and shortens the movement of the verb. Figure 2.2 provides some
examples of noun–verb pairs in ASL.

---

[2]Supalla and Newport (1978) are neutral as to whether nouns are derived from verbs or
vice versa.

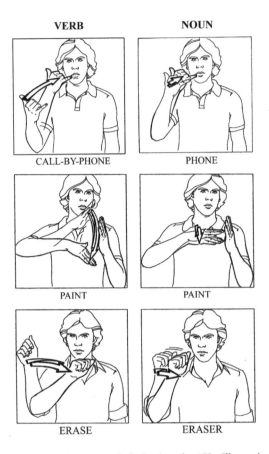

FIG. 2.2.   Examples of noun–verb derivations in ASL. Illustrations copyright © Ursula Bellugi, The Salk Institute.

Compounding, noun–verb derivation, and aspectual inflections are only a few examples of the morphological processes that are found in ASL (and in other sign languages). Verb agreement is another important morphological process in signed languages (it appears to be universal for these languages), but this phenomenon is considered later when we discuss syntactic structure.

Iconicity: Words That Look (or Sound) Like What They Mean

To express the concept of a tree, French speakers say *arbre*, English speakers say *tree*, and German speakers say *Baum*. The mapping between the sound of the word and its meaning is quite arbitrary, bearing no resemblance to an actual tree. Some linguists have cited the arbitrary mapping between words and meanings as a hallmark of human language (e.g., Hockett, 1960). Although some ASL signs exhibit an arbitrary mapping between their form and meaning (e.g., APPLE in Fig. 2.5), many more signs are iconic; that is, there is a relation between the form of the sign and its meaning. For example, the sign ERASE resembles the action of erasing a blackboard (Fig. 2.2), and PLAY-PIANO resembles the action of playing a piano (Fig. 2.6). Signs can be iconic in a number of different ways (see Mandel, 1977); for example, the hands can sketch an outline of the referent (in HOUSE, the hands trace the roof and sides of a canonical house) or the shape of the hands can resemble the shape of the referent (in BALL, the fingertips of both hands spread and touch, thus creating the shape of a ball). Does the iconicity of sign forms give rise to a fundamental distinction between signed and spoken languages?

The difference in iconicity between signed and spoken languages can be argued to be one of degree, rather than one of substance (Taub, 2001). Spoken languages also have iconic forms—words that resemble the sounds associated with their referents (e.g., onomatopoeic words; see Hinton, Nichols, & Ohala, 1994, for further discussion). For example, the English word *ding* resembles the sound of a bell, and *sizzle* and *pop* mimic the sounds associated with these actions (note also that the articulation of *pop* (rapid opening and closing of the mouth) iconically resembles a popping action). However, the auditory–vocal modality is an impoverished medium for creating iconic forms; many referents and actions have no associated auditory imagery, and the vocal tract is limited in the types of sounds it can produce. In contrast, the visual–gestural modality is rich with imagery that can motivate the form of signs because the hands and face are directly observable and many referents can invoke visual images. Thus, arbitrariness of form does not appear to be a basic or necessary characteristic of human language; in fact, iconically motivated word forms may be preferred, but the articulatory and perceptual resources of spoken languages limit the iconicity of spoken words.

Iconic signs and iconic words are not simply mimes—they must conform to constraints on form within a language (e.g., a throat clearing sound could not be part of an English onomatopoeic word and movement of the legs could not be part of an ASL iconic sign), and their meanings often cannot be guessed by naive observers or listeners (Klima & Bellugi, 1979; Pizzuto & Volterra, 2000). Furthermore, languages conventionalize iconic mappings in distinct ways: In English, roosters say *cock-a-doodle-doo*, but in French they say *cocorico*. In ASL, the sign for tree is made with the forearm upright and the fingers spread, schematically depicting the trunk and branches of a canonical tree; but in Danish Sign Language, the two hands outline the shape of a tree starting with a round top and ending with the trunk (Klima & Bellugi, 1979). Finally, iconicity is not fixed; historical change and morphological processes can obscure or reduce the iconic resemblance between form and meaning (Frishberg, 1975; Klima & Bellugi, 1979).

Is iconicity important? For some domains, the answer is "no." The prevalence of iconicity in sign language does not affect the pattern of language acquisition (although the initial acquisition of certain classifier forms may be an exception; see chap. 5), and iconicity does not appear to play a role in sign language processing (see chap. 4). There are no grammatical rules that refer to the iconicity of a sign. For other domains, however, the answer is "yes"—iconicity is important. For example, the prevalence of iconic forms in sign language must be taken into account when determining the genetic relationships among sign languages. Signed languages contain a certain percentage of similar signs based simply on shared iconicity (e.g., the sign for EAT is similar in many unrelated signed languages), and this percentage must be taken into account when estimating whether sign languages are historically related to each other (e.g., Currie, in press; McKee & Kennedy, 2000). In addition, the iconic use of signing space is critically involved in spatial descriptions and the use of classifier constructions, as we see in the next chapter. Finally, iconicity is integral to the nature of metaphor in sign languages, as discussed at the end of chapter 3 (and see Brennan, 1990; Taub, 2001).

The Composition of the ASL Lexicon

The structure of the lexicon of ASL is complex, exhibiting some properties that may be unique to signed languages, as well as properties found in spoken languages. The composition of the ASL lexicon is schematized in Example (1) (from Brentari & Padden, 2001; Padden, 1998):

(1) The ASL lexicon (the native lexicon is bolded)

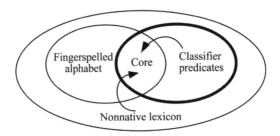

The nonnative lexicon contains English words that are fingerspelled, and these forms may be considered on the periphery of the ASL lexicon

(Padden, 1998). The fingerspelled alphabet is a set of signs for the English alphabet and consists of a set of handshapes that can be specified for orientation (H/U), orientation change (J), or movement (Z) (see Appendix A for handshape illustrations). ASL signers fingerspell English words in a variety of contexts; for example, to introduce a technical word that has no sign equivalent (e.g., fingerspelling H-Y-P-E-R-T-E-X-T in a discussion of Web technology). Fingerspelling is not a direct representation of English—it is a manual representation of the orthographic representation of English. Although fluent fingerspelling clearly involves sequencing handshapes in correspondence with written letter sequences, there are constraints on the nature of movement patterns and co-articulation effects for handshape sequences (Akamatsu, 1985; S. Wilcox, 1992). Fluent and correctly articulated fingerspelling is difficult to acquire for late learners of ASL.

As depicted by the arrow in Example (1), English words can be borrowed into ASL via fingerspelling (Battison, 1978). For example, the sign SAY-NO-TO is derived from fingerspelled N-O (see Fig. 2.3). Padden (1998) analyzed fingerspelled loan signs such as SAY-NO-TO as foreign vocabulary in ASL based on a proposal by Itô and Mester (1995) for spoken Japanese. For ASL and Japanese (as well as other languages), the lexicon is composed of both native and foreign vocabulary. Foreign vocabulary items vary in the degree to which they are constrained by formational rules applicable to the native lexicon. For example, in Japanese, only the native (Yamato) vocabulary adheres to certain constraints on the sequence of voiced sounds, whereas other phonological constraints are found for both the Yamato vocabulary and Sino-Japanese words, but not for words of European origin (e.g., a single [p] can occur in words borrowed from English but not in Sino-Japanese or Yamato words). Itô and Mester (1995) proposed a core-periphery structure in which native vocabulary exist primarily in the core, and foreign vocabulary can be mapped onto the core-periphery arrangement depending on the extent to which their phonological structure conforms to the constraints of the native vocabulary. Padden (1998) proposed a similar core-periphery structure for the ASL lexicon: At the core are native signs which obey all constraints, and extending out to the periphery are foreign signs that obey some, but not all constraints, and at the furthest boundary is foreign vocabulary that conforms to the least number of constraints.

For example, native ASL signs allow very restricted handshape change, and most fingerspelled signs violate this constraint—but the nativized sign, SAY-NO-TO, does not. Essentially, handshapes can only change from "open" to "closed" and must maintain the same active (selected) fingers (Brentari, 1990; Corina, 1993). The handshapes N and O in the fingerspelled form N-O involve distinct groups of fingers, violating this

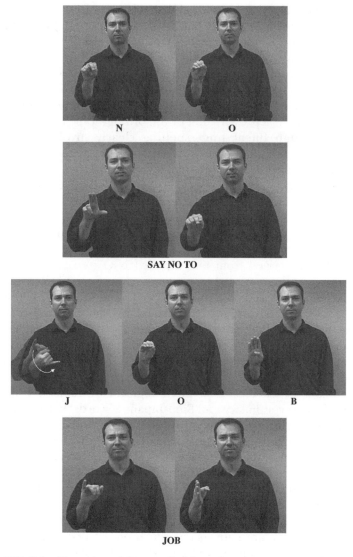

FIG. 2.3.   Illustration of fingerspelled loan signs SAY-NO-TO and JOB
and their fingerspelled counterparts N-O and J-O-B.

constraint (see Fig. 2.3). In contrast, SAY-NO-TO involves the same group
of fingers and changes from an open to a closed configuration, conform-
ing to constraints on handshape sequences found with native signs in the
core lexicon. Other signs with a fingerspelled origin violate the constraints
on handshape change, but adhere to other constraints, such as the al-
lowable number of orientation changes. For example, the loan sign JOB

shown in Fig. 2.3 violates the constraint on handshape change (the "I" to "B" handshape sequence involves two distinct groups of fingers), but it contains only a single orientation change, as do native signs (Brentari, 1998).[3] The fingerspelled word H-E-D-G-E violates both constraints on handshape change and on the number of orientation changes within a sign, and thus it would be considered on the far periphery of the ASL lexicon.

By organizing foreign and native vocabulary along a continuum from core to periphery within the lexicon, Padden (1998) argued that degrees of nativization and variation in conformity to formational (phonological) constraints can be more easily explained. Thus, fingerspelled forms are not completely independent of native ASL signs; rather, the formational constraints proposed for native signs apply to varying degrees to fingerspelled forms as well.

Finally, *classifier predicates* form a separate component within the ASL lexicon because these forms may violate formational constraints of the core lexicon (e.g., the symmetry and dominance constraints on two-handed signs that are discussed in the next section), and they have distinct morphological properties. Briefly, classifier predicates are complex forms in which the handshape is morphemic, and the movement and location of the hand may specify the movement and location of a referent. Classifier predicates are generally used to talk about the motion and position of objects and people or to describe the size and shape of objects. For example, to describe a person meandering along a path, a signer would use a classifier predicate in which the 1 handshape (referring to the person) moves forward with a zig-zag motion; to describe a weaving car, the signer would produce the same predicate but with a 3 handshape, which refers to vehicles (e.g., cars, bikes, motorcycles). Other handshapes refer to an object's size or shape, for example, "flat and round" (an F handshape), "flat and wide" (a B handshape), "cylindrical" (a C handshape; see Appendix A for handshape illustrations). These handshapes occur in predicates that specify the location of an object (e.g., the position of a coin, a sheet of paper, or a cup) and to specify the shape of an object (e.g., a long thin pole). Classifier predicates are described in much more detail in chapter 3.

An example of a classifier predicate entering the core lexicon is the sign FUNERAL shown in Fig. 2.4 (Valli & Lucas, 1995). FUNERAL appears to be derived from a classifier predicate in which the V handshape specifies two upright people with the meaning "people walk forward two-by-two." In the productive classifier form, the handshape could be changed to indicate three people, the movement could be altered to indicate that one pair moved away, and the orientation of the hands could be changed to indi-

---

[3]Native signs permit only one orientation change within a syllable; the next section describes syllables in signed languages.

FUNERAL

FIG. 2.4. Illustration of a "frozen" form derived from a classifier predicate.

cate that the pairs were facing each other. In the "frozen" form FUNERAL, none of these alterations is possible, and the formational components (the handshape and movement) are not morphemic—the sign means "funeral," not "pairs of people walk forward." Many, if not the majority, of signs in the core lexicon may have an origin in the classifier system (Brennan, 1990; McDonald, 1982; Shepard-Kegl, 1985), and lexical innovations frequently arise from classifier predicates, for example, the new signs LAPTOP and SNOWBOARD are derived from classifier forms.

To conclude, Padden's (1998) analysis of fingerspelled loan signs illustrates the similarity between spoken and signed languages with respect to how foreign vocabulary is organized within the lexicon. What is unique about many signed languages is that foreign vocabulary enters the language via a system that represents the *orthography* of the foreign language (see also Brentari, 2001). In Asia, written Chinese can be borrowed into signed languages via "character signs," which iconically represent Chinese characters, and the formational structure of these signs differs in varying degrees from that of native signs (Ann, 1998). The other modality specific aspect of sign language lexicons may be the separate system of classifier constructions, which participates so heavily in the formation of new words. Although the term *classifier* is used, these constructions differ from spoken language classifiers, and aspects of their structure are greatly influenced by the visual–spatial modality (see chap. 3). Nonetheless, when classifier predicates enter the core lexicon, they follow lexicalization patterns found in spoken languages, despite their modality specific nature. In spoken languages, when complex words (or phrases) become monomorphemic (or become single words) over time, there is a shift in meaning, a loss of morphological compositionality, and a conformity to the formational and rhythmic constraints on single words. For example, the word *cupboard* was originally a compound composed of *cup* and *board*, but it no longer is pronounced like a compound and has lost its morphological compositionality (a cupboard is a small cabinet, not a board for holding cups). Similar semantic and formational changes occurred with the lexicalization of the sign FUNERAL. Thus, although aspects of classifier predicates may turn out to be unique to signed languages, the same linguistic forces that shape lexical change and word formation in spoken languages apply to these constructions as well.

THE PHONOLOGY OF A SOUNDLESS LANGUAGE

Is it possible to have a phonological system that is not based on sound? In spoken languages, words are constructed out of sounds that in and of themselves have no meaning. The words "bat" and "pat" differ only in the initial sounds that have no inherent meanings of their own. Sounds may be combined in various ways to create distinct words: "Bad" differs from "dab" only in how the sounds are sequenced. Similarly, signs are constructed out of components that are themselves meaningless and are combined to create morphemes and words (see Fig. 2.5 and following text). Thus, sign languages exhibit a linguistically significant, yet meaningless level of structure (Stokoe, 1960), but should we call this level of structure *phonology*? S. R. Anderson (1993) argued that the use of this term obscures rather than clarifies matters because it prejudices investigators to find specious parallels between signed and spoken languages and to overlook informative differences. On the other hand, Sandler (1995) argued that there is much to be learned by applying what is known about spoken language phonology to understanding the formational level of structure of signed languages. Most linguists adopt Sandler's position, assuming that a similar cognitive system underlies the expression of both signed and spoken languages (for reviews, see Brentari, 1995; Corina & Sandler, 1993). In this section, we examine the formational structure of signed languages as a phonological system, exploring the extent to which representational units (e.g., segments or syllables), levels of organization, and constraints on form are based on comparable principles for spoken and signed languages.

Before discussing the nature of sign language phonology, it is important to point out a few basic characteristics of signs. Some signs are produced with one hand and some with two hands, but handedness is not distinctive in ASL (or perhaps in any sign language). That is, there are no ASL signs that differ only on the basis of whether they are made with the right hand or with the left hand. One-handed signs are produced with the signer's *dominant* hand—thus left-handers and right-handers differ in which hand is dominant (see chap. 4 for a discussion of hand dominance

in sign language production).[4] Signs may also have a nonmanual component, characterized by distinct facial expressions, head movements, or
both that occur with the manual sign(s). The nature of two-handed signs
and nonmanual features are discussed in separate sections.

Segments and Features

Signs are composed of three basic phonological categories: handshape, location (place of articulation), and movement (orientation of the hand is
another important aspect of sign structure discussed later in this section).
Figure 2.5 provides an illustration of three *minimal pairs*: signs that are
identical except for one component, and if you substitute one component
for another, it changes the meaning of the sign. The top illustration shows
two ASL signs that differ only in handshape. ASL contains over 30 different handshapes, but not all sign languages share the same handshape in-
ventory. For example, the T handshape in ASL does not occur in European sign languages. Chinese Sign Language contains a handshape,
formed with an open hand with all fingers extended except for the ring
finger, which is bent; this hand configuration does not occur in ASL. Signs
also differ according to where they are made on the body or face, and Fig.
2.5B shows two signs that differ only in their place of articulation. Signs
can also differ with respect to whether they are articulated within the vertical, horizontal, or sagittal planes within signing space (Brentari, 1998).
Finally, *movement* is another contrasting phonological category that distinguishes minimally between signs, as shown in Fig. 2.5C. Signs can differ in
the *path* of movement (e.g., straight vs. arc), and signs may differ in their
local (secondary) movement, such as wiggling or hooking the fingers.

   Early on, it was thought that these phonological categories were expressed simultaneously and that signs did not have a linear segmental
structure, as did spoken words (e.g., Klima & Bellugi, 1979). However, it
later became clear that some kind of linear structure was necessary to capture the sequential aspects of many ASL signs (see Liddell, 1984a). For example, the signs CHRISTIAN and COMMITTEE share an initial location,
but they differ in their final location (see Fig. 2.6A). The signs MOS-
QUITO and JOT-DOWN illustrate the importance of ordering with respect to handshape (see Fig. 2.6B). These signs share a final B handshape,
but differ in the initial handshape. With respect to movement, Newkirk
(1981/1998) observed that some signs have unidirectional movement (a
single path movement in one direction), whereas other signs have bi-

---

[4]Although it does not matter which hand is dominant, a *change* in dominance can have
meaning (see chap. 4).

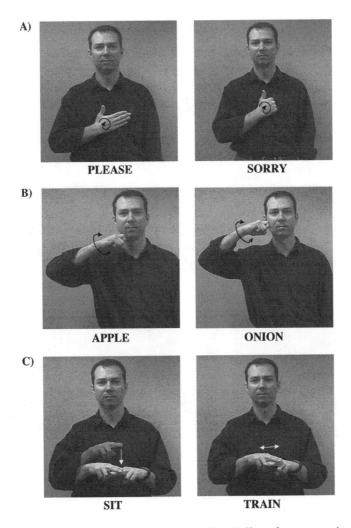

FIG. 2.5. Examples of minimal pairs in ASL: (A) Signs that contrast in hand configuration, (B) signs that contrast in place of articulation, and (C) signs that contrast in movement.

directional movement (a path movement from one location to another and back again). The signs FINGERSPELL (unidirectional) and PLAY-PIANO (bidirectional) exhibit this distinction (see Fig. 2.6C).

Spoken languages represent sequential structure in terms of the linear ordering of consonant (C) and vowel (V) segments. These segments are characterized by phonological features that are most often defined in articulatory terms, for example, the feature *labial* indicates that the lips

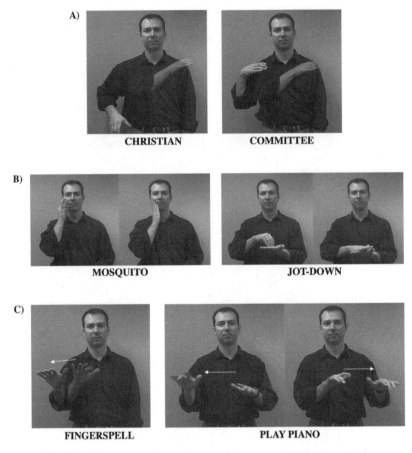

FIG. 2.6.   Illustration of several sequential aspects of ASL signs: (A) signs
that differ in the sequence of locations, (B) signs that differ in handshape sequence, and (C) signs that differ in the sequence of movements (unidirectional vs. bidirectional movement).

are used in the articulation of a sound. Phonological features constitute a
small set of elementary categories that combine to form the sounds of all
spoken languages. In earlier phonological models, all features were listed
separately for each segment (e.g., Chomsky & Halle, 1968), but more recent *autosegmental* models recognize that some phonological features are
best treated as spread across more than one segment (e.g., Goldsmith,
1976/1979). For example, high and low tones in languages like Thai or
Hausa can extend over more than one vowel. Thus, tone is represented on
a separate *tier* from the other features of consonants and vowels, as illustrated in Example (2). In this example, the vowels in the Shona word *hóvé*
are both produced with a high tone.

(2) An autosegmental representation of the high (H) tones in the word *hóvé* ("fish") from the African language Shona (from Odden, 1995):

CVCV
\/
H

This type of autosegmental representation explains how a single tone can be associated with two separate vowels. The representation also shows that tones are somewhat independent of the linear consonant and vowel segments. For example, if the final vowel in Example (2) were deleted when a suffix is added to the word, the high tone may remain—it is not necessarily deleted along with the vowel. In this case, the high tone would then be pronounced on the vowel of the added suffix.

Similarly, the linear structure of signs can be represented in terms of sequences of phonological categories that are somewhat akin to consonant and vowel categories. Most models of sign phonology propose a linear segmental structure for signs, although they differ in the precise characterization of segments (see Brentari, 1998, for a review).[5] For purposes of cohesion and ease of explanation, we focus on Sandler's *Hand Tier model* (Sandler, 1986, 1989). In this model, segments consist of Locations (Ls) and Movements (Ms). *Location segments* are defined as a specific location (in signing space or on the body) that the dominant hand must reach during the articulation of a sign, and *Movement segments* constitute the dynamic aspect of signs (akin to vowels). Evidence for two segment types is provided by patterns of derivation and inflection, which can differentially change features associated with one segment type, but not the other (e.g., Liddell, 1984a, 1984b; Sandler, 1990). Furthermore, like tone, handshape or *hand configuration* (HC) is represented on a separate autosegmental tier (Sandler, 1986, 1989). A schematic representation of signs like CHRISTIAN or COMMITTEE (see Fig. 2.6A) is given in Example (3):

(3) The phonological structure of CHRISTIAN (from Sandler, 1989):

HC

L   M   L

---

[5]Current phonological models include the *Movement-Hold model* of Liddell and Johnson (1986/1989), the *Hand Tier model* of Sandler (1989), the *Prosodic Model* of Brentari (1998), the *moraic model* of Perlmutter (1992), and the *phonological dependency model* of van der Hulst (1993, 1996). In contrast to these models, Wilbur (1993) proposed a nonsegmental representation of signs in which tiers of phonological features are organized and sequenced within a syllable, but no segmental units are hypothesized.

In the sign CHRISTIAN, the hand configuration (HC) is a C handshape, and the representation in Example (3) indicates that this handshape is articulated at the first Location of the sign (at the chest) and is maintained during the Movement to the second Location at the trunk (see Fig. 2.6A). Like consonants and vowels, Location and Movement segments are characterized by phonological features; however, these features are defined in terms of manual articulation, rather than in terms of oral articulation. For example, just as consonant segments can be specified as *labial*, Location segments can be specified as at the *trunk* (and as *ipsilateral* or *contralateral*), and Movement segments can be specified as *arc* or *straight*.

Placement of hand configuration (HC) on a separate tier captures the fact that all Location and Movement segments in a sign are characterized by the same handshape. In addition, the existence of an autosegmental tier for hand configuration can explain why handshape behaves as an independent unit in phonological rules (see following text) and in slips of the hand (analogous to slips of the tongue, see chap. 4). A further similarity between spoken and signed languages is that those phonological units that are represented on a separate phonological tier can also function as morphemes (McCarthy, 1981). For example, a high tone can function as a morpheme in Mixtecan, marking continuous or ongoing activity (Goldsmith, 1990). Similarly, handshape can function as a morpheme in classifier constructions (see chap. 3; Sandler, 1989).

Further parallels between spoken and signed languages can be found in how phonological features are organized and referred to by phonological rules. Before exploring these parallels, however, it is important to first understand a bit more about recent advances in feature theory for spoken language phonology, and we also work through a simple example of a phonological rule for English that provides an analogy for a phonological rule in ASL. First of all, rather than simply listing features with each segment, spoken language phonologists have proposed that features that function together as a unit in phonological rules should be grouped together into constituents (e.g., Clements, 1985). Specifically, features are organized into a hierarchical structure, called a *feature geometry*, that is hypothesized to be universal to all spoken languages. See Example (4):

(4) The (simplified) feature geometry for consonants:

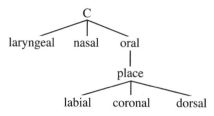

The features directly under the C segment specify which parts of the vocal tract are involved: the oral (mouth) cavity, the nasal cavity (for nasal sounds like /n/, air goes through the nose as well as the mouth), and the larynx (the voicing feature is represented under this node). The place constituent groups together the major articulatory features of the tongue: *Dorsal* sounds are made with the back of the tongue (e.g., /k/ or /g/), whereas *coronal* sounds are made with the tip of the tongue, (e.g., /t/ or /d/). This type of representation accounts for the fact that phonological rules apply to the features under the place constituent as a class, rather than as individual features.

An example of a phonological rule that refers to this class of features is *place assimilation*. Assimilation rules change the features of one segment to become more like another. An example of place assimilation is found with the English prefix, *in-*. When this prefix occurs before words that begin with a labial sound such as [b] or [p], the coronal segment /n/ becomes labial (i.e., [m]), as with *impolite*. When *in-* occurs before words that begin with a dorsal sound such as [g] or [k], then /n/ becomes dorsal (i.e., [ŋ]—the final sound in the word *sing*), as with *incomplete*. Finally, when *in-* occurs before words that begin with a coronal sound such as [d] or [n], then the /n/ segment remains coronal, as with *indecent*. Rather than referring to each place feature separately (i.e., labial, dorsal, coronal), the phonological rule need only refer to the place node within the feature geometry. An illustration of how this rule works for the place assimilation example just described is shown in Example (5). The first C segment represents the coronal /n/ segment, and the second C segment represents a labial [p] or [b] segment. Basically, the rule specifies that the features of the place node of the /n/ segment connect to (are associated with) the following consonant. The double lines indicate "de-linking" (disconnection), and the dotted line indicates the new association line which represents the assimilation.

(5) An example of place assimilation for spoken language (**coronal** /n/ becomes **labial** [m] before the **labials** [p] or [b])

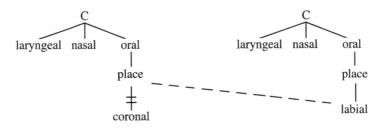

Similarly, for sign languages phonological features are also organized into a hierarchical feature geometry. For example, a simplified version of

the feature geometry for hand configuration within Sandler's model is
given in Example (6) (from Sandler & Lillo-Martin, in press).

(6) A simplified feature tree for hand configuration:

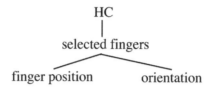

Selected fingers (including the thumb) are those that are selected during
the articulation of a sign; that is, selected fingers are those that make contact with the body and have a wider range of postures compared to the rest
of the fingers (*unselected* fingers can only be *open* (extended) or *closed*). *Finger position* refers to the posture of the fingers (e.g., bent, curved, spread).
The significance of orientation for sign structure was first recognized by
Battison (1978). Signs can be distinguished simply by the orientation of
the palm, as illustrated by the minimal pair CHILDREN and THING in
Fig. 2.7.

An enlightening example of phonological assimilation for sign language involves hand configuration and occurs with compound formation
in ASL (Sandler, 1987, 1989; see Fischer, 1982, for another example of assimilation). A compound noun is formed by concatenating two words, as in
the English compounds *blackboard* and *greenhouse*. In ASL lexicalized compounds, the hand configuration of the initial sign in a compound can exhibit either total handshape assimilation or just orientation assimilation.

CHILDREN   **THING**

FIG. 2.7.   Illustration of signs differing only in palm orientation.

One example of an ASL compound is the sign BLOOD, which is derived by combining the signs RED and FLOW, as shown in Fig. 2.8. Figure 2.8A shows the two signs in isolation before compounding. Figure 2.8B shows one possible articulation of the compound BLOOD in which total handshape assimilation has occurred—the phonological representation of this assimilation process is shown in Example (7). In this compound, you can see that the hand configuration of the sign RED (a 1 handshape) has been "replaced by" the hand configuration of the following sign, FLOW (an open 5 handshape); that is, the handshape of RED has assimilated to the following handshape. In Example (7) through Example (9), HC_1 refers to the hand configuration for the sign RED, and HC_2 refers to the hand configuration for the sign FLOW. In these examples, assimilation affects only the hand configuration of the first sign (RED)—the Location (at the chin) remains the same, and the outward path movement of RED is deleted by a separate compounding rule. Handshape assimilation is represented in Example (7) by the dotted line linking the selected fingers node of HC_2 (FLOW) to HC_1 (RED).

(7) Total handshape assimilation in compounds (see Fig. 2.8B):

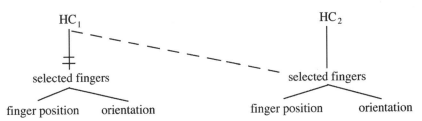

An alternate pronunciation of BLOOD is shown in Fig. 2.8C. In this variant, only orientation has assimilated, and not handshape (i.e., not the selected fingers). In this compound, you see that the hand configuration of RED (a 1 handshape) has not changed, but the orientation of the fingertip is similar to the orientation of the fingers in FLOW. That is, the orientation of the fingers (not the entire hand configuration) has assimilated to the sign FLOW. The phonological representation of this process is shown in Example (8).[6]

---

[6] The features upright and lateral are not from Sandler's (1989) Hand Tier model (they simply describe finger orientation in these examples). Sandler's (1989) orientation features are not specific enough to capture the subtle change in orientation observed in this example of compound formation. Other models represent orientation as a relation between a part of the hand and the body or planes in signing space, rather than by a set of features (Brentari, 1998; Liddell & Johnson, 1986/1989).

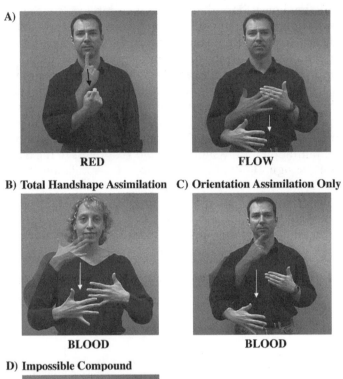

A)

RED   FLOW

B) Total Handshape Assimilation   C) Orientation Assimilation Only

BLOOD   BLOOD

D) Impossible Compound

*BLOOD

FIG. 2.8. Examples of phonological processes in ASL compounds. (A) The lexical signs that are input to the compound (RED, FLOW). (B) The compound BLOOD illustrating total handshape assimilation, (C) The compound BLOOD illustrating orientation assimilation alone, and (D) an impossible compound in which handshape assimilates, but orientation does not.

(8) Orientation assimilation in compounds (see Fig. 2.8C):

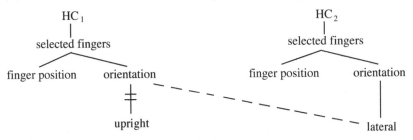

Finally, Fig. 2.8D shows an impossible compound sign in which hand-shape (selected fingers) has assimilated, but not orientation; that is, the first part of the compound maintains the hand orientation for RED (fingers pointing upward), but assimilates to the hand configuration of FLOW (a 5 handshape). This illegal form is represented in Example (9).

(*9) An illegal form, see Fig. 2.8D (the box symbolizes that the orientation features did not assimilate):

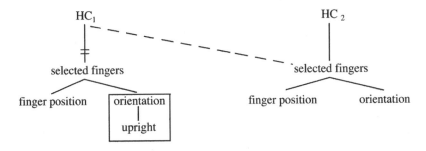

The reason that this form is illegal (although perfectly articulatable) is explained by the nature of feature geometry, which is universal to all human languages. Specifically, if a phonological rule (such as assimilation) applies to a constituent node (e.g., *selected fingers* in signed languages or *place* in spoken languages), it affects all of the dependent features of that node (e.g., *orientation* for signed languages or *labial* for spoken languages). Thus, although orientation features can assimilate alone as in Example (8), if handshape assimilates via the selected fingers node, then orientation features must assimilate as well, resulting in total assimilation as in Example (7). Crucially, this constraint is not a quirk about ASL or about sign language. Rather, it arises from the hierarchical nature of phonological systems, whether spoken or signed.

The hierarchical representation proposed by Sandler is not the only game in town. In fact, the organization of phonological features for sign language is a topic of much current research (see Brentari, 1998; Corina, 1993; and van der Hulst, 1995, for alternative proposals). However, one principle of phonology is that feature categories and their organization are universal. Therefore, it is hypothesized that just as there are not distinct feature geometries for English and for Swahili, there are not separate feature geometries for individual signed languages. The goal is to discover a hierarchical organization of features that can explain phonological patterns found across distinct signed languages, not just within ASL. Cross-linguistic research is crucial to determining the set of distinctive features and the manner in which they are grouped into larger constituents, and much investigation remains to be done. Of course, the features that explain phonological patterns in spoken language are distinct from those of sign language, but the basic organization of the feature system appears to be universal for both spoken and signed languages.

In addition, the examples presented thus far illustrate that there are non-obvious constraints on the form of signs and that signers have clear intuitions about what is permissible and what is ill formed. Such is not the case for gesture, and it may be that these types of form constraints are not observed even in the most "language-like" gesture systems, such as home sign. Thus far, there is little evidence that home sign gestures are composed of combinations of meaningless elements or that systematic restrictions on form apply to such elements.

Syllables

The *syllable* is a unit of structure that is below the level of the word but above the level of the segment. The question is whether such a level of structure is necessary to explain the form and patterning of signs. Sign phonologists have generally answered in the affirmative, but disagree about precisely how sign syllables should be characterized (e.g., Corina, 1990; Perlmutter, 1992; Sandler, 1993; Wilbur, 1993). However, there is general agreement that a sign syllable must contain a movement of some type. All signs in Fig. 2.5 contain one syllable (the majority of ASL signs are monosyllabic). Examples of bisyllabic signs are MOSQUITO, JOT-DOWN, PLAY-PIANO, LOCK, and CANCEL (see Figs. 2.6, 2.9, and 2.13). Brentari (1998) outlines several phonological constraints that must refer to the sign syllable (defined as one sequential movement). For example, Uyechi (1994/1996) discovered that only certain movement sequences are allowed in bisyllabic ASL signs: Circle + straight movements are permitted (e.g., LOCK), but straight + circle movements are not, as illustrated in Figure 2.9.[7] Crucially, although a straight + circle movement sequence is ill formed as a single word, it is well formed when it occurs in a phrase, such

---

[7]This constraint applies to monomorphemic signs.

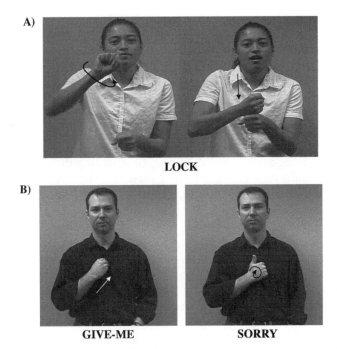

FIG. 2.9.   A) Example of a bisyllabic sign that contains a circle + straight movement sequence. B) Example of a phrase that contains a straight + circle movement sequence. If (B) were a sign stem, then it would be ill formed, even if both handshapes were the same as in (A).

as GIVE SORRY (Brentari, 1998; see Fig. 2.9). Thus, the constraint on movement sequences needs to refer to a level smaller than the word (the constraint does not hold across words), but larger than the segment.

Similarly, in spoken languages, constraints on segment sequences are stated with respect to the syllable. For example, only consonant clusters that begin a syllable can begin a word, and only clusters that end a syllable can end a word. In English, the sequence /str/ can begin a word, but /stl/ cannot. However, such a sequence would be allowed in a phrase, for example, "fast lane." Another constraint found in both spoken and signed languages is that all words must consist of at least one syllable. For sign language, no sign is well formed unless it has a movement of some type (e.g., Brentari, 1998; Wilbur, 1987).

The syllable also constrains the nature of handshape change in ASL. Specifically, changes in handshape are temporally coordinated with respect to movement at the level of the syllable, not at the level of the lexical item or morpheme (Brentari, 1998). To understand this constraint, it is important to know that when handshape changes during the movement *between* lexical signs (e.g., changing from the 1 handshape of RED to the H handshape of TRAIN in the phrase RED TRAIN), then the change in handshape may be completed before the end of the transitional movement. However, when handshape change occurs within a lexical sign (e.g., in MEMORIZE, the handshape changes from a 5 to an S handshape; see Fig. 2.16C), then the handshape change is coordinated with the path movement and is rarely completed before the end of the movement (Brentari & Poizner, 1994). Crucially, if a sign has two movements (two syllables), then handshape change is coordinated with only one of the movements. For example, a variant of the sign LOCK (Fig. 2.9A) has a handshape change in the first syllable, that is, during the first circle movement, the handshape changes from a hooked 5 to an S handshape. The sign would be considered ill formed if the handshape change occurred across both movements. Thus, handshape change is coordinated with sign syllables, not with morphemes or with the sign.

These examples illustrate that an intermediate level of representation, such as the syllable, is needed to determine what counts as a well-formed articulation of a sign and to describe constraints on segment sequences and other phonological patterns. The syllable also appears to play a role in the manual babbling of deaf infants (see chap. 5). However, sign syllables differ from syllables in spoken language because there is little evidence of an onset-rhyme distinction for sign. Spoken syllables can be divided into onsets (usually, the first consonant or consonant cluster) and rhymes (the vowel and final consonants). Such internal structure does not appear to be present for sign syllables (although some linguists have argued for weight distinctions, i.e. "heavy" vs. "light" syllables, based on differences in movement types). Because of the lack of internal structure, there do not appear to be processes such as resyllabification in sign language (a segment from one syllable becomes part of another syllable). The basic parallel is that both signed and spoken languages have an intermediate prosodic level of structure that is above the segmental-featural level and below the word level.

Constraints on the Structure of Two-Handed Signs

One of the most striking differences between signed and spoken languages is that speech involves one major articulator (the tongue), whereas sign involves two independent anatomically identical articulators: the two hands. However, for linguistic expression, the two hands are not independent in their articulation (even within the limits of motor coordination). For example, Battison (1978) discovered two major constraints on the nature of two-handed signs in ASL, which appear to be universal to all sign languages studied thus far. Signs that illustrate these two conditions are shown in Fig. 2.10.

A) Signs illustrating the Symmetry Condition

| SINCE | WITH |

B) Signs illustrating the Dominance Condition

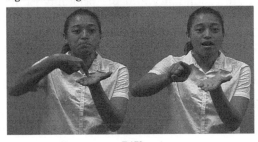 

| PAY | VOTE |

C) Signs violating the A) Symmetry Condition and B) Dominance Condition

 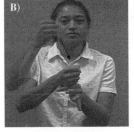

| An illegal sign | An illegal sign |

FIG. 2.10. (A) Signs illustrating the symmetry condition: Both hands move and are specified for the same handshape, movement and orientation. (B) Signs illustrating the dominance condition: The nondominant hand does not move and has an unmarked hand configuration. (C) An illegal lexical sign that violates A) the symmetry condition: The two hands have distinct hand configurations, and an illegal lexical sign that violates B) the dominance condition: The nondominant hand has a marked hand configuration.

The Symmetry Condition.   If both hands of a sign move independently during its articulation, then both hands must be specified for the same location, the same handshape, the same movement (whether performed simultaneously or in alternation), and the specifications for orientation must be either symmetrical or identical. (Battison, 1978, p. 33)

The Dominance Condition.   If the hands of a two-handed sign do not share the same specification for handshape (i.e., they are different), then (a) one hand must be passive while the active hand articulates the movement, and (b) the specification of the passive handshape is restricted to be one of a small set: A, S, B, 5, 1, C, O. (Battison, 1978, p. 35; see Appendix A for illustrations of handshapes)

These constraints illustrate redundancy and predictability within the system. For example, the symmetry condition basically specifies that information related to the dominant hand (i.e., its handshape, orientation, movement) can be "copied" to the nondominant hand—the implication for phonological models is that this information does not have to be represented twice. In fact, van der Hulst (in press) suggests that the universality of these constraints across signed languages may be due to the principle that there is essentially only one major articulator in language (either the tongue or the dominant hand). The fact that these constraints can be systematically violated by certain types of signs (specifically, in classifier constructions; see chap. 3) indicates that they do not arise solely from physiological constraints on bimanual coordination.[8] Finally, as discussed in chapter 9, evidence from neural imaging studies and from sign language aphasia indicates that despite the fact that separate hemispheres control the motor functions of each hand, only the left hemisphere controls linguistic production (as it does for speech).

Nonmanual Components of Signs

Some ASL signs have an obligatory nonmanual component that is timed to co-occur with distinct parts of the manual sign. For example, the nonmanual component of AT-LAST (Fig. 2.11) consists of a compression of the lips associated with the beginning of the sign, followed by the opening of the mouth, which is synchronized with the movement of the sign (Brentari, 1995). The nonmanual component is not a trivial aspect of sign language structure—facial expression, head/body tilt, and eye gaze all

---

[8]However, van Gijn, Kita, and van der Hulst (in press) recently suggested that the symmetry condition may be a phonetic effect, rather than a phonological constraint. They found that the spontaneous gestures that hearing people make when speaking also conform to the symmetry condition.

AT-LAST

FIG. 2.11. Illustration of the nonmanual component of signs.

have extremely important functions within ASL morphology, syntax, and discourse, as we will see. However, the representation of nonmanual features has received much less attention than the manual features of sign. For example, no proposal for nonmanual phonological features has yet been put forward, although Sutton-Spence and Day (in press) propose a feature-based system for coding mouth articulations, and Bergman and Wallin (in press) propose a distinctive feature analysis for some mouth patterns in Swedish Sign Language.

Linguists studying European sign languages have analyzed *mouth patterns*, which are mouthings and mouth gestures produced simultaneously with manual signs (e.g., Ebbinghaus & Hessmann, 1996; Schermer, 1990; Vogt-Svendsen, 1983; see papers in Boyes-Braem & Sutton-Spence, in press), but little ASL research has been conducted on these topics. *Mouth gestures* refer to mouth activity that is unrelated to spoken words (e.g., the mouth articulation for the ASL sign AT-LAST), whereas *mouthing* refers to the production of a spoken word (or part of a word), usually without voice, while simultaneously producing a corresponding manual sign or signs. Examples of mouthing in ASL can be seen in Fig. 2.10B for the signs PAY and VOTE. The signer silently mouthed the English word "pay" and the syllable "vo" from "vote" (the final consonant was not produced). Mouthing can be used to disambiguate signs that are manual homonyms, that is, signs that have the same form but different meanings (e.g., NATION and OF-COURSE; see Fig. 4.4 in chap. 4). Mouthing occurs when Deaf signers converse with each other, but the degree of mouthing varies with the individual and with sociolinguistic context (e.g., it occurs more often when conversing with nonfluent signers). Mouthing may be acquired by Deaf children as a part of some signs before they know the corresponding English word: For example, a young Deaf child may produce the "fsh" mouthing with FINISH (to mean "all done!") before he or she knows the English word "finish" (see Reilly, McIntire, & Bellugi, 1990b; see Keller, in press, for examples from the acquisition of German Sign Language). In cases like this, the mouthing is part of the phonological form of the sign— it is not the simultaneous production of a spoken English word and a manual ASL sign that is observed with Total Communication or contact signing (see chap. 1).

Mouthing in European sign languages occurs much more often with nouns than with verbs, possibly because verbs occur with mouth gestures (e.g., facial adverbials, see following text). Mouthing can also be "stretched" across more than one manual sign (Boyes-Braem, 2001). One function of such stretched mouthing is to prosodically bind constituents (Boyes-Braem, in press; Sandler, 1999a). For example, in Swiss German Sign Language (DSGS), when signers produce a noun followed by a plural marker, the spoken language mouthing spreads over both the noun and the plural marker, for example, the mouthing of "Doktor" is stretched over the signs DOKTOR PERSON[plural] in the phrase SECHS DOKTOR PERSON[plural] meaning 'six doctors'. (PERSON[plural] is the DSGS person classifier (see chap. 3) that is repeated horizontally in slightly shifted locations to indicate plurality). Mouthing may function similarly to prosodic intonation in spoken languages because it groups signs into a unit (see the discussion of superarticulation to come).[9] However, the linguistic status of mouthings remains controversial and not well understood, for example, are mouthings obligatory? Are they borrowings or examples of code mixing? Or do they simply reflect the attempted suppression of sign language in an environment of oral education? (for a discussion, see Sutton-Spence & Boyes-Braem, in press). Clearly, this aspect of sign language production deserves further investigation, particularly for ASL.

With respect to mouth gestures (mouth patterns that are unrelated to the spoken language), the term *echo phonology* has been used to refer to those gestures in which the mouth articulation parallels the manual movement, that is, opening mouth movements accompany hand opening or movement away from the body (AT-LAST in Fig. 2.11), whereas closing mouth movements accompany hand closing or movement toward the body (Woll, in press; Woll & Sieratzki, 1998). Such parallelism may be due to the tight coordination between manual and oral gestures in general (e.g., try mouthing "pah" while repeatedly closing your hand, compared to opening your hand. Which is easier?). Another function of mouth gestures is *enactment* (Schermer, 1990; Sutton-Spence & Woll, 1999). For signs like BITE in ASL, the mouth gesture enacts or imitates the real ac-

---

[9]Sandler (1999a) argued that this type of mouthing is the equivalent to marking a prosodic word in spoken language. For example, *did not* can be contracted to form *didn't*, which is a single prosodic word in English. Similarly, in Israeli Sign Language, a noun and related pronoun can become "coalesced" (articulated roughly at the same time), and the mouthing of the noun occurs throughout.

tion, often in a stylized way, for example, a clamping of the jaw. These gestures are not always universal—in BSL, an enactment mouth gesture (a biting action) accompanies the sign APPLE (Woll, in press), but no such mouth gesture accompanies the ASL sign APPLE (see Fig. 2.5B).

Finally, a proposal put forth independently by Wilbur studying ASL and Sandler studying Israeli Sign Language (ISL) is that aspects of nonmanual expression correspond to prosodic intonation in spoken language (Nespor & Sandler, 1999; Sandler, 1999b, 1999c; Wilbur, 1991, 2000). Sandler (1999c) coined the term *superarticulation* to describe the "intonational" system of sign language. For spoken languages, intonational phrasing is marked by changes in pitch and pausing. For signed language, superarticulation is expressed by variations in facial expression. For example, raised eyebrows throughout a sentence indicates a yes–no question in many signed languages (just as rising pitch does in many spoken languages). Changes in head position and eye blinks frequently mark the boundaries of syntactic phrases in ASL (Wilbur, 1994). These prosodic analyses must interface with syntactic analyses of nonmanual markers discussed in the next section (e.g., Neidle, Kegl, MacLaughlin, Bahan, & Lee, 2000, show that nonmanual syntactic markers for WH questions and negation extend only over certain syntactic domains).

An interesting modality specific distinction between intonation and superarticulation discussed by Sandler (1999c) is that intonational melodies can be described solely as sequences of high and low tones (although the perceived melodies contain a wide range of pitches); in contrast, superarticulation involves several distinct articulators (e.g., the eyebrows, eyelids, mouth, head), which are independent of the manual articulators that express lexical information. For speech, the vocal channel must express both lexical and prosodic information at the same time, and to accomplish this, spoken languages appear to universally create intonation patterns using sequences of high and low tones (e.g., Pierrehumbert, 1980). Sandler (1999c) suggests that such combinatorial sequencing may be a modality effect and that this aspect of intonational structure is not a requirement of the linguistic system per se.

To conclude, we find that despite the tremendous difference between the major articulators (the hands and the tongue), most linguists agree that sign languages exhibit a level of structure that can be fruitfully analyzed as phonology. Signed and spoken languages exhibit some surprising structural parallels, which suggests that there are common principals underlying the organization of linguistic expression. The research strategy of comparing signed and spoken languages makes it possible to tease apart which phonological entities arise from the modality of articulation and perception and which properties arise from the nature of the expression system of human language, regardless of modality. The results thus far suggest that basic phonological entities such as distinctive features, segments, and syllables do not arise because language is spoken; that is, they do not arise from the nature of speech. Although the detailed structure of these entities differs (e.g., distinctive features in signed languages are based on manual, rather than oral, articulation), they appear to play the same organizational role for both signed and spoken languages.

However, it is also important to recognize significant distinctions between signed and spoken language phonology. For example, the degree to which phonological elements are realized simultaneously appears to be much greater in signed language compared to spoken language. Cross linguistically, signs tend to be monosyllabic with few segments, whereas spoken languages commonly allow multisyllabic words with several segments. This distinction in degree of simultaneity seems to be directly related to the auditory–oral and visual–manual modalities of speech and sign. The auditory system is adept at distinguishing quick sequential distinctions (e.g., the sequence /ba/ is typically less than 100 msec long), and the tongue can produce several quick gestures in succession. In contrast, the visual system is adept at parallel processing, and hand configuration and place of articulation can be perceived simultaneously within the visual field (see chap. 4). In addition, S. R. Anderson (1993) pointed out that when simultaneous gestures do occur in speech, the gestures often must be converted into sequential events because the sound could not otherwise be distinguished acoustically. For example, labiovelar sounds in West African languages are produced by simultaneously closing the lips and touching the back of the tongue to the soft palate, but these sounds are distinguished by first opening the lips and then lowering the tongue. In contrast, simultaneous gestures by the hands and face are easily distinguished by the visual system. Furthermore, the sign articulators are fully in view and do not obstruct one another, unlike speech where the lips obscure the tongue, which is why "reading lips" is so difficult. Thus, sign languages are quite free to represent elements of phonological structure simultaneously, rather than sequentially. In fact, the slower movement of the manual articulators may discourage a great reliance on sequentially expressed elements. (A further discussion of the nature of sign perception and production will be presented in chap. 4.)

Finally, as S. R. Anderson (1993) remarked, the discovery that the formational units of both signed and spoken languages are organized into hierarchical levels of representation (e.g., features, segments, and syllables) does not by itself indicate that these parallels are necessarily *linguistic* in nature. Many types of complex motor activities, from playing the piano to walking, have a similar type of hierarchical organization (e.g., Lashley, 1951). The broad parallels outlined here between signed and spoken language phonology may arise because both signing and speaking involve skilled motor control of a vast array of complex articulatory gestures. A key research endeavor for both signed and spoken language phonologists is to uncover what phonological phenomena can be explained solely in terms of the articulatory, acoustic, or visual properties of the linguistic expression system and what phenomena must be attributed to specifically linguistic principles not found in nonlanguage domains.

SYNTAX: THE STRUCTURE OF SENTENCES

As with all human language users, signers can distinguish grammatical from ungrammatical combinations of words in their language. For example, ASL signers accept MAN OLD SLEEP-FITFULLY ('The old man sleeps fitfully') as a well-formed sentence, but they judge OLD SLEEP-FITFULLY MAN as ill-formed. This judgment is not based on meaning—signers judge IDEA GREEN SLEEP-FITFULLY ('The green idea sleeps fitfully') as also well-formed grammatically, but nonsensical. Signs combine to form sentences that are governed by phrase structure rules and syntactic principles. In this section, we examine some universal properties of sentence structure found in both signed and spoken languages, and we explore some aspects of ASL structure that appear to be influenced by the visual–gestural modality.

Word Order and Universal Constraints on Structure

The basic word order of ASL is subject–verb–object or SVO (Fischer, 1975; Liddell 1980). The ASL sentence GIRL PUSH BOY unambiguously means 'The girl pushes the boy,' and BOY PUSH GIRL means 'The boy pushes the girl.' The SVO word order is not necessarily the most frequent order in the language, rather, this is the order that occurs if there have been no prosodically marked changes to the underlying order of elements. One way that the basic word order can be changed is by topicalization, as illustrated in Example (10b). The blank line represents the underlying object position of the topicalized noun. *Topicalization* is a phenomenon in which an element of a sentence is singled out as the topic by the use of a marked construction (e.g., fronting the topicalized element to the beginning of the sentence). The ASL topicalization marker is a combination of a backward head tilt and raised eyebrows, timed to co-occur with the manual sign(s) (Liddell, 1980), as shown in Fig. 2.12. The line

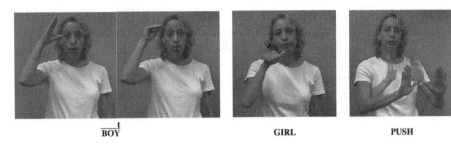

$$\overline{\underset{\text{BOY}}{\hspace{2em}}}^{t} \qquad\qquad \text{GIRL} \qquad\qquad \text{PUSH}$$

FIG. 2.12. Illustration of an ASL sentence with a topicalized object (Example 10b).

above BOY in (10b) indicates the scope of the facial expression (i.e., it continues throughout the articulation of BOY), and "t" stands for topic.[10]

(10a) Basic word order
GIRL PUSH BOY.
'The girl pushed the boy.'

(10b) Topicalized object

$$\overline{\hspace{3em}}^{t}$$
BOY, GIRL PUSH _____
'As for the boy, the girl pushed him.'

Topicalization in ASL is subject to the same universal "island" constraints that apply to spoken languages (Ross, 1967; see Fischer, 1974). For example, the *coordinate structure constraint* is a universal constraint on the ability to move an element out of a coordinate structure. A coordinate structure is one in which a word such as *and* or *or* joins together categories of the same type (e.g., nouns, verb phrases, or clauses). Padden (1983) showed that ASL also obeys this constraint, as illustrated in Example (11). The subscripts on the pronoun (glossed as PRO)[11] and the verb PERSUADE in Example (11) indicate the direction of movement, that is, toward the addressee (second person) or the signer (first person). The direc-

---

[10]Aarons (1994) argued that not all topics result from movement—some are base-generated in a sentence initial topic position, rather than moved to this position (see also Neidle et al., 2000). These different types of topics are distinguished by variations in the nonmanual markers that accompany them. Although the English translation of the topics in these examples is "as for X," this should not be interpreted as indicating a change in discourse topic, which Aarons (1994) associates with base-generated topics.

[11]PRO here is simply an abbreviation for PRONOUN and does not refer to "big PRO." (Within Minimalist syntactic theory, PRO refers to an empty category that is the subject of infinitival verb phrase complements of control verbs such as *want* or *decide*.)

tion of motion of the verb marks the role of these referents in the clause (see following).

(11) Example of a violation of the coordinate structure constraint (from Padden, 1983):

    a) $_{2nd}$PERSUADE$_{1st}$ BUT PRO$_{1st}$ BUY HOUSE.
      'You persuaded me, but I bought the house (anyway).'

            _____t
    b) * HOUSE, $_{2nd}$PERSUADE$_{1st}$ BUT PRO$_{1st}$ BUY _____.
      *'As for the house, you persuaded me, but I bought ____ (anyway).'

In (11a), the conjunction BUT joins two coordinate clauses: $_{2nd}$PERSUADE$_{1st}$ ('You persuaded me'), and PRO$_{1st}$ BUY HOUSE ('I bought the house'). Example (11b) illustrates that HOUSE cannot be topicalized and moved out of the conjoined clause, PRO$_{1st}$ BUY HOUSE.

Similarly, Lillo-Martin (1991) showed that ASL obeys the WH island constraint, which states that an element cannot be moved out of a clause with an embedded WH question. WH questions involve question words like WHO, WHAT, WHERE, or WHY. An English example is shown in Example (12)—the embedded WH clause is bracketed.

(12) Example of a violation of the WH island constraint in English
    a) Pat wonders [what Bob wants].
    b) *It's Bob that Pat wonders [what ____ wants].

Example (12b) is ungrammatical because the subject *Bob* appears outside of the embedded WH question. An ASL example of a similar violation is shown in (13). The embedded subordinate clause is bracketed.

(13) Example of a violation of the WH island constraint in ASL (from Lillo-Martin, 1991):

    a) PRO$_{1st}$ DON'T-KNOW ["WHAT" MOTHER LIKE].
      'I don't know what mom likes.'

            _____t
    b) *MOTHER, PRO$_{1st}$ DON'T-KNOW ["WHAT" _____ LIKE].
      *'As for mom, I don't know what ____ likes.'

In (13b), the subject MOTHER has been topicalized out of the embedded WH clause, and this movement creates an ungrammatical sentence.

Both the coordinate structure constraint and the WH island constraint can be unified under more general constraints on structure (e.g., Chomsky, 1981, 1995). These few examples illustrate that ASL not only has rules for constituent ordering, but also exhibits subordinate clause structure and follows universal constraints on syntactic form. Such findings should not be particularly surprising, given that there is no obvious hypothesis regarding how the visual–gestural modality of sign language would influence the nature of constituent structure or syntactic constraints.

Grammar on the Face:
Nonmanual Grammatical Markers

The visual–gestural modality provides a unique two-channel system in which distinct linguistic information can be expressed simultaneously by the face and by the hands. Both hearing and Deaf people use their face in the same way to convey emotion—expressions of happiness, sadness, and anger are universal (Ekman, 1992). However, ASL signers also use facial expressions and changes in head and body position to convey linguistic contrasts (Liddell, 1980). Linguistic and emotional facial expressions differ in their scope and timing and in the facial muscles that are used (Baker-Schenk, 1983; Reilly, McIntire, & Bellugi, 1991). Facial expressions that function linguistically have a clear onset and offset, and they are coordinated with specific parts of the signed sentence, as we have already seen in the phonology section that discussed the nonmanual components of signs. In contrast, emotional expressions have more global and inconsistent onset and offset patterns, and their timing is not linked to specific signs or sentential structures.

Grammatical facial expressions are critical to the syntax of ASL because they distinguish several different syntactic structures. We have already seen that a distinct facial expression marks topicalized structures (see Fig. 2.12). In addition, coordinate and subordinate clausal structures can be distinguished solely by nonmanual marking. For example, the ASL sentence SNOW, CLASS CANCEL ('It's snowing, and class is canceled') consists of two coordinate main clauses. However, if the first clause is produced with a conditional facial expression (the eyebrows are raised, the head is tilted slightly to the side, and the shoulders move slightly forward), the syntactic structure is altered (Baker & Padden, 1978). The first clause is then a conditional subordinate clause, and the meaning changes to 'If it snows, class will be canceled'. The only difference between the two structures is the nonmanual marking that co-occurs with the first clause, as illustrated in Fig. 2.13.

WH questions must also be accompanied by a specific facial expression: furrowed brows, squinted eyes, and a slight head shake (Baker & Cokely,

A) Two co-ordinate clauses

SNOW

CLASS

CANCEL

B) A conditional subordinate clause and a main clause

cond
SNOW

CLASS

CANCEL

FIG. 2.13. An illustration of grammatical facial expression in ASL. (A) illustrates two coordinate clauses, whereas (B) contains a subordinate conditional clause marked by specific nonmanual markers that co-occur with the first clause. An English translation for (A) is 'It's snowing, and class is canceled.' An English translation for (B) is 'If it snows, class will be canceled.'

1980). Furthermore, this facial expression usually co-occurs with the entire WH phrase, as shown in Example (14):[12]

     <u>   wh   </u>

(14) a. BOB LIKE WHAT?   "What does Bob like?"

        <u>   wh   </u>

    b. WHO LOVE BOB?   "Who loves Bob?"

        <u> wh </u>

   *c. *WHO LOVE BOB?

The WH facial expression can also occur without a manual WH sign. For example, <u>COLOR?</u> would mean 'What color is it?' (Lillo-Martin & Fischer, 1992). This form contrasts with the yes–no question <u>COLOR?</u>, which means 'Is there color?' Yes–no questions are marked by raised eyebrows and a forward head tilt (Baker & Cokely, 1980). This facial expression may be an example of superarticulation that has a syntactic function, perhaps akin to the syntactic function of question intonation in spoken languages.

Facial behaviors also represent adverbials that appear in predicates and carry various specific meanings (Liddell, 1980). For example, the facial expression notated as *mm* (lips pressed together and protruded) indicates an action done effortlessly; whereas the facial expression *th* (tongue protrudes between the teeth) means 'awkwardly' or 'carelessly.' When these two facial expressions accompany the same verb (e.g., DRIVE), two quite different meanings are conveyed, that is, 'drive effortlessly' or 'drive carelessly'. Facial expressions that function as adverbs are limited to the lower face and generally co-occur with a single lexical sign. Table 2.1 provides a fairly extensive list of facial adverbs in ASL compiled by D. Anderson and Reilly (1998). It is possible that *pah* and *pow* are not actually facial adverbs, but examples of ASL mouth gestures, which would explain why the meaning of these forms has been difficult to determine.

The use of facial expressions to mark grammatical contrasts is unique (and apparently universal) to signed languages. The linguistic use of the face raises several intriguing questions that we explore throughout this book: Are linguistic facial expressions perceived categorically, as are emotional expressions? (chap. 4). How do Deaf children acquire facial morphemes? (chap. 5). Signers must rapidly discriminate among distinct facial

---

[12]The syntactic analysis of WH questions is a topic of current linguistic debate (see Neidle et al., 1998; and Petronio & Lillo-Martin, 1997). These accounts disagree on the direction of the WH movement operation (rightward or leftward) and on the conditions under which the spread of WH marking is obligatory.

TABLE 2.1

Facial Adverbs in ASL (From Anderson & Reilly, 1998). FACs stands for Facial Action Coding System (Ekman & Friesen, 1978)

Adverbial Gloss	Description of Facial Adverb	Meaning (according to Baker & Cokely, 1980)	Examples
puff	both cheeks filled with air (FACS AU 13)	a large amount; a very large mass of; too much too many;	$\overline{\text{puff}}$ PEOPLE MANY FLOOR COLLAPSE 'there were too many people and the floor collapsed' $\overline{\text{puff}}$ 2h: HS:5 SCADS-OF 'a lot of something'
		or	
		far away in time or space;	$\overline{\text{puff}}$ FUTURE 'far into the future'
mm [see Fig. 4.2]	lips pressed together; the bottom lip may protrude in a slight pout (FACS AU 15 + 22B)	normally, regularly;	$\overline{\text{mm}}$ WALK CL: 1 'person moving' 'a person is walking along normally'
		or	
		with pleasure, enjoyment;	$\overline{\text{mm}}$ CHAT 'someone is chatting with enjoyment'
int	tightened lips are drawn back and teeth are clenched together (FACS AU 20 + 25 + 31)	surprisingly large; unusually great degree;	$\overline{\text{int}}$ CAT 2h:HS:5 'hoard of' 'there was a huge group of cats'
		or	
		extremely far away in time or space	$\overline{\text{int}}$ FUTURE 'awfully far in the future'

49

TABLE 2.1
(Continued)

Adverbial Gloss	Description of Facial Adverb	Meaning (according to Baker & Cokely, 1980)	Examples
ps	lips are pressed together and drawn slightly back with a small opening in the center (FACS AU 23 + 25)	just missed; very thin; smooth	J-E-T CL: $\overline{\text{J-E-T CL}}^{\text{ps}}$ 'fly over the tree', 'the jet just missed hitting the tree' BOX $\overline{\text{HS:B arc}}^{\text{ps}}$ 'top', 'the box has a smooth top'
th [see Fig. 4.2]	jaw is relaxed and lips part slightly to show protruding tongue (FACS AU 19 + 26)	carelessly; without attention; incorrect, wrong	$\overline{\text{DRIVE}}^{\text{th}}$ 'driving carelessly' ENTER SEE KID FLOOR $\overline{\text{SLEEP-ON}}^{\text{th}}$ 'I entered a room and saw the kids incorrectly sleeping on the floor'
sta	lips are slightly open; teeth are clenched; jaw opens and closes (FACS AU 22T + 25, 26)	over and over, too much, hard	$\overline{\text{WORK}}^{\text{sta}}$ +++ 'work hard over and over'

cha	lips are slightly opened; teeth are clenched; jaw drops suddenly (FACS AU 22T + 25 + 27)	relatively large	<u>cha</u> BOOK LARGE 'the book was really thick'
cs	tightened lips are drawn back on one side of the face; teeth are clenched together (FACS AU 20R + 25R + 31)	very close to present time or place; recently;	<u>cs</u> ARRIVE 'just arrived' <u>cs</u> PAST 'just yesterday'
pah [see Fig. 2.11]	tightly pressed lips open suddenly to form the (unspoken) word "pah" (FACS AU 24, 27)	meaning still under investigation;	<u>pah</u> SUCCESS 'finally succeeded' [also glossed as AT-LAST] <u>pah</u> PERFECT 'exactly perfect'
pow	tightly pressed lips open suddenly to form the (unspoken) word "pow" (FACS AU 24, 27, 18 + 26)	meaning still under investigation;	<u>pow</u> CAT SCATTER 'the cats dispersed everywhere' <u>pow</u> MOTHER BECOME-ANGRY 'Mom became really angry'

Note. From "PAH! The Acquisition of Non-manual Adverbials in ASL," by D. Anderson and J. S. Reilly, 1998, *Sign Language and Linguistics, 1*, pp. 123–124. Copyright © 1998 by John Benjamins Publishing Company. Reprinted with permission.

expressions during language comprehension. Does this unusual perceptual and cognitive experience with the face affect general face processing
mechanisms for signers? (chap. 8). Are emotional and linguistic facial expressions controlled by the same neural systems within the brain? (chap. 9).

Pronouns: A Unique Effect of Modality

The expression of pronominal reference is also an area in which sign languages are clearly conditioned by the visual–gestural modality. In ASL
(and other sign languages), personal pronouns have essentially the same
form as pointing gestures used by all people and are no doubt historically
related to such gestures. For example, to indicate "I" the signer points to
his or her own chest and to indicate "you," the signer points to the addressee (wherever that person may be located). Similarly, when other referents are physically present, ASL pronouns are directed toward these referents. However, ASL pronouns differ from pointing gestures because
they have been grammaticized into a linguistic system (see chap. 5 for a
discussion of how ASL pronouns are acquired by Deaf children). Specifically, ASL pronominal signs are compositional, unlike pointing gestures, and the component parts convey different grammatical distinctions.
Handshape (B vs. 1 hand configuration) contrasts grammatical case (possessive vs. nominative/accusative) and movement (an arc vs. pointing) indicates grammatical number (plural vs. singular). Hand orientation (toward the chest vs. away from the chest) indicates grammatical person (first
vs. non-first person). It is in this last category that ASL (and possibly all
signed languages) differs from spoken languages.

Meier (1990) was the first to point out that ASL does not comply with
one of the universal properties of (spoken) language observed by
Greenberg (1966): "All languages have pronominal categories involving
at least three persons and two numbers" (p. 96). The ASL pronominal system distinguishes two numbers (plural and singular) but does not distinguish between the three categories of first person ("I"), second person
("you"), and third person ("he/she/it"). Meier (1990) argued that the category of first person exists in ASL because first person plural pronouns (WE
and OUR; see Fig. 2.14) have a phonological form that must be specified
in the lexicon, and these signs do not point toward the physical locations
of their referents. That is, the sign WE is not directed toward the locations
of the speaker and another person(s). The second argument for the category of grammatical person in ASL is based on the nature of personal pronouns as "shifters." (Engberg-Pedersen, 1993, makes the same argument
for Danish Sign Language.) The referent of the first person pronoun shifts

| I | WE | OUR |

FIG. 2.14.   Illustration of first person pronouns in ASL.

depending on who is signing, but the phonological form is the same (a point to the chest). Furthermore, under direct quotation, the referent of "I" is not necessarily the signer, for example, if Mary makes the following statement: *John said, "I'm hungry,"* the pronoun "I" refers to John not to Mary. That is, a point to the chest in ASL does not always refer to the person who is signing (see Fig. 2.18B for an example).

Although Meier (1990) argued that ASL has a formationally distinct first person pronoun, he contended that there is no evidence for a distinction between second and third person pronouns. Because an addressee or a nonaddressed individual (a "third person" referent) can be located at any place within the environment, the signer can point to anywhere in the environment to specify either an addressee or a nonaddressed individual. Thus, there is no phonological distinction between a pronoun indicating second versus third person that can be specified in the lexicon. Some have suggested that eye gaze toward the addressee obligatorily accompanies a second person pronoun (e.g., Berenz & Ferreira Brito, 1987). However, Meier (1990) provided several counterexamples and concluded that although gaze toward an addressee is an important feature of signed (and spoken) conversation, it does not grammatically mark second person in ASL.

When referents are not physically present, signers may associate discourse referents with a location in signing space, and a pronoun directed toward that location refers to the associated referent. The association between a referent and a spatial location is typically made by producing a nominal sign at a location in space, gazing toward a location in space while producing the sign, or by pointing to a location while producing a nominal sign. This pointing (indexing) sign has been analyzed as a determiner when it is produced prior to the noun and as a locative adverbial when produced after the noun (MacLaughlin, 1997; see also Zimmer & Patschke, 1990). In this book, I use the term *spatial location* rather than *spa-*

tial locus because more and more evidence suggests that pronouns and
verbs are not directed toward *points* in space.[13]

Thus, ASL pronouns pick out specific referents as their antecedents
(e.g., "Mary"), rather than a class of possible referents (such as singular,
third person females). In addition, the number of possible referents associated with locations in signing space is unlimited, at least in principle,
and thus there is an unlimited set of possible third person pronouns
(Lillo-Martin & Klima, 1990). Meier (1990) concluded that

> the linguistic category of third person is not itself sufficient to distinguish
> among the available pronominal forms. . . . In contrast, deictic reference to
> the spatial loci associated with an array of referents is a far more powerful
> descriptive device than is a contrast between second and third person. More-
> over, indexing of spatial loci is sufficient to distinguish the loci associated
> with the addressee from those associated with the nonaddressed individuals
> in a conversation (p. 188–189).[14]

It appears then that ASL has a person category that consists of a distinction between first and non-first person.

Nonetheless, Liddell (2000b) rejects a two person grammatical system
in which there is an open number of possible non-first person forms. He
proposes instead that all pronouns are simply deictic points. The fact that
non-first person pronominal forms are not listable or phonologically
specifiable is problematic for grammatical theory, as argued by Liddell in
several papers (Liddell, 1990, 1994, 1995, 2000a, 2000b). A major problem is phonological implementation—how to specify the full phonological
form of a non-first person pronoun. The orientation (the direction of
pointing) of the pronoun is specified by *nonlinguistic* factors, namely by
where the referent is located in space.[15] For example, to refer to a present
referent, Mary, a signer, would direct a pronoun toward Mary, wherever
she happened to be—sitting at the top of the stairs or under the table. Although Neidle et al. (2000) proposed a primary distinction between first
and non-first person, they suggest that "non-first person can be further
subclassified into many distinct person values" (p. 257, fn. 14). The prob-

---

[13]For example, MacLaughlin (1997) argued that indefinite referents are associated with
areas in space; Liddell (1990, 1994) presented evidence that during referential shift, verbs
and pronouns are directed toward conceptualized referents (see following); and Padden
(1990) argued that first, and non-first person categories are characterized by distinct vectors,
rather than points in space. Padden (1990) suggests that agreement morphology "accesses
broader chunks of space" (p. 126).

[14]Deictic reference means reference to a location in the immediate environment of the
speaker or signer (e.g., *there* and *here* are deictic pronouns in English).

[15]The same arguments hold for nonpresent referents. Signers can associate a referent
with any number of possible locations in signing space, and the choice of location is often determined by pragmatic factors (see chap. 3 and Engberg-Pedersen, 1993).

lem is that such "person values" correspond to actual persons and their locations for present referents, and these are nonlinguistic entities.[16]

However, with no person category, it is not clear how to account for (a)
the distinct phonological form of *first* person pronouns in ASL (e.g., the
sign glossed as "I" is phonologically specified as a point to the center of
the chest); (b) the fact that WE does not point to its referents; and (c) the
shifting nature of first person pronoun referents under direct quotation. If
the person category analysis of Meier (1990) is correct, then there must be
a nonlinguistic process that aligns the direction of the non-first person
pronoun with the physical location of a present referent (or with the location in signing space associated with a referent). Liddell (1998; 2000a) argued that this process is gestural—that is, ASL pronouns are combinations
(blends) of linguistic and gestural elements. The handshape (marking
case), the movement (marking number), and I would suggest the facing
orientation (marking person) are linguistic features of the pronoun that
can be specified phonologically and morphologically, but the specific direction of movement and orientation constitute a gestural component of
the non-first person pronoun.

This process is not unique to signed languages. Spoken utterances can
also exhibit a composite of linguistic and gestural elements, but it is easy
to distinguish between the linguistic signal and deictic gestures because
they occur in different modalities (Liddell, 2000a). In addition, the gestural component does not influence the form of individual spoken words
as it does for signed languages. Liddell (2000a) suggested "the one difference [he is] proposing between signed languages and spoken languages, is
that signed languages have all developed in ways which allow the gestural
component to combine with the linguistically specified features of some
classes of signs without interfering with the ability to recognize the signs
themselves" (p. 354). Both speakers and signers produce utterances that
combine words concurrently with gestures; but for signed languages, the
deictic gesture is superimposed on the word and thus alters its form be-

---

[16]For nonpresent referents, Neidle et al. (2000) proposed that a pronoun is articulated by
"the index finger pointing to the location in space associated with the person features of the
intended referent" (p. 31). However, the evidence suggests that *referents* are associated with
locations in space, not the person features themselves. For example, the association between
a spatial location and a referent can change if the signer describes the referent moving to a
new physical location (e.g., see Padden, 1988, and Example [15]). The signer may use a new
location in signing space to refer to the same referent in this new location, but the person features of the referent presumably have not changed. Referents can be located in different
physical locations, which influences how signers choose to associate a particular location in
signing space with a particular referent (e.g., a signer may direct a pronoun toward an office
chair to refer to the person who normally occupies that chair; Engberg-Pedersen, 1993).
Thus, person features may be associated with referents, but there is no evidence that person
features are directly associated with locations in signing space. A person feature can only be
associated with a location in signing space via its relationship to a referent.

cause the word and gesture are in the same modality (see chap. 4 for further discussion of gesture and sign language).

Finally, it has often been claimed that ASL pronouns are unambiguous because they specify particular referents, rather than a class of possible referents (e.g., Emmorey & Lillo-Martin, 1995; Lillo-Martin & Klima, 1990; Neidle et al., 2000). However, ASL pronouns can be ambiguous with respect to whether they specify a referent or the physical location of that referent (Janis, 1992). Furthermore, van Hoek (1992) discovered that under certain circumstances, two distinct spatial locations can be associated with a single referent (see also Padden, 1988). She provides the following example (the relevant pronominal contrast is highlighted; the subscripts *a* and *b* indicate distinct locations in signing space):

NIGHT, WE-TWO$_a$ TALK THERE$_a$ HIS$_a$ ROOM. PRO$_a$ $_a$BAWL-OUT$_{1st}$. I $_{1st}$TELL$_a$ I SORRY. PRO$_a$ FORGIVE ME. MORNING, I GO$_b$ OUT$_b$ Y-A-R-D$_b$ $_{1st}$SEE$_b$ PRO$_b$ AGAIN. $_b$BAWL-OUT$_{1st}$ AGAIN. STRANGE. BEFORE, **PRO$_a$** $_a$TELL$_{1st}$ **PRO$_a$** FORGIVE ME. MORNING **PRO$_b$** ANGRY AGAIN.

English Translation: "In the evening, we talked, in his room. He bawled me out. I told him I was sorry, and he forgave me. In the morning, I went out to the yard and saw him again. He bawled me out again. It was strange. Before, **he** told me **he** forgave me, but in the morning **he** was angry again."

(from van Hoek, 1992, p. 185; subscripts are substituted for semicircles representing signing space in the original and bolding is added).

In this example, one pronominal form was used to refer to the referent in one context (in his room) and the other form was used to refer to the referent in a different location (in the yard). The choice of pronominal form reflected the conceptual location of the referent. In general, if the same referent participates in two events that have two distinct spatial settings, the signer may use two locations in signing space for that referent.

When an entity and its location are equally salient (and the signer has not chosen to use separate locations in signing space for the entity and the location), the ASL pronoun can be ambiguous as to whether it refers to the entity or to the location of the entity. This appears to be true for present referents as well. This ambiguity is illustrated in Example (15) and in Fig. 2.15. In Example (15), it is only the following discourse that disambiguates whether the pronoun refers to a referent (*dad*) or to a location (*Australia*). The pronoun itself is ambiguous. Such ambiguity is easily overlooked because distinct types of assertions are usually made for entities compared to locations. In the example in Fig. 2.15, both the referent (*the girl*) and her location (*a friend's home*) are equally salient, and the assertion could be made of either the referent or her location, thus creating a clear ambiguity.

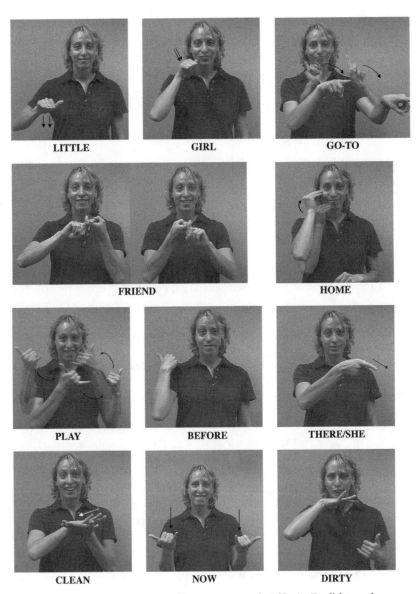

FIG. 2.15. Example of an ambiguous pronoun in ASL. An English translation of this discourse is: 'A little girl went to play at a friend's house. She played and played all around the house. Before, she/it was clean, now (she/it) is dirty.'

(15) 1960, DAD$_a$ VISIT$_a$ AUSTRALIA$_a$. DRIVE-AROUND$_a$. FINISH,
$_a$FLY$_b$ INDIA. REFUSE DRIVE-AROUND$_b$. WHY?
A) PRO$_a$ LOST$_{[continually]}$. SICK-OF-IT.
B) PRO$_a$ HAVE STRICT LAWS. THINK MAYBE SAME INDIA.

'In 1960, my dad visited Australia. He drove all around, and then
he flew to India. He refused to drive there because
A) he (in Australia) was continually getting lost. He was sick of it.'
B) it (Australia) had strict (traffic) laws, and he thought it would
be the same in India.'

In sum, ASL pronouns exhibit properties that are universal to all languages (e.g., number distinctions and shifting reference), but they also exhibit properties that reflect the visual–gestural nature of signed language.
Specifically, spoken languages distinguish among (at least) three person
categories: first, second, and third person. In contrast, ASL appears to distinguish only first and non-first person. Non-first person pronouns obligatorily combine with a nonlinguistic gestural component, which serves to direct the pronoun toward the specific location of a present referent or
toward a location in signing space associated with a referent. The obligatory
combination of a spoken form and a gesture is rare in spoken languages,
but it does occur. Pragmatic anaphors are an example (e.g., "It was about
yea high" must be accompanied by a specific measuring gesture; see
Jackendoff, 1983).[17]

However, the gestural component of ASL pronouns is controversial (see
Aronoff, Meir, & Sandler, 2000; and Neidle et al., 2000, for alternate views).
The controversy revolves in part around whether it is necessary to specify
spatial locations within a syntactic representation or whether the syntax
need only specify referential indices (e.g., Mathur & Rathmann, in press;
Lillo-Martin, 2000b; Lillo-Martin & Klima, 1990). Within a syntactic representation, a referential index is attached to each noun phrase (NP) and
conventionally indicates what entity that NP refers to in a real or conceptual
world (Trask, 1993). Nouns and pronouns (NPs) bearing the same referential index are by definition coreferential, according to the notational convention illustrated in Example (16). The referential indices *i* and *j* specify
which pronouns refer to *Lisa* and which pronouns refer to *Mary*. Thus, when
a pronoun and noun are coindexed, they are coreferential.

(16) Illustration of referential indices marking co-reference (from
Trask, 1993).

After she$_i$ arrived, Lisa$_i$ asked Mary$_j$ to give her$_i$ an account of her-
self$_j$.

---

[17]Gestures often accompany deictic (nonanaphoric) demonstratives in spoken language,
as in "Give me that book." However, it is not clear that the gesture is obligatory (e.g., context
might provide enough information that a gesture is not required).

Further research will help to determine whether the syntax must refer to the actual locations toward which pronouns are directed (and if so, how these locations are to be specified phonologically), or whether the syntax need only specify constraints on coindexation, and the direction of the pronoun is "filled in" by a gestural component sensitive to nonlinguistic factors such as the physical location of present referents.

Verb Agreement and Space

Padden (1983) observed that ASL verbs can be characterized as belonging to three classes: agreeing[18] verbs, spatial verbs, and plain verbs. *Agreeing verbs* can be directed toward locations in signing space to indicate the arguments of the verb (see Fig. 2.16A). *Spatial verbs* are also directed toward locations in signing space, but these verbs specify locative information (see Fig. 2.16B), and *plain verbs* are not directed toward spatial locations (see Fig. 2.16C). Janis (1995) argued that verb class membership is predictable from the semantics of the verb (e.g., based on the type of semantic roles associated with the verb) and from the phonology of the verb (e.g., whether the verb is body anchored; see Janis, 1995, for details).

It has been generally argued that agreeing verbs mark agreement with the subject and object of the sentence. The beginning location of the verb marks the subject and the end location marks the object (e.g., Wilbur, 1987).[19] Thus, in Fig. 2.16A, the verb BLAME begins at the location for a first person subject (near the signer's body) and moves toward the location of the addressee (the syntactic object), and the verb means 'I blame you'. However, some researchers have recently argued that the direction of movement of agreeing verbs is related to the semantic roles associated with the arguments of the verb, rather than to the syntactic subject and object (Janis, 1995; Meir, 1998; Taub, 2001). Evidence from so-called "backwards verbs" suggests that the direction of movement marks source and goal arguments that represent the start and end points of figurative or physical motion (see also Friedman, 1975; Shepard-Kegl, 1985). For example, Meir (1998) pointed out that the movement of the verbs SEND and TAKE (a "backwards" verb) both begin at a location associated with the source argument of the verb, rather than the subject. As illustrated in Fig. 2.17, both verbs begin at the location associated with the referent that is the source (the beginning point) of the sending/taking, not the location as-

---

[18] These verbs have also been called *inflecting verbs* (Padden, 1983) and *indicating verbs* (Liddell, 1995).

[19] The spatial location itself is not the subject or object.

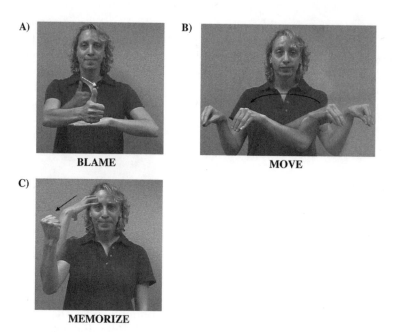

A)

BLAME

B)

MOVE

C)

MEMORIZE

FIG. 2.16.   Illustration of A) an agreeing verb, B) a spatial verb, and C) a plain verb. The verbs can be translated as A) 'I blame you', B) 'to move from here to there', C) 'to memorize'.

sociated with the referent that is the subject (first person in both cases). This type of analysis also explains why the same verbs are also "backwards" in sign languages unrelated to ASL (e.g., TAKE, INVITE, and BORROW are all backwards verbs in ASL, Israeli Sign Language, and British Sign Language).

Meir (1998) presented further evidence that the facing of the hands is toward the location associated with the referent that is the object of the verb.[20] For example, the palm of the hand in both verbs SEND and TAKE in Fig. 2.17 face toward the (indirect) object of the verb (the addressee), and in order for the sign BLAME in Fig. 2.16A to mean 'you blame me', the knuckles of the hand would orient to face the signer (and the movement of the verb would be from the location of the addressee toward the signer). Evidence for this analysis comes from the fact that the facing of the hands determines which referent location cannot be omitted.[21] That is,

[20]Facing is defined as the direction toward which either the palm or the fingers are oriented.

[21]Meir (1998) stated the generalization as follows: "The agreement marker (i.e., reference point) which is not marked by the facing of the hands can be deleted" (p. 25).

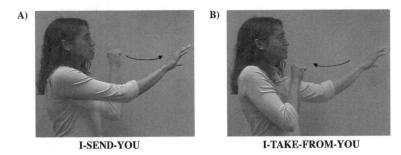

I-SEND-YOU   I-TAKE-FROM-YOU

FIG. 2.17.   Illustration of A) a regular agreeing verb and B) a "backwards" verb.

the verb must be articulated with respect to the location associated with the referent that is the syntactic object, regardless of the semantic role of that referent (goal or source). In contrast, a neutral location can be substituted for a specific location associated with the subject referent (Padden, 1983).[22] This generalization needs to be stated in terms of a syntactic role (i.e., the object), rather than in terms of a semantic role (either goal or source).

Bahan (1996) argued that verb agreement can also be expressed with nonmanual markers (see Neidle et al., 2000). For transitive sentences (e.g., "John hates Mary"), head tilt toward the location associated with the referent who is the subject ("John") marks subject agreement, and eye gaze toward the location associated with the referent who is the object ("Mary") marks object agreement. For intransitive sentences (e.g., "John is bathing"), eye gaze, head tilt, or both are toward the location associated with the subject referent ("John"). Bahan (1996) argued that these nonmanual markers occur with all verbs in the language, including plain (nonagreeing) verbs like LOVE and BATHE. However, nonmanual agreement markers are not generally required for grammaticality, and the use of eye gaze as an agreement marker can be overridden by other functions, such as turn taking and signaling referential shift (see following).

In contrast to these analyses, Liddell (2000b) argued that agreeing verbs (which Liddell terms indicating verbs), do not exhibit *agreement*, as most often defined by linguists (e.g., Lehmann, 1988). Basically, agreement is traditionally defined as a grammatical phenomenon in which the appearance of one item in a sentence (e.g., a third person subject, "she") requires that a second item that is grammatically linked to it appear in a particular form (e.g., the verb must have a third person suffix, "-s"; Trask,

---

[22] The neutral location is near the signer's body when the object is non-first person and in front of the signer in neutral space when the object is first person; the opposite pattern applies for backwards verbs.

1993).[23] Agreement occurs with respect to a grammatical category (e.g., number, gender, or person), which is morphologically marked on certain classes of words. Example (17) illustrates subject–verb agreement in English. The form of the copula ("to be") and the verb *read* agree with the person features of the subject (first, second, or third person).

(17) I am happy. I read books.
　　 You are happy. You read books.
　　 He is happy. He reads books.

Most ASL agreement analyses assume that, like English, the agreement category for verbs is person and number (e.g., Padden, 1990). However, the person category in ASL (first vs. non-first person) cannot be the basis for the directionality of agreeing verbs because non-first person does not distinguish between locations associated with distinct referents (Meier, 1990). For example, in the ASL sentence translated as 'You blamed him', the *locations* of the addressee and the nonaddressed individual determine how to direct the sign BLAME, not the *person features* of the subject and object—both are non-first person. One solution is to propose that non-first person can be subdivided into multiple distinct "person features" associated with distinct referents (Neidle et al., 2000). Another solution is to treat location (termed *locus*) as a grammatical category for sign languages (e.g., Engberg-Pederson, 1993). However, these solutions are problematic because both person features and the members of the locus category (i.e., the spatial locations associated with referents) are unlimited, are not phonologically specifiable, and are not a property of a noun (or pronoun) that can be specified in the lexicon (as number, gender, and the usual notion of person can be; Liddell, 2000b).

However, the morphology of ASL agreeing verbs clearly exhibits the anaphoric function of agreement found in spoken languages. That is, agreement morphology of the predicate-argument type serves to coindex salient arguments of a verb and has some of the same referential properties as pronouns (e.g., S. R. Anderson, 1992; Croft, 1988). Like pronouns, agreeing verbs pick out referents by where they are directed in space, and Lillo-Martin (1986) presented evidence that agreement morphology functions syntactically like an overt pronoun. It may be that ASL agreeing verbs perform the anaphoric function of agreement, but they do so in a way conditioned by the modality of the language. As just suggested for

---

[23]The element that controls agreement does not need to be overt. For example, in Spanish, one can simply say *habla* to mean 'I speak' or *hablo* to mean 'he speaks'. In this case, the verb agrees with the person features of a phonologically null pronominal element (i.e., the unexpressed first or third person subject).

pronouns, agreement may be marked within the syntax in the form of referential indices that are coindexed with arguments of the verb (Lillo-Martin, 2000b). These referential indices can serve as the semantic interface with a gestural or indexical component that directs verbs toward present referents or toward locations associated with nonpresent referents. However, this proposal is controversial, and more research is needed to solve the problems raised by Liddell (2000b), if an agreement analysis of ASL verbs is to be maintained.

To conclude, sign languages follow universal constraints on syntactic form that have been proposed on the basis of data from spoken languages (e.g., constraints on coreference relations and embedded structures). However, they also exhibit effects of the visual–gestural modality with respect to the nature of the pronominal system and agreement morphology. These modality effects are evident in the fact that, cross-linguistically, sign languages exhibit strong typological homogeneity in their pronominal and agreement systems (Newport & T. Supalla, 2000). Signed languages primarily encode person and number distinctions in personal pronouns, whereas spoken languages exhibit great variability in the type of information encoded in these forms, for example, gender, kinship, proximity, formality, logophoricity, and so on (McBurney, in press).[24] Furthermore, Mathur and Rathmann (in press) reported that sign languages exhibit uniformity in the form of agreement, as well as uniformity in the exceptions to agreement (gaps in the paradigm), in contrast to spoken languages that exhibit extensive variability in the form of agreement and in what morphological gaps appear in the system. Within the domain of agreement and pronominal reference, randomly selected sign languages resemble each other much more than any random group of spoken languages (Newport, 1996; Sandler & Lillo-Martin, in press).

DISCOURSE AND LANGUAGE USE

Signers, like speakers, use language to tell stories, to converse, and for artistic expression. In this section, we briefly explore issues in language use and discourse structure. As with other levels of linguistic structure, we largely find similarities between spoken and signed languages, with a few intriguing domains that are influenced by the visual–gestural modality.

---

[24]Although Japanese Sign Language marks gender on indexical classifier forms, the distinction is not generally marked on personal pronouns (S. Fischer, personal communication, June, 2000; Fischer & Osugi, 2000).

Conversations

During conversations, it may appear that people take turns with only one person talking at a time, but the actual interactions between conversation partners are much more complicated. Speakers[25] must know how to initiate a conversation, how to maintain their turn, and how to relinquish the floor. Addressees must know how to indicate that they understand the speaker (how to "back channel"), as well as when and how to take their turn or to interrupt the speaker. Speakers and addressees make use of a number of linguistic and nonlinguistic signals that indicate the initiation and termination of a turn, as well as the desire to take or maintain a turn (Baker, 1977; Duncan, 1972; Sacks, Schegloff, & Jefferson, 1974).

Signed conversation differs from spoken conversation in that a speaker cannot initiate a conversation until the desired addressee *looks* at the speaker (see chap. 5 for the implications of this for children learning sign language). For spoken language, a speaker can simply start talking to initiate a conversation, even while looking at a newspaper, the television, or other object of interest. In contrast, for signing, the speaker must first ensure that he or she has an addressee's visual attention. Baker (1977) reported that signers have a variety of ways to get another's attention in order to initiate a conversation: waving a hand within the addressee's field of view, lightly touching the addressee, or engaging a third person near the addressee to attract the addressee's attention. Once signers are engaged in conversation, eye gaze becomes the most powerful regulator of turn taking because it determines when one can speak. Once a speaker has the floor, then eye gaze away from the addressee is permitted and even desirable if competition for the floor is aggressive (Baker, 1977). That is, a speaker can maintain a turn by not looking at the addressee (this is true for spoken conversations in Western cultures as well). The speaker will return gaze to the addressee to check that the addressee is following, to "signal the boundary of an information package" (p. 223) and to signal the termination of a turn (Baker, 1977). It is considered rude for an addressee to look away during a speaker's turn.

An addressee can signal the desire for a turn by raising the hands from a rest position into signing space or by an increase in head nodding; the latter also occurs during spoken conversations to indicate that the addressee understands and has something to add (Baker, 1977). To interrupt a speaker, an addressee may start signing and repeat the first few signs until the speaker looks at the addressee. Once eye contact has occurred, the addressee (now speaker) may look away to maintain the turn. A speaker may refuse to relinquish the floor by holding an upturned palm toward the addressee (meaning "stop, wait"). As with speech, the signing

---

[25]In this context, "speaker" refers to the person who is signing or speaking.

of speakers and addressees may overlap in time, for example, an addressee may begin signing before the speaker has finished. Addressees can project or predict when a speaker's turn is ending, and thus fluent conversation has few gaps between turns (Sacks et al., 1974). This particular conversational skill develops late in childhood for both signers and speakers (see chap. 5).

A final issue in sign language conversations is how signers negotiate signing space. For example, when a referent is associated with a location in the speaker's signing space, how does the addressee refer to that referent? Does the signing space of the addressee and the speaker overlap? These and related questions will be taken up in the next chapter.

Narratives

Sign narratives share the same features as spoken narratives: scene setting, plot development, complicating actions, and conflict resolutions (e.g., Gee & Kegl, 1983; Bahan & S. Supalla, 1995). A narrative technique that is extremely common in sign language is the use of *referential shift* or *role shift* to express direct quotations, as well as to convey actions from a particular point of view (Bahan & Petitto, 1980; Engberg-Pedersen, 1993; Padden, 1986). When either a speaker or a signer produces a direct quote within a narrative, he or she is illustrating or demonstrating the speech of a character within the story, often producing the intonation and facial expression of that character (see H. Clark & Gerrig, 1990). The narrator "takes on the perspective" of that character during the quotation. In ASL, a narrator can also take on the perspective of a character while describing the character's *actions* (rather than quoting the character's words). When describing the actions of a character, narrators often portray the facial expression, eye gaze, and head movements of the character performing the action they describe. In this sense, the storyteller demonstrates aspects of the action from the attitudinal or affective perspective of that character. Sign linguists refer to both direct quotation and what has been called *reported action* as examples of referential shift or role shift (e.g., Padden, 1986; Poulin & Miller, 1995).

Direct quotation and reported action can be contrasted with *plain narration* (sometimes called *third person narration*). During plain narration, the nonmanual affective behaviors (e.g., facial expressions, body posture, nonlinguistic gesture) are attributed to the narrator (the person signing). The content of the discourse indicated by manual signs can be actions, descriptions, or the speech (sign) of the narrator. In contrast, for direct quotation the nonmanual affective behaviors are attributed to the character who is being quoted, and the content of the discourse (expressed by the manual signs) is the speech of the character. Similarly, for reported action, the nonmanual affective behaviors are attributed to the character whose actions are being described, but, unlike direct quotation, the content of the discourse are actions described by the narrator. In this case, the narrator is "reporting" the actions from the perspective of a particular referent by producing nonmanual behaviors that reflect that referent's attitude and that demonstrate selected aspects of the action itself.

Referential shift is indicated by a break in eye gaze with the addressee, a shift in head and body position (not obligatory), and often with a change in facial expression. A referential shift indicates that the following discourse should be understood from the point of view of the referent associated with the shift. Figure 2.18A and 2.18B illustrate an example of plain narration and a direct quote in ASL using referential shift. In Fig. 2.18A, the signer neutrally describes the situation ('she (the student) hates that class'), whereas in Fig. 2.18B, the signer provides a direct quote from the student ('I hate that class'). It is not necessary to use a phrase like "she said," to indicate quotation. The quoted referent (the student) is indicated by the direction of the body/head shift (toward the location associated with the student) and the direction of eye gaze. In this example, the referent of PRO_{1st} is not the signer, but the student. The use of the first person pronoun indicates unambiguously that the discourse within the referential shift is a direct quote (see Engberg-Pedersen, 1995). The use of a first person pronoun is ungrammatical during reported action; that is, if PRO_{1st} is used, signers interpret the discourse as speech (or thought) rather than as a description of action (Poulin, 1995). Lillo-Martin (1995) and Lee, Neidle, MacLaughlin, Bahan, and Kegl (1997) provided (differing) syntactic accounts of direct quotation at the level of the clause.

At a discourse level, Tannen (1986), describing spoken language discourse, introduced the term *constructed dialogue* to replace *reported speech* because speakers do not provide verbatim quotations, but rather construct dialogues to depict aspects of an interaction they want to portray (see also H. Clark & Gerrig, 1990). Constructed dialogue is often used in ASL stories, but it is also found in other narrative formats, such as lectures. Roy (1989) provided an example from a lecture on the mating habits of the stickleback fish in which the lecturer invents thoughts and speech for the fish. The dialogue is marked by changes in eye gaze and changes in facial expression (e.g., when describing the female fish's response $FINE_{wgl}$ with a "Mae West" facial expression). As in the example in Fig. 2.18, verbs like SAY or THINK were not used or were rare. Constructed dialogue serves to make a narrative more vivid and entertaining.

Figure 2.19 provides an example of reported action within a referential shift. This example is from a retelling of the picture book story *Frog, Where Are You?* by Mayer (1969).[26] The signer is describing the scene in which a

---

[26]I thank Judy Reilly for providing me with this example.

Introductory discourse:

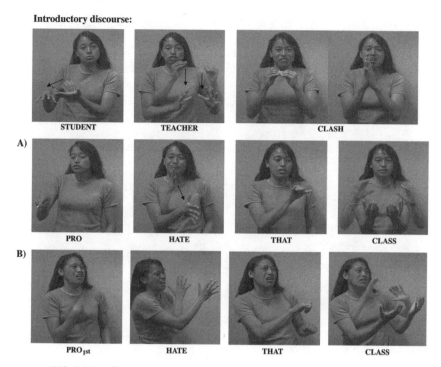

FIG. 2.18. Illustration of A) *plain narration* (sometimes referred to as *third person narration* and B) a direction quotation. An English translation for the introductory discourse is: 'A student and teacher clashed together (were arguing)'. An English translation for A) is 'He (the student) hates that class'. An English translation for B) is '(The student said) 'I hate that class' '.

small boy is holding onto what seem like branches while looking for his lost frog. The "branches" are in fact the antlers of a deer, and when they start to move, the boy falls onto the deer's head. During this description, eye gaze is away from the addressee, and the facial expression and nonlinguistic body movements (e.g., turning of his head and squinting his eyes when signing LOOK) are attributed to the boy in the story, rather than to the narrator. Engberg-Pedersen (1993, 1995) referred to this phenomenon as *shifted attribution of expressive elements*. Furthermore, signers can rapidly shift between distinct character points of view. For example, after signing FALL-ON-HEAD (from the boy's perspective) in Fig. 2.19, the signer then indicates that the deer raises his head by signing DEER and moving his head forward with an angry expression. Shifts are indicated by a change in facial expression, a change in body position, and almost always with a change in eyegaze. Poulin and Miller (1995), studying Langue des Signes Québécoise (LSQ), showed that the scope of the referential shift is critical to semantic interpretation. Neutral comments cannot

LOOK-AROUND   GRASP-OBJECT

FALL-ON-HEAD   DEER-RAISE-HEAD

FIG. 2.19.   Illustration of reported action (or constructed action) in an
ASL narrative (see text).

be expressed within a referential shift, which can only express an "internal
point of view" (that of the character with whom the signer identifies).

Liddell and Metzger (1998) referred to reported action within a referential shift as *constructed action*, which they define as providing "a visual example of the actions of the characters [in a narrative]" (p. 665). However,
in Fig. 2.19, the sign LOOK is not an action, but a lexical item that refers
to an action—only the facial expression and searching head movement
are gestural depictions of the action of the character (see chap. 4 for further discussion of the combination of gesture and signing). Nonetheless, if
constructed action is defined more broadly as actions depicted or described from a character's point of view, the term avoids the awkwardness
of "reported" with respect to conveying the actions of characters. Thus,
constructed action will be adopted for the remainder of the book.

Another aspect of referential shift is that pronouns and agreeing verbs
appear to be directed toward referents that are conceptualized as present,
rather than toward loci in signing space (Liddell, 1990, 1994). For example, certain agreeing verbs are lexically specified as being directed toward
specific heights with respect to a present referent: ASK is directed toward
the chin, HAVE-TELEPATHY-WITH is directed toward the head, and

GIVE is directed toward the chest of a present referent (Liddell, 1990). Similarly, during a referential shift, these signs are directed toward the conceptualized location of the body of a nonpresent referent. For example, if a signer was describing an interaction with a small child, the verb ASK would be directed downward toward the imagined child, but if the signer was describing an encounter with a very tall person, ASK would be directed upwards toward the face of the imagined referent (see chap. 8 for further discussion). Liddell (1995, 1998) offered an explanation for this discourse phenomenon in terms of Fauconnier's theory of mental spaces (Fauconnier, 1985, 1997).

Finally, we have seen that referents can be associated with locations in signing space, but it is also possible for discourse topics (and subtopics) to be associated with such spatial locations. Winston has shown that *spatial mapping* is a powerful strategy for structuring discourse in ASL (Mather & Winston, 1998; Winston, 1993, 1995). In this context, spatial mapping refers to the cohesive use of signing space at a discourse level rather than to the topographic use of space to describe a spatial scene (Poizner, Klima, & Bellugi, 1987; also see chaps. 3 and 9). For example, in a comparative discourse, Winston (1995) found that the signer mapped one concept, the art of ASL poetry, on one side of signing space and another, the science of ASL poetry, on the other side. As the signer described his understanding of the two concepts, he used various techniques to evoke a comparison between them: shifting his body toward one side or the other while signing, gazing toward one location or the other, or switching hands in order to articulate a sign nearest the appropriate space. Furthermore, signers can also "suspend" a spatial discourse map during an aside or digression and then reinvoke the original spatial map. In an analysis of a children's story, Mather and Winston (1998) found that the entire narrative could be divided into two main discourse spaces that structured the main points of the story (events that occurred inside a house and interactions with a wise man); these spaces could be further "chunked" into subspaces that mapped to subtopics in the narrative. Such spatial structuring is not in terms of individual associations between referents and locations in space. Rather, spatial mapping provides a more global visual patterning of the discourse that groups events together and allows an audience to make comparisons and inferences.

CONCLUSIONS AND IMPLICATIONS

The study of the linguistic structure of signed languages has revealed (and continues to reveal) significant insights into the nature of human language. At the level of phonology, which has been traditionally defined as the *sound* patterns of language, we find meaningful parallels between signed and spoken languages with respect to the patterns of linguistic form. At the same time, these investigations also reveal domains in which the articulatory and perceptual mechanisms of speech and sign affect linguistic patterning at the phonological level. With respect to word structure, we again find parallels between signed and spoken languages with respect to the basic architecture of the system, with language modality affecting preferences for particular types of morphological processes (e.g., affixation vs. nonconcatenative processes). At the level of syntax, signed languages conform to universal constraints on movement and syntactic structure, but the gestural modality impacts the nature of pronominal and agreement systems in ways that are not observed for spoken languages. At the level of discourse, both signed and spoken languages exhibit rich narrative mechanisms, but signers can also manipulate signing space to structure events and discourse topics (hints of this use of space may be found in the gestures of hearing people when they talk; see McNeill, 1992).

Finally, this review has shown that ASL makes use of spatial contrasts to express linguistic information from phonology to discourse. In the remaining chapters of this book, we explore the ramifications of such extensive spatial encoding for, among other things, the neural organization of language, verbal working memory, the relation between language and cognition, language processing, the acquisition of language, and in chapter 3, the expression of spatial and nonspatial information.

SUGGESTIONS FOR FURTHER READING

Brentari, D. (1998). *A prosodic model of sign language phonology.* Cambridge, MA: MIT Press.

Brentari's book presents a comprehensive theory of sign language phonology. In addition to laying out the Prosodic Model, Brentari places it in the context of other phonological models, pointing out shared assumptions and analyses, as well as discussing critical differences among current models. In the final chapter, Brentari discusses the contribution of sign language phonology to phonological theory and cognitive science.

Neidle, C., Kegl, J., MacLaughlin, D., Bahan, B., Lee, R. G. (2000). *The syntax of American Sign Language: Functional categories and hierarchical structure.* Cambridge, MA: MIT Press.

Neidle and colleagues present an in-depth analysis of ASL syntax within a formal linguistic framework. The analysis of agreement is different from that presented in this chapter—their proposal accounts for manual and nonmanual agreement in terms of distinct subject and object projections within the clause. Other chapters cover the nature of tense markers, determiners and determiner phrases, and WH questions. In addition, the authors also discuss important methodological issues in collecting and analyzing sign language data.

Sandler, W., & Lillo-Martin, D. (in press). *Sign language and linguistic universals*. Cambridge, England: Cambridge University Press.

This book is designed to illustrate the value of sign language research in advancing our understanding of linguistic universals. The overview focuses on theoretical linguistic research within the domains of phonology, morphology, and syntax, with extensive examples from both American Sign Language and Israeli Sign Language.

The following are excellent examples of ASL literature and poetry:

Bahan, B., & Supalla, S. (1992). *American Sign Language literature series: Collector's edition*. [Videotape available from DawnSignPress, 6130 Nancy Ridge Dr., San Diego, CA 92121].

Dannis, J. (Producer). (1995). *ASL poetry: Selected works of Clayton Valli*. [Videotape available from DawnSignPress, 6130 Nancy Ridge Dr., San Diego, CA 92121].

Lentz, E. M. (1995). *The treasure*. [In Motion Press (producer); videotape available from DawnSignPress, 6130 Nancy Ridge Dr., San Diego, CA 92121].

Chapter 3

The Confluence of Language and Space

Because signed languages are perceived visually and are articulated by movements of the hands in space, signers have a rich spatial medium at their disposal to express both spatial and nonspatial information. Signers can schematize signing space to represent physical space or to represent abstract conceptual structure. For sign languages, *spatial language*—the linguistic devices used to talk about space—primarily involves the use of classifier constructions, rather than prepositions or locative affixes. These constructions appear to be universal to sign languages (see Appendix B for the pattern of emergence of classifier handshapes in Nicaraguan Sign Language), and they exhibit some properties that may turn out to be typologically unique and arise from the visual–spatial modality. In this chapter, we first review and discuss these structures for ASL and then examine how ASL signers structure signing space to express spatial–locative information. We also explore how signing space functions to convey abstract information about time and to depict other abstract concepts and mental models.[1]

CLASSIFIER CONSTRUCTIONS

Classifier constructions are complex predicates that express *motion* (e.g., "The car meandered up a hill"), *position* (e.g., "The bicycle is next to the

---

[1]Portions of this chapter appeared in Emmorey and Falgier (1999b) and Emmorey (2001).

tree"), *stative-descriptive* information (e.g., "It's long and thin"), and *handling* information (e.g., "I picked up a spherical object"; T. Supalla, 1982, 1986). Although classifier predicates are quite frequent in ASL, their linguistic structure is not well understood. Most research has focused on the semantics and morphological structure of these forms, with little exploration of their syntactic or phonological structure, and our discussion thus reflects this distribution of research.

Figure 3.1 provides an illustration of how classifier predicates can be used in a discourse. The example is from a larger discussion about hanging pictures. In Fig. 3.1A, the signer indicates the square shape of the picture using a "tracing" classifier predicate. Figure 3.1B illustrates several classifier predicates. An English rendition of this discourse might be "Sometimes when people walk by and doors slam, the picture can shift position." The three classifier predicates indicate the movement of objects (a person, a door, and a picture). The final classifier predicate in Fig. 3.1C could be translated as "You simply readjust the picture," and the predicate indicates how a person held and moved an object (the picture).

Classifier predicates differ from the types of verbs discussed in chapter 2 (agreeing, spatial, and plain verbs) because the handshape functions as a morpheme and a "classifier" (we will discuss the use of this term in a later section). Classifier handshapes combine with various types of movement morphemes, and there are morphosyntactic constraints on these combinations (T. Supalla, 1982). In this chapter, the categorization system for classifier handshapes and movement morphemes proposed by Engberg-Pedersen (1993) for Danish Sign Language will be applied to ASL. Table 3.1 presents a modified version of this system for ASL.[2] Movement morphemes are expressed by the shape of the path traced by the hands or by the quality of the movement of the hand, but they do not necessarily denote motion of the referent object. For clarity, the term *movement* will be used here to refer to movement of the hand, and *motion* to refer to the motion denoted by the movement of the hand. Unlike Engberg-Pedersen, I use the term *position* rather than *location* as a cover term for movement morphemes that denote "be located," a change in orientation, or posture.[3] The classifier categories presented in Table 3.1 share similarities with the proposal presented by Liddell and Johnson (1987), partially summarized in Valli and Lucas (1995).

---

[2] The terminology in Table 3.1 differs from Engberg-Pedersen's (1993) terminology because Engberg-Pedersen rejects the term *classifier* and analyzes handshape morphemes as stems. A further difference is that Engberg-Pedersen proposes a *distribution* movement morpheme, but it is not clear whether this morpheme occurs in ASL.

[3] *Location morphemes* can also be misunderstood as treating locations in signing space as morphemic (parallel to treating movements as morphemic), which is not intended.

FIG. 3.1. Illustration of classifier predicates in ASL (see text). The discourse could be translated as A) "The picture is square," B) "Sometimes when people walk by and doors slam, the picture can shift position," and C) "You simply readjust the picture." These examples are based on an excerpt from "Hanging pictures: How to hang pictures evenly" from the videotape *Pursuit of ASL: Interesting facts using classifiers* (Interpreting Consolidated, 1998).

TABLE 3.1
Categories of Handshape and Movement Morphemes for ASL
(Based on Engberg-Pedersen, 1993)

Handshape	Movement
Whole entity classifiers are used to predicate something about whole entities, such as a person or a coin or a group of entities regarded as a whole, such as a mound of coins. These morphemes refer to an object as a whole, such as a car, a person, a pencil, or a piece of paper.	*Position morphemes.* "To be located at X location" (*loc*) is expressed by a short downward movement (identical to T. Supalla's (1982) *contact* morpheme). A change in hand orientation indicates either a change in object orientation or a noncanonical orientation. A *hold* morpheme (no motion) indicates a backgrounded verb and can combine with limb or handling classifiers to indicate posture.
Handling/instrument classifiers are used in verbs that denote an animate agent using the hand(s) to handle an entity or handling an instrument other than the hand (e.g., a knife, a gun). Instrument classifiers iconically represent a whole entity, but semantically they imply an agent handling the entity.	*Motion morphemes.* Path movement of various sorts is indicated by movement of the hand (e.g., *move-line, move-arc*). Movement indicates that an object moves or appears to move along a path of a particular shape. Motion morphemes can combine with position and manner morphemes.
Limb classifiers. Handshape represents limbs of humans or animals (e.g., legs, feet, or paws).	*Manner morphemes.* Movement indicates manner of motion, without specifying path (e.g., speed of movement, random motion).
Extension and surface classifiers. For extension classifiers, the handshapes represent the depth or width of an object. For surface classifiers, the handshape represents thin, narrow, or wide surfaces (e.g., a wire, the top of a board, or roof of a car). These classifiers are used to predicate the state of an entity or mass.	*Extension morphemes.* Movement does not denote motion, but depicts the outline of an entity or mass. In some cases, movement traces the perimeter of an object. Movement can also indicate the configuration of an unspecified number of whole entities (e.g., books lined-up on a shelf).

Morphosyntactic Constraints on Classifier Predicates

Whole Entity Classifiers. These classifier handshapes can combine with all four types of movement morphemes, as shown in Fig. 3.2. The choice of classifier depends on either the semantic or the physical attributes that are inherent or ascribed to the referent object (see Wilbur, Bernstein, & Kantor, 1985). For example, signers most often use the vehicle classifier when talking about the movement or location of cars (as illustrated in Fig. 3.2). However, a signer could also use a B handshape (thumb touching palm), which denotes a flat two-dimensional object, to describe

A)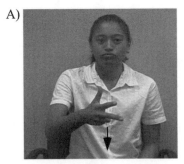

"A car is located here."

B)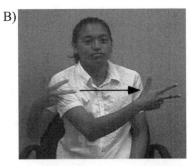

"The car moves in a straight line."

C)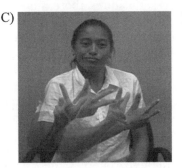

"The car moves randomly."

D)

"There is a row of cars."

FIG. 3.2.   The English sentences under each example represent a possible translation of the classifier predicate. The figure illustrates the whole entity classifier for vehicles combined with A) a *loc* position morpheme, B) a *move-linear* motion morpheme, C) a *random* manner morpheme, and D) a *linear* extension morpheme.

the motion of cars (palm horizontal) or motorcycles (palm vertical). These more general whole entity classifiers are chosen when the signer wants to focus on the path of motion (T. Supalla, 1990). When whole entity classifiers combine with extension movement morphemes, the verb indicates the spatial arrangement of multiple entities (e.g., "cars in a row"; Fig. 3.2d).[4]

Whole entity handshapes can also refer to the intrinsic features of an object, such as its front or back. For the vehicle classifier, the front of the vehicle is represented roughly by the tips of the extended fingers (see Fig. 3.2); when the 1 handshape is used for humans, the back of the hand cor-

---

[4]Engberg-Pedersen (1993) analyzes such examples as a whole entity stem + *loc* morpheme + *distribution* morpheme. This analysis captures the similarity of this form with other examples in DSL in which motion and *distribution* morphemes combine, for example, in the DSL translation of "go into many shops (on a street)." Further research is necessary to determine whether this is the correct analysis for ASL.

responds to the back of the body, but when the inverted V handshape (the "legs classifier") is used, the back of the hand corresponds to the front of the body. However, unmarked forms without orientation change or motion morphemes do not necessarily refer to intrinsic features of the referent object. For example, in Figs. 3.2A and 3.2D, the cars described are not necessarily facing away from the viewer (represented by the signer's body). In addition, whether parts of a handshape are interpreted as corresponding to inherent features of an object depends on whether the object itself is considered to have an intrinsic front or back.[5] For example, when the C handshape is used to refer to a dresser or chest of drawers, the back of the hand corresponds to the front of the dresser, but when this handshape is used to refer to a box which has no inherent features, there is no such attribution of sidedness to the classifier handshape. Such an interaction between classifier handshape and type of object suggests that a strict morphemic analysis of handshape parts for object features is problematic.

The entities referred to by classifier handshapes do not have to be concrete, physical objects. Liddell (1995) provides an example from a signer who describes the concept of *culture*, using the C classifier handshape to represent "a container holding the linguistic and cultural behaviors that people carry with them as part of their culture" (p. 36). Wilcox (1993, 2000) discusses another example in which the 1 handshape (index finger extended) is used to represent an idea. In these examples, there is a metaphorical mapping in which conceptual elements (e.g., culture, an idea) are mapped to the concrete domain (e.g., a container, a straight object) through the use of classifier handshapes (Taub, 2001). Furthermore, motion morphemes do not necessarily indicate actual motion. For example, to indicate "telephone poles rushed past me," a signer rapidly moves 1 classifier handshapes (for long thin objects) past the sides of his head (Lucas & Valli, 1990). Because the telephone poles are not actually moving, such motion is called *perceived motion* or more generally, *fictive motion* (Talmy, 1996).

Liddell and Johnson (1987) observed that whole entity classifiers do not allow other classifier morphemes to be located on them. For example, it is ungrammatical in ASL to place the hooked V handshape used to represent small animals on top of the vehicle classifier to indicate "the cat was on top of the car." Instead, a surface morpheme must be used to represent the roof of the car—in this case, a B handshape (palm down). Surface morphemes are the only morphemes that allow other classifiers to be located on them, and they make up a subset of extension morphemes in Engberg-Pedersen's system. Finally, when whole entity classifier predicates interact with body locations, they appear to be constrained by the relative scale of

---

[5]I thank Edward Klima for this observation.

the hand with respect to the body. For example, the hooked V handshape can be placed on the signer's head to describe a small boy riding on top of a deer's head (as when describing a scene from the *Frog Story*), but the vehicle classifier cannot be placed on top of the signer's chest to describe a car running over someone (T. Supalla, 1982).

Finally, the category of whole entity classifiers contains the category of *semantic classifiers* and a subset of the *size and shape specifiers* (SASS classifiers) proposed by T. Supalla (1982, 1986). T. Supalla (1982) argued that semantic classifiers indicate the semantic category of an object and that SASS classifiers are distinct because they "consist not of a single handshape morpheme, but of a group of simultaneous hand-part morphemes: each finger as well as the thumb and forearm is a possible morpheme which can combine in specifiable ways to form a handshape (p. 36)." This analysis predicts that the C handshape classifier ("deep and round") is morphologically more complex than the baby-C handshape classifier ("flat and round") because the C handshape has additional finger morphemes. In fact, there is little evidence for such morphological complexity (see McDonald, 1982). Although increasing hand size is iconically motivated as referring to objects of increasing depth, there does not appear to be evidence for a morphemic analysis of hand-internal structure in these forms. In contrast, Schick (1990c) characterizes SASS classifiers as denoting "the visual-geometric features of the nominal referent by categorizing the referent according to salient visual-geometric properties" (p. 26). The difficulty with this semantic definition is that it creates a heterogeneous class with respect to the movement morphemes that can combine with SASS classifier handshapes. For example, the 1 handshape (extended index finger) is considered a SASS classifier for "long thin objects" and could be used in a range of constructions indicating, for example, motion ("The spear arced through the air"), location ("The pencil lay there"), a narrow surface ("The bird sat on a wire"), but it could not be used to describe a narrow stripe on a shirt (a G handshape in a tracing construction would be used instead). The usefulness of this type of semantically based division for SASS and semantic classifier handshapes has not been clearly established. Thus, some linguists have argued that SASS classifiers do not form a uniform category (e.g., Engberg-Pedersen, 1993; Zwitserlood, 1996).

Handling and Instrument Classifiers. These handshape classifiers are distinct from whole entity classifiers because an outside agent is interpreted as causing the motion. For example, when describing someone using a knife to spread jam on bread, the H handshape (an instrument classifier) would be used to refer to the knife, but when describing a knife falling off a table, the 1 handshape (a whole entity classifier) would be used. When the classifier handshape represents how the hand holds an object, the implied agent (i.e., who is holding the object) is not necessarily the signer; that is, the classifier verb and the signer's body can be associated with two different referents (Engberg-Pedersen, 1993). For example, in retelling a story in which a girl paints on a boy's face, signers often used an instrument classifier for the paint brush and articulate the sign as if painting on their own face (see Fig. 5.6A in chap. 5). In this construction, the classifier handshape refers to the girl (as the agent of painting), but the signer's face is associated with the boy. Recent research suggests that predicates with *instrument* classifiers (the handshape iconically represents the instrument itself) are subject to different syntactic constraints than predicates with *handling* classifiers (the handshape iconically represents how the human hand holds or manipulates an object; Brentari & Benedicto, 1999).

Handling and instrument classifiers can combine with some position, motion, and manner morphemes, as illustrated in Fig. 3.3, but they cannot combine with extension movement morphemes. For example, the H handshape (representing a knife) could not be substituted for the vehicle classifier in Fig. 3.2D to denote "a row of knives." Handling classifiers also cannot combine with the position morpheme indicating "to be located" because of the implied agency in these predicates—such a combination would be interpreted as indicating the placement of an object at a location (McDonald, 1982). Handling or instrument classifiers also do not necessarily refer to concrete entities. For example, in chapter 2, we discussed an ASL lecture in which a signer compared the art and science of ASL poetry (Winston, 1995). Near the beginning of the lecture, the signer used a handling classifier predicate to indicate that he was separating these two abstract concepts (two C handshapes contacted at the thumbs and then separated, moving laterally from the center). Similarly, some predicates glossed as LOOK turn out to be instrument classifier predicates in which

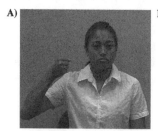
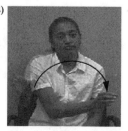
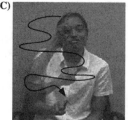

"Someone holds a spear."   "Someone moved the cup."   "Someone spray-painted randomly."

FIG. 3.3. The English sentences under each example represent a possible translation of the classifier predicate. The figure illustrates various handling classifier handshapes combined with A) a *hold* position morpheme, B) a *move-arc* motion morpheme, and C) a *random* manner morpheme.

the V classifier handshape metaphorically represents an instrument of visual perception (Engberg-Pedersen, 1993; Liddell & Johnson, 1987). Like other instrument classifiers, the agent implied by LOOK (the one who is looking) can be distinct from the referent associated with the signer, as in the predicate translated as "he looked me over." When combined with motion morphemes, LOOK can indicate the line of sight. For example, to indicate "look down into a well," LOOK is articulated with an arc motion into a C handshape referring to the well; the motion here is fictive, rather than actual (see Talmy, 1996, for extensive discussion of fictive motion).

Limb Classifiers.   These handshapes are used in predicates to denote the motion or state of an animate referent's limbs, and it is not always clear whether a particular handshape should be categorized as a handling or limb classifier. The major distinction is that handling, but not limb classifiers, can denote a referent different than the one associated with the signer's body. In ASL, limb classifiers can only combine with manner morphemes, and T. Supalla (1990) termed these predicates *verbs of locomotion*. As illustrated in Fig. 3.4, to indicate a person limping in a circle, the signer must first indicate the manner of motion ("limping") with the limb classifier for human legs (one hand remains stationary while the other hand hops). The signer then indicates the circular path and direction of motion with a separate verb (a motion morpheme combined with a general whole entity classifier handshape). Although it is physically possible (and iconically motivated) to produce the limping motion with the limb classifier along a circular path, this combination is ungrammatical in ASL (T. Supalla, 1990). The limb classifier predicates are an exception to the general pattern in which path and manner of motion are conflated within the

FIG. 3.4.   Illustration of the serial verb construction to describe a human limping in a circle. From T. Supalla (1990), "Serial Verbs of Motion in ASL." In S. D. Fischer and P. Siple (Eds.), *Theoretical Issues in Sign Language Research*, Chicago, IL: University of Chicago Press. Illustration copyright © The University of Chicago Press. Reprinted with permission.

predicate. These predicates are also clear examples of a morphemic analysis of movement because a single motion event is represented not by analogue movement but by two separate concatenated verbs, one indicating manner of locomotion and the other indicating path motion.

Extension Classifier Handshapes. These classifier handshapes refer to the width or depth of an entity or outline the extent of an entity, as illustrated in Fig. 3.5. These classifier handshapes can only combine with extension movement morphemes, which do not indicate either fictive or actual motion. If the movement ends with a brief hold, the object is specified as bounded (e.g., a length of pipe), but if the movement does not end with a hold, then the object is unbounded (e.g., a pipeline that goes on and on; Schick, 1990a). For extension predicates that trace the outline of an object, the movement always starts with both hands together in one place, and then either both hands move in opposite directions (tracing a symmetrical shape) or one hand moves while the other hand remains in space (e.g., Fig. 3.5C; T. Supalla, 1986). This two-handed structure is also found when whole entity classifiers occur with extension movement morphemes (see Fig. 3.2D). Such phonological constraints on form distinguish tracing constructions from the tracing gestures that sometimes accompany speech, arguing against Marschark's (1994) suggestion that these tracing forms may be gestures rather than ASL predicates.

**Gradient Versus Categorical Properties
of Classifier Constructions**

An early unpublished experiment by Schwartz (1979), conducted with Newport and T. Supalla, was the first to investigate whether aspects of classifier constructions were treated as categorical morphemes or as gradi-

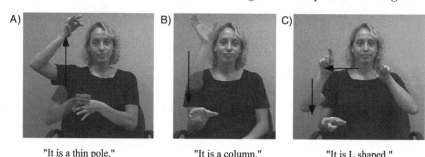

"It is a thin pole."   "It is a column."   "It is L shaped."

FIG. 3.5. The English sentences under each example represent a possible translation of the classifier construction. The figure illustrates various extension classifier handshapes combined with *linear* extension movement morphemes. Example (C) is a complex construction with two movement morphemes.

ent, analogue representations. In this study, Deaf signers were shown pictures of dots that varied continuously in size (along with several other distractor pictures) and were asked to produce a sign for each picture. The question of interest was whether signers produced gradient and continuous variation in handshape size in order to capture the continuous variation in dot size. To answer this question, another group of Deaf signers was shown the videotaped ASL productions and asked to choose the matching picture from the continuum of dots of various sizes. The results revealed a significant correlation between the picture-choices of the Deaf judges and the pictures described by the Deaf signers across size categories, but not within a size category (the medium-sized category was the only category with enough members to test for a correlation). This finding suggested that continuous variation in size was not expressed by analogue or gradient alterations of handshape size and that size was encoded categorically by classifier handshapes.

Emmorey and Herzig (in press) presented further support for this conclusion using a similar task design. A set of pictures was created illustrating a round medallion at the end of a necklace, and the size of the medallion varied continuously from quite small (¼ inch in diameter) to very large (2½ inches). A group of Deaf signers was asked to describe only one of the medallion pictures (embedded in a set of distractor pictures), and these descriptions were shown to a second group of Deaf judges, who were asked to determine which size medallion had been described. As with the Schwartz (1979) study, the Deaf judges were not able to correctly identify individual target medallion sizes within the continuum. However, in a separate experiment, another group of Deaf judges and a group of hearing nonsigners were shown a videotape of an ASL signer who described the size and shape of the medallions. This signer purposefully (as part of the experiment) produced a continuum of handshape sizes from a "squeezed" F to a wide baby C handshape. The Deaf and hearing subjects saw all of the productions (in random order). They were asked to chose from a set of stickers that varied continuously in size, and to place the sticker at the end of a necklace to indicate the size described by the signer on the videotape (the hearing subjects were told that the person on the videotape was producing a gesture to describe each medallion). In contrast to the first study, there was a strong correlation between choice of medallion size and classifier handshape size, but only for the Deaf judges. Hearing nonsigners were generally insensitive to the relation between handshape form and medallion size. Unlike the hearing nonsigners, the Deaf signers knew which aspect of the linguistic form could be manipulated in an analogue fashion to indicate gradient size information. Similarly, hearing English speakers know which part of a word can be manipulated to convey analogue gesture-like information; for example, speakers know to lengthen the vowel rather than the consonants of a word to convey variation in duration or length; for example, we say *looooong* not *llllllong* or *longngngngng* (Okrent, in press). Together the results from the ASL experiments suggest that classifier handshapes indicating size (and shape) are normally treated as categorical morphemes, but they can be specially manipulated to express analogue information.

Emmorey and Herzig (in press) conducted a parallel study investigating whether Deaf signers treated locations in signing space as categorical or gradient representations. T. Supalla (1978, 1982) proposed that classifier verbs of location are expressed with a limited set of *base point* or *placement morphemes* comprising a *base grid system* of contrasting locations. Within Supalla's model, locations in signing space are morphemic and categorical. To investigate this hypothesis, Emmorey and Herzig (in press) asked Deaf signers and hearing nonsigners to watch a videotape of a signer describing the location of a dot using the F classifier handshape. The dot was described as above or below a bar (expressed with a B handshape) in one of 30 distinct locations. Subjects then placed a round sticker in relation to a bar on a response sheet in response to each signed description (presented in random order). We found that signers and nonsigners performed identically on this task and were able to distinguish almost all spatial locations. This result suggests that Deaf signers interpret locations in signing space as analogue representations and do not group similar locations together as members of a linguistic category. Furthermore, both groups of subjects exhibited a bias for placing stickers at locations away from the central vertical axis, just as Crawford, Regier, and Huttenlocher (2000) found in a nonlinguistic spatial memory task (subjects had to reproduce the location of a dot on the computer screen). Crawford et al. (2000) hypothesize that the bias for reproducing locations away from the central vertical axis arises because this axis constitutes a nonlinguistic spatial category boundary.

To investigate whether Deaf signers produce categorical or gradient expressions of location, Emmorey and Herzig (in press) asked 30 different Deaf signers to describe just one of the 30 "dot and bar" pictures (embedded within a set of distractor drawings). Each person saw a different target picture, and no one saw the entire set. Again, to determine whether signers produced analogue or categorical descriptions of locations, a videotape of all of the subjects' descriptions (created by digitizing and editing the master tapes) was shown to another group of Deaf judges who performed the sticker-placement task. In contrast to the results with the size continuum and classifier handshapes, Deaf judges were able to correctly identify most of the target spatial locations. As with the first experiment investigating the interpretation of locations in signing space, the results of the second study indicated that locations were treated as analogue, gradient representations and that signing space was susceptible to the same spatial category effects observed for "nonlinguistic" space (specifically, a bias away from the central vertical axis, a spatial category boundary) and toward the diagonal quadrants, hypothesized to be nonlinguistic spatial categories; Crawford et al., 2000).

Finally, when the spatial location description study was conducted with English speakers, Emmorey (2000) found very different results. English-speaking judges were not able to correctly identify the 30 target locations described in English by another set of speakers (parallel to the ASL study, speakers described only one of the 30 "dot and bar" pictures, and their descriptions were randomized and played to the judges who performed the sticker-placement task). Unlike the ASL descriptions, the English descriptions did not preserve the relative locations in space; rather, the descriptions tended to categorize space primarily along a vertical dimension (describing the dot as either *above* or *below* the bar) and secondarily along a horizontal dimension (describing the bar as above/below and to the *right* or *left*).

Overall, these experiments indicate that some aspects of classifier constructions are clearly categorical morphemes, specifically whole entity handshapes, but other components, specifically locations within signing space, are gradient and analogue representations. Thus, spatial language in signed languages (or at least in ASL) differs dramatically from spoken languages because for the latter, spatial information is conveyed categorically by a small set of closed-class forms, such as prepositions and locative affixes (Talmy, 2000). Spoken languages do not have a way of phonologically altering a preposition or affix to mean "upward and to the left" versus "upward and slightly to the left" versus "upward and to the far left." In ASL, such spatial information is indicated in an analogue manner by where the hands are located in signing space. This is not to say that there are no linguistic constraints on where or how the hands are positioned in signing space. As noted earlier, certain whole entity classifiers do not allow other classifiers to be located on them, and there are constraints on perspective and relative scale that affect choice of classifier handshape. However, the gradient and analogue descriptions of spatial locations that can be produced by signers stand in stark contrast to the categorical nature of spatial descriptions produced by speakers (see also Talmy, in press).

Simultaneous Constructions

To express a locative relation and/or a motion event involving two (or more) referents, classifier predicates can be combined to create a simultaneous construction in which two predicates are expressed at the same time (see Engberg-Pedersen, 1994; Miller, 1994). Such simultaneous constructions are unique to signed languages and may occur because of the availability of two independent articulators (see chap. 4). However, there are strong constraints on the form of these constructions. For example, the two simultaneous predicates cannot contain distinct movement morphemes, as one would need to describe a woman walking past a zigzagging car. To describe such a situation, the signer first indicates the zigzagging car with a vehicle classifier predicate, then produces a simultaneous construction. The simultaneous construction consists of the vehicle classifier with a *hold* morpheme, which indicates a backgrounded element and the 1 classifier (for an upright person) with a *move-line* motion morpheme (see Table 3.1); the 1 handshape moves past the vehicle classifier held in signing space. The *hold* morpheme is neutral with respect to the semantic distinction between location and motion (Engberg-Pedersen, 1993); that is, the described car is still understood as zigzagging as the woman passes by, but the classifier handshape does not move (i.e., the *hold* morpheme does not specify either "be located" or "no motion"). Other examples of simultaneous constructions in which one predicate contains a *hold* morpheme and the other contains a motion or position morpheme can be found in Figs. 3.6, 3.7A, and 3.7B (in these examples, the *hold* predicate refers to a static rather than a moving object).

If both hands move, the motion morphemes within each predicate must be the same, for example, if the woman and car were both moving with a linear motion, a simultaneous construction could be used in which each predicate contained a *move-line* morpheme. These constraints on form are subsumed under the *symmetry condition* for two-handed signs proposed by Battison (1978; see chap. 2). However, classifier constructions permit other handshapes for the stationary hand, and they permit sequences of movements that are not allowed for nonclassifier verbs (Engberg-Pedersen, 1993).

For locative expressions, simultaneous constructions involve two types of referents: a figure object (the located object) and a ground object (the reference object).[6] In the sentence, "The bike is near the house," the bike is the figure and the house is the ground (Talmy, 1983). In English, the figure is the subject of the sentence (mentioned first), and the ground is expressed as the object of the preposition. To express this locative relation in ASL, however, the ground object is indicated first with a separate classifier predicate, as illustrated in Fig. 3.6. The location of the figure object with respect to the ground is indicated by a second simultaneous classifier construction. This ordering of mention for figure and ground may be an

---

[6] T. Supalla (1982) used the term *central object* for the figure and separates the ground into a *secondary object* (a reference object) and a *ground* (a background surface). It is not clear whether such a distinction between types of ground objects is required.

HOUSE   whole-entity CL + *loc*   BIKE   whole-entity CL + *loc*

FIG. 3.6.   A possible English translation would be "The bike is near the house."

effect of the visuospatial modality of sign languages (Emmorey, 1996). For example, to present a scene visually by drawing a picture, the ground object tends to be drawn first, and then the figure is located with respect to the ground. Thus, if drawing a picture of a bike next to a house, most people draw the house first; similarly, for a cup on a table, the table is drawn first.

Why Are They Called "Classifiers"?

We now turn to the problematic term *classifier* as it is applied to spoken and signed languages. In his influential survey of classifier systems in spoken languages, Allan (1977) defined classifiers with respect to two criteria: (1) "they occur as morphemes in surface structures under specifiable conditions," and (2) "they have meaning, in the sense that a classifier denotes some salient perceived or imputed characteristic of the entity to which an associated noun refers (or may refer)" (p. 285). The first criterion rules out analyzing English verbs such as *jab* as a classifier for "actions of stabbing with a pointed object" or *meander* as a classifier for "movement by a winding or indirect course." There is no morpheme that can be identified as referring to any referent nouns with which such verbs co-occur, and one cannot specify the type of construction within which such a classifier may occur. The second criterion rules out such systems as gender marking in German, where gender classifications are relatively arbitrary categories that do not refer to the actual gender of the noun (e.g., *Mädchen* ('young girl') requires the neuter, rather than feminine, gender marking). By these two criteria, ASL has classifiers, but so does English. English examples such as *flock of* birds, *herd of* cows, or *school of* fish qualify as classifiers. However, Allan would categorize ASL, but not English, as a "classifier language" because (a) ASL appears to belong to a particular type of classifier language (a predicate classifier language like Navajo), and (b) because ASL contains forms that refer to the inherent properties of an entity. Classifiers that refer to the arrangement of an entity or group of entities or that refer to the quantity of an entity (as in the English examples just cited) are found in both classifier and nonclassifier languages, but classifiers that refer to inherent properties of an entity (such as its shape or semantic class) are confined to classifier languages.

Engberg-Pedersen (1993) argued that Allan's first criterion actually rules out predicate classifier languages such as Navajo because the classificatory and predicative meanings are merged within the verb. For example, the Navajo stem -tá is used for long slender objects that are in a rest position, -tííh is used for long slender objects that are moved or handled, -t'è? is used when such objects are dropped or thrown, and -kèès is used when such objects are free moving (Davidson, Elford, & Denny, 1963). Although most of these forms appear to be morphologically related, one cannot point to a *classifier morpheme*, which refers to the properties of the referent noun (just as one cannot do so for the English words *stab* or *jab*). Linguists generally refer to these Navajo verbs as *classificatory verb stems* rather than as predicate classifiers.

In contrast to Allan (1977), some linguists only use classifier to refer to separate words in noun phrases. For example, in Trask's (1993) *A Dictionary of Grammatical Terms in Linguistics*, *classifier* is defined as "One of a set of specialized grammatical words which, in certain languages, typically or obligatorily form constituents of certain types of noun phrases, especially those containing numerals, the choice of classifier being determined by the semantic characteristics of the head noun" (p. 44). Under this definition, ASL does not have classifiers because ASL classifier forms are not part of a noun phrase.[7] So, does ASL have classificatory verb stems, classifiers, or something else? Well, it depends on your definition of *classifier* and your morphological analysis of ASL classifier predicates.

T. Supalla (1978, 1982, 1986) adopted an analysis in which classifier forms contain a root morpheme that expresses motion or location. Handshape is a morpheme (or set of morphemes) that is affixed to this verb root. The handshape morpheme(s) refers to inherent properties of an object and would thus be considered a classifier by some linguists, as just noted. However, both McDonald (1982) and Engberg-Pedersen (1993) questioned whether the proposed motion and location morphemes are actually the true stem of classifier verbs. Engberg-Pedersen noted that the main argument in favor of such an analysis is based entirely on semantics. That is, classifier verbs express motion and location information, and such information is conveyed by the movement or placement of the hand,

---

[7]Bergman and Wallin (2001) have argued that Swedish Sign Language does have classifiers that are part of the noun phrase. The noun classifiers are formationally related to SLS nouns and/or to classifier predicates that specify size and shape, but they are distinguished from these forms in meaning, in distribution, and in the co-occurring mouth patterns.

not by handshape. The problem is that the interpretation of the movement of the hand can crucially depend on the handshape morpheme; for example, a linear movement can be interpreted as indicating motion of an object, extent of an object, or caused motion, depending on the handshape.

Similarly, McDonald (1982) suggested that the handshape morpheme has a much more central role in determining the meaning of a classifier verb than is implied if handshape is simply an affix that is superimposed on a verb stem denoting motion. That is, under the affixal analysis, one would predict that substituting one classifier handshape for another would not alter the meaning of the motion but rather indicate that the same motion is now being predicated of a different sort of object. Such a prediction does not appear to be true. For example, the same movement (e.g., an arc) can have radically different interpretations depending on which handshape co-occurs with the movement. McDonald (1982) illustrated this point with two classifier forms that have the same movement, each with a different handshape, as shown in Fig. 3.7. The construction in Fig. 3.7A could be translated as "Someone put the book on the shelf," and the construction in Fig. 3.7B as "The cat jumped on a shelf." In Fig. 3.7A, the motion is caused by an outside agent, and in Fig. 3.7B, the motion is self-generated. Wallin (1994) also finds that it is the classifier handshape that distinguishes between nonagentive motion and self-agentive motion for Swedish Sign Language. Furthermore, Schembri (in press) provides evidence from Auslan (Australian Sign Language) that handshape does not exclusively classify the properties of a referent (e.g., whether it is human or animal), and choice of handshape cannot be clearly separated from the conception of the motion event being described. The fact that the meaning of a classifier form depends on a complex interaction between move-

A)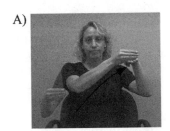

B)

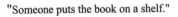

"Someone puts the book on a shelf."   "The cat jumps on a shelf."

FIG. 3.7. The English sentences under each example represent a possible translation of the classifier construction. A) Illustration of a classifier handshape used for handling thick flat objects combined with an *arc* motion morpheme. B) Illustration of a classifier handshape used for small animals combined with an *arc* motion morpheme.

ment and handshape and the fact that movement does not have a stable, identifiable meaning suggests that movement is not the stem, with handshape as a classificatory affix.

It is becoming apparent that we cannot maintain an analysis of classifier verbs in ASL as composed of a movement stem with handshape as a classifier affix that can be substituted within the verb. In addition, handshape does not appear to be a *classifier* in the sense used by many linguists. Specifically, handshape morphemes do not form part of a noun phrase, are not affixes attached to a verb stem, and are not classificatory verbs as found in Navajo and other Athapaskan languages (see Engberg-Pedersen, 1993, and Schembri, in press, for further discussion).

For these reasons, Engberg-Pedersen (1993) proposed that we abandon the term *classifier* and characterize these forms as *polymorphemic*. However, this term is vague because many nonclassifier verbs are polymorphemic, in the sense of containing more than one morpheme. Wallin (1994) proposed that these verbs be termed *polysynthetic*, but this term is used typologically to characterize languages that exhibit properties not observed in ASL (or in other sign languages), such as the incorporation of noun stems into verbs (e.g., Baker, 1988). It may indeed turn out that this type of predicate is unique to sign languages—in fact, classifier forms of the sort described in this chapter have been found in all sign languages documented to date, regardless of historical relation.

Although the term *classifier* may be problematic when applied to sign languages, it is in widespread use among sign language linguists, not to mention ASL instructors and students, and no clear alternative terminology has been proposed or widely accepted. The initial use of *classifier* to refer to the handshape in ASL verbs of motion and location may have arisen because of an early misinterpretation of the Navajo verb system—it was thought that Navajo verbs contained identifiable classificatory morphemes (Schembri, in press). The term *classifier* may remain popular for ASL researchers because the handshapes do in some sense "classify" referents based on their physical or semantic characteristics, and they form a closed set with specific morphosyntactic properties. Given the terminological void and the use of the term *classifier* both currently and historically by those studying sign languages, the term will not be abandoned here. However, readers should now understand that the term has a unique meaning for sign languages and that sign language classifiers differ in many (but not all) properties that are ascribed to classifiers in spoken languages.[8]

Another unresolved issue within sign linguistics is whether the handshape or the movement (or perhaps both) should be considered the

---

[8]At a recent workshop on classifier constructions, the term *property marker* was proposed as an alternative to handshape classifier. A *property marker* indicates the relevant property of a referent.

stem of a classifier predicate. Most analyses propose that movement is the stem on semantic grounds, that is, it is the movement that denotes motion or location in these verbs (Schick, 1990a; T. Supalla, 1982, 1986; Wallin, 1994). However, as noted, handshape and movement appear to jointly determine the meaning of a classifier predicate (see also T. Supalla, 1990). McDonald (1982) and Engberg-Pedersen (1993) proposed that handshape, rather than movement, should be considered the stem of a classifier verb. However, there is something semantically odd about this proposal because handshape primarily conveys information about a noun referent, and classifier handshapes can be interpreted as coreferential with a nominal element in the discourse. In fact, some analyses treat classifier handshapes as a type of pronoun (Baker & Cokely, 1980; Kegl & Wilbur, 1976). Therefore, rather than assuming an analysis in which classifier handshapes are affixes attached to movement stems or vice versa, we considered classifier handshapes and movement as morphological units that combine to create classifier predicates, and neither have been treated as primary. Future linguistic research may provide a clearer analysis of the internal morphological structure of these complex predicates.

TALKING ABOUT SPACE WITH SPACE

In the ASL version of the sentence, "The bike is near the house," shown in Fig. 3.6, the locative relation expressed by the classifier construction is not encoded by a separate word as it would be in English with the preposition *near*. Although ASL has lexicalized locatives such as NEAR, ON, or IN, signers prefer to use classifier constructions when describing spatial relationships. As we have already discussed, rather than encoding spatial information with prepositions or locative affixes, such information is conveyed by a schematic and isomorphic mapping between where the hands are placed in signing space and the locations of objects being described. The ramifications of this spatialized form for how signers describe spatial environments is explored next.

Spatial Formats, Perspective Choice, and Frames of Reference

When English speakers describe environments, they often take their listener on a "mental tour," adopting a *route* perspective, but they may also adopt a *survey* perspective, describing the environment from a "bird's eye view," using cardinal direction terms (Taylor & Tversky, 1992, 1996). Route and survey perspectives differ with respect to (a) point of view (moving within the scene vs. fixed above the scene), (b) reference object (the addressee vs. another object/landmark), and (c) reference terms (right–left–front–back vs. north–south–east–west). Route and survey perspectives also correspond to two natural ways of experiencing an environment (Emmorey, Tversky, & Taylor, in press). A route perspective corresponds to experiencing an environment from within, by navigating it, and a survey perspective corresponds to viewing an environment from a single outside position. The following are English examples from Linde and Labov's (1975) study of New Yorker's descriptions of their apartments:

> *Route perspective:* As you open the door, you are in a small five-by-five room which is a small closet. When you get past there, you're in what we call the foyer . . . If you keep walking in that same direction, you're confronted by two rooms in front of you . . . large living room which is about twelve by twenty on the left side. And on the right side, straight ahead of you again, is a dining room which is not too big . . . (p. 929)

> *Survey perspective:* The main entrance opens into a medium-sized foyer. Leading off the foyer is an archway to the living room which is the furthermost west room in the apartment. It's connected to a large dining room through double sliding doors. The dining room also connects with the foyer and main hall through two small arches. The rest of the rooms in the apartment all lead off this main hall which runs in an east–west direction. (p. 927)

Emmorey and Falgier (1999b) found that ASL signers also adopt either a route or survey perspective when describing an environment and that signers structure signing space differentially, depending on perspective choice. Following Taylor and Tversky (1992, 1996), we asked 40 fluent ASL signers to memorize one of two maps (the town or the convention center; see Fig. 3.8) and then to describe the environment such that someone unfamiliar with the environment could find all of the landmarks. We found that if signers adopted a survey perspective when describing an environment, they most often used a *diagrammatic* spatial format, but when a route perspective was adopted, they most often used a *viewer* spatial format. The term *spatial format* refers to the topographic structure of signing space used to express locations and spatial relations between objects. Table 3.2 summarizes the properties associated with each spatial format.

Diagrammatic space is somewhat analogous to Liddell's notion of *token space* (Liddell, 1994, 1995) and to Schick's (1990a) *Model space*. Model space is characterized as "an abstract, Model scale in which all objects are construed as miniatures of their actual referents" (Schick, 1990a, p. 32). Liddell (1995) describes tokens as "conceptual entities given a manifestation in physical space," and states that "the space tokens inhabit is limited to the size of physical space ahead of the signer in which the hands may be located while signing" (p. 33). Diagrammatic space is also so limited, and under Liddell's analysis, signers could conceptualize tokens as representing

TABLE 3.2
Properties Associated With Spatial Formats in ASL

Diagrammatic Space	Viewer Space
Signing space represents a map-like model of the environment.	Signing space reflects an individual's view of the environment at a particular point in time and space.
Space can have either a 2-D "map" or a 3-D "model" format.	Signing space is 3-D.
The vantage point does not change (generally a bird's eye view).	The vantage point can change.
Relatively low horizontal signing space or a vertical plane.	Relatively high horizontal signing space.

objects and landmarks within a description of an environment. However, tokens are hypothesized to be three-dimensional entities, and the data from Emmorey and Falgier (1999b) contained some examples in which the spatial format was 2-D, representing a map with points and lines.

Figure 3.8 provides an example of the use of diagrammatic space, illustrating the pointing signs produced by one participant in the experiment to indicate the locations of the outer rooms of the convention center. The locations within signing space map isomorphically to the locations of the rooms on the convention center map. This particular signer is unusual because she did not rotate the map. That is, most signers "shifted" the map so that the entrance was located at the chest and the bulletin board extended outward on the left of signing space. This pattern may reflect a convention for spatial descriptions of buildings (and rooms) in ASL: Position a main entrance at the front of the body.

Within a diagrammatic spatial format, signers can use either a horizontal (as seen in Fig. 3.8) or a vertical plane (the surface is parallel to the signer). Signers can shift back and forth from a horizontal to a vertical plane, either rapidly (e.g., between sentences) or slowly, for example, changing from the vertical plane to the horizontal plane across one or two sentences. The horizontal plane can be a true two-dimensional plane, or it can represent a three-dimensional model of space (in which case it is not a true plane). However, the vertical plane appears to be limited to two dimensions (see Emmorey & Falgier, 1999b).

Viewer space is similar to *surrogate space* described by Liddell (1994, 1995) and *Real-world space* described by Schick (1990a). The term *Real-world space* is problematic because it implies the actual physical space surrounding the signer, rather than indicating a larger scale, as intended by Schick. It is important to distinguish between "real" space and viewer space because in the first case, the signer actually sees the environment be-

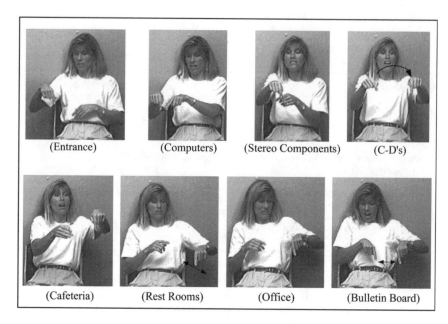

| (Entrance) | (Computers) | (Stereo Components) | (C-D's) |

| (Cafeteria) | (Rest Rooms) | (Office) | (Bulletin Board) |

CONVENTION CENTER

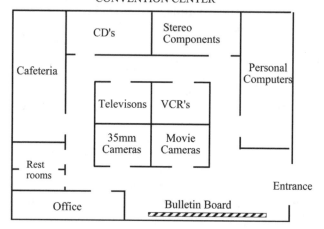

FIG. 3.8.   Illustration of the diagrammatic spatial format in ASL. The figure shows pointing signs used in a survey description of the outer rooms of the convention center. The intervening lexical signs are not shown, and the lexical and pointing signs for the inner rooms are also omitted. The rooms associated with the pointing signs are given in parentheses. The map of the convention center is reprinted with permission from Taylor and Tversky (1992), copyright © 1992 by Academic Press. The ASL figure is from "Talking About Space With Space: Describing Environments in ASL" by K. Emmorey and B. Falgier in *Storytelling and Conversation: Discourse in Deaf Communities*, edited by E. Winston (1999): 3–26. Washington, DC: Gallaudet University Press. Reprinted by permission of the publisher. Copyright © 1999 by Gallaudet University Press.

ing described, and in the second case, the environment is conceptualized as present and observable (see also Liddell, 1995).

Figure 3.9 illustrates a route description of the convention center and shows the pointing signs and classifier signs used to indicate the locations of the outer rooms. In contrast to Fig. 3.8, the locations in signing space map to what the signer would observe as she describes moving along the corridor. The vantage point is not fixed, but changes with motion through space. For example, the signer indicates that the CD room would be in front of her (as she stands next to the cafeteria), but later she indicates that the personal computer room is in front of her because she has described

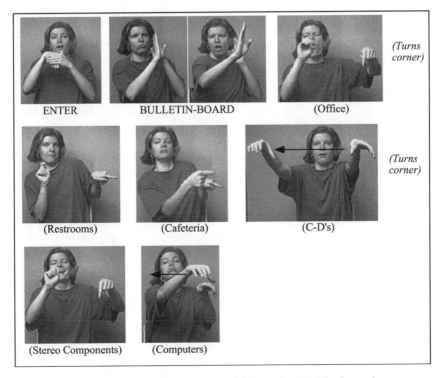

FIG. 3.9.   Illustration of the viewer spatial format in ASL. The figure shows pointing and other signs used in a route description of the outer rooms of the convention center. The intervening lexical signs for the rooms are not shown, and the lexical and pointing signs for the inner rooms are also omitted. The rooms associated with the pointing signs are given in parentheses. A map of the convention center is shown in Fig. 3.8. Figure 3.9 is from "Talking About Space With Space: Describing Environments in ASL" by K. Emmorey and B. Falgier in *Storytelling and Conversation: Discourse in Deaf Communities,* edited by E. Winston (1999): 3–26. Washington, DC: Gallaudet University Press. Reprinted by permission of the publisher. Copyright © 1999 by Gallaudet University Press.

going around the corner. The spatial interpretation of signing space changes with the description. Now compare the location of these rooms as given by the signer in Fig. 3.8; in that example, signing space represents a model of the entire convention center, and the spatial relationship among locations does not change during the description.

Note also the relatively high signing plane used in the description shown in Fig. 3.9. Lucas and Valli (1990) hypothesized that signs articulated above the chest can engage a "perspective system," and that the height of these signs has the meaning "from signer perspective." For example, they found that when the classifier construction glossed as SURFACE-PASS-UNDER-VEHICLE is signed at eye level versus mid-chest level, it does not indicate the relative height of the surface or vehicle being described. Rather, the height indicates whether the action is being described from the signer's perspective or whether the action is being described more generally, with no reference to the signer.[9] The data from Emmorey and Falgier (1999b) supported and elaborated the findings of Lucas and Valli (1990). When signers described environments as if they were moving through those environments, they articulated signs at a relatively high plane, thus indicating that the description reflected their own imagined view of the environment.

ASL signers can articulate both viewer-relational terms (e.g., LEFT, RIGHT) and cardinal directional terms (e.g., NORTH, SOUTH) to correspond with the particular spatial format adopted within a description. Thus, lexical spatial terms and the frames of reference that they invoke are not dependent on a particular spatial format. In the context of spatial language, *frame of reference* refers to the spatial coordinate system invoked by a particular lexical item or sentence. The following summarizes Levinson's (1996) characterization of the three frames of reference that are linguistically distinguished:

Intrinsic frame of reference involves an object-centered coordinate system, where the coordinates are determined by the "inherent features," sidedness or facets of the object to be used as the ground. English examples: 1) "The man is in front of the house" (meaning at the house's front). In this example, the house is the ground, and the man is the figure. 2) "The ball is in front of me." In this example, the speaker is the ground and the ball is the figure.

Relative frame of reference presupposes a "viewpoint" (given by the location of a perceiver), and a figure and a ground which are both distinct from the viewpoint. Thus, there is a triangulation of three points (the viewpoint, the figure, and the ground), and the coordinates for assigning directions to the

---

[9]Lucas and Valli (1990) noted that the perspective is not necessarily that of the actual signer; rather, the signer may have signaled a referential shift (e.g., by a change in eyegaze), and the perspective is that of the referent associated with the shift.

figure and ground are fixed on the viewpoint. English example: "The ball is to the left of the tree." In this example, the viewpoint is the speaker (the perceiver of the scene), the ball is the figure, and the tree is the ground.

Absolute frame of reference involves fixed bearings (cardinal directions or gravity), and the coordinate system is anchored to these fixed bearings with the origin on the ground object. English example: "The ball is to the north of the tree."

Spatial formats in ASL are clearly not the same as frames of reference. Rather they are specific ways of structuring signing space within a discourse. It appears that signers can adopt an intrinsic, a relative, or an absolute frame of reference when using either diagrammatic or viewer space. For example, using diagrammatic space, the signer could indicate that a man was in front of a car by positioning the 1 classifier handshape for an upright person in front of the vehicle classifier, that is, at the finger tips of the 3 handshape. Such an expression uses the intrinsic reference frame: The ground is the car, and the figure (the man) is located with respect to the features of the car. When viewer space is used with an intrinsic reference frame, the ground would always be the signer (or another referent within the discourse if the expression was within a referential shift). For example, the signer could indicate that the car was in front of her, by positioning the vehicle classifier at eye level (see Lucas & Valli, 1990); the English translation would be "the car is in front of me."

When viewer space is used within a relative frame of reference, the description is similar, but a figure and ground object are related to each other from the viewpoint of the signer (or other referent if within a referential shift). For example, to express the equivalent of "the picture is to the right of the window" using viewer space, a signer would first describe the window on the left of signing space and then the picture on the right, both at eye level (the order of expression indicates which object is figure and which is ground). An example using diagrammatic space and a relative reference frame is shown in Fig. 3.10. In this example, the signer describes a man on a hill looking down on a house behind a lake. The viewpoint is that of the man (not the signer), the ground is the lake, and the figure is the house. The signer indicates that the house is behind the lake from the man's viewpoint by directing the sign LOOK toward the location of the house from the location of the man, that is, he indicates that the man is the perceiver of the scene. The signer is not expressing his own view of the scene—that is, he is not indicating that the man is on his right, the lake is in the center of view, with the house to his left.

Signers can specify an absolute frame of reference using cardinal direction signs within either a viewer or diagrammatic spatial format. For example, within viewer space, the sign EAST can be articulated outward

| Location of the man | Location of the lake | Location of the house |

FIG. 3.10.   Illustration of discourse with a relative frame of reference using diagrammatic space. The intervening lexical signs are not shown (see text for a description of the discourse). Illustration from "Talking About Space With Space: Describing Environments in ASL" by K. Emmorey and B. Falgier in *Storytelling and Conversation: Discourse in Deaf Communities*, edited by E. Winston (1999): 3–26. Washington, DC: Gallaudet University Press. Reprinted by permission of the publisher. Copyright © 1999 by Gallaudet University Press.

from the body at a relatively high plane to indicate the eastward direction of a road that stretches in front of the signer (i.e., the viewer of the scene).[10] Within diagrammatic space, cardinal direction signs can be articulated with respect to a "map" created in signing space. Emmorey and Falgier (1999b) described an example in which a signer traced the path of a road along the horizontal plane in signing space from right to left, and then articulated the sign NORTH along this same path (with horizontal leftward movement)—the citation form of NORTH moves upward along the vertical plane.

What may be unique to signed languages is that relative and intrinsic frames of reference can be expressed simultaneously (Emmorey, 1996). For example, adopting a relative frame of reference, a signer could indicate that a car is behind a tree from the signer's viewpoint. Now suppose that the signer indicates *in the same construction* that the car is facing away from the tree (i.e., the tree is in back of the car), by articulating the vehicle classifier with the palm facing sideways and the fingertips facing outward (away from the signer). In this expression, the intrinsic frame of reference is expressed via the intrinsic properties of the classifier handshape for vehicles. The fact that ASL can express two frames of reference simultaneously indicates that spatial reference frames are not mutually exclusive (see also Levinson, 1996).

---

[10] The citation form of EAST is articulated with movement toward the right.

Finally, when a route or survey perspective is adopted for an extended spatial description, it does not necessarily mean that a particular frame of reference has been adopted for that description. For example, motion through space is not a property of a particular reference frame, but it characterizes route descriptions. Survey descriptions tend to adopt an absolute reference frame, but only when cardinal direction terms are used, and English speakers are much more likely to use these terms than ASL signers (Emmorey et al., in press). Instead, signers adopt either an intrinsic or relative frame of reference, and a survey perspective is conveyed with the diagrammatic spatial format, along with locative classifier constructions (rather than motion constructions). Signers also tend to adopt an intrinsic frame of reference for route descriptions, but the reference object (the ground) is the signer as the viewer of the scene, rather than another object, as for survey descriptions.

Shared Space

For the spatial descriptions we have discussed thus far, signers produced a monologue, and neither the signer nor the addressee is observing the actual environment being described. In such narratives, the spatial description is from the point of view of the signer, and the addressee, if facing the signer, must perform a mental transformation of signing space. For example, in Fig. 3.9, the signer indicates that the bulletin board in the convention center is to the left by articulating a classifier construction appropriate for the bulletin board on the left in signing space. Because the addressee is facing the signer (like you, as the reader), the location of the bulletin board is actually *observed* on the right. There is a mismatch between the location of the bulletin board in the room being described (the bulletin board is on the left as seen from the entrance) and what the addressee actually observes in signing space (the classifier construction for the bulletin board is produced to the addressee's right). In this case, the addressee must perform what amounts to a 180° mental rotation to correctly comprehend the description. Emmorey, Klima, and Hickok (1998) found that such a transformation is not difficult for ASL signers (see also chap. 8).

One might consider this situation analogous to that for English speakers who must understand the terms *left* and *right* with respect to the speaker's point of view. The crucial difference, however, is that these relations are encoded spatially in ASL, rather than lexically. The distinction becomes particularly clear in situations where the signer (the "speaker") and the addressee are both in the environment, observing the same scene. In this situation, English speakers most often adopt their addressee's point of view, for example giving directions such as, "Pick the one on your right," or "It's in front of you," rather than "Pick the one on my left" or "It's farthest from me" (Schober, 1993; Mainwaring, Tversky, & Schiano, 1996).

However, when jointly viewing an environment, ASL signers do not adopt their addressee's point of view but use what Emmorey and Tversky (2001) termed *shared space*. Figure 3.11 provides an illustration of what is meant by shared space in this case. In the situation depicted, the speaker and addressee are facing each other, and between them are two boxes (for simplicity and clarity, "speaker" will be used to refer to the person who is signing in these conversational contexts). Suppose the box on the speaker's left is the one that he wants shipped. If the speaker uses signing space (rather than just pointing to the actual box), he would indicate the box to be shipped by placing the appropriate classifier sign on the left side of signing space. In this situation, no mental transformation is required by the addressee. The speaker's signing space is simply "mapped" onto the jointly observed physical space—the left side of the speaker's signing space maps directly to the actual box on the right side of the addressee. However, if the speaker were to adopt the addressee's point of view, producing the classifier sign on his right, the location in signing space would conflict with the location of the target box observed by the addressee.

In fact, in situations where the signer and addressee are both observing and discussing a jointly viewed physical environment, there is no true speaker versus addressee point of view in signed descriptions of that environment. The signing space is *shared* in the sense that it maps to the physi-

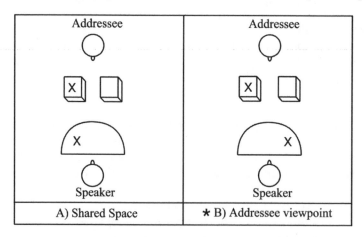

FIG. 3.11.   Illustration of a speaker using A) shared space and B) using the addressee's spatial viewpoint to indicate the location of the box marked with an "X" (the asterisk indicates that signers reject this type of description). The half circle represents the signing space in front of the signer. The "X" represents the location of the classifier sign used to represent the target box (e.g., a hooked 5 handshape).

cally observed space and to both the speaker's and addressee's view of the physical space. Furthermore, the signer's description of the box would be the same regardless of where the addressee happened to be standing (e.g., placing the addressee to the signer's left in Fig. 3.11 would not alter the signer's description or the nature of the mapping from signed space to physical space). Thus, in this situation, ASL signers do not need to take into account where their addressee is located, unlike English speakers who tend to adopt their addressee's viewpoint. This difference between languages derives from the fact that signers use the actual space in front of them to represent observed physical space.

We now turn to situations in which two signers are conversing about a spatial scene that they are not currently observing. In a study by Emmorey (in press), pairs of signers discussed the invented town from Taylor and Tversky (1992). One member of a pair memorized the map of the town and then described the town such that their partner could subsequently draw a map. The addressee could ask questions throughout the speaker's description. As expected, addressees generally performed a mental reversal of observed signing space when redescribing the town or asking a question. For example, if the speaker indicated that Maple Street looped to the left (observed as motion to the right for the addressee), the addressee would trace the Maple Street loop to his or her left in signing space. It was rare for an addressee to mirror the speaker's space, for example, by tracing Maple Street to the right. Addressees also used a type of shared space by pointing toward a location within the speaker's space to ask a question or comment about the landmark associated with that location. Figure 3.12 provides an illustration of these different possibilities.

Mirroring the speaker's signing space as in Fig. 3.12B led to left–right errors in comprehension. For example, one addressee mirrored the direction of Maple Street when redescribing that part of the town, and then drew the map with Maple Street incorrectly looping to the right. In a different type of example, the speaker specifically told his addressee that he would describe the map of the town from the addressee's point of view (as if the addressee were looking at the map on a blackboard). Thus, the speaker reversed the left–right locations of landmarks, which was very difficult for him, and he made several errors. When the addressee redescribed the town, he did not reverse the speaker's signing space, but correctly mirrored the speaker's space. Mirrored space was correct in this case because the speaker had already reversed the spatial locations for his addressee.

Figure 3.12C provides two illustrations of the use of shared space during conversations. Example (a) in Fig. 3.12C is designed to illustrate the situation in which the addressee uses a pronoun to refer to a location (or associated referent) within the speaker's signing space (indicated by the dotted arrow in the figure). Such shared space is common for nonspatial discourse

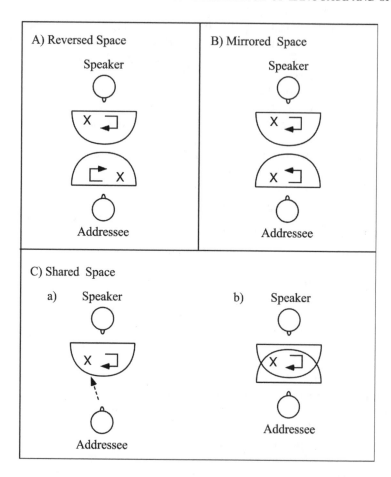

FIG. 3.12.   Illustration of A) reversed space, B) mirrored space, and C) two examples of the use of shared space for nonpresent referents. The half circles represent signing space, the solid arrow represents the direction of the Maple Street loop, and the "X" represents the location of the town hall with respect to Maple Street. The dotted arrow in example (a) of C) indicates the direction of a pointing sign used by the addressee to refer to the town hall.

when an addressee points toward a location in the speaker's space in order to refer to the referent associated with that location; for example, if the referent "John" has been associated with a location on the speaker's right, then the addressee would direct a pronoun toward this location, which is on his or her left, to refer to John (cf. Fig. 3.4 of Neidle et al., 2000). However, when the speaker's signing space is structured topographically to represent the location of several landmarks, the addressee generally reverses the speaker's space, as shown in Fig. 3.12A. Such reversals do not occur for nonspatial conversations because the topography of signing space is not generally complex and does not convey a spatial viewpoint.

Example (b) in Figure 3.12C illustrates an example of shared space in which the signing space for the addressee and speaker actually overlap. For example, in one situation, two signers sat across from each other at a table, and the speaker described the layout of the town by signing on the tabletop, for example, tracing the location of streets on the table. The addressee then used classifier constructions and pronouns articulated on the table to refer to locations and landmarks in the town with the same spatial locations on the table—the signing space of the speaker and addressee physically overlapped. In another similar example, two signers (who were best friends) were seated side by side, and the addressee moved her hands into the speaker's space in order to refer to landmarks and locations— even while her partner was still signing! This last example is rare, with both signers finding such "very shared space" amusing. Physically overlapping shared space may only be possible when there is an object, such as a table, to ground signing space in the real world or when signers are well known to one another.[11]

Özyürek (2000) used the term *shared space* to refer to the gesture space shared between spoken language users. However, Özyürek focuses on how the speaker changes his or her gestures depending on the location of the addressee. When narrators described "in" or "out" spatial relations (e.g., "Sylvester flies *out* of the window"), their gestures moved along a front–back axis when the addressee was facing the speaker, but speakers moved their gestures laterally when the addressee was to the side. Özyürek (2000) argued that speakers prefer gestures along these particular axes so that they can move their gestures into or out of a space shared with the addressee. In contrast, shared space as defined here for ASL is not affected by the spatial position of the addressee, and signers do not alter the directionality of signs depending on where their addressee is located. For example, OUT is signed with motion along the horizontal axis (outward from the signer), regardless of the location of the addressee. The direction of motion can be altered to explicitly refer to the addressee (e.g., to express 'the two of us are going out') or to refer to a specific location within signing space (e.g., to indicate the location of an exit). The direction of motion of OUT (or of other directional signs) is not affected by the location of the addressee, unless the signs specifically refer to the addressee. The use of shared space in ASL occurs when the speaker's signing space maps to his or her view of the spatial layout of physically present objects (as in Fig. 3.11) or to a mental image of the locations of nonpresent objects (as in Fig. 3.12C). The addressee shares the speaker's signing space either

---

[11]In one pair of signers, the speaker clearly attempted to use overlapping shared space with his addressee, but she adamantly maintained a separate signing space.

because it maps to the addressee's view of present objects or because the addressee uses the same locations within the signer's space to refer to nonpresent objects.

Furuyama (2000) presented a study in which hearing subjects produced collaborative gestures within a shared gesture space, which appears to be similar to shared space in ASL. In this study, a speaker (the instructor) explained how to create an *origami* figure to a listener (the learner), but the instructor had to describe the paper-folding steps without using a piece of *origami* paper for demonstration. Similar to the use of shared space in signed conversations, Furuyama (2000) found that learners pointed toward the gestures of their instructor or toward "an 'object' seemingly set up in the air by the instructor with a gesture" (p. 105). Furthermore, the gesture space of the two participants could physically overlap. For example, learners sometimes referred to the instructor's gesture by producing a gesture near (or even touching) the instructor's hand. In addition, the surface of a table could ground the gesture space, such that instructors and learners produced gestures within the same physical space on the table top. These examples all parallel the use of shared space in ASL depicted in Fig. 3.12C.

Finally, shared space, like spatial frames of reference, is independent of the spatial format used to describe an environment. For the examples discussed thus far, all involved diagrammatic space, but viewer space can also be shared. For example, suppose a speaker uses viewer space to describe where she wants to place a new sofa in her living-room (i.e., the spatial description is as if she were in the room). Her addressee may refer to the sofa by pointing to its associated location in the speaker's space, for example, signing the equivalent of, "No, move it over toward that side of the room."

Because spatial language is instantiated visually, rather than auditorily, the interface between language and visual perception (how we talk about what we see) has an added dimension for signers (they also see what they talk about). This spatialization of linguistic expression affects whether the speaker or addressee or neither should be considered as the ground (the reference point) in certain spatial descriptions (e.g., in Fig. 3.11, neither the speaker nor the addressee should be considered the reference point). It also affects the nature of language comprehension by requiring addressees to perform a mental transformation of the linguistic space under certain conditions (as in reversed space, Fig. 3.12A; see also Emmorey, Klima, & Hickok, 1998).

NONLOCATIVE FUNCTIONS OF SIGNING SPACE

Spatial locations serve a referential function by virtue of their association with specific referents, and they have a topographic function when representing the location of their associated referents. Chapter 4 presents psycholinguistic evidence that these two functions are not encoded in memory in the same way. However, referential and topographic functions of signing space are not mutually exclusive. In fact, Engberg-Pedersen (1993) argued that the distinction between locative and nonlocative functions of signing space is not all or none and that "there is rather a continuum between using space to express locative notions and using space to express other kinds of semantic and pragmatic notions" (pp. 310–311). We now explore the other end of this continuum by delineating some of the nonlocative functions of signing space.

Articulatory Functions

First of all, locations within signing space serve an articulatory function (Liddell, 1990). Locations can be phonologically significant, but they need not have any semantic import. For example, the signs SIT, SUNDAY, and THROW can be phonologically specified as having *neutral space* as their place of articulation, but each is articulated with respect to a different plane within signing space: SIT is articulated within the horizontal or transverse plane with respect to the body, SUNDAY within the frontal or vertical plane, and THROW within the midsagittal plane (Brentari, 1998). Brentari (1998) argued that specifying the plane of articulation within signing space is not merely a notational convenience because some phonological rules must refer to a specific plane of articulation. However, within a particular plane, distinct locations are not relevant for phonological rules, and there is currently no accepted way to phonologically represent the potentially unlimited number of location distinctions within signing space. For example, a teacher might sign the equivalent of "Amy, you sit over there, and Joe, you sit over there," articulating the sign SIT toward the left corner of the classroom when talking to Amy and toward the right corner for Joe. Both instances of SIT are articulated within the horizontal plane, but the specific location of each verb is dictated by nonlinguistic factors (i.e., the corners of the classroom where the teacher wants each student to sit), and although these locations within signing space serve an articulatorily function (and perhaps a deictic function), they are not phonologically specified in the lexical representation of the verb SIT.

**Discourse Conventions: Signing Space
as Semantically Loaded**

Signing space has been characterized as having a syntactic function, often referred to as *spatialized syntax* (Bellugi, 1988; Poizner et al., 1987). Within this context, the association between referents and spatial locations is often characterized as arbitrary. However, Engberg-Pedersen (1993) presented strong evidence that the choice of a location in signing space for a particular referent is rarely arbitrary.[12] She proposed the following semantic–pragmatic conventions for organizing signing space:

The convention of semantic affinity: Referents with semantic affinity are represented by the same locus[13] unless they need to be distinguished for discourse reasons. Semantic affinity covers many possible semantic relations. Examples of this convention include using the same spatial locus for a person and the place where he or she works or using the same locus for a possessor and the thing possessed. Thus, ambiguities can arise with respect to whether a pronoun refers to a person or a place or to the possessor or thing possessed (see Fig. 2.15 in chap. 2 for an example).

The convention of the canonical location: This convention is a variant of the semantic affinity convention. A canonical location is the place where a referent is typically found or a place conventionally associated with a referent. For example, signers may direct a pronoun toward a location where a referent is typically, but not currently, for example, referring to someone by pointing to his or her desk in an office even when that person is absent.

The convention of comparison: When comparing or contrasting two referents, signers often use a side-to-side (left, right) dimension in signing space. Winston (1995) provides a detailed analysis of this convention in ASL (in Winston's example, the art and the science of ASL poetry are contrasted and are associated with the locations on the left and right of signing space; see chap. 2).

The iconic convention: This convention states, "the spatial relation between the locus of a referent A and the locus of a referent B reflects the location of A in relation to B in the described situation on an appropriate scale and leaving out irrelevant detail" (Engberg-Pedersen, 1993, p. 74). This convention is at the heart of spatial language just discussed.

The authority convention:[14] Referents with perceived or actual authority (e.g., a boss, the school principle, the government) are frequently associated with loci in the upper portion of signing space, reflecting the general metaphor "power is up" (G. Lakoff & Johnson, 1980).

Choice of locus and point of view: The side-to-side dimension in signing space is used when two referents have equal discourse weight. The diagonal dimensions (extending from near the signer diagonally toward either the left or

---

[12]Engberg-Pedersen's (1993) evidence is based on data from Danish Sign Language, but her observations hold for ASL as well.

[13]Engberg-Pedersen (1993) used the term *locus* rather than *location* (see chap. 2 for discussion of these terms).

[14]Engberg-Pedersen (1993) did not list this convention separately but subsumed it under a section headed "standard choices of loci." However, the pattern is relatively common and is worth noting as a separate convention.

right) are used when the signer empathizes with one of the referents. Signers choose a distal location along the diagonal for referents with which they empathize the least, for example, if discussing a disliked university course compared to a preferred course, the preferred course would be associated with a location nearer the signer.

These discourse conventions indicate that the association between a particular referent and a location in signing space is not random or arbitrary. Although not completely predictable, signers choose locations in signing space to reflect a semantic affinity between two referents, to indicate the authority of a referent, or to reflect empathy with a particular referent. To quote Engberg-Pedersen (1993), "signing space is semantically loaded from the moment the signer starts signing" (p. 78).

Does signing space have a syntactic as well as a semantic function? Generally, the term *spatialized syntax* is used to refer to the role of signing space in the production of agreeing verbs and with respect to person agreement (first vs. non-first person pronouns). As discussed in chapter 2, there is no evidence that locations within signing space actually represent syntactic elements such as "subject" or "object," and there is an unlimited number of possible non-first person forms—thus, distinct locations within signing space do not distinguish among grammatical subcategories of person. Whether locations in signing space have a purely syntactic function is a matter of current debate (Liddell, 2000b; Meir, 1998). The neurolinguistic data suggesting a dissociation between spatialized syntax and spatial mapping (the topographic function of signing space) is discussed in chapter 9.

Time Lines and Temporal Reference

Time is an abstract nonspatial construct, but we often adapt spatial structures to convey temporal information (e.g., spatial metaphors, charts, and graphs; see papers in Gattis, 2001b). Similarly, signers adapt signing space to express temporal information both at the lexical level and at the discourse level.

In ASL, temporal signs utilize the "future is ahead" metaphor, which is consistent with both the ego-moving metaphor in which the observer moves toward the future and the time-moving metaphor in which time is conceived of as a type of river that flows from the future toward the observer. Within both types of metaphor, the future is conceptualized as ahead of the observer or ahead of the person signing for ASL (Taub, 2001). Similarly, the past is conceptualized as behind the signer, and the present is co-located with signer. The deictic signs TOMORROW, NOW, and YESTERDAY illustrate this space–time metaphor: The sign TOMOR-

ROW moves ahead of the signer; the sign NOW is articulated at the body, and the sign YESTERDAY moves backward (i.e., toward the signer's back). In addition, the movement of some temporal signs can be altered to indicate past and future (Cogen, 1977; Friedman, 1975). For example, when the sign WEEK is articulated such that the hand moves ahead of the signer, it means "next week," and when the hand moves toward the signer, the sign means "last week." Certain temporal verbs and adverbs are also articulated with respect to the temporal structure associated with signing space (e.g., WILL, PAST, POST-PONE and PRE-PONE).

Such examples illustrate how the form of certain lexical signs reflects a mapping between spatial structure and temporal structure. The mapping appears to be based on a spatial metaphor in which future time is mapped to space ahead of a reference point, and the past is mapped to space behind this point. The temporal reference point can be represented either by the signer's body (as for the deictic adverbs TOMORROW and YES-TERDAY) or by the nondominant hand (as in the verbs POST-PONE [seen in Fig. 3.14] and UNTIL).

Time lines are spatial constructs within signing space that represent distinct types of temporal information. When a referent is associated with a location along a time line, the entire line is invested with specific referential potential, and nontemporal referents associated with the time line take on temporal meaning (Engberg-Pedersen, 1993). Time lines are always available, and they have a variety of meanings. Engberg-Pedersen (1993) first identified several distinct time lines for Danish Sign Language: a deictic, an anaphoric, and a sequence time line.[15] Emmorey (2001) and Winston (1989) found that these time lines also exist for ASL, as illustrated in Fig. 3.13.

Deictic Time Line. The deictic time line extends forward from the dominant shoulder and is perpendicular to the body. The reference point for the time line is the signer's body, and the default meaning is *deictic*, that is, referring to the time of utterance. "After now" is associated along the line outward from the signer, and "now" is associated with locations near the signer. For example, if the sign FRIDAY is articulated with the arm extended, the form would mean "next Friday" (see Fig. 3.14). To indicate "this Friday," signers can point to a location on the time line near the body and articulate the sign FRIDAY at this location (usually with an adverbial facial expression glossed as 'cs', which indicates recent time). It

---

[15]Engberg-Pedersen (1993) also observed a *mixed time line* for Danish Sign Language, which is a mixture of the deictic, anaphoric, and sequencing lines. The mixed time line is used when "expressing a sequence of moments in time or a period of time seen from a point before its start" (p. 88). However, whether this time line exists for ASL is not clear.

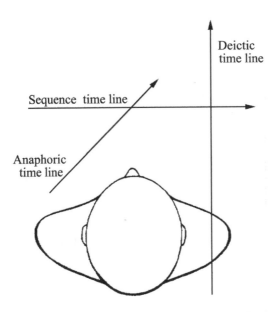

FIG. 3.13.   Time lines in ASL. From "Space on Hand: The Exploitation of Signing Space to Illustrate Abstract Thought," by K. Emmorey, 2001, Cambridge, MA: MIT Press. Copyright © 2001 by MIT Press. Reprinted with permission.

FIG. 3.14.   Illustration of the deictic time line from the following ASL discourse (only the bolded signs are pictured): **TUESDAY**, MUST PASS OUT REVIEW PAPERS. WHY? **NEXT-FRIDAY** TEST. IF NOT-YET PASS-OUT, **TEST POST-PONE**. An English translation would be "On Tuesday, I must pass out the review papers because the test is on Friday. If I haven't yet passed them out, Friday's test will be postponed."

is interesting to note that Danish Sign Language and ASL differ in how "before now" is represented. In Danish Sign Language, "before now" is behind the signer such that a determiner can point to a location behind the signer to refer to a past event (e.g., a conference held last January; Engberg-Pedersen, 1993). In ASL, such deictic reference to a location behind the signer cannot be temporal; it can only have spatial meaning (i.e., referring to a location, person, or object that is behind the signer). To refer to "last Friday," ASL signers produce the phrase PAST FRIDAY, and the sign FRIDAY is produced in its citation form (i.e., roughly in the middle section of the time line). In ASL, it is not possible to associate a referent with a location on the time line behind the signer.

Nominals without inherent temporal meaning can be associated with the deictic time line and thereby take on temporal meaning (Engberg-Pedersen, 1993). Figure 3.14 provides an example in which the sign TEST is associated with a location on the deictic time line. TEST is not a time expression, but it takes on temporal meaning ("next Friday's test") by virtue of its spatial location.

Anaphoric Time Line. The anaphoric time line extends diagonally across signing space (see Fig. 3.13). The default meaning of this time line is not "now" (i.e., the time of the utterance); rather, the temporal reference point is determined within the discourse. The time line is *anaphoric* in the sense that temporal meaning is derived from the narrative, and there is no default temporal reference point.

Winston (1989, 1991) provided an example from an ASL lecture about sign poetry in which the signer actually shifts his body along the anaphoric time line. He signs the following centrally: "Why were there deaf poets after the 1970s but not before? I doubt that is what really happened. I believe that before that no one had noticed their existence. Why? You're right." Then he steps left and backwards signing "Before, in the late 1960s, Stokoe recognized ASL as a language. He tried to tell people about this, but he was resisted at first. Then his ideas began to be accepted and . . ." The signer then moves back to the center while signing "over the years they spread, and now they have been widely accepted." He then moves backward and left again signing, "Before, maybe they had (ASL) poetry but no one noticed it. I believe that it existed but no one noticed it." In this example, the anaphoric time line was used to express changes in time frames within the discourse.[16] Chunks of discourse, rather than single signs, were associated with locations along the time line.

---

[16]If the discourse described here were produced by a seated signer, the signer's upper body would lean along the anaphoric time line, and signs would be articulated at appropriate locations along this time line, but the location of the signer's body would not change.

Sequence Time Line. The sequence time line is parallel to the body and extends left to right, representing early to later periods or moments in time. Unlike lexical signs, the left-to-right direction of the sequence time line is not reversed in left handers. The directionality of the sequence time line may reflect language culture because the sequence time line in Jordanian Sign Language extends right to left (Dan Parvaz, personal communication, November, 1998; see Tversky, Kugelmass, & Winter, 1991, for evidence of left-to-right temporal mapping for English speakers and right-to-left temporal mapping for Arabic speakers).

Like the anaphoric time line, the temporal reference point is established within the discourse. Winston (1989) provides an example in which a signer associates 1960 with a location on the left and 1980 with a location on the right, tracing a line between the two locations. The signer then refers to specific events in time (e.g., marriage, divorce, and remarriage) by articulating signs near the appropriate locations on the time line (e.g., closer to one of the locations associated with the endpoints, 1960 or 1980). As with the other time lines, nontemporal signs can take on temporal meaning when associated with the sequence time line. For example, when the sign MARRY is articulated to the left (i.e., at or near the location associated with 1960), it indicates an earlier event compared to when MARRY is articulated to the right, near the location associated with 1980. The sequence time line is used when signers refer to ordered events that are not related to the utterance time.

The deictic, anaphoric, and sequence time lines all appear to have distinct temporal functions. In general, the deictic time line is used to refer to points in time related to the immediate context of an utterance (as in English, "next Friday"). The sequence time line appears to be used when signers want to talk about the temporal order of events, and the reference point is established within the discourse (as in English, "the following Friday"). Finally, the anaphoric time line appears to be used to contrast or compare time periods related to the topic of discourse. Further research may reveal additional semantic characteristics associated with these timelines, as well as constraints on their use.

Calendar Plane. The calendar plane is a two dimensional plane with the surface parallel to the body (Engberg-Pedersen, 1993). In Danish Sign Language, it can be used for the year, but in ASL, it appears to be most often used for weeks within a month. As shown in Fig. 3.15, the signs for the days of the week are associated with a relatively high location on the plane (as if "labeling" the columns on a calendar page for a week), and like the sequence line, time moves from left to right. The example in Fig. 3.15 is parallel to the example in Fig. 3.14, which illustrated the deictic time line.

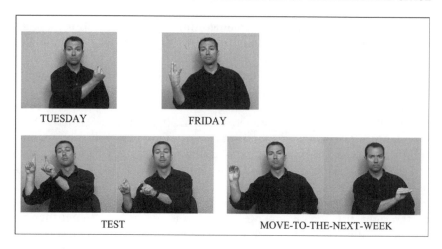

FIG. 3.15.   Illustration of the calendar plane from the following ASL discourse (only the bolded signs are pictured: **TUESDAY**, PASS OUT REVIEW PAPERS. **FRIDAY** TEST. IF NOT-YET PASS-OUT, **TEST MOVE-TO-THE-NEXT-WEEK**. An English translation would be "On Tuesday, I pass out review papers because tests are on Friday. If I haven't yet passed them out, the test is moved to the next week."

However, the sign POST-PONE cannot be used here, perhaps because its form, which requires forward motion, conflicts with the structure of the calendar plane. The calendar plane tends to be used when signers are describing the general structure of events within a week, whereas the deictic time line is used when describing events with respect to a particular time (by default, the time of the utterance). Thus, the example using the calendar plane (Fig. 3.15) could be interpreted as a description of events that occur every week, but the example using the deictic time line (Fig. 3.14) could not.

The mapping from space to time appears to be semantically quite rich. As in other cognitive domains, signers map time to a line or plane in space. The mapping to a plane is based on how time is represented on a Western calendar, and the mapping to a line may be based on the conceptualization of time as a one-dimensional construct with a direction (see Gentner, 2001). The semantics of time lines may differ for distinct sign languages, and not all sign languages utilize time lines (Ferreira Brito, 1983). However, when time lines are used by signers, they appear to preserve a basic structural mapping between space and time in which a spatial direction (e.g., forward from the body) is mapped to a temporal direction (e.g., toward the future), and spatial reference points (e.g., the signer's body) are mapped to temporal reference points (e.g., the time of speaking).

Space to Represent Abstract Relations and Concepts

Signers can create spatial models within signing space to represent both abstract and concrete information. Within the abstract domain, signers adhere to general cognitive constraints for mapping conceptual and spatial schemas (see Gattis, 2001a). For example, signers associate conceptual elements with locations in signing space and manipulate the form of signs to indicate relations between these elements. Emmorey (2001) described a science lecture by a Deaf teacher who created a model in signing space to explain physical and chemical change to her Deaf third-grade students. When discussing the physical forms of matter, the teacher associated the concept of *gas* with a location about shoulder height in signing space, *liquid* with the middle of signing space, and she signed SOLID at a very low location in space. Thus, different locations within signing space were associated with different states of matter. In addition, the teacher articulated certain verbs such that they moved between these locations, illustrating changes in state. For example, the signs EVAPORATE and STEAM were moved upward from the location associated with a liquid state to the higher location associated with a gas state. The teacher also used the sign B-A-C-K to indicate changing from a gas state back to a liquid state by moving the sign downward from the spatial location associated with gas to the location associated with liquid. The phonological and morphological structure of these verbs allows the teacher to map them onto the model of physical change she created in signing space. However, the phonological structure of the sign MELT is not congruent with this model because the movement of the sign is downward, rather than upward. This form is iconically motivated by the visual perception of the height of a solid decreasing as it melts. However, within the model created in signing space by the teacher, the liquid state is above the solid state, but it is ungrammatical to articulate MELT with upward motion to illustrate change from a solid to a liquid. Nonetheless, the teacher uses the sign MELT in its grammatical form, and it does not create confusion or conflict. Thus, the teacher refers to the spatial model within signing space only to the extent allowed by linguistic constraints, and the spatial model does not override these constraints.

    Through metaphorical mapping, signers can extend the use of classifier constructions and signing space to describe abstract concepts and relations. In *conceptual* metaphors, the elements of an abstract domain are consistently described in terms of the elements of a concrete domain (e.g., G. Lakoff & Johnson, 1980; G. Lakoff & Turner, 1989). For example, the abstract domain of communicating is often mapped to the concrete domain of sending, for example, "We tossed some ideas back and forth" or "That went right by me." In this metaphorical mapping, *ideas* correspond to *objects*, and the act of *communicating* corresponds to *sending*. Taub (2001) showed that conceptual metaphors in ASL involve a double mapping: (1) a metaphorical mapping from an abstract target domain to a concrete source domain (e.g., concepts are mapped to objects), and (2) an iconic mapping from the concrete domain to the linguistic form (e.g., objects map to handshapes). For example, ASL signers also use the "communicating as sending" metaphor, but there is an additional iconic mapping between the concrete domain (objects) and the articulators (the hands). Taub (2001) illustrated this point with the sign glossed as THINK-BOUNCE, which indicates a failure to communicate and consists of an iconic depiction of a projectile bouncing off a wall (the 1 handshape moves from the head and bounces off the nondominant hand). The sign is roughly equivalent to the English "I didn't get through to him," but in English, there is no iconic mapping between the form of the words and the concrete domain they express, unlike in ASL.

Such double mapping occurs for signing space as well. For example, the metaphorical mapping between power and height ("power is up") has an additional iconic mapping between height and signing space. This metaphor is found in the authority convention described earlier. Similarly, signers employ the "intimacy is proximity" metaphor and may associate known or preferred objects/people with locations near their body and less preferred objects/people with locations away from their body. This metaphor is also instantiated as a discourse convention. Spoken and signed languages appear to share many of the same schematic mappings between abstract conceptual domains and concrete spatial domains (see Emmorey, 2001). Moreover, Taub's (2001) research indicates that sign languages exhibit an additional mapping between the concrete domain and the linguistic form itself.

In sum, individual signers can create spatial models for specific purposes within a discourse, as the science teacher did in her explanation of physical change and states of matter. In addition, the mapping between signing space and an abstract domain can become conventionalized. For example, time lines are not invented by individual signers but are always available for use. ASL signers can evoke a time line by articulating a temporal sign at a particular location in signing space, and each time line has particular temporal semantics associated with it.

CONCLUSION

The confluence of space and language in signed languages provides a rich domain for exploring the interface between spatial concepts and linguistic expression. Classifier constructions are the primary linguistic structure used to express both concrete and abstract concepts of motion and location. ASL signers also exploit signing space to schematically represent spatial relations, time, and aspects of conceptual structure. When signers describe spatial relations, there is a structural analogy between the form of a classifier construction and aspects of the described scene. Specifically, physical elements in ASL (the hands) map to physical elements within the scene (objects); movement of the hands maps to the motion of referent objects; and locations in signing space map to relative locations within the scene. Signers structure signing space differently, depending on their perspective of the scene (i.e., as an outside observer or within it), using either diagrammatic or viewer spatial formats. These spatial formats are independent of spatial frames of reference, and they are also independent of whether signing space is shared, reversed, or mirrored by the addressee. How signers negotiate the mapping between signing space and observed or imagined space is an area that is sure to yield further insights into the relation between spatial cognition and language.

SUGGESTIONS FOR FURTHER READING

Engberg-Pedersen, E. (1993). *Space in Danish Sign Language: The semantics and morphosyntax of the use of space in a visual language*. Hamburg, Germany: Signum-Verlag.

Engberg-Pedersen presents groundbreaking research on how space is used in Danish Sign Language to express locative relations, transitivity, time lines, and point of view. Her analysis of polymorphemic (classifier) verbs and time lines was applied in this chapter to American Sign Language.

Emmorey, K. (Ed.). (in press). *Perspectives on classifier constructions in sign languages*. Mahwah, NJ: Lawrence Erlbaum Associates.

This volume contains papers on classifier constructions in thirteen different sign languages. The issues that are discussed include the acquisition of classifier constructions, the relation between gesture and classifier constructions, similarities and differences between classifiers in spoken and signed languages, crosslinguistic variation in classifiers, and the syntax and morphology of classifier constructions.

Chapter 4

Psycholinguistic Studies of Sign Perception, Online Processing, and Production

The different perceptual and productive systems of signed and spoken languages may result in differing constraints on the nature of linguistic processing. Sign languages present a natural opportunity to explore how the modality in which a language is expressed crucially affects the psychological mechanisms required to decode and produce the linguistic signal. One goal of this chapter is to examine what aspects of language processing and production may be universal and what aspects are affected by the particular characteristics of audition versus vision or by the specific constraints on gestural versus vocal articulation. Another aim is to provide a review of what is currently known about the psychological processes involved in sign language comprehension and production. We compare sign language processing to speech, rather than to reading, because unlike written text, which can be characterized as "visual language," sign language consists of dynamic and constantly changing forms rather than static symbols. In addition, neither sign language nor spoken language comes presegmented into words and sentences for the perceiver. Finally, in contrast to written language, sign and speech are both primary language systems (see chap. 7), acquired during infancy and early childhood without formal instruction (see chap. 5).

SIGN PERCEPTION AND VISUAL PROCESSING

A critical distinction between speech perception and sign perception is that the articulators are entirely visible for sign, but not for speech. For sign language, "what you see" is "what you produce" in terms of the relation between perception and production. In contrast, a major challenge for speech perception research is to understand the relation between the acoustic signal perceived by a listener and the movements of the vocal articulators. This is a complex problem because the same segment can have different acoustic realizations depending on the surrounding context, speaking rate, and the individual speaker. Furthermore, different articulatory gestures can give rise to the same acoustic perception, and a simple invariant mapping between acoustic features and perceived phonemes has been extremely difficult to find, despite intense research efforts (Stevens & Blumstein, 1981). For the visual signal, the problem of invariance takes the form of a problem in high level vision: How are objects (e.g., the hands) recognized as "the same" when seen from different views and distances or in different configurations? It turns out that this is not an easy problem to solve. Furthermore, vision researchers are struggling with the problem of how information about object motion, object shape, and object location are integrated (the so-called "binding problem"). Thus, although mapping between the perceived visual signal and mental representations of signed segments may appear straightforward, how such perceptual mapping is achieved is not well understood.

The early perceptual stages of language processing may be the most affected by the visual–gestural modality, although even here the effects are not dramatic. As will be detailed, sign articulation is much slower than speech, and movement cues may play a different role in segmentation for the two modalities. Visual perception of hand configuration, place of articulation, and movement exhibit linguistically relevant patterns of discrimination, and there is even some recent evidence suggesting that categorical perception occurs in sign language.

Segmentation

In natural speech, segments overlap and are coarticulated to achieve transmission rates of about 10 to 15 segments per second (Liberman, 1996). In an informal study, I found that the transmission rate for ASL is approximately 7–11 segments per second.[1] The average number of words per second in running speech is about 4 to 5, compared with 2 to 3 signs per second for fluent signing (Bellugi & Fischer, 1972). The slower rate of sign transmission is due largely to the fact that the hands and arms are larger and thus slower articulators compared to the lips and tongue. De-

---

[1] Three signers were filmed producing a small set of sentences at normal speed and at a fast rate. Sandler's (1989) model was used to count Location and Movement segments. The average number of segments per second for the normal rate was 7.0, and 10.75 for the fast rate.

spite the difference in segment and word transmission rates, the proposition rate for sign and speech is the same, roughly one proposition every 1 to 2 seconds (Bellugi & Fischer, 1972). In addition, the intelligibility of both sign and speech breaks down when either signal is time compressed to about 2.5 to 3 times the normal rate, suggesting a modality independent upper limit for the ability to accelerate language processing (Fischer, Delhorne, & Reed, 1999).

With respect to segmenting the signed linguistic signal, the actual movement of the articulators does not appear to carry the same type of segmentation information that it does for speech. In speech, articulatory transitions provide the most salient information for phonological processing (e.g., Tallal, Miller, & Fitch, 1993). Temporal changes provide strong cues to phoneme identity for both vowels and consonants. In contrast, the identification of phonological structure for sign does not rely as heavily on the transitions of the articulators. Hand orientation, place of articulation, and hand configuration can all be observed simultaneously in the signed visual signal. In contrast to speech, movement transitions do not provide essential cues to phonological features, such as hand configuration, because the visual system can perceive these features statically without reference to movement. That is why signers can easily recognize many static drawings of signs which contain no information about movement.

Visual Discrimination

Several studies have investigated visual perception for the major phonological parameters of sign: hand configuration (Lane, Boyes-Braem, & Bellugi, 1976), place of articulation (Poizner & Lane, 1978), and movement (Poizner, 1981). Lane et al. (1976) modeled their study of the visual perception of hand configurations after Miller and Nicely's (1955) investigation of the auditory perception of English consonants. Miller and Nicely asked subjects to identify CV syllables (e.g., *ba, da, ga, na, ma*) masked with differing levels of white noise. They found that consonants that shared several phonetic features were confused more often than consonants that shared few features (e.g., *ba* was often confused with *va* but not with *sa*, which differs in voicing, place of articulation, and consonant type). In addition, some phonetic features, such as voicing, were more salient than others. Using a similar technique with visual noise ("snow" on a television screen), Lane et al. (1976) found that "compact" hand configurations— those without extended fingers—were easily confused with each other (e.g., the A, O, and C handshapes; see Appendix A), and the number and type of selected fingers were particularly salient (e.g., the I handshape was rarely confused with the 3 handshape). The goal of the Lane et al. (1976) study was to provide a binary feature analysis for hand configuration; however, internal linguistic evidence (whether a proposed feature explains phonological patterns) has proven to be more useful for the development of phonological feature analyses for sign language (see chap. 2). Finally, both Deaf signers (native and nonnative) and hearing nonsigners make the same types of visual confusions among handshapes, suggesting that linguistic experience does not affect the saliency of the visual features critical to handshape identification and discrimination (Richards & Hanson, 1985; Stungis, 1981).

Poizner and Lane (1978) used the same visual noise technique to investigate the perception of place of articulation for ASL signs by both signers and nonsigners. Three different handshapes (A, B, and U; see Appendix A) were presented with various movements at 14 different locations on the body and face, under varying levels of visual noise. Deaf signers were found to be more accurate in perceiving locations that are frequent places of articulation in ASL (the chin and the nondominant hand, palm up), and hearing nonsigners were more accurate in perceiving less frequent locations (the neck and wrist). This group difference was not due to response bias, and it suggests that linguistic knowledge can affect perceptual accuracy for location. However, only the perception of linguistically relevant body locations may be affected, because signers and nonsigners do not appear to differ in the perception of visual locations in general (see chap. 8). Further, the scaling and clustering analyses of the similarity structure for places of articulation yielded essentially the same results for signers and nonsigners.

The perception of linguistic movement in ASL signs was also investigated by Poizner and colleagues (Poizner, 1981, 1983; Poizner, Bellugi, & Lutes-Driscoll, 1981; Poizner, Fok, & Bellugi, 1989; see also chap. 8). To isolate movements of the hand and arm, small light-emitting diodes were placed at the major joints of the body (shoulders, elbows, wrists, index fingertips). Thus, when signing was recorded in a darkened room, only the patterns of moving points of light were seen against a black background. Poizner, Bellugi, and Lutes-Driscoll (1981) found that signers were able to identify signs (with a constant hand configuration) from such point-light displays and that the more distal the joint (particularly the fingertips), the more crucial its movement for lexical recognition. In addition, Poizner (1983) found that the dimensions underlying the perception of *lexical* movement were distinct from those underlying *inflectional* movement. This result provides perceptual evidence for a separation between lexically specified movement and movement specified by morphological processes (see chap. 2). Finally, unlike the perception of hand configuration and place of articulation, the perceptual saliency of movement is affected by linguistic experience, such that signers and nonsigners provide different similarity judgments for point-light motion displays. (See chap. 8 for a discussion of the impact of sign language experience on motion perception.)

Categorical Perception in Sign Language?

Categorical perception refers to the finding that certain stimuli (particularly speech) appear to be perceived categorically rather than continuously, despite a continuous variation in form (Liberman, Cooper, Shankweiler, & Studdert-Kennedy, 1967; but see Massaro, 1987). To demonstrate categorical perception, stimuli are created that vary in small steps between two endpoints of a continuum. For example, in English "ba" and "pa" constitute endpoints for a voicing continuum, and synthetic speech can be created in which the time delay before voicing begins varies in set increments from 0 to 60 msec (this delay is known as *voice onset time* or VOT). When English speakers are presented with these continuously varying stimuli in random order and asked to identify them, their performance is discontinuous. That is, they uniformly identify one end of the continuum as "ba" (VOTs from 0 to 20 msec) and the other end as "pa" (VOTs from 40 to 60 msec). Performance on this labeling task is compared to a discrimination task in which subjects simply decide which one of two stimuli matches a target stimulus (the ABX paradigm), and no overt categorization is involved. Crucially, speakers are able to easily discriminate between stimuli that fall across a category boundary (e.g., between 20 and 30 msec VOT), but perform more poorly when discriminating within a category (e.g., between 10 and 20 msec VOT).

Recently, McCullough, Brentari, and Emmorey (2000) investigated categorical perception in ASL for place of articulation and hand configuration. Deaf signers and also hearing nonsigners were presented with computer generated sign stimuli that varied continuously in either place of articulation (e.g., a continuum along the side of the face between the endpoint signs ONION and APPLE) or hand configuration (e.g., a continuum between the B and A handshapes with PLEASE and SORRY as the sign endpoints). We used a 3D animation program to "morph" one endpoint image to another, thus creating two continua of still images that consist of equally spaced steps between the two hand configuration or the two place of articulation categories (see Figs. 4.1A and 4.1B). Discrimination and identification tasks were used to determine whether subjects demonstrated categorical perception for either hand configuration or place of articulation.

When asked to identify the stimuli, both signers and nonsigners exhibited discontinuous (sigmoidal) performance and categorized nonidentical stimuli together at each end of the perceptual continuum.[2] Given that we already know that place of articulation and hand configuration categories exist for signers based on linguistic data, this result was not surprising for

---

[2]Subjects indicated whether a given stimulus was most like image #1 or image #2, which were the endpoint images of each continua (thus, nonsigners did not have to label the stimulus with an ASL sign).

A) B and A handshapes (PLEASE and SORRY)

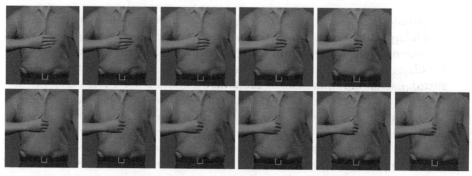

B) upper cheek and chin (ONION-APPLE)

FIG. 4.1.   Illustration of stimulus continua varying in (A) hand configuration (from the sign PLEASE to the sign SORRY) and (B) place of articulation (from the sign ON-ION to the sign APPLE). These stimuli were created with Poser software from Metacreations.

signers. The finding that hearing nonsigners performed similarly suggests that these categories have a perceptual as well as a linguistic basis. The results thus correspond to those of Lane et al. (1976) and of Poizner and Lane (1978) who, as noted, found similar perceptual groupings by Deaf signers and hearing nonsigners for hand configuration and for place of articulation.

Crucially, for hand configuration, the discrimination task revealed that only Deaf signers exhibited better discrimination across the category boundary compared to within categories, thus demonstrating categorical perception. An earlier investigation of categorical perception in ASL by Newport and T. Supalla (reported in Newport, 1982) may have failed to find categorical perception for hand configuration because of a lack of statistical power (only four or fewer subjects were tested) or because computer generated stimuli were not used (thus, the steps may have not been truly equal along the continuum). For place of articulation, McCullough et al. (2000) found that both signers and nonsigners exhibited similar discrimination abilities across and within categories, thus failing to demonstrate categorical perception for this parameter. Overall, these preliminary findings suggest that visual discrimination of spatial location is unaffected by linguistic input, but linguistic experience can affect the perception of the configuration of the hand. In addition, the results suggest that categorical perception may not be unique to the auditory modality or to speech. Experience with a visual language can affect how at least some components of that language are perceived.

Further evidence for visual categorical perception of sign language stimuli has been found in the domain of linguistic facial expression. First of all, several studies using computer morphing techniques have demonstrated categorical perception effects for *emotional* facial expressions (Calder, Young, Perrett, Etcoff, & Rowland, 1996; Etcoff & Magee, 1992; Young et al., 1997). Systematic morphing between images of endpoint emotions (e.g., happy and sad expressions) yielded discontinuous discrimination and identification performance, with better discrimination across category boundaries than within categories. McCullough and Emmorey (1999) and Campbell, Woll, Benson, and Wallace (1999) investigated whether *linguistic* facial expressions are perceived categorically for American Sign Language or for British Sign Language, respectively. Both studies examined a continuum between the facial expressions that mark yes–no and WH questions, and McCullough and Emmorey also examined a continuum between the *mm* and *th* facial adverbials in ASL, as illustrated in Fig. 4.2 (see chap. 2 for a description of these facial morphemes). Both the British and American studies found evidence for the categorical perception of linguistic facial expressions for *both* Deaf signers and hearing nonsigners for all continua investigated. Both groups of subjects showed better discrimination for stimuli that straddled the category boundaries (although the effects were weaker and less consistent for the Campbell et al., 1999, study).

The finding that hearing nonsigners demonstrated categorical perception for ASL linguistic facial expressions suggests that the categorical perception effects observed for Deaf signers are not due to linguistic experience. Furthermore, the results indicate that categorical perception effects are not limited to emotional facial expressions. That is, hearing and Deaf people perceive facial expressions that do not convey basic emotions (e.g., those expressions shown in Fig. 4.2) as belonging to distinct categories. It may be that humans have evolved a perceptual mechanism for classifying facial displays that allows for efficient discrimination and recognition of communicative expressions, even when these expressions are unfamiliar. Sign languages may capitalize on this mechanism by employing facial expressions to mark grammatical and lexical functions.

TH-MM (adverbial facial expressions)

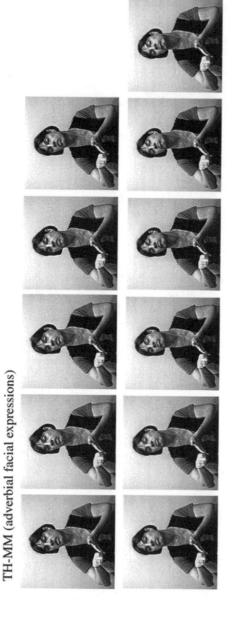

FIG. 4.2. Illustration of a computer "morphed" continuum of grammatical facial expressions from the *th* adverbial to the *mm* adverbial (from McCullough & Emmorey, 1999). The signer is producing the sign WRITE (still images were presented). The *th* adverbial marks the action as careless, whereas the *mm* adverbial marks the action as regular or easily done. These stimuli were made with *VideoFusion* software.

In sum, these few studies of categorical perception indicate that signers categorize nonidentical sign stimuli into linguistically relevant categories, but they do so in ways that are not particularly distinct from hearing nonsigners, suggesting that many linguistic categories in ASL take advantage of naturally occurring perceptual groupings (movement categorization may be an exception). However, the results of McCullough et al. (2000) indicated that Deaf signers (but not hearing nonsigners) exhibit categorical perception for hand configuration. In this domain, language experience does appear to affect perceptual categorization of the shape of the human hand, such that discrimination is better across a category boundary than within a handshape category. Whether the lack of categorical perception for place of articulation is due to the more continuous nature of location (akin to the continuous nature of vowels), to the nature of the visual system's encoding of space, or to some other factor requires further research. These types of studies provide an unusual window into the interplay between linguistic and perceptual systems, and illuminate how language capitalizes on natural perceptual categories and how linguistic processing may (or may not) affect perception.

LEXICAL ACCESS AND SIGN RECOGNITION

Although nonsigners may interpret the visual signed signal simply as a collection of rapid hand and arm motions, signers quickly extract complex meaning from the incoming visual signal. One aspect of this process is the recognition of individual signs using both perceptual and contextual information. Perceptual information comes from visual processing of the signed input, and contextual information may come from the preceding linguistic context (either sentences or signs) or world knowledge. Theories of lexical access and sign recognition attempt to explain how these two types of information are used to identify signs in isolation or in context. In what follows, we see that the same general models of lexical access proposed for speech apply to sign as well, with some intriguing variations in the pattern of lexical access (due to the special role of movement in sign recognition) and in the organization of the lexicon (with respect to the type of morphological affixation and the rarity of lexical ambiguity).

Early Sign Recognition Processes:
The Unique Role of Movement

Several models of spoken word recognition hypothesize that an acoustic–phonetic representation is sequentially mapped onto lexical entries, and lexical candidates that match this initial representation are activated (e.g., the cohort model proposed by Marslen-Wilson (1987) or the TRACE model of McClelland & Elman, 1986). As more of a word is heard, activation levels of lexical entries that do not match the incoming acoustic signal decrease. The sequential matching process continues until only one candidate remains, which is consistent with the sensory input. At this point, word recognition can occur. This process is clearly conditioned by the serial nature of speech perception. Because signed languages are less dependent on serial linguistic distinctions (see chap. 2), visual lexical access and sign recognition may differ from spoken language. Grosjean (1981) and Emmorey and Corina (1990b) used a gating technique to track the process of lexical access and sign identification through time. In this task, isolated signs are presented repeatedly, and the length of each presentation is increased by a constant amount (e.g., one videoframe or 33 msec). After each presentation, subjects report what they think the sign is and how confident they are.

The gating studies found that Deaf signers produced initial responses that shared the place of articulation, hand configuration, and orientation of the target sign but differed in movement. The movement of the sign was identified last and coincided with lexical recognition. This pattern of responses suggests that similar to the speech signal, the visual input for sign activates a cohort of potential lexical candidates that share some initial phonological features. This set of candidates narrows as more visual information is presented until a single sign candidate remains. L. Clark and Grosjean (1982) showed further that sentential context did not affect this basic pattern of lexical recognition, although it reduced the time to identify a target sign by about 10%.

However, unlike spoken word recognition, sign recognition appears to involve a two-stage process of recognition in which one group of phonological features (hand configuration and place of articulation) initially identifies a lexical cohort, and then identification of phonological movement leads directly to sign identification. Such a direct correlation between identification of a phonological element and lexical identification does not occur with English and may not occur for any spoken language. That is, there seems to be no phonological feature or structure, the identification of which leads directly to word recognition. Movement is the most temporally influenced phonological property of sign, and more time is required to resolve it. For speech, almost all phonological components have a strong temporal component, and there does not appear to be a single element that listeners must wait to resolve in order to identify a word.

The Speed and Time Course of Lexical Identification

Both Grosjean (1981) and Emmorey and Corina (1990b) found that signs were identified surprisingly rapidly. Although signs tend to be much longer than words, only about 240 msec or 35% of a sign had to be seen before the sign was identified (Emmorey & Corina, 1990b). This is significantly faster than word recognition for English. Grosjean (1980) found that approximately 330 msec or 83% of a word had to be heard before the word could be identified. There are at least two reasons why signs may be identified earlier than spoken words. First, the nature of the visual signal for sign provides a large amount of phonological information very early and simultaneously (or nearly simultaneously). Emmorey and Corina (1990) found that signers could identify place of articulation and orientation of the hand after about 145 msec, and hand configuration was identified about 30 msec later. The early availability of this phonological information can dramatically narrow the set of lexical candidates for the incoming stimulus. Second, the phonotactics and morphotactics of a visual language such as ASL may be different than those of speech. In English, many words begin with similar sequences, and listeners can be led down a garden path if a shorter word is embedded at the onset of a longer word—for example, "pan" in "pantomime." This phenomenon does not commonly occur in ASL. Furthermore, sign initial cohorts seem to be much more limited by phonotactic structure. Unlike English in which many initial strings have large cohorts (e.g., the strings [kan], [mæn], and [skr] are all shared by 30 or more words), ASL has few signs that share an initial phonological shape (i.e., the same hand configuration and target location). This phonotactic structure limits the size of the initial cohort in ASL. The more constrained phonotactics and the early and simultaneous availability of phonological information may conspire to produce numerically and proportionally faster identification times for ASL signs.

Emmorey and Corina (1990) also investigated whether certain phonological factors influenced the time course of sign recognition. For example, we hypothesized that hand configuration might be identified earlier than place of articulation for signs produced near the face because visual cues to hand configuration might be available during the transition from the resting position in the lap to the face. However, this hypothesis was not supported, suggesting that transitional information is minimal when a sign is produced in isolation. In contrast, signers were able to predict changes in hand configuration before they actually saw the change in articulation; for example, signers were able to anticipate the change from closed to open in signs like EXPENSIVE and UNDERSTAND. These findings suggest that signers are able to utilize some visual cues to anticipate lexical structure, but the basic two-stage pattern of lexical access and sign recognition seems to hold for a variety of different lexical signs.

Sign Frequency and Lexicality Effects

The *word frequency effect* refers to the finding that words with a high frequency of occurrence are recognized faster and more accurately than words with a low frequency of occurrence in either speech (Savin, 1963) or

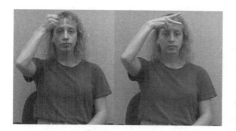

FIG. 4.3. Examples of three nonsigns used in lexical decision experiments. All are formationally possible, but nonoccurring forms.

print (Forster, 1978). To determine a word's frequency, most studies utilize frequency counts from written texts (e.g., Kucera & Francis, 1967) or spoken corpora (e.g., Dahl, 1979). Currently, no such resources exist for sign languages, and researchers have relied on ratings from native signers to estimate sign frequency. For example, signers indicate perceived sign frequency using a rating scale (e.g., 1 = quite rare, 10 = very common), and interrater reliability has been found to be about .70 (Emmorey, 1991; Emmorey, Norman, & O'Grady, 1991). Emmorey (1990) found that ASL signs with high frequency ratings (e.g., FINE, LIKE) were recognized faster than signs with low frequency ratings (e.g., DRAPES, DYE).[3] Most models of word recognition propose that frequency effects arise from variation in the thresholds or resting activation levels of lexical representations. High frequency words or signs have lower activation thresholds (or higher resting levels of activation), and thus less stimulus information is required for recognition, leading to faster recognition times (for example, Morton, 1969, the Logogen model; Luce, Pisoni, & Goldinger, 1990, the Neighborhood Activation model).

Word recognition is often measured by a *lexical decision* task in which subjects decide as quickly as possible whether a given item is a real word or a nonword (e.g., "pardack"). For sign-based lexical decision, nonsigns are created by changing the location, movement, and/or hand configuration of a real sign to create a possible, but nonexisting form. Figure 4.3 provides some examples of ASL nonsigns (compare these examples with the formationally illegal signs illustrated in several figures in chap. 2). Like nonwords, response times to nonsigns in a lexical decision task are much longer than to real signs (Corina & Emmorey, 1993; Emmorey, 1991). In addition, nonsigns that are similar to existing signs take longer to reject

---

[3] The task was lexical decision, and the stimuli were the filler (nonprimed) signs in Experiment 1 of Emmorey (1991). The mean response time of native Deaf signers was 1003 msec for low frequency signs (N = 20; mean rating = 2.9) compared to 885 msec for high frequency signs (N = 24; mean rating = 7.3). This difference in response time was significant (t(42) = 3.49, p < .002).

(Emmorey, 1995). These effects are referred to as *lexicality effects* and are generally explained by assuming that nonsigns (and nonwords) do not have lexical representations. Thus, long response times reflect either an exhaustive (unsuccessful) search of the lexicon before rejection (Forster, 1978), or nonsign rejection occurs when no lexical representation has reached a criterion level of activation. Nonsigns that are similar to real signs take longer to reject because the lexical representation of real signs have been partially activated.

LEXICAL REPRESENTATIONS AND ORGANIZATION

Models of sign and word recognition must explain not only how lexical information is accessed from memory, but also how this information is represented and organized. Knowledge about words is not randomly structured, and the representation of this knowledge is considerably more complex than that found in an ordinary dictionary. The same is true for signs.

Semantic Organization and the Rarity of Lexical Ambiguity

One organizing principle within the lexicon appears to be semantic associations between words. Meyer and Schvaneveldt (1971) were the first to discover that words are recognized more quickly when they are preceded by semantic associates. Similarly, Corina and Emmorey (1993) found that when a sign such as PENCIL is preceded by a semantically related sign such as PAPER, lexical decision times are faster than when PENCIL is preceded by an unrelated sign (e.g., MOTHER). Bosworth and Emmorey (1999) replicated this result and showed that sign iconicity played no role in the semantic priming effect. One hypothesized mechanism for semantic priming is "spreading activation" through the links connecting closely associated words, which then facilitates (primes) recognition of the associated words (Collins & Loftus, 1975; for discussion, see Neely, 1991). Together, these studies indicate that the lexicons of both signed and spoken languages exhibit a semantic organization that facilitates language processing.

But what happens when a word has more than one meaning such as *straw* (a type of hay vs. a drinking implement)? Are all meanings accessed or just the meaning that is appropriate for the context? A great many psycholinguistic studies have been conducted with English in an attempt to answer this question. One reason for such enthusiasm is that the answer bears directly on the issue of modularity and language (Fodor, 1983). For example, if multiple meanings of an ambiguous word are initially accessed

EVERYTHING/INVOLVE   PERSON/BOOTH   OF-COURSE/NATION

FIG. 4.4.   Illustration of lexically ambiguous ASL signs.

regardless of sentential context, it suggests that lexical access processes are insulated from higher level semantic and cognitive processes. But if context has an immediate and selective effect on lexical access, it suggests a more interactive model of language processing is correct. While this debate rages on (and may have outlived the debate's usefulness; Simpson, 1994), one is struck by the rarity of ambiguous signs in ASL.[4] In attempting to elicit such signs from native signers, I have found that facial expression (specifically mouth patterns) would often disambiguate meanings for a potentially ambiguous sign. For example, the sign glossed as TASTE or FAVORITE can be disambiguated by whether the teeth contact the lower lip (as if producing an "f"), which would mark the sign as FAVORITE. Some examples of signs that are truly ambiguous are given in Fig. 4.4, but even for these signs, the meanings could be disambiguated by mouthing the appropriate English word while producing the sign.

Is the rarity of lexical ambiguity in ASL real? And if so, is it a fact about ASL or about signed languages in general? To address these questions, I conducted a small sampling study using dictionaries from four different languages: *A Dictionary of American Sign Language on Linguistic Principles* (Stokoe, Casterline, & Croneberg, 1965), *The Random House College Dictionary* (Stein, 1984), *Dictionary of British Sign Language/English* (Brien, 1992), and *Navajo-English Dictionary* (Wall & Morgan, 1958/1994). To achieve roughly 250–300 words/signs per sample, items were randomly selected as follows: *ASL and BSL*: the first sign listed at the top of each page; *English*: the first word listed at the top (right-hand column) of every fifth page; *Navajo*: the top word on each column of every page. The following forms were excluded from sampling: multiple word entries, abbreviations, archaic and rare forms, technical terms, proper names, foreign words, and compounds. A word or sign was considered ambiguous if two distinct entries were listed or two distinct meanings were given within the list of definitions or English glosses. Fitting the anecdotal evidence, 20% of the Eng-

---

[4] The phenomenon here is ambiguity involving quite distinct meanings (homonyms) rather than polysemy (words or signs with multiple related meanings).

lish words, but only 6% of the ASL signs, were clearly ambiguous.[5] However, the rarity of lexical ambiguity does not appear to be an effect of language modality because both British Sign Language and Navajo had similar rates of ambiguity: 7% and 4%, respectively. Whether percentage of lexical ambiguity is affected by language history, vocabulary size, morphological complexity, or some other factor(s) awaits future research.

Nonetheless, sign languages may be unique in their ability to minimize lexical ambiguity by presenting distinguishing information on a separate channel. Many ambiguous signs can be disambiguated through mouth patterns borrowed from the surrounding spoken language. However, the use of such mouth patterns may vary depending on the degree of bilingualism in the community and on other social and cultural factors (see papers in Brentari, 2001).

Morphological Organization

The representation of morphologically complex words and signs is another issue that lexical theories need to address. Poizner, Newkirk, Bellugi, and Klima (1981) showed that morphologically complex signs were organized in memory not as holistic forms, but in terms of a base form and an inflection. They presented short lists of signs for immediate serial recall (see chap. 7) and found that signers sometimes added or deleted inflections from a list item or recombined morphological components within the list. For example, BEAT[reciprocal] and SHOOT[multiple] were misrecalled as SHOOT[reciprocal] and BEAT[multiple]; in this example, the base forms are switched. Another error type involved switching the inflections, leaving the base forms in the same serial position in the list. These error patterns were taken as evidence that signers were encoding the base form and inflectional morphology separately. However, these findings do not address the question of how morphological structure is organized and represented within the ASL lexicon.

For example, what is the primary unit of representation, the sign or the morpheme? Are morphologically complex signs represented as decomposed units or as whole sign structures that represent internal morphological structure? *Repetition priming* is frequently used to investigate these questions and refers to the finding that lexical decisions (and other lexical responses) are faster when a word has been previously seen in the experiment. For example, when the two words are morphological variants of each other (*walking, walk*), priming has been found that is equal to identity

---

[5] The percentage of ambiguous signs for ASL did not take into account disambiguation via mouthing (see Schermer, in press, for a discussion of the implications of mouthings for the production of sign language dictionaries).

priming (*walk, walk*), indicating that a single root morpheme (*walk*) has been activated (Fowler, Napps, & Feldman, 1985; Stanners, Neisser, Hernon, & Hall, 1979). Repetition priming effects are argued to be due to morphological structure, rather than to shared semantics or phonological structure, because the priming effect occurs over very long lag times (unlike semantic priming, which is short-lived), and it occurs between words that have little phonological overlap, for example, *heal, health* (Fowler et al., 1985; Henderson, Wallis, & Knight, 1984). Repetition priming can be interpreted as an index of the interrelation among morphologically related forms in the lexicon (see Marslen-Wilson, Tyler, Waksler, & Older, 1994, for a review).

Emmorey (1991) used the repetition priming technique to investigate the organization of morphologically complex signs in the ASL lexicon. Two separate experiments showed that verbs inflected with aspect morphology produced strong facilitation; for example, ASK[habitual] and SIT[continual] facilitated later recognition of the citation forms ASK and SIT.[6] However, agreeing verbs did not facilitate recognition of the base form of the verb. That is, verbs such as ASK[dual], BEAT[multiple], and SHOOT[reciprocal] did not prime their citation forms. Repetition priming was not observed for nonsigns, which indicates that the facilitation effect produced by verbs with aspect marking was a true lexical effect and not due to episodic memory or to facilitation at a phonological level. The explanation for the difference in morphological priming for the two verb types is not completely clear. Differential productivity, that is, variation in how many verbs allow a particular affix, may provide part of the answer (see Emmorey, 1995). The reciprocal, dual, and multiple are less productive morphological affixes compared to the habitual or continual (e.g., more verbs can be marked with habitual than with reciprocal). Stronger morphological priming indicates a stronger morphological association between related forms within the lexicon, and this association may be modulated by the productivity of the affixes (see Frauenfelder & Schreuder, 1992, for a discussion of the role of productivity in morphological processing).

In addition, Hanson and Feldman (1989) found that for bilingual signers, the lexical organization of ASL reflects the morphological relationships of ASL signs, not English words. They found significant morphological priming when subjects were asked to make sign-based decisions for words that were morphologically related in ASL, but were not morphologically related in English, for example, noun–verb pairs such as SHOOT/GUN (see chap. 2 for a discussion of noun–verb derivations in ASL). However, when signers were presented with these same words, but an English

---

[6]The task was continuous lexical decision and approximately one minute (30 items) intervened between the prime and target signs.

word-based decision was required, no morphological priming was observed.[7] The long lag times between the prime and target words rule out an explanation based on semantic association or phonological form.[8] The facilitation effect found with the sign-based task provides additional support for a morphological organization within the ASL lexicon, and further, the absence of facilitation in the English task indicates that the English lexicon for these bilingual signers is not organized with respect to morphological relations inherent to ASL.

The Preference for Nonconcatenative Morphology: A Processing Explanation

Sign languages appear to show a marked preference for nonconcatenative morphological processes, in contrast to the preference for linear affixation exhibited by spoken languages. ASL contains a few suffixes: the multiple suffix (Wilbur, 1987), the agentive suffix, -ER, and a negative suffix, ZERO, recently documented by Aronoff, Meir, Padden, and Sandler (in press). However, the majority of morphological processes in ASL are nonconcatenative (see chap. 2). Bergman (1982) claimed that Swedish Sign Language has neither suffixation nor prefixation, but exhibits several types of reduplication and nonconcatenative morphological processes. Similarly, Sutton-Spence and Woll (1999) described only nonconcatenative morphological processes for British Sign Language, with the exception of compounding. Thus far, the data from numerous signed languages indicates that linear affixation is rare and that simultaneous expression of a base form and its morphological markings is the preferred linguistic encoding.

In contrast, for spoken languages, simultaneous affixation, such as template morphology, infixation, or reduplication, is relatively rare, and linear affixation is the preferred linguistic encoding for morphological processes. Cutler et al. (1985) argued that processing constraints underlie the rarity of morphological processes, which alter the phonological integrity of the base form (e.g., infixation, which inserts an affix into the middle of a word). Languages avoid processes that disrupt the structural integrity of linguistic units. Hall (1992) also argued that the rarity of nonconcatenative morphology is due to the processing complexity associated with dis-

---

[7]For the sign-based decision task, subjects decided if the ASL sign corresponding to a given English word was made with one hand or two hands. For the English word-based response, subjects made lexical decisions to the English words.

[8]In addition, Hanson and Feldman (1991) found no evidence of form-based or associative priming for ASL signs under the same experimental conditions, indicating that the priming effects observed in their earlier study were due to morphological relationships between ASL signs.

continuous elements in general (e.g., center embedding or verbs with particles). Concatenative morphology requires much less computational complexity because of the straightforward mapping between the surface form of a word and its underlying representation (S. R. Anderson, 1992). Given these arguments, why do signed languages prefer nonconcatenative morphology and does it pose the same processing challenges that it does for spoken languages?

First, signed languages appear to favor nonconcatenative morphology because the visual modality affords parallel processing. Vision can easily encode spatially distinct information in parallel (unlike audition), and as we noted, the hand configuration, place of articulation, and orientation of signs are all perceived simultaneously. Second, universal constraints on working memory and a slower articulation rate may induce sign languages to disfavor linear affixation (see chap. 7). Evidence for this hypothesis comes from S. Supalla's (1991) finding that when the linear morphology of a spoken language is transferred to the visual modality, Deaf children exposed to this artificial language do not acquire the system and alter it to create simultaneous (spatial) morphological encoding. As discussed in chapter 1, Manually Coded English (MCE) borrows heavily from the lexicon of ASL, but its inflectional morphology is strictly sequential and based on English morphology. S. Supalla (1991) found that children exposed only to MCE modify the inflectional morphology to take advantage of the visual modality. That is, these children produce spatial nonlinear modifications to base verbs and pronominals in order to mark person and verb arguments, despite the fact that they were exposed only to linguistic input that produced these distinctions linearly. The children's spatial morphological creations were idiosyncratic, but they were systematic within a child and similar to the grammatical morphology found in signed languages of the world. Stack (1999) also found that Jamie, a young child exposed only to MCE, failed to acquire the nonspatial pronouns and linear inflections of MCE; rather, she created a pronominal system that utilized space and innovated nonlinear morphology to express linguistic notions such as plurality (by reduplication), reciprocal aspect (the second hand mirrors the first), and verb arguments (indicated by the beginning and endpoints of a verb). These results suggest that not only does the visual modality easily afford nonlinear affixation, but visual processing may actually demand it.

Finally, unlike infixation or circumfixation, the morphological processes of ASL (and possibly other signed languages) do not "interrupt" the base form and do not involve discontinuous affixes. Figures 2.1 and 2.2 in chapter 2 illustrate several examples of ASL nonconcatenative morphology. In no case is the base form of the sign actually interrupted by the morphological marking. The morphological marking appears to be *super-imposed* onto the base form of the verb, and Sandler (1989, 1990) analyzed these forms as instances of templatic or autosegmental morphology. Thus, the morphological parsing difficulties that arise from nonconcatenative processes in spoken languages do not seem to arise for signed languages.

Phonological Organization

Recently, Corina (2000a) conducted a series of experiments investigating whether phonological aspects of ASL signs are activated online during sign recognition. Using a lexical decision task, Corina explored whether the major class segments, Movement and Location (see chap. 2), have independent representations that can be primed during sign recognition. Phonological priming is indicated by faster response times when a sign is preceded by a phonologically related sign, compared to an unrelated sign. In these experiments, native Deaf ASL signers viewed two sign stimuli in succession (separated by either 100 msec or 500 msec), and they were asked to decide whether the second item was a true sign or a nonsign. The sign pairs either shared the same Movement or the same Location, or they were unrelated (shared no phonological segments). Corina (2000a) found no evidence of phonological priming for either Movement or Location segments, which contrasted with the earlier results of Corina and Emmorey (1993). In this earlier study, we found evidence of facilitation when signs shared Movement, inhibition for shared Location, and no priming effects for shared hand configuration. However, subject response times in this experiment were particularly long (over 1,000 msec), suggesting that the priming effects occurred postlexically. That is, these earlier results may have been due to response strategies, rather than to effects that occur during lexical recognition.

However, lack of phonological priming in ASL is not at odds with results from spoken language. For spoken word recognition, phonological primes (e.g., bull-beer) may produce facilitation when subjects are given a post-lexical task, but no priming effects are observed when subjects participate in online tasks (Lively, Pisoni, & Goldinger, 1994). In fact, phonetically similar words (words sharing a single segment with similar features, e.g., bull-veer) may actually produce inhibition, that is, slower response times for the target word (Goldinger, Luce, & Pisoni, 1989). Corina (2000a) observed a similar trend for inhibition in the ASL data. Several models account for inhibition effects by assuming that activated words or phonemes inhibit similar items (e.g., Luce, 1986; McClelland & Elman, 1986). However, more research on the nature of phonological processing during sign recognition is necessary before we can determine whether these models of phonological inhibition can be applied to signed languages.

To conclude, lexical access and word recognition are generally quite similar for spoken and signed languages. For both language types, we observe effects of word frequency and lexicality, similar semantic and morphological organization within the lexicon (as evidenced by semantic and morphological priming), and an initial lexical access process in which sensory input (visual or acoustic) activates a cohort of potential lexical candidates that narrows until a single candidate remains. Language modality effects are observed in the speed of sign identification and in the preference of signed languages for nonconcatenative morphological processes.

ONLINE COMPREHENSION OF SIGNED UTTERANCES: PSYCHOLINGUISTIC STUDIES OF COREFERENCE

Online comprehension refers to the interpretation of signed utterances as they are being perceived in real time. One can ask whether the visual modality places any special demands on the processing mechanisms required for online sentence comprehension, and the interpretation of pronouns and coreference processing are domains where language modality might be expected to have an effect. As described in chapter 2, pronominal reference in ASL involves the association of a referent with a location in signing space, and a pronominal sign directed toward this location refers back to the associated referent. My colleagues and I have conducted several studies investigating how signers understand and maintain the association between referents and spatial locations during real-time language processing. For these experiments, we adapted a probe recognition technique in which subjects view signed ASL sentences on videotape and judge as quickly as possible whether a probe sign has occurred in the sentence. In the English version of the task, subjects usually read sentences and probe words on a computer screen. This technique has been shown to be sensitive to coreference conditions between clauses or sentences. In general, we have found that the same processing mechanisms are required to interpret coreference in signed and spoken languages, but for signed languages, the type of information represented by the spatial location can influence how coreference relations are processed and represented in memory.

Antecedent Activation and Spatial Anaphora

Studies using the probe recognition technique suggest that pronouns and other anaphoric elements "reactivate" their antecedents during processing (e.g. Chang, 1980; Corbett & Chang, 1983; Gernsbacher, 1989). For example, Chang (1980) presented sentences such as "Mary and John went to the store and he bought a quart of milk." Response time to the probe word "John" (the antecedent of the pronoun in the second clause) was faster than response time to "Mary" (the nonantecedent). In addition, when a noun phrase in a sentence or clause is later referenced by a pronoun, responses to that noun in the probe task are faster than when the noun appears in a sentence with no pronoun (e.g., MacDonald & MacWhinney, 1990). These results suggest that comprehension of the pronoun invokes the backward activation of its antecedent. In addition, several studies have also found evidence for inhibition or suppression of activation for the nonantecedent (Gernsbacher, 1989, 1990; MacDonald & MacWhinney, 1990).

Comparing signed and spoken languages with respect to antecedent activation and nonantecedent suppression is particularly appealing because of the nature of coreference in ASL. For example, ASL pronouns usually pick out specific antecedents, rather than a class of possible antecedents (such as singular third person females). Thus, reference to spatial locations allows explicit coreference, which is almost always unambiguous. Gernsbacher (1989) found that unambiguous pronouns in English produce stronger nonantecedent suppression. To investigate coreference processing in ASL, Emmorey et al. (1991) presented videotaped ASL sentences in which the first clause established two possible noun antecedents, and the second clause either contained a pronoun which referred to one of the nouns in the first clause, or it lacked a pronoun. For example:

Pronoun Condition:

A-FEW REALLY STRICT LIBRARY-AGENT$_a$ FORBID BIG-HEAD STU-DENT$_b$ TAKE-OUT BOOK, HAPPEN THEY$_b$ CONTACT PRINCIPAL COMPLAIN.

"A few really strict librarians refused to allow arrogant students to check out books, as it happens they (students) contacted the principal and complained."

Probe signs: STUDENT (antecedent), LIBRARY-AGENT (nonantecedent)

No-Pronoun Condition:

A-FEW REALLY STRICT LIBRARY-AGENT$_a$ FORBID BIG-HEAD STU-DENT$_b$ TAKE-OUT BOOK, HAPPEN PRINCIPAL FIND-OUT PISSED-OFF.

"A few really strict librarians refused to allow arrogant students to check out books, as it happens the principal found out and was upset."

Probe signs: STUDENT (antecedent), LIBRARY-AGENT (nonantecedent)

Probe signs were edited in either immediately after or one second following the pronoun in the pronoun condition or following the second word of the second clause in the no-pronoun condition.

At the one second delay, Deaf signers were faster at recognizing a probe sign that was the antecedent of a pronoun (STUDENT) compared to a probe sign that was a nonantecedent (LIBRARY-AGENT). Subjects were also faster at recognizing a probe sign when it was the antecedent of a pronoun compared to when the probe appeared in the no-pronoun control condition. These results indicate that ASL pronouns activate their antecedents, thus making these nominals more accessible during language comprehension (Gernsbacher, 1990). In addition, the results suggest that some rise time is required for antecedent activation because at zero delay (i.e., immediately after the pronoun), no evidence of antecedent activation was observed.

Some studies with English have also found activation at a one second delay (MacDonald, 1986)—although most studies report earlier activation. Given that signs take nearly twice as long to articulate, we might expect some differences in the absolute time for antecedent activation to occur. MacDonald (1986) found that 500 msec was an optimal delay between a pronoun and presentation of a probe word to observe antecedent activation. An average of two to three words are read in 500 msec, but 1,000 msec would be required for two to three ASL signs to be viewed in a sentence context. Thus, the critical variable may not be the absolute amount of time following the pronoun, but how much additional information follows the pronoun before antecedent activation occurs. These findings, in conjunction with research on spoken language, suggest that antecedent activation is a robust, modality independent, psychological process.

Emmorey et al. (1991) further investigated the strength of the relationship between a spatial location and its associated referent by examining interference effects in the probe recognition task. In a second experiment, probe signs were articulated either at a location that was congruent with the test sentence or at an incongruent location. For example, if STUDENT in our example sentence were articulated to the left in signing space, the *congruent* probe sign STUDENT would be also articulated to the left, and the *incongruent* probe sign STUDENT would be articulated to the right. Subjects were instructed to make their decisions based on lexical content and ignore the spatial information (thus, the decision would be *yes* for both spatially congruent and incongruent probes because the sign itself (STUDENT) appeared in the sentence). Assuming that the association between a nominal and its spatial location must be maintained in memory for future discourse reference, we predicted that it should take subjects longer to recognize a probe that had been marked for an incorrect spatial location with respect to the test sentence.

However, the results did not support this prediction—response times were very similar for probes articulated at congruent and incongruent spatial locations. There was little evidence of an interference effect for probes produced with an incorrect spatial location. However, Emmorey, Corina, and Bellugi (1995) found that such interference effects may only occur when spatial locations function semantically as counterparts to physical locations in the world (or in an imagined world), rather than to simply convey referential distinctions within a discourse. Figures 4.5 and 4.6 provide illustrations of test sentences and probe signs used in this experiment. In the sentence in Fig. 4.5, the spatial locations represent a topographic mapping of a scene in which the spatial locations stand in specific relationships to each other, and these relationships are meaningful. Figure 4.6 illustrates a sentence in which the spatial locations bear no inherent relation to each other and function primarily to convey referential distinctions. The probe sign was articulated simultaneously with an index (a determiner; see chap. 2) that was directed toward the correct or incorrect location. Subjects were told to decide whether the probe sign itself was used in the sentence regardless of indexation.

Emmorey et al. (1995) found that the amount of interference caused by a spatially incongruent probe was three times as great when locations functioned topographically. Thus, when spatial locations do not convey spatial information but merely serve to indexically distinguish among referents, there appears to be a much weaker relation between referents and locations in signing space, such that signers are easily able to ignore a spatially incongruent probe sign. However, when spatial locations in signing space convey information about the spatial location of associated referents, signers maintain a stronger representation of this association in memory and are unable to suppress incongruent spatial information.

Further support for this hypothesis is provided by a second experiment in which the same sentences were presented in a continuous recognition memory task. Subjects were shown lists of videotaped ASL sentences and had to decide for each sentence whether it had been previously seen. Some sentences were altered by reversing the spatial locations associated with two referents. We predicted that for sentences in which the locations functioned topographically, subjects would notice the spatial changes much more frequently than for sentences in which the locations functioned purely as referential indices (see Figs. 4.5 and 4.6). The results supported this prediction: When locations in signing space functioned topographically, subjects were significantly more likely to notice a spatial change. Thus, locations that convey information about the spatial location of their associated referent may be specifically encoded and maintained in memory, perhaps as part of a semantic representation; whereas spatial locations that function primarily to distinguish referents may not be encoded in the same way and may be more likely to fade from memory once their referential function is no longer required by the discourse.

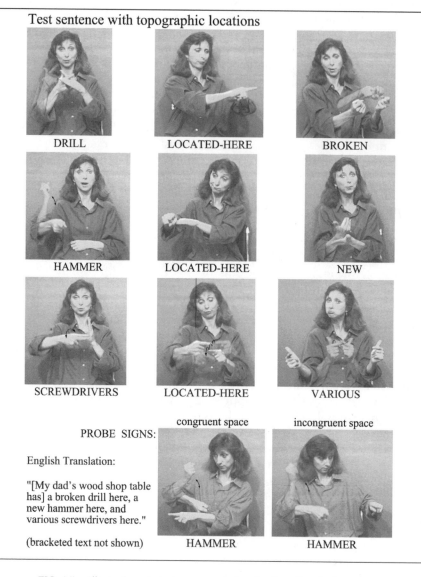

FIG. 4.5.   Illustration of a test sentence and probe signs from K. Emmorey, D. Corina, and U. Bellugi (1995). The spatial locations in this sentence provide topographic information about the associated referents. Copyright © 1995 by Lawrence Erlbaum Associates. Reprinted with permission.

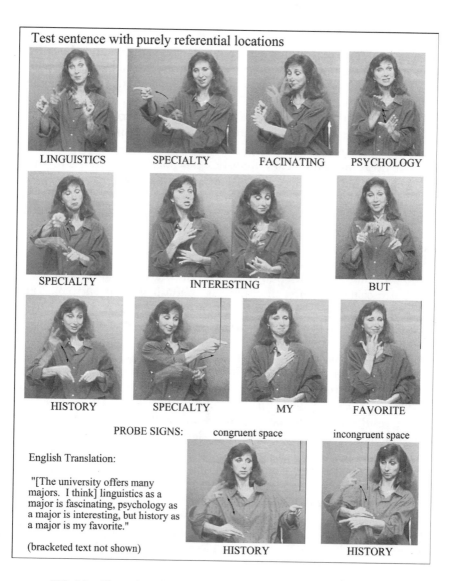

Test sentence with purely referential locations

LINGUISTICS	SPECIALTY	FACINATING	PSYCHOLOGY
SPECIALTY	INTERESTING		BUT
HISTORY	SPECIALTY	MY	FAVORITE

PROBE SIGNS: congruent space   incongruent space

English Translation:

"[The university offers many majors. I think] linguistics as a major is fascinating, psychology as a major is interesting, but history as a major is my favorite."

(bracketed text not shown)

HISTORY   HISTORY

FIG. 4.6.   Illustration of a test sentence and probe signs from K. Emmorey, D. Corina, and U. Bellugi (1995). The spatial locations in this sentence function primarily to distinguish referents. Copyright © 1995 by Lawrence Erlbaum Associates. Reprinted with permission.

Processing Overt Versus Null Pronouns in ASL

Unlike English (but similar to Italian and Chinese), ASL permits phono-logically null pronouns in tensed clauses. That is, subjects and objects can appear as null elements that do not have an overt lexical form (e.g., a pro-noun or lexical noun phrase), as illustrated in Fig. 4.8. Emmorey and Lillo-Martin (1995) explored how such null pronouns are associated with their antecedents. Null pronouns are permitted to occur because of the morphological marking of agreeing verbs, and they display the character-istics of the category *pro* (see Chomsky, 1982); that is, they act syntactically just like overt pronouns. They are licensed by marking on the verb, which makes use of the same locations in signing space as overt pronouns. Lillo-Martin (1986) provided linguistic evidence that null pronouns in ASL pat-tern like overt pronouns, and the study by Emmorey and Lillo-Martin (1995) was designed to investigate whether null pronouns are also proc-essed similarly to overt pronouns.

Three types of sentences were compared: those with an overt pronoun, those with null pronouns, and those with no anaphora. All stimuli began with a two-clause discourse that spatially established two participants (Fig. 4.7), and there were three possible continuations (Fig. 4.8), which con-tained either (a) an overt pronoun, coreferential with one of the two possi-ble antecedents; (b) null pronouns licensed by verb morphology, corefer-ential with both of the two possible antecedents; or (c) no anaphora (the control condition). Probe signs (the two possible antecedents) were pre-sented either at the end of the continuation sentence (Experiment 1) or 1,000 msec after the pronoun (Experiment 2).

The results indicated that both overt and null pronouns activate their antecedents. Response time to a probe sign that was the antecedent of ei-ther an overt or null pronoun was faster than response time to the same probe sign appearing in the control sentence containing no anaphora. However, when the probe sign was presented at the end of the sentence, response time to the nonantecedent probe sign was unexpectedly faster in the overt pronoun condition. We hypothesized that this result may have been due to so-called "wrap-up" effects (e.g., Balogh, Zurif, Prather, Swinney, & Finkel, 1998). That is, subjects may have been reviewing the sentence for integration, and the presence of the pronoun may have led to the activation of all possible antecedents at the end of the sentence. When probes were presented before the end of the sentence (at the 1,000 msec delay), no activation of the nonantecedent was observed.

In addition, the amount of antecedent activation was similar for both overt and null pronouns. This finding provides additional support for the existence of an empty category with pronominal characteristics. Overt and null pronouns both activate their antecedents. Furthermore, subject null

Introductory Discourse

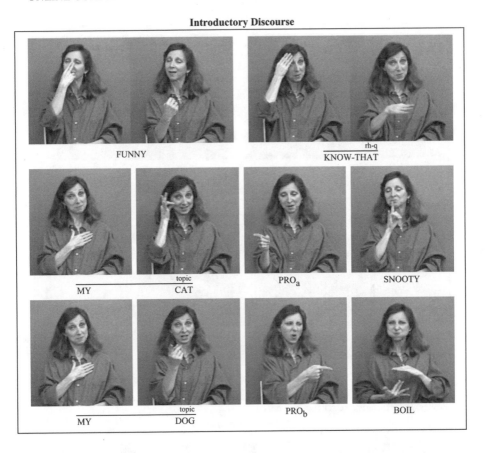

FIG. 4.7. Illustration of the introductory discourse for a stimuli set (Fig. 4.8 provides the possible continuations). An English translation is: "It's funny—you know that my cat is reserved and snooty, and my dog is boiling mad." The illustration is from K. Emmorey and D. Lillo-Martin, 1995, "Processing Spatial Anaphora: Referent Reactivation with Overt and Null Pronouns in American Sign Language." *Language and Cognitive Processes, 10*(6), 631–664. Copyright © 1995. Reprinted by permission of Psychology Press Limited, Hove, UK.

pronouns and object null pronouns produced similar amounts of activation. This finding suggests there is no "first mention" advantage for null pronouns within these constructions. Gernsbacher (1990) argued that within a clause, the first mentioned participant has a higher activation or accessibility level. In our study, the subject *pro* always preceded the object *pro*; however, we did not find faster response times for the subject probe sign. There are at least two possible explanations. The advantage of first mention may apply only to explicit noun phrases and not to pronouns (either overt or null). Another possibility is that although the subject *pro* pre-

Continuation Sentences
Control

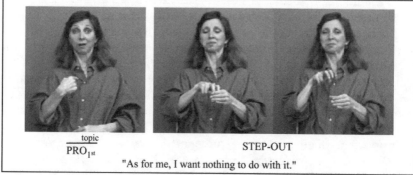

$$\overline{\text{PRO}_{1st}}^{\text{topic}} \qquad\qquad \text{STEP-OUT}$$

"As for me, I want nothing to do with it."

Probes: DOG, CAT

Overt Pronoun

PRO$_b$ FED   U-P

"He (the dog) is fed-up."   (not shown)

Probes: DOG (referent), CAT (nonreferent)

Null Pronouns

$_b$HATE$_a$ WOW!

"He (the dog) really hates him (the cat), wow!"

Probes: DOG (subject referent), CAT (object referent)

FIG. 4.8. Example of three possible continuation sentences. The illustrations are from K. Emmorey and D. Lillo-Martin, 1995, "Processing Spatial Anaphora: Referent Reactivation with Overt and Null Pronouns in American Sign Language." *Language and Cognitive Processes, 10*(6), 631–664. Copyright © 1995. Reprinted by permission of Psychology Press Limited, Hove, UK.

cedes the object *pro* within the verb phrase, there are phonological cues to the object referent that are produced at the beginning of the verb. That is, the orientation of the hand often signals the beginning location (associated with the subject referent) and the end location (associated with the object referent). As already discussed, hand orientation is perceived very early before the sign movement is resolved. Thus, the subject and object referents may be identified simultaneously by the verb morphology.

Nonantecedent Suppression

Neither the Emmorey et al. (1991) study nor the Emmorey and Lillo-Martin (1995) study found any evidence of nonantecedent suppression. That is, response time to nonantecedent probe signs was not slower in the pronoun condition compared to the control condition. One effect of nonantecedent suppression is to improve the accessibility of the coreferent nominal by suppressing the activation of those nominals that are not antecedents. In particular, Gernsbacher (1989) argued that the more unambiguous and explicit a coreferential element is, the more quickly it can be used to suppress nonantecedents. The fact that neither of our studies found evidence for nonantecedent suppression in ASL raises some questions: Is nonantecedent suppression a universal processing mechanism or is it language specific? Is this process dependent upon the type of pronominal system within a language?

Emmorey (1997b) investigated these questions and found that when the appropriate baseline measure is used, nonantecedent suppression occurs with ASL pronouns. The previous experiments measured suppression with respect to a sentence that contained no anaphoric element. In Emmorey (1997b), nonantecedent suppression was measured by comparing response times to probes presented either prior to or after the pronoun. The same sentences from Emmorey et al. (1991) were presented, but probe signs were presented either before the pronoun (after the last word of the first clause) or one second after the pronoun. Response times to nonantecedent probe signs were significantly slower when the probe was presented after a noncoreferential pronoun, compared to before the pronoun. This result provides evidence that ASL pronouns suppress the activation of nonantecedent nominals, thus making the antecedent nominal more accessible in memory. Emmorey (1997b) argued that the *no pronoun sentence* baseline is more sensitive for measuring antecedent activation effects (but not for measuring nonantecedent suppression), whereas the *"before pronoun"* baseline is more sensitive to nonantecedent suppression effects (but not to antecedent activation).

In conclusion, these experiments show that the same suppression and activation processes are involved in interpreting anaphors in a language that uses spatial representations as part of its coreference system. The evidence indicates that ASL pronouns activate their antecedents and suppress nonantecedents. The results also suggest that within the probe recognition paradigm, the spatial indexing of ASL pronouns is similar to gender marking in English with respect to picking out an unambiguous antecedent and suppressing nonantecedents. In addition, our findings indicate that when the association between a referent and a spatial location functions primarily as an indexation device, the association may not be retained long in memory. However, when the association also specifies the spatial relation between one referent and another, the spatial locations may be encoded as part of the semantic representation of the sentence and are thus more accurately maintained in memory. These studies reveal some unique aspects of processing coreference in sign language, but in general they indicate that despite the considerable differences in surface form, signed and spoken languages use many of the same processing mechanisms in resolving and interpreting coreference relations.

SOME ISSUES IN SIGN LANGUAGE PRODUCTION

Thus far, we have been exploring the perception and comprehension of sign language. We now turn to issues related to sign production. Several models of speech planning and speech production have been proposed (e.g., Dell, 1986; Garrett, 1975; W. J. M. Levelt, 1989), but little research has been conducted regarding the mechanisms involved in the online production of signed utterances. No models of sign production have been proposed, and the extent to which speech production models can be applied to sign is unknown. In this section, we discuss some aspects of sign production that are unique to the visual–manual modality and review some provocative parallels and contrasts between the nature of speech production and sign production.

Two Independent Articulators: A Unique Aspect of Sign Language Production

The two arms and hands are anatomically equivalent and independent articulators that could, in principle, produce two distinct messages simultaneously. However, signers never express distinct propositions using the two hands, except as a type of parlor trick requiring extensive practice (e.g., fingerspelling two different words on each hand). This result falls out of constraints on bimanual coordination and limitations on human language processing (i.e., two different messages cannot be attended to simultaneously). In all cases where the two hands simultaneously produce distinct signs, the two signs are related to a single predication (W. J. M. Levelt, 1980), and generally one hand is held motionless. For example, a determiner can be articulated simultaneously with a noun (see the probe signs in Figs. 4.7 and 4.8), and in chapter 3, we saw examples of locative expressions in which the ground object was expressed simultaneously with the figure object in two-handed classifier constructions (e.g., Fig. 3.6).

In addition, under certain discourse contexts, a signer can maintain the articulation of a classifier handshape while continuing to sign with the dominant hand, as illustrated in Fig. 4.9. In such examples, the classifier sign does not represent the ground object in a locative relation; rather it represents backgrounded information within the discourse. Several researchers have proposed that these simultaneous constructions create text coherence by using the nondominant hand to indicate backgrounded information while the dominant hand expresses focused information (Engberg-Pedersen, 1994; Friedman, 1975; Gee & Kegl, 1983; Miller, 1994). Signers may use this backgrounding device to help maintain the topic of discourse, particularly when the focused discourse represents a potential topic shift, as in Fig. 4.9. Signers may use this device to indicate to their addressee that they will return to the theme represented by the held sign. Furthermore, Emmorey and Falgier (1999a) found that sign addressees are sensitive to this backgrounding device. Using the probe recognition technique, we found that the activation level of the referent associated with the held classifier sign was maintained during processing (compared to sentences in which the classifier sign was dropped). This finding highlights a modality specific aspect of language processing: the ability to visually perceive a backgrounded element while processing focused information within a discourse.

Miller (1994) reviewed other examples of simultaneous constructions that do not involve classifier signs. For example, a common simultaneous construction involves enumeration morphology (ordinal tip loci; see Liddell, 1990) in which the thumb and finger tips of the nondominant hand represent numerical order (1st, 2nd, 3rd, etc.). The nondominant hand is held in space while the dominant hand produces signs associated with each ordinal tip locus (e.g., listing birth order of siblings, items on a menu, or the order of topics to be discussed). In simultaneous event constructions, a verb sign can be held with one hand while the other hand produces a clause expressing another event, and this construction expresses the notion, "while doing X, Y happened." For example, "I LOOK-AROUND(to right), MAN COME-UP-TO-ME(from left)" in which the sign LOOK is held during the second clause; the ASL sentence would mean, "While I was looking around (at something on the right), a man came up to me (from the left)." The phonological and syntactic constraints on simultaneous constructions are not well understood, and further re-

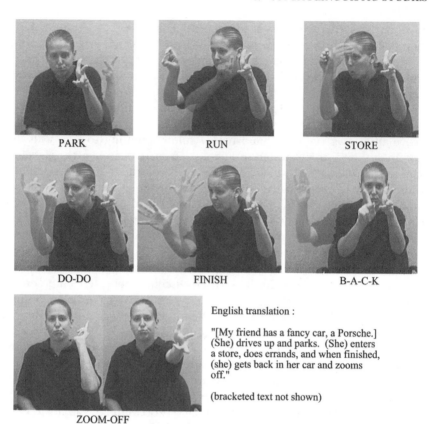

FIG. 4.9. Illustration of a simultaneous construction in which the ASL vehicle classifier is held in space as a backgrounding device maintaining the "fancy car" as the discourse topic, while the dominant hand produces the current focused discourse (from Emmorey & Falgier, 1999a).

search may illuminate when and how signers are able to exploit this unique aspect of sign production.[9]

Related to simultaneous constructions is the phenomenon of *dominance reversal*, first described by Frishberg (1983). Dominance reversal occurs when a normally right-handed signer produces a sign (or string of signs) with the left hand as the dominant hand (and vice versa for a left-handed signer). Like some simultaneous constructions, dominance reversal can be

---

[9]The mouth is also somewhat independent of the hands, and Vogt-Svendsen (in press) reports examples from Norwegian Sign Language in which a nominal sign co-occurs with mouthing of a Norwegian color adjective (e.g., mouthing *hvit* ("white") while producing OMRÅE ("area") to mean "white area"). The phonological and syntactic constraints on these simultaneous constructions are not well understood either.

used to background material; for example, an "aside" or parenthetical information may be signed with the nondominant hand to set it apart from the main narrative. Dominance reversal can also serve to highlight contrasts and comparisons; for example, signing CHILDREN with the right hand and PARENTS with the left in order to contrast the two. Frishberg (1983) also found that the tendency to shift dominance was much greater for left-handed than for right-handed signers. The fact that individual variation in motor control can affect the nature of language usage at a discourse level may be particular to sign language, with no obvious parallel in spoken language.

Monitoring and Self-Repair: "Ums" and "Uhs" in Sign Language

Psycholinguistic research has shown that speakers monitor their speech, and when they detect an error or an ill-chosen word, they interrupt themselves and repair the utterance (W. J. M. Levelt, 1983, 1989; Schegloff, Jefferson, & Sacks, 1977). During the pause in speech before the repair, speakers often produce *editing expressions* to indicate that they are having trouble. The type of editing expression depends on the type of trouble (W. J. M. Levelt, 1983). For example, *no, sorry*, and *I mean* are most often produced when the speaker has made an error, as in Example (1a). Editing expressions such as *rather, that is*, and *you know* are used when the speaker is correcting a word that is not wrong, but simply inappropriate, ambiguous, or underspecified (Clark & Gerrig, 1990; W. J. M. Levelt, 1989). See Example (1b). The most frequent editing expressions for spoken English are so-called "filled pauses" such as *um* and *uh*, which occur after errors (before the repair) and when speakers have word-finding or other difficulties, as in Example (1c).

(1) Examples of editing expressions and repairs in English (from spoken descriptions of the town and convention center from Emmorey, Tversky, & Taylor, in press):

   a) bordering the town, on the south is the white high—no the river highway.
   b) and it's a it's a fairly big you know partitioned area.
   c) there's going to be, um, there's going to be a room which has, uh, movie cameras, on the right.

Signers also appear to monitor their signing, interrupt themselves and produce editing expressions and repairs (Dively, 1998). The following are examples from signed descriptions of the convention center from Emmorey and Falgier (1999b; see Fig. 3.8 in chap. 3).

(2) Examples of error detections, editing expressions, and repairs in ASL

a) THERE$_a$ 35-mm CAMERA [describes locations of TVs and VCRs] THERE$_b$
                           __headshake__
THERE$_b$ . . . . HAND-WAVE 35-MM CAMERA, BACK-THERE$_a$ - WRONG - THERE$_a$ MOVIE-CAMERA

"There [location a in space] are the 35-mm cameras [describes locations of TVs and VCRs]. There, there [location b in space] . . . no not the 35-mm cameras, back there [location a] - I was wrong - there [location a] were the movie cameras"

                    __headshake__
b) NEXT$_a$ UM MOVIE----------------- NEXT$_b$ MOVIE M-O-V-I-E [See below for an explanation of UM. The extended line indicates that the sign MOVIE was held during the headshake]

"The next room [location a] has um movies, no, the room next to that [location b] has movies"

In Example (2a), the signer uses a manual gesture (a slight hand wave, palm outward) and the sign WRONG to signal that she had detected an error. In both examples, a nonmanual headshake also signaled that an error had occurred. The hand wave, the sign WRONG, and the headshake all appear to be editing expressions that are used when a signer wants to repair an error. Signers also produced appropriateness repairs, for example, "NEXT BATHROOM . . . RESTROOM,"—"Next are the bathrooms, restrooms." (The sign BATHROOM is more common, but the room on the map was labeled *Restrooms*.) Further investigation may indicate whether there are manual or nonmanual editing expressions that are specific to appropriateness repairs (e.g., there appeared to be a slight head nod that accompanied the correction, RESTROOM, in this example). However, these are anecdotal examples; there has been little systematic study of editing expressions or repairs in ASL (but see Dively, 1998).

  W. J. M. Levelt (1983, 1989) proposed that speakers monitor their internal speech and can intercept errors before they are overtly uttered—he termed this *prearticulatory editing*. It is reasonable to hypothesize that signers also have such an internal monitor. In chapter 7, we discuss evidence for a nonovert, articulatory based system of sign rehearsal that is used during short-term memory tasks. This rehearsal system appears to be equivalent to subvocal rehearsal for speech and provides evidence for a type of inner signing. Like speakers, signers may be able monitor this internal signing, catching errors before they are actually articulated. Sometimes errors or inappropriate words nonetheless do slip through, and speakers also monitor their overt speech and can catch errors by listening to their own voice. Herein lies a potentially interesting difference between sign and speech. Speakers hear their voices, but signers do not look at their hands and cannot see their own faces. W. J. M. Levelt (1989) cited studies by Lackner and Tuller (1979), showing that when speakers are prevented from hearing their own voices (e.g., by wearing headphones emitting loud white noise), they are much less likely to detect certain types of speech errors compared to when they can hear themselves (specifically, voicing and vowel quality errors are missed). In contrast, it may turn out that pre-articulatory and postarticulatory editing are basically identical for signers. Further, W. J. M. Levelt (1989) proposed that the monitor for both internal and overt speech operates via the language user's speech-understanding system. However, this cannot be the entire story for sign language monitoring because the sign-understanding system operates on the basis of visual input, which is unavailable to the person who is signing (the signer does not see him or herself signing). Thus, the nature of the perceptual loop for sign monitoring may be quite different from that for speech monitoring, but again the relevant studies have not yet been conducted.

Finally, what about "ums" and "uhs"? Are such filled pauses specific to speech or do we find them in signed languages as well? To answer this question, I again examined the signing of Deaf subjects who described the town and convention center from Emmorey and Falgier (1999b). These data are ideal because we found that speakers produced many "ums" and "uhs" while describing the layout of these environments (Emmorey et al., in press), and thus we might expect signers to also produce such expressions, if they exist. For a given articulation to be considered an "um" or a "filled pause," there had to be a cessation of fluent signing (a pause) and some type of movement or change in hand configuration that could not be interpreted as a false start. In addition, the potential filled-pause articulation had to be relatively consistent across signers and not idiosyncratic to an individual signer. At least one expression clearly fit these criteria: a slight wiggling of the fingers in a loose 5 handshape.

Figure 4.10 shows an example of this UM gesture from three signers. The gestures were produced during the following utterances:

Example A (left-handed signer): CORNER THERE[repeated point] **UM** STEREO-SPEAKERS.
"At the corner, there are um stereos."

Example B: TURN-LEFT **UM** LEFT-(false start) WILL SEE- YOU DRIVE-STRAIGHT
"Make a left turn um lef-. You will see- you drive straight."

FIG. 4.10.   Illustration of UM produced by three signers (from examples
A, B, and C in the text). The drawings were done by Jonas Schurz-Torboli, a
Deaf artist.

Example C: BUILDING CL:hooked-5 **UM** ROAD-TURNS-LEFT
"A building is there, um, the road turns left like this."

Over half of the signers in the study produced this gesture at least once,
and it was always made with the dominant hand, although there were a few
examples when it was produced on both hands. The intuitions of several
sign consultants indicate that producing UM with the nondominant hand
is distinctly odd. The duration of the UM expression varied from quite
short (about 100 msec or 3 videoframes) to more than a second, and the
shorter the duration, the less pronounced the finger wiggling. There were
several other candidates for filled pause gestures: a circling of the hand
with a loose 5 handshape, a slight downward motion of the hand (palm
up) with a loose C or 5 handshape (similar to the gesture glossed as
WELL), and a bouncing or jabbing movement with the index finger extended. However, none of these gestures were produced as consistently
across signers as the wiggling-fingers gesture.

Spoken "ums" and "uhs" rarely occur in scripted or rehearsed speech.
For example, television newscasters rarely produce these expressions.
Similarly, the hosts of *Deaf Mosaic* (a half-hour television program) produced no UM expressions (finger wiggle, 5 handshape) during Episode
#1005. However, at the very end of this program, after signing off and
during what is presumably nonscripted signing, Gil Eastman turned to his
cohost and signed "NICE IF UM R-A-R -" and then the TV image fades
before we can see the rest of his sentence. Thus, as with speech, when signers are paying attention to the form of their signing (as in a newscast),
UMs are much less frequent, but when signers are attending more to content (as is the usual case) then the UM gesture is more likely.

Finally, UM tended to appear when signers were searching for the name of a landmark in the environment being described (see Example A in Fig. 4.10) and when signers were faced with direction choices in their descriptions. For example, in both Examples B and C in Fig. 4.10, the signer was describing a crossroad in the town map and could have described two possible routes. These data fit with the results of Christenfeld (1994), who found that the number of options available to a speaker in part determined the use of "um." The fact that filled pauses occur in a visual–gestural language indicates that "ums" and "uhs" are not unique to speech, and they may universally function to cue an addressee as to the cognitive state of the language producer (e.g., "I'm thinking"). In addition, UM appears to be linguistic rather than gestural because none of the 40 hearing speakers from the Emmorey et al. (in press) environment description study produced a gesture that resembled the UM of ASL signers.

Whispering and Shouting in Sign

People whisper when they do not want to be overheard or when they must be quiet. For spoken language, whispering involves a cessation of phonation or voicing, such that whispered words sound breathy but are still quite understandable. Signers are faced with similar communication demands: Sometimes they don't want others to observe their talk and other situations demand that they be visually "quiet." How do signers adjust to these conditions? Like speakers, they whisper, producing less visible signing. Table 4.1 provides a list of features that contrast whispering with

TABLE 4.1
Features That Characterize Whispering and Shouting in Sign Language

Whispering	*Shouting*
• Signing space is reduced.	• Signing space is enlarged.
• Signing space is moved down and to the side or to a location not easily observed.	• Signing space is elevated.
• The body may move to block an observer's view.	• The body and head are lifted upward.
• Movement is distalized and reduced.	• Movement is proximalized and exaggerated.
• Coarticulation effects abound.	• Coarticulation is minimized.
• Two-handed signs tend to become one-handed.	• Two-handed variants are preferred.
• Fingerspelling may replace native signs.	• Fingerspelling disfavored.
• Eye gaze or head movement may substitute for indexical signs like pronouns.[10]	• Head movements and nonmanual markers may be exaggerated.

---

[10]Neidle et al. (2000), footnote 21, p. 183.

shouting, the other end of the visibility continuum, and Fig. 4.11 provides an illustration.

Shouting in sign, as illustrated in Fig. 4.11, does not refer to angry signing,[11] but to the type of signing one would use to communicate across a crowded room or whenever a large distance separates the signer and addressee. The functional dimension here is visibility, and as such, some of the features listed in Table 4.1 also characterize other *registers* or language styles in ASL (see chap. 1). For example, in a formal register such as a lecture or a sermon, signing must be made more visible for an audience and thus signers may prefer two-handed variants of signs and use a larger signing space, although signing space is generally not raised (Baker & Cokely, 1980). In intimate or casual signing, signers may reduce signing space, but unlike whispering, signing space is not displaced to the side or out of the view of others. As we see in chapter 5, "motherese" in sign sometimes involves movement proximalization in which the movement of a distal articulator (far from the torso, such as the wrist) is transferred to a proximal articulator (close to the torso, such as the shoulder). Figure 4.11 shows this phenomenon in the sign NOT in which the movement from the elbow (a proximal joint) replaces the distal movement of the wrist seen in normal signing. The shouting–whispering contrast is based more on visibility than style and provides a fruitful domain for investigating the relation between sign articulation and visual perception.[12]

Lexical Retrieval: Is There a Tip-of-the-Fingers Phenomenon?

A tip-of-the-tongue (TOT) experience refers to the state in which a speaker is temporarily unable to retrieve a word from memory, although sure that he or she knows the word (see A. Brown, 1991, and Schwartz, 1999, for reviews). Often, speakers are able to retrieve the first letter and sometimes the number of syllables, which provides evidence for the organization of spoken language lexicons. The TOT phenomenon indicates that semantic information can be retrieved independently of phonological information. TOTs may arise when there is a breakdown in the connection between semantic and phonological representations, suggesting a two-stage access process for lexical retrieval (W. J. M. Levelt, 1989). Marsh and

---

[11]See Reilly, McIntire, and Seago (1992) for a description of how emotional state (angry, happy, sad) is conveyed in the manual (as opposed to facial) channel of sign production.

[12]See Crasborne (2000) for a quantitative articulatory analysis of the shouting and whispering in Sign Language of the Netherlands. Crasborne also argues for a distinction between articulatory and perceptual representations of signs.

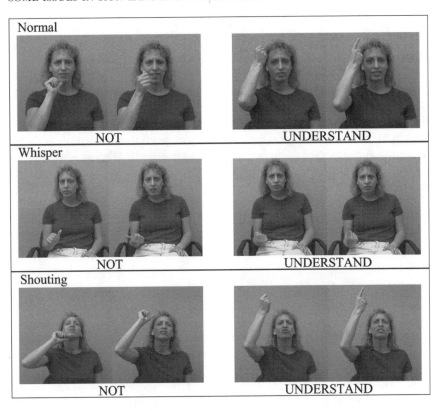

FIG. 4.11.   Illustration of the ASL sentence "NOT UNDERSTAND" ("[I]
don't understand") produced normally, in a whisper, and shouted. The
negative headshake is produced in all three versions, although it may not
be apparent from the illustrations.

Emmorey (2000) investigated whether a parallel tip-of-the-fingers (TOF)
experience occurs for Deaf ASL signers and whether TOFs are similar to
TOTs. To elicit a TOF experience, native signers were (a) shown pictures
of celebrities and asked to name them, and (b) given several English words
and asked to provide the corresponding sign (the English words were
names of countries or cities or had uncommon sign translations). In an
exit interview, subjects were also asked about the nature of their own TOF
experiences, if they had them.

We found that all subjects reported having a TOF experience with varying degrees of frequency, but they could not indicate what aspect of signs
they tended to retrieve. The celebrity naming task produced the most
TOF experiences (similarly, TOTs are frequently elicited by proper names).
Like speakers, signers were more likely to remember the first letter of a

fingerspelled name, suggesting that word onsets have a special status for fingerspelled words, as they do for spoken words. When in a TOF state for a lexical sign, signers tended to retrieve all but one of the major phonological parameters of the target sign, for example, retrieving the movement and handshape of SCOTLAND, but not the location (at the shoulder) or retrieving the movement and location of MINNEAPOLIS, but not the handshape (substituting an F for the target D handshape). We did not find that one phonological parameter was preferentially retrieved, although there was a suggestion that movement may be slightly less likely to be retrieved than either handshape or location. These results suggest that unlike ASL dictionaries, the ASL mental lexicon is not organized by a single phonological parameter (such as handshape) that guides lexical retrieval. The results further indicate that, as with spoken languages, semantic information can be retrieved independently of phonological information (e.g., signers may know all about a target sign but are unable to access its phonological form).

Slips of the Hand

In a well-known paper "The Non-Anomalous Nature of Anomalous Utterances," Fromkin (1971) demonstrated that slips of the tongue (speech errors) were not random mistakes in speaking, but revealed something about speech planning and the nature of the mental representation of phonology. Fromkin (1971) argued that speech errors provide evidence for the underlying units of speech production, suggesting that ". . . [D]espite the semi-continuous nature of the speech signal, there are discrete units at some level of *performance* which can be substituted, omitted, transposed, or added" (p. 217; emphasis in the original). The following English errors provide evidence that phonemes (both consonants and vowels) are discrete units that may be misselected during speech production (from Fromkin, 1971, pp. 32–33):

Exchange errors:
  (a) keep a tape → teep a cape
  (b) turn the corner → torn the kerner

Anticipation errors:
  (a) week long race → reek long race
  (b) available for exploitation → avoilable for . . .

Perseveration errors:
  (a) John gave the boy → . . . gave the goy
  (b) first and goal to go → first and girl to go

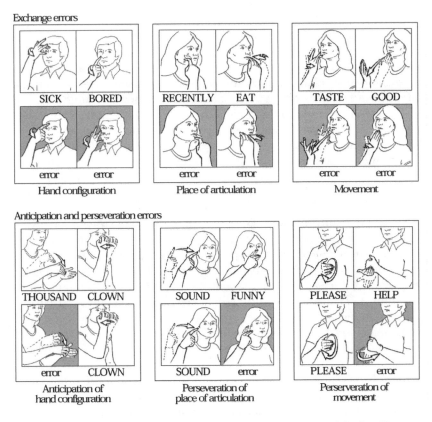

FIG. 4.12. Illustration of errors in sign production ("slips of the hand") from Newkirk et al. (1980). Illustrations copyright © Ursula Bellugi, The Salk Institute.

Errors of sign production provide similar evidence for the status of the major phonological parameters as discrete units involved in sign production. Newkirk, Klima, Pedersen, and Bellugi (1980)[13] reported exchange errors involving hand configuration, place of articulation, or movement. These same parameters can also take part in anticipation and perseveration errors, as illustrated in Fig. 4.12. Furthermore, these errors are highly constrained in that they almost always result in a phonologically possible ASL sign.[14]

---

[13]An earlier version of this paper appeared in Klima and Bellugi (1979).

[14]Newkirk et al. (1980) reported that 4% of the errors in their corpus (5 out of 131) resulted in impossible signs. In contrast, speech errors that result in an impossible word are not attested, for example, "slip of the tongue" would not be erroneously produced as "tlip of the sung" (Fromkin, 1973). Whether these few "impossible" sign errors indicate weaker output monitoring or more flexible motoric production for signers awaits future research.

The existence of such errors suggests that these phonological parameters constitute units in the production of signed utterances. The fact that movement exchange errors occur (see Fig. 4.12) argues for a phonological representation in which movement is represented as a separate unit, rather than derived from articulation constraints, as in Uyechi (1996). The data also support the analysis of place of articulation as a high-level unit within the representation of a sign, rather than as a phonetic feature(s) associated with a segment slot (as place of articulation is often represented for consonants). This argument derives from recent evidence indicating that phonetic features do not operate as units in speech production and rarely participate in speech errors (see Roelofs, 1999). Thus, because place of articulation in sign participates in exchange and other types of errors, it suggests that this parameter is a unit rather than a feature for the purposes of sign production. Finally, as discussed in chapter 2, models of sign language phonology place hand configuration on a separate autosegmental tier, much like tone is represented for tone languages. The speech error data from tone languages suggests that *tones* are independent units that can participate in exchange, anticipation, or perseveration errors (Gandour, 1977)—just as we find for hand configuration in sign language.

One striking difference between sign and spoken language errors is the percentage of errors that result in real words, often referred to as the *lexical bias effect*. Garrett (1988) estimated that 40% to 45% of spontaneous speech errors result in existing words (e.g., "first and girl" for "first and goal").[15] Newkirk et al. (1980) report "at least a dozen clear examples of actual, commonly used signs resulting from substitution of parametric values in intended signs with values from other signs" (p. 188). However, a dozen out of their total corpus of 122 phonological errors is only about 10% of errors that result in existing signs. The explanation for this impressive difference may lie in the base rate of errors that would be expected to result in real words or signs based on chance. To estimate the chance probability that an error will result in an existing word, Dell and Reich (1981) paired words from their corpus of phonological errors at random, exchanging initial phonemes (one from each word pair), and found the proportion of word outcomes was 33%. Using a similar method with the Newkirk et al. (1980) corpus, I estimated the chance rate that a sign error would produce an existing sign to be about 16%, which is similar to the observed rate.[16]

---

[15]The lexical bias effect is much stronger for experimentally induced slips (e.g. Baars, Motley, & MacKay, 1975), but this greater proportion of word errors may arise from a monitoring process that prevents nonwords from being output, particularly during an experiment where the task focuses on speech production.

[16]Fifty-six signs that participated in sign errors were randomly paired. For each sign pair, handshape, place of articulation, and movement were exchanged. Exchanges that resulted in

Now we are left with the question: Why do speech errors have a lexical bias, but sign errors do not? It turns out that the lexical bias effect may be language specific, and it may only exist for experimentally induced slips. Del Viso, Igoa, and Garcia-Albea (1991) failed to find evidence of a lexical bias effect in the spontaneous errors of Spanish speakers (chance estimate of a word outcome was 37%, and the actual proportion of errors that produced existing words was 35%). Del Viso et al. (1991) suggested that the difference between English speakers and Spanish speakers may be the rate of speech production (i.e., Spanish speakers talk faster) because the lexical bias effect disappears at high-speaking rates (Dell, 1988). However, this hypothesis cannot account for the lack of a lexical bias effect for ASL because sign production is demonstrably slower than speech production.

Finally, the ASL error corpus analyzed by Newkirk et al. (1980) contained very few whole word errors (9 out of 131); for example, "LIKE, MAYBE TASTE" instead of "TASTE, MAYBE LIKE" ('Taste it, and maybe you'll like it'). Such word exchanges are argued to take place at a separate stage of sentence planning (Garrett, 1975; W. J. M. Levelt, 1989). The dearth of such errors may reflect a bias by the ASL investigators who considered phonological errors much more significant because they revealed "the nature of signs and the constraints on their formational properties" (Newkirk et al., 1980, p. 173). That is, phonological errors showed that signs were not simply holistic gestures. However, recent evidence from Happ, Hohenberger, and Leuninger (in press), studying slips of the hand in German Sign Language (DGS) indicates that the rarity of word exchange errors in sign languages is real, and not due to a bias on the part of early researchers studying ASL. In their corpus of elicited slips of the hand, only 1% of the errors were sign exchanges, compared to 15% found in the Frankfurt corpus of spoken German errors.

In addition, Happ et al. (in press) did not find evidence for stranding errors in slips of the hand, and no stranding errors were reported by Newkirk et al. (1980). Examples of stranding errors in English are given below (from Garrett, 1988, p. 76):

Morpheme stranding errors:

   (a) That's why they sell the drinks cheap → That's why the sell the cheaps drink

   (b) Make it so the tree has more apples → Make it so the apple has more trees

In these examples, the *s* suffix is "stranded" or left behind when the two words exchange. The fact that stranding errors do not occur in sign lan-

---

illegal sign forms were not counted. The exchanges resulted in 62 possible sign forms, and of these 10 were existing signs. I thank Ursula Bellugi and Edward Klima for making the sign error transcripts available to me.

guages is most likely due to the fact that morphological processes are nonconcatenative rather than affixal. Stranding errors may only occur when morphemes are arranged linearly, rather than articulated simultaneously.

Happ et al. (in press) also found that sign errors were repaired much faster than speech errors. The locus of repairs for speakers is most often after the word, but for DGS signers, the error was preferentially caught somewhere within the sign, that is, before the signer finished articulating the sign containing the error. Happ et al. (in press) hypothesized that the longer articulation time for signs allows for earlier detection of sign errors compared to speech errors. Early repair of errors also explains the lack of sign exchange errors because the slip is detected before the second exchanged sign is produced.

This new data from DGS is beginning to reveal some fascinating modality effects on language production. The slower rate of sign articulation may lead to earlier error repairs for signers, and the linear affixation processes found in most spoken languages lead to production errors that are not observed in sign languages. Further research may illuminate how signers and speakers monitor their language output and whether models of spoken language production need to be modified to account for sign language production.

Lexical Selection During Sign Production

For spoken language production, W. J. M. Levelt (1989) argued that phonological encoding strictly follows lexical selection—that is, first a word is chosen and then it is given a pronounceable phonological form. Evidence for this procedural sequence comes from so-called "picture naming" tasks (see Glaser, 1992, for a review). In this task, subjects are presented with a picture that they must name, and a distractor name is presented either prior to, at the same time, or after the presentation of the picture. Subjects are told to ignore the distractor item, which they find difficult to do. If a semantically related word (e.g., *goat* for a picture of a sheep) is presented at the same time or slightly (100 msec) before the presentation of the picture, subjects are much slower to name the picture. That is, semantic inhibition occurs, and speakers are slow to produce the name of the object. In contrast, if a phonologically related word (e.g., *sheet* for a picture of a sheep) is presented at the same time or shortly (100 msec) after presentation of the picture, subjects are quicker to name the picture. That is, phonological facilitation occurs, and speakers are faster at producing the object name (this effect does not occur if the phonologically related word is presented prior to the picture). This pattern of early semantic inhibition and later phonological facilitation supports a production model in which lexical items are first selected and then given phonological form.

Corina and Hildebrandt (in press) conducted an investigation of picture naming in ASL in order to investigate the nature of sign production. In this initial study, subjects were asked to sign the name of a picture, and response time was measured as the time between picture presentation and when the subject's hands moved from a rest position, breaking a light beam. Superimposed on the picture was an image of a signer producing a sign that was either phonologically or semantically related to the picture, for example, MATCH–cigarette (a semantically related sign–picture pair) or ORANGE–ice cream (a phonologically related sign–picture pair; the signs ORANGE and ICE-CREAM are both made with an S handshape at the mouth). Both the distractor sign and the picture were clearly visible because the overlaid image of the signer was semitransparent (but still quite recognizable). Corina and Hildebrandt (in press) found that, like speakers, signers exhibited semantic interference when they had to name a picture with a semantically related sign presented at the same time. However, unlike for speakers, there was no evidence of phonological facilitation. There are several possible hypotheses for why signers failed to exhibit phonological facilitation. For example, the timing between lexical selection and pronunciation may not be the same for signed and spoken languages; that is, the more linear segmental structure of speech may allow for phonological facilitation, whereas the fact that signs have few segments may restrict the amount of phonological facilitation. Corina is currently investigating whether phonological facilitation might be found if the distractor sign is presented slightly after the picture (rather than at the same time). Corina's preliminary results are quite intriguing and stress the importance of studying sign language production to our understanding of language production in general.

Do Signers Gesture?

The final issue we explore in this chapter is the relation between gestures and signing. However, before we can answer our question, "Do signers gesture?," we must first elucidate what makes sign language *different* from gesture. This analysis depends entirely on one's definition of gesture. If gesture is defined sufficiently broadly, then the answer is "nothing." For example, Armstrong, Stokoe, and Wilcox (1995) defined gesture as "a *functional* unit, an equivalence class of coordinated movements that achieve some end" (p. 46; emphasis in the original). Under this definition, speech itself, the gesticulation accompanying speech, pantomime, emblems, and sign language are all examples of gesture. However, the question we wish to address here is whether signers produce forms that are a parallel to the gestures that hearing people use when they talk.

Kendon (1980) referred to this phenomenon as *gesticulation*, which is distinct from pantomime and emblems (conventionalized gestures such as "thumbs-up"). Gesticulation is spontaneous, and speakers are generally unaware of the gestures they produce. McNeill (1992) categorized speakers' gestures as follows: (a) *iconic gestures* illustrate some concrete aspect of the scene described in speech; (b) *metaphoric gestures* represent an "image" of abstract concepts and relationships that refer to the discourse meta-structure; (c) *beat gestures* mark the accompanying word or phrase as significant for its discourse–pragmatic content, and (d) *deictic gestures* are pointing gestures that function to indicate objects or events in the physical environment surrounding the speaker. Figure 4.13 provides several examples from McNeill (1992).

Table 4.2 lists some critical differences between signs and the gestures that co-occur with speech (see Emmorey, 1999, and McNeill, 1992, for further review).

As outlined in Table 4.2, signs are clearly not the same as the gestures of speakers. Given this background, we can now explore whether signers produce the kinds of gestures that hearing people produce as they speak and whether they do so in the same way. One major difference between signers and speakers is that signers do not produce idiosyncratic, spontaneous movements of the hands and arms while they are signing. The constraint on such movements is fairly obvious: Both hands are involved in producing the linguistic utterance, and constraints on bimanual coordination and motor resources hinder the production of a lexical sign with one hand and the production of a wholistic nonlinguistic gesture with the other.

However, signers do produce what can be called *component* gestures (H. Clark, 1996). Such manual gestures are produced as a separate component of a signed utterance, and signers stop signing while they produce the gesture (Emmorey, 1999). Figure 4.14 provides an illustration in which the signer produces a sign (LOOK), holds the sign with the nondominant hand, and produces a series of gestures with his dominant hand. The signer is retelling a scene from the *Frog, Where Are You?* story (Mayer 1969), in which a boy peers over a log, sees a group of baby frogs, and gestures to the dog to be quiet and come over to the log.[17] The sequence is purely gestural with no hierarchical or componential structure.

Notice that the sign LOOK remains loosely articulated on one hand while the signer produces the gesture with his other hand. This is as close as one gets to simultaneous gesture and signing. However, this example differs crucially from concurrent speech and gesture because, although cotemporal, the signs and gestures are not coexpressive. That is, the sign LOOK does not refer to the same referent as the "come-on" or "shh" gestures. In contrast, McNeill (1992) found that the gestures that accompany

---

[17]I thank Judy Reilly for providing me with this example from her collection of Frog story narratives.

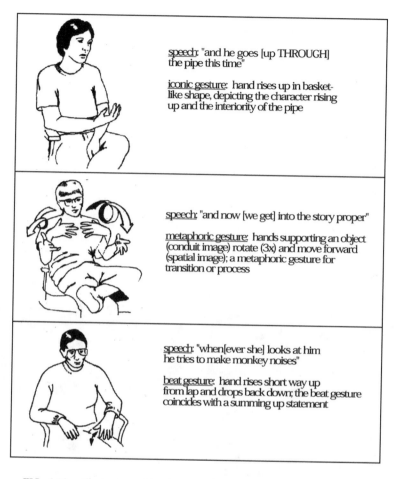

speech: "and he goes [up THROUGH] the pipe this time"

iconic gesture: hand rises up in basket-like shape, depicting the character rising up and the interiority of the pipe

speech: "and now [we get] into the story proper"

metaphoric gesture: hands supporting an object (conduit image) rotate (3x) and move forward (spatial image); a metaphoric gesture for transition or process

speech: "when[ever she] looks at him he tries to make monkey noises"

beat gesture: hand rises short way up from lap and drops back down; the beat gesture coincides with a summing up statement

FIG. 4.13. Illustration of iconic, metaphoric, and beat gestures that accompany speech. Brackets mark the extent of the gesture. Reprinted with permission from McNeill (1992), *Hand and Mind: What Gestures Reveal About Thought*. The University of Chicago Press. Illustration copyright © The University of Chicago Press.

speech always refer to the same object, relation, or event. Furthermore, LOOK was not initially produced at the same time as the gesture; rather, LOOK was first signed and then maintained while the gestures were produced. Figure 4.14 also provides an example of a metaphorical gesture. The gesture described as "well-what" is an abstract gesture in which information (what can be seen behind the log) is supported by the hands (the conduit metaphor, see McNeill, 1992).

Further illustrations of gestures alternating with signs are given below (these are also excellent examples of constructed action). The examples

TABLE 4.2
Distinctions Between Gestures and Signs

Signs	Gestures Accompanying Speech
• Exhibit a phonological structure	• Wholistic without internal structure
• Participate in a hierarchical constraint based system of generative lexical processes	• No standards of form
• Combine into sentences and subject to language specific and universal constraints on grammatical form	• Rarely occur in combination, and successive gestures do not form a larger hierarchical structure.
• No coexpressive system	• Timed to coincide with a structural element (the prosodic stress peak) of a separate coexpressive system (speech)
• Communication as the primary function	• May function to facilitate lexical access
• A community of users	• Idiosyncratic individual expressions

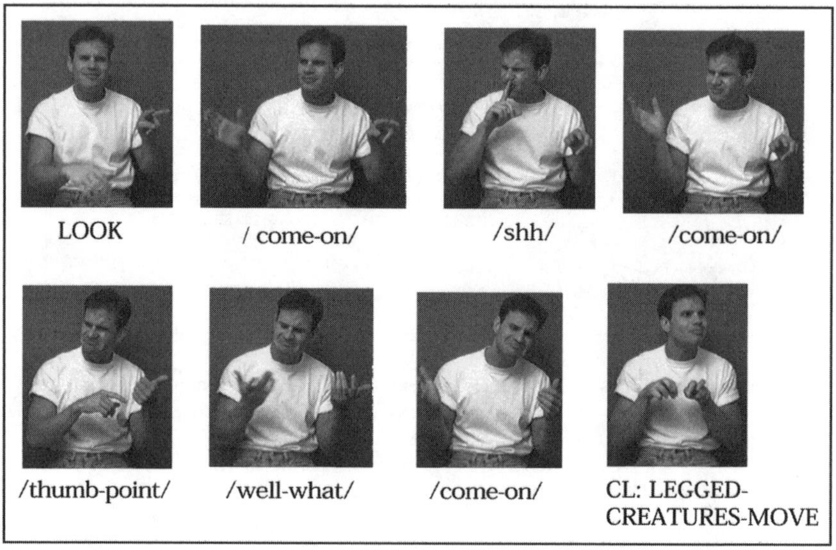

LOOK   / come-on/   /shh/   /come-on/

/thumb-point/   /well-what/   /come-on/   CL: LEGGED-CREATURES-MOVE

FIG. 4.14.   Illustration of manual gestures produced while signing. Gestures are indicated by back slashes. An English translation is: "Look over here. (gesture: come-on, shh, come-on, thumb-point, well what?, come-on). The two crept over (to the log)." Illustration from K. Emmorey (1999), "Do Signers Gesture?" In L. Messing and R. Campbell (Eds.), *Gesture, Speech, and Sign*. Copyright © 1999 by Oxford University Press. Reprinted with permission.

are from another signer telling James Thurber's Unicorn story in which a man sees a unicorn in his garden, but his wife doesn't believe him (gestures are indicated by back slashes):

(1) CL: RUN[two-handed limb classifier, 1 hs] /taps as if to wake imagined body/ WIFE THAT$_a$ /taps repeatedly at location a/

'He ran. (gesture: taps location where wife is sleeping) His wife is there. (gesture: taps imagined body more vigorously)'

(2) CL: KNEEL-ON-SURFACE[hooked V hs on flat B hs] /rests head on his hand/

'He knelt down. (gesture: head rests on his hand and his face has a contemplative expression)'

The meanings of these manual gestures tend to be fairly clear even outside of the sign context, and this is true for the majority of manual gestures that occur in alternation with signing. In contrast, the gestures of speakers are generally uninterpretable without the accompanying speech (Krauss, Morrel-Samuels, & Colasante, 1991).

Unlike manual gestures, body and facial gestures can be produced simultaneously with signing. The following examples provide illustrations of concurrent body and facial gestures. Brackets mark the extent of the gesture during signing, and the gestures are described in italics:

Body gesture (from a signer telling the Cinderella story):

(3) DECIDE DANCE. [DANCE+++] THEN GIRL THINK, "PRO$_{1st}$ MUST GO HOME, PRO$_{1st}$ MUST GO HOME."
Body sways as if to music.

'They decide to dance. They dance all around, and then the girl realizes, 'I must go home, I must go home.' '

Facial gestures (from another signer telling the *Frog, Where Are You?* story):

(4) CL: LARGE-ROUND-OBJECT-FALLS[2 hands with C hs]·
[CL:SWARM. MAD.]
Eyes squint, angry expression
[DOG CL:RUN$_{a[hooked V hs]}$·]   [BEE CL:SWARM-MOVES$_a$].
Tongue out, fearful expression   Eyes squint, angry expression

'The beehive fell to the ground. The bees swarmed out. They were mad. The dog ran away, and the bees chased him.'

Body gestures express how referents move their bodies during the action described by the concurrent signing. The duration of the body motion does not necessarily correspond to the actual duration of the referent's motion, for example, Cinderella is still dancing while thinking "I must go home," but the signer does not sway during the quotation. The facial gestures are examples of nonlinguistic facial expressions that illustrate the emotional state of the referent described in the signing (Liddell, 1980). In the Frog story example, the signer rapidly alternates between a facial expression that depicts the anger of the bees and one that depicts the fear of the dog. The facial expressions are understood as reflecting the attitude of the bees or the dog—the signer herself is neither angry nor afraid (see Engberg-Pedersen, 1993, for an analysis of shifted attribution of expressive elements). Facial gestures do not necessarily illustrate only an emotional state or evaluation. In Example (4), the signer sticks her tongue out slightly when describing the dog running. This aspect of her facial gesture depicts the panting of the dog rather than an emotion.

Although English speakers produce affective facial expressions and other facial gestures during narratives, they do so much less frequently than ASL signers. Provine and Reilly (1992) found that English speaking mothers produced significantly fewer affective facial expressions compared to signing mothers when telling the same story to their children. Instead of using their face, speakers rely more heavily on intonation and voice quality to convey affective and evaluative information. Furthermore, just as speakers vary in their tendency to use their voice to depict different characters or to convey affective information, signers vary in the extent to which they use affective facial expressions. However, signers do not vary in their use of obligatory grammatical facial expressions.

Finally, signers do not appear to produce manual beat gestures. For speakers, beat gestures generally have the same form regardless of the speech content (unlike iconic and metaphoric gestures). The typical beat is a quick flick of the hand or fingers up and down, or back and forth (see Fig. 4.13), and they tend to be associated with metanarrative functions such as introducing new characters, summarizing actions, introducing new themes, and signaling changes in narrative structure (McNeill, 1992). Given the discourse marking functions of beat gestures, it is not surprising that signers never interrupt the signing narrative to produce a manual beat gesture. However, it is possible that something akin to a beat gesture is produced by a change in the rhythmic stress of a sign or produced nonmanually, perhaps in the form of a head nod. If so, then one must determine whether the stress pattern or the nonmanual form should really be categorized as a beat gesture rather than as a linguistic discourse marker.

One other potential contrast between the gesture of speakers and that of signers is the frequency of gesturing. Liddell argues that ASL pronouns, many types of verbs, and classifier constructions are combinations (blends) of linguistic and gestural elements (Liddell, 1998; Liddell & Metzger,

1998). That is, some aspects of these signs are characterized by linguistic features (e.g., handshape, types of movement), but the direction and goal of the movement may constitute a gestural component of the sign (this proposal is discussed in more detail in chap. 2). Because signs incorporating this deictic movement are extremely common in ASL, signers are constantly incorporating gestural elements into their signing. Words and phrases that require a deictic gesture (e.g., "It's yea long") are much rarer, and furthermore, there are many speakers who never gesture within a given discourse or produce only an occasional identifiable gesture. In addition, speech is quite understandable in the absence of gesture, but sign would be incomprehensible without the gestural component proposed by Liddell (1998). These differences are clearly due to the fact that gesture and sign occur in the same modality, but gesture and speech do not.

A final question to be addressed is whether gestures perform the same function for signers that they do for speakers. Some researchers argue that the primary function of gesture is to convey information to the addressee (e.g., Kendon 1983). Others argue that the primary function of gesture is to facilitate lexical retrieval (Krauss & Hadar, 1999), whereas still others suggest that gestures are linked to speech hesitations and repair (Butterworth & Beattie, 1978). In particular, Krauss and colleagues questioned the communicative function of gestures that co-occur with speech (Krauss, Dushay, Chen, & Rauscher, 1995; Krauss et al., 1991). For example, speakers produce gestures even when they cannot be seen by their addressee (e.g., when speaking on the telephone), and the ability to see a speaker's gestures does not appear to enhance comprehension by an addressee (Krauss et al., 1995). Krauss and colleagues concluded that a primary function of gestures is to facilitate speech production. Evidence for this hypothesis stems from the effect of preventing gesture on speech and from the temporal relation of gesture to speech. Preventing gesture appears to lead to difficulties associated with word retrieval (Rauscher, Krauss, & Chen, 1996), and the initiation of gestures almost always precedes the word associated with that gesture (its "lexical affiliate"), suggesting that gesture production is an aid to word retrieval (Morrel-Samuels & Krauss, 1992).

It seems unlikely that the manual, body, or facial gestures produced by signers function to facilitate lexical access for signers. Their gestures are not tied to a particular lexical item, and the body and facial gestures do not have the spatiodynamic features that would be needed to prime an associated lexical representation (see Rauscher et al., 1996). Signers simply do not produce the type of gesture that has been purported to aid lexical retrieval; namely, manual gestures concurrent with (or slightly preceding) associated lexical signs. In contrast, H. Clark (1996) argued that although gestures may be facilitative, their main function is, in fact, communicative, and signers' gestures certainly appear to be communicative. For the most part, the gestures discussed here depict how someone's hands or body move during an event described by the signer.

To summarize, signers do gesture, but not in the same way, that speakers do. Unlike speakers, the manual gestures of signers occur in alternation with the linguistic signal (rather than concurrently with it), and signers' gestures tend to be more conventional and mimetic, rather than idiosyncratic. In addition, signers' manual gestures are not synchronized to co-occur with a particular sign related to the gesture's meaning; rather, these gestures function as components of an utterance or as independent expressions. Signers frequently produce facial and body gestures that are articulated simultaneously with signing (particularly during narratives), and such gestures are more rare for speakers. In contrast, metaphorical (abstract) gestures are quite common for speakers (McNeill, 1992), but appear to be much less common for signers, perhaps because their gestures are intentionally communicative. In addition, signers may frequently incorporate gestural elements into lexical signs, unlike speakers. Finally, it is questionable whether signers produce the equivalent of beat gestures. Potential nonmanual candidates are more likely to be analyzed as linguistic discourse markers or prosodic aspects of sign production.

SUGGESTIONS FOR FURTHER READING

Gernsbacher, M. A. (Ed.) (1994). *Handbook of psycholinguistics*. San Diego, CA: Academic Press.

This large volume is an excellent resource describing basic results in psycholinguistic research. The chapters cover such topics as speech perception, spoken and written word recognition, lexical ambiguity, reading processes, sentence parsing, discourse processing (including figurative language, inference processes, mental models, and text understanding), first- and second-language acquisition, the neuropsychology of language, and language production at both the word and discourse levels.

Levelt, W. J. M. (1989). *Speaking: From intention to articulation*. Cambridge, MA: MIT Press.

Levelt provides a detailed model of speech planning and speech production. His book brings together data and theory from many diverse disciplines: linguistics, psychology, speech science, acoustic phonetics, discourse analysis, and artificial intelligence. The model describes the generation of messages (from macroplanning to microplanning), the generation of surface structure and grammatical encoding, the generation of phonetic plans for words and connected speech, actual articulation, and self-monitoring and self-repair. The book is essential for anyone interested in language production.

McNeill, D. (1992). *Hand and mind: What gestures reveal about thought*. Chicago, IL: The University of Chicago Press.

Hand and Mind is the handbook for gesture researchers. McNeill presents a theoretical framework for studying the gestures that accompany speech and presents a standard methodology for analysis and transcription. McNeill hypothesizes that gestures form an integral and inseparable part of language and further that gestures have an impact on thought itself.

Chapter 5

Sign Language Acquisition

A child acquiring a sign language appears to be faced with a quite different task than a child acquiring a spoken language. A completely different set of articulators is involved and the language is perceived with a different sensory system. Do the properties of sign languages affect the course and timing of language acquisition? For example, do the iconic properties of sign languages aid in their acquisition? Do the spatial properties of sign language present special challenges for the acquisition process? The studies addressing these questions have investigated Deaf and hearing children acquiring ASL as a native language from their Deaf parents. Deaf children who have hearing parents may be exposed to ASL later in childhood, and we examine the effects of such late acquisition on adult language competence and processing in chapter 6.

The general finding of many, many studies is that Deaf children of Deaf parents acquire sign language in the same way that hearing children of hearing parents acquire a spoken language: Both groups of children pass through the same developmental stages at about the same time and make the same sorts of errors (for reviews, see Bellugi, 1988; Lillo-Martin, 1999; Meier, 1991; Newport & Meier, 1985). These results suggest that the capacities that underlie language acquisition are maturationally controlled and that the psychological, linguistic, and neural mechanisms involved in language acquisition are not specific to speech or audition. In this chapter, we review the nature of language milestones and highlight domains where the study of sign language acquisition helps to unveil the mystery of our uniquely human ability to master complex linguistic systems within the first few years of life.

EARLY DEVELOPMENT

We begin by examining the early stages of language development, from infancy to about age 2, when children start to combine words (or signs) into sentences. Investigations of how Deaf children begin acquiring sign language have provided essential insights into the acquisition process. For example, results from sign language research indicate that babbling is *not* determined by the anatomy of the vocal tract, that there may be an early advantage for gestural communication (for both Deaf and hearing children), and that parental input ("motherese") is modified to fit the demands of language modality. The overarching finding is that even the earliest stages of language development are unaffected by whether the language to be acquired is signed or spoken.

Manual Babbling

Just as hearing babies babble prior to producing their first word, Deaf babies babble with their hands prior to producing their first sign.[1] Petitto and Marentette (1991) found that Deaf babies exposed to sign language from birth produced "manual babbles" from 10 to 14 months, but hearing babies exposed only to speech did not produce such manual movements. Manual babbling, like vocal babbling, is characterized by a syllabic structure (path movement or change in handshape or orientation; see chap. 2), which is often reduplicated (e.g., "bababa" for spoken language or cyclic movements for signed languages). Babbling is produced without meaning or reference and is not communicative. Figure 5.1 provides an illustration of manual babbles from Petitto and Marentette (1991). The fact that babbling occurs in babies exposed to sign language indicates that babbling does not arise from the maturation of articulatory mechanisms that are specific to speech. Furthermore, syllabic manual babbling has been observed in Deaf babies exposed to Japanese Sign Language (Masataka, 2000) and to Langue des Signes Québécoise or LSQ (Petitto, 1997), suggesting that manual babbling may be as universal for babies exposed to sign language as vocal babbling is for speech-exposed babies. Petitto and Marentette (1991) contended that babbling is "the mechanism by which infants discover the map between the structure of language and the means for producing this structure (p. 1495)." Hearing babies map their vocal articulations to patterns in auditory speech input, whereas Deaf babies map their manual articulations to patterns in their visual signed input.

Deaf babies are reported to produce vocal babbles, but because they have no auditory feedback from their own vocalizations or any auditory

---

[1]The use of "Deaf" rather than "deaf" in this context is meant to emphasize the key fact that the babies were exposed to sign language, not that the babies were audiologically deaf.

A)   B)

FIG. 5.1. Illustrations of two types of manual babbles. In real time, there are no pauses between the hand configurations, and the sequence is reduplicated. (A) is a two-handed handshape change syllabic babble and (B) is a unimanual bisyllabic, handshape change production involving four handshapes. Reprinted with permission from "Babbling in the Manual Mode: Evidence for the Ontogeny of Language," L. A. Petitto and P. F. Marentette, 1991, *Science, 251*, 1493–1496. Copyright © 1991, American Association for the Advancement of Science.

experience with the speech of others, reduplicated babbling begins late (generally after 1 year), and the babbling has a very low rate of cyclicity (Oller & Eilers, 1988). In contrast, Meier and colleagues report that hearing babies exposed only to speech (not to sign), produce manual "babbles" starting at about 7 months and continue past 1 year (Cormier, Mauk, & Repp, 1998; Meier & Willerman, 1995). Meier (2000) argued that, unlike deaf children producing vocal babbles, hearing children receive visual feedback from their own gestures and see nonlinguistic gestures produced by adults around them. Unlike Petitto, Meier and colleagues suggest that manual babbles are rooted in the stereotypic rhythmic motor actions that are produced by all infants (e.g., Thelen, 1979, 1991).

How can we reconcile Meier's results and conclusions with Petitto's? One possible explanation is variation in coding criteria for counting manual babbles—precise phonetic definitions of a sign syllable (and thus a manual babble) have not yet been proposed. Another possibility is simply individual variation among the children studied. However, a more satisfying explanation may lie in the temporal structure of manual babbling. Both Meier and Willerman (1995) and Petitto and Marentette (1991) found that Deaf infants produce significantly more manual babbles with repetitive, multicycle movements than hearing infants. Further, using an optic system to track movement patterns, Petitto (2000) reported that syllabic manual babbling in Deaf infants is produced at a slower velocity, in a more constrained space, and in isolation (i.e., with no accompanying leg movements), compared to other rhythmic hand activities. Thus, although both vocal and manual babbling may emerge in part as a function of neuromuscular development, linguistic input from the environment and perhaps an inherent temporal sensitivity to rhythmic patterns within that input affect the structure of both manual and vocal babbling. In line with this hypothesis, Schley (1991) found that 4-month-old hearing infants are sensitive to the movement classes inherent in ASL signs (as defined by Poizner, 1981).

At one time it was claimed that vocal babbling was unrelated to language development (Jakobson, 1968), but Oller, Wieman, Doyle, and

Ross (1976) showed that preferences observed in babbling are predictive of the phonological patterns found in early words. For example, initial stop consonants (e.g., b, d, k) are preferred over fricatives (e.g., s, z, v) in both babbling and early words (e.g., a stop will be substituted for a fricative in a target early word). The same is true for manual babbling. Petitto and Marentette (1991) reported that there is "a continuity between the phonetic and syllabic forms used in deaf infants' manual babbling and their first signs" (p. 1494). For example, the most frequent locations and handshapes observed in babbling were also the most frequent in the babies' first signs. Cheek, Cormier, and Meier (1998) replicated this result; they found that the 5 handshape was favored in manual babbling and was substituted most frequently in early signs and that downward palm orientation was most frequent during babbling and also a common error in early sign productions.

All babies begin to discover the phonological structure of their language, whether signed or spoken, through babbling. The fact that both vocal and manual babbling begin at the same time during development suggests that babbling is not linked to inborn mechanisms for producing speech that may have evolved with our species (e.g., Lieberman, 1984); rather, babbling may reflect the maturation of a more general mechanism that maps patterned perceptual input (either auditory or visual) to related motoric output (either vocal or manual). The development of this perceptual–motor connection allows human infants to discover the units that serve to express linguistic meaning, whether encoded in speech or in sign.

First Words—Is There an Advantage for Sign Language?

Several early studies of ASL acquisition suggest that first signs are produced earlier than first words (Bonvillian, Orlansky, & Novack, 1983; McIntire, 1977; Orlansky & Bonvillian, 1985; P. M. Prinz & E. A. Prinz, 1979; Schlesinger & Meadow, 1972; Siple & Akamatsu, 1991). For example, Deaf parents report that their signing children produced their first signs at about 8½ months (Bonvillian et al., 1983). In contrast, first words are reported to appear between 10 and 13 months (J. G. de Villiers & P. A. de Villiers, 1978; Ingram, 1989). In addition, hearing children who are simultaneously acquiring ASL and spoken English begin to sign before they begin to speak (Bonvillian & Folven, 1987; P. M. Prinz & E. A. Prinz, 1979).[2] The apparent early appearance of first signs is not due to iconicity because the majority of first signs are not particularly iconic (Orlansky & Bonvillian, 1984).

---

[2]Note, however, that it is not clear whether these children are receiving equal sign and speech input at this early age.

The apparent precocious development of first signs has been hypothesized to be due to the earlier motor development of the hands than of the vocal tract, earlier maturation of visual cortex than of auditory cortex, the larger size of the manual articulators, the ability of the child to see his or her own articulators, or even the ability of parents to directly manipulate the child's hands to form signs (Meier & Newport, 1990; Orlanksy & Bonvillian, 1985).[3] Meier and Newport (1990) suggested that under this account, sign is not advantaged, but rather speech is disadvantaged. That is, all children may be cognitively and linguistically ready to produce their first lexical item during their eighth or ninth month, but the perceptual and articulatory difficulties associated with speech delay the onset of first words for speaking children. Deaf children are not so constrained, and, thus, first signs appear earlier.

However, what may actually appear earlier than spoken words are not lexical (symbolic) signs, but prelinguistic communicative gestures that are produced by both hearing and Deaf children (Acredolo & Goodwyn, 1988; Capirci, Montanari, & Volterra, 1998; Petitto, 1988, 1992, 1994; Volterra & Caselli, 1985; Volterra & Iverson, 1995). Petitto (1988) pointed out that the studies cited earlier were inherently biased to find a sign language advantage for first words because early communicative gestures are counted as lexical items for signing children but not for speaking children. For example, in these studies, the general criteria for counting a given manual gesture as a sign was simply that it was recognizably related to an adult sign and produced in an appropriate context. Of course, under such a criterion, the communicative gestures of speaking children would not be counted as lexical items—only vocal utterances that resemble adult words would be counted. Nonetheless, hearing children who have never been exposed to sign language produce communicative gestures before they utter their first words (e.g., Bates, Benigni, Bretherton, Camaioni, & Volterra, 1979). For example, a hearing child might make a gesture for a pacifier by pretending to suck on something or pat his head for a hat (Caselli, 1990). Such gestures would not be counted as "first words" for a hearing child, but they might be for a Deaf child acquiring ASL. Volterra and Iverson (1995) concluded that the gestural modality is a powerful medium of communication during the early stages of communicative development, even for children with no exposure to sign language. In other words, the "sign advantage" may reflect a more general advantage of the gestural over the vocal modality for early communication in *all* normally developing children.

When symbolic and referential criteria are used to assign word status to a given utterance, then first signs and first words both appear somewhere

---

[3]Another possibility is that the first attempts at signs are easier for parents (and researchers) to recognize than the first attempts at spoken words (Meier & Newport, 1990).

around the first birthday (Petitto, 1988, 1992; Volterra & Caselli, 1985). Symbolic use can be defined as using a lexical item in more that one context, in the absence of the referent, or to refer to a class of related referents. Such usage reflects the ability to use symbols (either words or signs) independently of a particular context and not tied to a unique referent (e.g., just using "doggie" for the family pet). Bonvillian and colleagues also report that referential signs (signs that are not imitative or context-dependent) appear at about 1 year of age (Bonvillian & Folven, 1993; Bonvillian, Orlansky, & Folven, 1990). Finally, Petitto (1992) provided evidence that symbolic gestures and symbolic signs can be differentiated in the Deaf signing child. Specifically, signs (and words for hearing children) are not used across lexical types (e.g., object names, property words, event words); in contrast, symbolic gestures are used in ways that cross these boundaries. For example, two Deaf children produced a "twist" gesture to refer to a jar, objects within a jar, and the action of opening or closing a jar, but they used the ASL sign OPEN only to refer to the act of opening a container (Petitto, 1992).

In sum, the timing of the one-word stage, in which lexical items are used symbolically, is identical for both sign and speech, indicating that the maturational mechanisms underlying early lexical development are independent of the articulatory and perceptual systems of the two modalities.

Baby Talk and the Acquisition of Phonology

Signing children produce "baby signs" just as speaking children produce "baby words" in which the adult forms are simplified and altered. For example, a child acquiring English might say "baba" for "bottle," and a child acquiring ASL might produce the sign MOMMY with an A hand configuration rather than the 5 hand configuration used in the adult sign (see Fig. 5.2A). The phonological alterations in both sign and speech tend to reflect articulatory ease, with more difficult sounds and segments acquired later. For example, liquids (e.g., r, l) and fricatives (e.g., s, "th") are more difficult to produce than stop consonants (e.g., b, d, g), and some of these sounds may give children trouble even into the school years. For ASL (and probably for other sign languages), hand configuration turns out to be the most difficult of the major phonological parameters to acquire.

Conlin, Mirus, Mauk, and Meier (2000) studied the early signs of three Deaf children with Deaf parents from ages 7 months to 17 months and found that nearly 80% of early signs were produced with the correct place of articulation and about 45% had the correct movement. In contrast, only 25% of these early signs were produced with the correct hand configuration. Furthermore, errors in place of articulation were consistent (e.g., producing the sign for DOLL consistently at the upper lip, rather than the

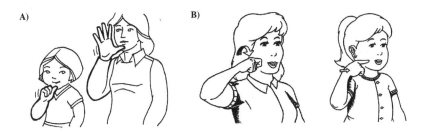

FIG. 5.2.　Examples of "baby signs" in which children simplify and alter the adult form. In (A), the child substitutes an A handshape for the 5 handshape in the sign MOTHER (Illustration copyright © Ursula Bellugi, The Salk Institute). In (B), the child substitutes a 1 handshape for the X handshape in the sign APPLE and produces a "contact" movement rather than the twisting movement in the adult sign (Illustration by Michael Shang, from Marentette & Mayberry, 2000, copyright © Rachel Mayberry & Paula Marentette). Example (B) also provides an example of the deletion of a distal movement—the twisting movement of the wrist (see text).

nose), but hand configuration errors were much less systematic (e.g., one child substituted three different hand configurations (C, baby-O, and 1) for the X handshape of DOLL). Early success with place of articulation in conjunction with high error rates for hand configuration is a pattern consistent with parental reports (Siedlecki & Bonvillian, 1993) and is most likely due to differences in the development of fine versus gross motor control (Bonvillian & Siedlecki, 1996; Conlin et al., 2000).[4] The gross motor ability to reach toward a location is solidly in place by 1 year. Children can easily reach toward toys and other objects in their environment at this age, and all that is required to produce a sign with the correct place of articulation is to reach a target location on the child's own body. In contrast, children at this age have not yet developed the fine motor control necessary to articulate the diversity of distinct hand configurations that occur in ASL.

Children first produce those hand configurations that are easy to articulate, easy to perceive, and are most frequent in the language (Boyes-Braem, 1990; Conlin et al., 2000; Marentette & Mayberry, 2000; McIntire, 1977; Siedlecki & Bonvillian, 1997). In general, the first handshapes produced by children are the following: 5, 1, A, B, C, and (baby-)O. (See Appendix A for illustrations.) The handshapes that are more difficult to articulate are acquired late (sometime in the fourth year) and include the following: R, W, 8, X, T (see Ann, 1996, for physiological principles that

---

[4]In addition, Marentette and Mayberry (2000) proposed that place of articulation may be easier because the child can rely on an emerging cognitive representation of the body (a body schema) that can be used to distinguish places of articulation for signs. Such a representation may not be available for hand configuration.

specify articulatory ease/difficulty). However, it is not merely articulatory complexity that creates problems for the production of hand configuration. Siedlecki and Bonvillian (1997) described one child who could form all of the letters of the manual alphabet, but substituted simpler handshapes for the more complex ones when producing signs. Thus, when a hand configuration must be produced within a lexical sign that contains additional specifications for place of articulation and movement, the task of articulating a complex handshape becomes too difficult and substitutions occur.

When children make phonological errors, they do not do so randomly. For example, speaking children tend to substitute stops for fricatives ("that" becomes "dat"), delete final consonants ("dog" becomes "da" not "og"), and reduce consonant clusters ("stop" becomes "top") (Jakobson, 1968). Recent phonological investigations utilizing Optimality Theory find that children systematically adhere to a set of markedness constraints (e.g., "syllables should have onsets"), which gradually become less strong as the child acquires the articulatory ability to produce forms that are faithful to the adult model (see Bernhardt & Stemberger, 1998; Smolensky, 1996).[5] Children first produce unmarked segment and syllable types, and the sequence of acquisition can be predicted by how various constraints interact during development (e.g., C. C. Levelt, Schiller, & W. J. M. Levelt, 2000). Similarly, signing children develop phonological systems with internal consistency that seem to follow general phonological constraints. For example, with respect to hand configuration, children substitute unmarked handshapes (e.g., 5, A) for marked handshapes (e.g., X, 8; Boyes-Braem, 1990; Conlin et al., 2000). Further, data from Marentette and Mayberry (2000) suggested that handshape substitutions are based on phonological similarity and are unidirectional (e.g., the 5 handshape may replace the C handshape, but not vice versa). In addition, a single handshape may substitute for a set of handshapes. Such error patterns are indicative of a developing phonological system.

With respect to movement, Meier, Mauk, Mirus, and Conlin (1998) discovered that children systematically alter the movement of target signs by *proximalizing* the movement. This means that children change which part of their body articulates a movement by substituting an articulator that is closer to (proximal to) their torso, such as the shoulder, for an articulator that is farther (distal) from their torso, such as the wrist or fingers. For example, the articulation of GRANDFATHER involves a path movement

---

[5] The markedness constraints are the same as for adults, but they are ranked differently for children, for example, the (violable) constraint against producing VC syllables is much stronger for young children than for adults. Markedness constraints initially outrank faithfulness constraints for children (Demuth, 1995; see Kager, 1999, for an introduction to Optimality Theory).

FIG. 5.3. Illustration of the adult sign GRANDFATHER from *Basic Sign Communication* (1983), National Association of the Deaf: Silver Spring, MD. Reprinted with permission. When children produce this sign, they may drop the twisting motion of the forearm (a more distal articulator) and articulate the path movement from the shoulder (a proximal articulator), rather than from the elbow, as shown here.

outward from the forehead that is articulated by extending the elbow (see Fig. 5.3). Rather than bending the elbow (a more distal articulator), one child described by Meier et al. (1998) articulated GRANDFATHER by raising her arm at the shoulder, a proximal articulator. In addition, the child omitted the simultaneous twisting motion of the forearm (a distal articulator). Deletion of the movement of a distal articulator was another pattern observed by Meier et al. (1998); see also Fig. 5.2B. It is interesting to note that Mirus, Rathmann, and Meier (2001) found that *adult* learners of sign language also produce more proximalized movements when imitating new signs. Thus, the tendency for movement proximalization may be an aspect of the acquisition of new motor skills, and not solely a product of the immature motor systems of young children.

The study of the acquisition of sign language phonology is only just beginning. We know very little about phonological or articulatory processes that occur beyond age 2. However, the research thus far suggests that the acquisition of phonological systems proceeds similarly for the aural–vocal and visual–manual modalities, from babbling to early words. Furthermore, the study of how very young children learn the complex motoric patterns required for sign articulation may provide novel insights into the nature of motor development and may also inform us about possible constraints on the phonological systems of signed languages. Signed languages, like spoken languages, must be learnable by children, and we may find universal phonological tendencies that arise from developmental constraints on articulation (Meier et al., 1998).

Finally, research on the acquisition of sign phonology has focused primarily on articulatory development, at least thus far. Two studies have examined hearing infants' perception of signs. Carroll and Gibson (1986) found that hearing babies could distinguish straight versus arced movement (LEFT vs. LIBRARY), but failed to discriminate the plane of articulation (sagittal plane vs. the vertical plane, WHERE vs. SCOLD). As mentioned earlier, Schley (1991) found that hearing infants were able to perceive movement distinctions in ASL (e.g., aspectual movement patterns). These two studies suggest that hearing infants possess certain prerequisite perceptual abilities necessary to acquire a sign language.

For spoken language, researchers have discovered that infants and young children develop specific perceptual abilities for listening to speech. For example, studies have shown that adult speakers of Japanese have difficulty distinguishing /l/ and /r/ (e.g., Eimas, 1975); whereas adult English speakers have difficulty distinguishing between dental and retroflex stops (/da/ vs. /Da/) found in languages like Hindi (Werker & Tees, 1983). In contrast, 6-month-old hearing infants in Japan, India, and the United States can all distinguish these sound contrasts. By about 1 year of age, however, infants are performing like their adult counterparts, reliably distinguishing only those speech sounds relevant to their language. Kuhl (1991, 1998) proposed that babies do not simply lose their ability to perceive nonnative sounds, rather they develop representations of prototypical sounds in their language (see also Werker, 1994). These prototypical representations serve to "filter" sounds in ways unique to a particular language, making it difficult to hear some of the distinctions of other languages. Whether sign-exposed babies develop perceptual prototype representations for handshapes or for movement patterns is a fascinating question for future research (and one could also ask whether sign-exposed babies might be able to distinguish planes of articulation for signs, unlike hearing infants not exposed to a signed language).

Motherese

Motherese is not just produced by mothers, as reflected in the more politically correct (and more accurate) label, *child-directed talk*. When adults talk to babies, they modify their speech in very systematic and characteristic ways. For example, they talk more slowly, use a higher pitched voice, employ a wider range of prosodic contours, produce longer pauses, and add emphatic stress (e.g., Garnica, 1977). Furthermore, crosslinguistic evidence suggests that these prosodic and rhythmic patterns are universal for users of spoken language (Fernald et al., 1989). Why do adults spontaneously and naturally talk this way to children? Some researchers hypothesize that these particular prosodic patterns help babies to detect and discriminate word and clause boundaries (Kemler-Nelson, Hirsch-Pasek, Jusczyk, & Wright-Cassidy, 1989); whereas other researchers suggest that motherese is primarily used to attract and hold an infant's attention (e.g., Fernald, 1984). In fact, when given a choice, babies prefer to listen to motherese rather than to adult-directed talk (Fernald, 1985).

Given that motherese is generally characterized by the acoustic properties of speech (e.g., changes in pitch and pitch contours), is it even possible

to have the equivalent in a signed language? The answer is unequivocally
yes. Several studies have found that Deaf mothers and fathers systematically alter their signing when communicating with their Deaf babies
(Erting, Prezioso, & O'Grady-Hynes, 1990; Holzrichter & Meier, 2000;
Maestas y Moores, 1980; Masataka, 1992). Signs produced for babies are
longer in duration, contain more movement repetitions, and are relatively
larger in size. Holzrichter and Meier (2000) found that parents may add
path movement to signs and produce proximalized movements that result
in longer and larger signs.[6] Furthermore, motherese occurs in other
signed languages. Masataka (1992, 2000) found that Deaf mothers using
Japanese Sign Language (JSL) produced signs with a longer duration and
with more repetitions; in addition, the mothers angled their signs so that
they were more visible to the baby. Thus, the systematic alteration of the
form of language for young infants appears to be a robust language universal that is not specific to speech.

Moreover, motherese appears to perform the same functions for sign
language acquisition that it does for the acquisition of spoken language.
For example, Holzrichter and Meier (2000) suggested that the rhythmic
alterations of signs observed in ASL motherese may help Deaf babies segment the visual input and detect individual signs, particularly because
these alterations help to regularize the linguistic input. Furthermore, the
larger and longer signs produced in sign motherese are well suited to
gaining the baby's visual attention. In support of the attention-getting
properties of sign motherese, Masataka (1996, 1998) found that both Deaf
and hearing babies prefer to watch JSL motherese over adult-directed
JSL. The fact that hearing babies (who have never seen JSL before) prefer
to watch signed motherese suggests that human infants may be inherently
attracted to input with a particular rhythmic pattern, regardless of modality and independent of prior experience.

However, Deaf babies do differ from hearing babies in that hearing babies are able to listen to a word and look at an object at the same time. This
ability is important because researchers have found that the rate and size
of early vocabulary development are related to how often mothers name
objects that the child is (visually) attending to (Harris, Jones, Brookes, &
Grant, 1986; Tomasello & Farrar, 1986). Thus, young hearing children
spend a significant amount of time NOT looking at their mothers. For the
Deaf child, however, the linguistic input and the nonverbal context are all
within the same modality. For the Deaf child to observe the relationship

---

[6]One could hypothesize that children produce early signs with proximalized movements
because the signed input contains such movements (Meier et al., 1998). However, since
Mirus et al. (2001) found that adult learners also proximalize movements (and these adults
are not exposed to ASL motherese), it is unlikely that children proximalize movements simply because they observe them in the input.

between a sign and its immediate context, he or she might have to alternate attention between the sign input and the nonverbal context—such an asynchrony in attentional timing has been shown to have adverse affects on early language development for hearing children acquiring a spoken language (Harris, 1992). So why do we not observe difficulties or delays in early sign development for Deaf children? The answer may lie in the nature of motherese.

In addition to the prosodic alterations just described, Deaf parents may displace their signs so that they fall within the view of the child or wait until the child spontaneously looks at them before signing, and sometimes they may produce a sign on the child's body, for example, producing the sign CAT on the child's face rather than on their own face (Holzrichter & Meier, 2000; Maestas y Moores, 1980; Spencer, Bodner-Johnson, & Gutfruend, 1992). In addition, mothers may move an object to a position where both the object and the signing can be perceived, or they may sign directly on or near an object (Harris, Clibbens, Chasin, & Tibbitts, 1989). All of these strategies enable the Deaf child to jointly attend to both the language addressed to her and to relevant aspects of the nonverbal context. Apparently, Deaf parents intuitively modify their signing and interactions to accommodate the constraints of a single input modality.[7]

Finally, spoken motherese, unlike adult-directed discourse, is almost always grammatical with very few false starts, sentence fragments, errors, or incomplete utterances (Newport, H. A. Gleitman, & L. A. Gleitman, 1977). However, Reilly and Bellugi (1996) found that Deaf mothers consistently produced ungrammatical ASL expressions under very specific circumstances: when emotional facial expressions conflicted with grammatical facial expressions. By the age of 1 year, babies are able to produce and comprehend a range of emotional facial expressions (Nelson, 1987), and both hearing and Deaf parents frequently use facial expressions to communicate positive affect to their babies (Erting et al., 1990). However, for Deaf parents, the grammatical facial expression required for WH questions resembles the affective expression indicating anger (or puzzlement), for example, both involve furrowed brows. Furthermore, WH questions are quite common in speech (and signing) to children (e.g., "Where's the ball?" and "What's that?"). Reilly and Bellugi (1996) therefore asked the question, "when deaf mothers communicate with their toddlers, do they use facial expression primarily to convey affective information or to signal grammatical distinctions?" (p. 225).

---

[7]Hearing mothers with Deaf children may experience more difficulty modifying their signing and getting the visual attention of their Deaf babies, perhaps because their own communicative experiences affect their spontaneous interactional strategies (Koester, Karkowski, & Traci, 1998; Waxman & Spencer, 1997).

Reilly and Bellugi (1996) found that when children are age 2 or younger, parents opt for affect over grammar when asking WH questions. Parents choose not to produce the required WH facial expression, which could be interpreted as negative affect and instead produce WH questions with either an (ungrammatical) neutral facial expression or with an expression of positive affect (eyebrows raised, rather than furrowed). Interestingly, Reilly and Bellugi (1996) found that parents were totally unaware of this strategy. "When we later asked the deaf mothers about their facial behaviour, and the frequent absence of the grammatical morphology, they were incredulous. Initially, they refused to believe us. In fact, they were only convinced after reviewing their own videotapes" (p. 232). After age 2, there is a dramatic shift in parental input. At this age, Deaf children begin to produce WH questions themselves, using manual signs (e.g., BRUSH WHERE++? "Where's (my) brush?"), and it is at this point that parents begin to produce grammatical WH facial expressions with furrowed brows.[8]

Thus, ASL motherese, like spoken language motherese, is attuned to the communicative competence of the child (Snow, 1972), but because there is an unusual competition on the face between affect and grammar, there appears to be a specific developmental period in which ASL motherese, unlike spoken language motherese, contains systematically ungrammatical input. As we see in the next sections, this ungrammatical input does not hamper the child's acquisition of the morphology or syntax of ASL.

WHAT DOES THAT "MISTAKE" MEAN?
ACQUISITION OF SYNTAX AND MORPHOLOGY

Children do not learn language by simple imitation, instruction, or reinforcement, as illustrated by the following dialogue between a parent and child (McNeill, 1966, p. 69):

---

[8]An alternative explanation for this phenomenon has been suggested independently by Woll, Hoiting, and Pyers (personal communication, May, 2000). Before age 2, mothers often ask questions that they already know the answer to (e.g., "What's that?" pointing to a picture book). In such situations, WH questions may not require furrowed brows because they are not information requesting speech acts. As the child gets older, the pragmatics of the situation changes, and mothers may begin producing WH questions in which they are asking true questions (i.e., the mother does not already know the answer). Further investigation of the pragmatics of questions in motherese (and in adult–adult conversations) may determine whether Deaf mothers are avoiding negative facial affect or are producing a type of rhetorical WH question that does not require furrowed brows (see Neidle et al., 2000).

CHILD: Nobody don't like me.
MOTHER: No, say "Nobody likes me."
CHILD: Nobody don't like me.
              (dialogue repeated eight times)
MOTHER: Now, listen carefully, say *"Nobody likes me."*
CHILD: Oh, nobody don't likes me

This dialogue shows that children do not imitate adult utterances but instead have an internal system of rules that may or may not match the adult grammar. The "mistakes" children make (and do not make) provide a window into their developing grammar and into the principles that guide language acquisition. The study of sign language acquisition has been particularly insightful regarding the nature of acquisition principles. Researchers have explored whether children use prelinguistic gesture as a bridge to linguistic signs, whether children transfer knowledge about affective facial expressions to grammatical facial expressions, and whether principles of iconicity aid language acquisition. All of the evidence indicates that the same principles of language acquisition that have been proposed on the basis of data from spoken language are evident in the acquisition of ASL by Deaf children. Furthermore, some potentially advantageous aspects of sign language, such as iconicity and the relation to early communicative gesture, do not seem to alter or affect the timing or course of acquisition.

The Transition From Gesture to Sign:
The Acquisition of ASL Pronouns

Children learning English (and other spoken languages) sometimes make errors with personal pronouns, substituting "you" for "me" and vice versa. Pronoun reversals are not that surprising in child speech, given the shifts that occur between speakers and listeners using "I" and "you." For ASL, one might predict a different course of acquisition for these pronouns because of their iconic properties, that is, "you" is indicated by pointing to the addressee and "me" is indicated by pointing to oneself. Both hearing and Deaf children use pointing gestures prelinguistically (Bates et al., 1979; Petitto, 1987), and this raises the question of how Deaf children move from prelinguistic gestural communication to linguistic–symbolic communication when the form (pointing) is identical. Is the acquisition of pronouns early and error free for children acquiring ASL? Do they capitalize on the iconic nature of ASL pronouns?

Petitto (1987) discovered that the surprising answer is *no*. Despite the transparency of pointing gestures, Deaf children do not use ASL pronouns earlier than children acquiring English, and they sometimes make pronoun reversals in early signing (see also Hoffmeister, 1978; Jackson, 1989; and Pizzuto, 1990; but see Ahlgren, 1990). Children acquiring ASL pronouns appear to go through three stages: (1) gestural (nonlinguistic) pointing to people and objects (beginning at about 9 months), (2) pronoun reversal errors may occur and names may be used instead of pronouns (ages 1;6 to 2;0),[9] (3) the correct use of personal pronouns (ages 2;0 to 2;6). Both speaking and signing children begin to use personal pronouns at the same age (around 18 months) and make the same kinds of errors.

Why does the Deaf child "ignore" the iconic properties of ASL pronouns? Petitto (1987, 1993) argued that Deaf children differentiate between language and gesture, and that at about 18 months, children begin to analyze the pointing gesture as a lexical sign, not as a point. The Deaf child may initially interpret pronouns as ordinary signs, rather than as "shifting" signs in which the referent changes with the speaker (i.e., when I say "me," it refers to a different person than when you say "me"). The young child may thus interpret the pronoun YOU as a lexical item that is equivalent to his or her name. Hearing children may make the same error with English pronouns (see E. Clark, 1978). Petitto's results indicate that children are attuned to linguistic regularities (such as the fact that lexical items tend to refer to classes of referents and generally do not shift reference) and do not rely on the transparency of the form-meaning relation (i.e., the iconic relation between a point and a referent). The results also suggest a discontinuity between prelinguistic and linguistic forms, rather than a continuum from early communicative gestures into first words and language. However, this broad conclusion should be tempered by recent work on the acquisition of classifier constructions, which suggests that there may be no clear break between early gesture and the production of certain classifier forms (see later discussion of the acquisition of classifier constructions).

Baby Faces: The Acquisition of Nonmanual Grammatical Markers

Emotional facial expressions are produced consistently and universally by children by 1 year of age (Nelson, 1987). Affective facial expressions also appear to be the source for the grammaticization of linguistic facial expressions (Janzen, 1999; MacFarlane, 1998; see also Appendix B for the emergence of linguistic facial expressions in Nicaraguan Sign Language). Reilly and colleagues investigated whether Deaf children might use their early ability to comprehend and produce affective facial expressions as a way to bootstrap their way into the gramatical system of ASL (Anderson &

---

[9]Following convention, ages are written as years;months.

Reilly, 1997, 1998; Reilly, 2000; Reilly, McIntire, & Bellugi, 1990a, 1990b, 1991). The grammatical functions of ASL facial expressions and other nonmanual markers include negation, adverbials, WH and yes–no questions, conditionals, and topics. Descriptions and examples of these nonmanual markers in the adult model are given in chapter 2.

Negation. As any parent knows, all children shake their heads to mean "no" at a very early age (before 2). Because this communicative headshake is physically identical to the grammatical headshake used to signal negation in ASL, Deaf children might recruit this early communicative headshake into their emerging linguistic system and thus easily produce the required headshake with manual negative signs like NO, NOT, or CAN'T. This hypothesis assumes that the communicative and linguistic headshakes stem from the same underlying symbolic system. However, D. Anderson and Reilly (1997) found evidence that communicative and linguistic headshakes are mediated by two independent systems, each with a different developmental course. Beginning at about 1 year, Deaf children, like hearing children, produce isolated headshakes in response to questions or to reject requests. Manual negative signs begin to emerge at about 18 months, but Deaf children do not generalize the use of the communicative headshake to these new linguistic contexts. Surprisingly, as each new negative manual sign is acquired, it is consistently (and ungrammatically) produced *without* the negative headshake. D. Anderson and Reilly (1997) observed a 1- to 8-month delay before the nonmanual negative headshake was added to the manual sign (over an age span from 1;6 to 3;4). This pattern follows the linguistic tendency for children to first acquire freestanding lexical items (i.e., the manual negative signs) before bound morphology (markers that cannot occur in isolation, such as the English possessive "-s" or in this case, the linguistic negative headshake, which is bound to the manual sign). D. Anderson and Reilly's (1997) results indicated that children do not attempt to adopt a communicative behavior that is similar in form and function to a grammatical marker; rather, they acquire the grammatical marker gradually, as part of a linguistic system—just as Petitto (1987) observed for the acquisition of ASL personal pronouns.

Adverbials. It is possible that young Deaf children initially fail to produce a negative headshake with manual negation because of the dual function of headshakes for both communicative and syntactic functions. To investigate this possibility, D. Anderson and Reilly (1999) studied the acquisition of facial adverbs, which have no prelinguistic communicative facial expression that could compete with the linguistic morphology. They found that, like negation, children initially produce bare manual predicates before adding the co-occurring facial morphology. The first productive facial adverb emerged at age 1;11 (*puff*)—see chapter 2, Table 2.1, for a description of these facial adverbs. Under age 3;0, children produced three facial adverbs: *puff*, *mm*, and *th*; and between 3;0 and 4;0, several additional facial adverbs were acquired: *pah*, *pow*, *int*, and *ps*. Finally, *cha* did not appear until 4;8, and the facial adverbs *sta* and *cs* had not yet appeared by 4;11. Crucially, in all cases when a child produced a facial adverb, D. Anderson and Reilly (1999) were able to find examples of the corresponding manual sign produced by a younger child without the facial morphology. This result again supports the general acquisition pattern in which lexical items are acquired before bound morphology. To give another English example, children say "two shoe" before "shoes." D. Anderson and Reilly (1999) argued that the particular order of acquisition of facial adverbs is dictated by the regularity of the individual adverbials (*puff*, *th* and *mm* can modify many predicates, whereas *cs* and *cha* are more constrained) and by semantic complexity/accessibility (children have the concept *a lot* (encoded by *puff*) by 18 months, but the concept of *recency in time or space* (encoded by *cs*) is acquired late).

WH and Yes–No Questions. Yes–no questions are marked with raised brows and a slight forward head tilt, whereas WH questions are marked with furrowed brows. Yes–no questions are marked only with the non-manual marker, whereas WH questions may also contain a WH sign, such as WHAT, WHERE, or HOW. Reilly and colleagues found that children produce the nonmanual morphology for yes–no questions as early as 1;3, and children begin to produce WH questions with WH signs slightly later, at 1;6 (Reilly, McIntire, & Bellugi, 1991). However, the development of the facial morphology that signals WH questions appears to follow a U-shaped acquisition pattern: First, some children produce WH signs with the correct facial expression, but these signs are produced as unanalyzed gestalts or amalgams; next, children produce WH questions with "blank faces" until about age 3;6, when they begin to produce the correct WH facial expression (Reilly & McIntire, 1991). Such a U-shaped pattern has been described for the acquisition of English past tense. For example, some children may initially produce the verb *came* correctly, then develop an analysis of past-tense morphology but overgeneralize it and produce *comed*, and finally they learn the exceptions and again produce the correct verb *came*. Similarly, Deaf children appear to reanalyze early correct productions of WH morphology, eliminating the WH facial marking as they grapple with the system.

Notably, all children go through a stage in which WH questions are produced without the required nonmanual marking. Prior to and during this stage, however, Deaf children do use furrowed brows to indicate general puzzlement. Thus, children do not generalize the affective use of furrowed brows to indicate uncertainty to the linguistic task of marking WH questions with furrowed brows (Reilly & McIntire, 1991). Deaf children may continue to occasionally omit the required facial morphology for WH questions until relatively late in development (age 6; see Lillo-Martin, 2000). In contrast, children do not omit the obligatory facial morphology for yes–no questions.[10] The differential acquisition of the nonmanual marking of yes–no versus WH questions may arise because of the additional complexity and variability associated with WH questions. For yes–no questions, facial expression is the only marker, and it is not associated with a particular manual sign. In contrast, the nonmanual morphology signaling WH questions can occur with or without a WH sign, and the WH sign can appear clause initially or finally (or both). Furthermore, children must learn that the WH facial marking occurs not only with the WH sign, but sometimes must spread to the entire clause (see chap. 2; and Lillo-Martin, 2000a). Thus, the complexity of the nonmanual marker for WH questions may delay its acquisition (formal complexity delays the acquisition of morphemes in spoken languages as well; e.g., Slobin, 1973).

Conditionals and Topics.   Topics are marked solely by a nonmanual marker, and it is difficult to determine whether a child is expressing the notion of "topic." However, if the child preposes an object phrase to sentence initial position, then there is at least some evidence that the child is expressing a topic. Reilly et al. (1991) reported that topics first appear around age 3. An example is shown in (1) from Reilly et al. (1991, p. 15):

(1) From Corinne (3;4):

> $\overline{\text{AU } 1+2+5}$
> STRAW-HOUSE WOLF BLOW.

'The straw house, the wolf blew (on it).'

(AU 1+2+5 are "action units" used to code facial expressions from Ekman and Friesen's (1978) facial action coding system (FACS): 1 = inner brow raise; 2 = outer brow raise; and 5 = upper lid raise).

Deaf children begin to produce conditional clauses at about the same age, but although they can use facial expression to mark topics, they mark conditionals only with (optional) manual signs such as I-F or SUPPOSE

---

[10]It is possible that children produce yes–no questions without the required facial morphology, but such omissions would be easily missed. Such failed productions would be interpreted as statements (to the frustration of the child!). Similar communication failures may occur when hearing children fail to use intonation correctly when it is the sole marker of yes–no questions (Lillo-Martin, personal communication, July 1999).

(Reilly, McIntire, & Bellugi, 1990a; Reilly et al., 1991). In addition, Reilly et al. (1990a) found that 3-year-old children initially misinterpret conditional clauses marked only with nonmanual morphology as two conjoined clauses (e.g., "The milk spilled and Mom's mad") rather than as conditionals ("If the milk spills, Mom will be mad"). That is, at this age, children do not yet comprehend or produce the nonmanual morphology associated with conditional clauses. By age 5, both manual and nonmanual conditional markers are understood and produced, although the timing of the facial expression with the manual clause may not be completely correct (Reilly et al., 1990a).

Reilly et al. (1991) proposed that Deaf children are following Slobin's (1973) principle of *unifunctionality*, which states that if a language has a single form that signals two similar (but still distinct) meanings, then children will initially try to distinguish the two meanings with distinct markers. Thus, because topics and conditionals are both marked with similar facial expressions (see Figs. 2.13 and 2.14 in chap. 2) and they have similar functions, children initially distinguish topics using facial expression (the only means the language provides) and conditionals with manual signs.

The overarching generalization that arises from the research of Reilly and colleagues is that children acquire "hands before faces" for all of the domains investigated thus far, from single signs to complex clauses. This pattern of acquisition appears to fall out from principles of language development that have been independently proposed for spoken languages. In addition, Reilly et al. (1991) argued that the hands are the primary linguistic articulators and are perceptually more salient. Slobin (1973) proposed that all children assume underlying semantic relations should be marked overtly and clearly, and thus "a child will begin to mark a semantic notion earlier if its morphological realization is more salient perceptually" (p. 202). Thus, Deaf children initially mark lexical and syntactic structures with manual morphology before they add the less salient nonmanual component. Crucially, signing children do not assume that communicative and affective facial expressions can be generalized to mark linguistic structures within their emerging grammar; the development of affective and linguistic facial expressions follow different maturational trajectories (Reilly, 2000).

Directing Verbs Toward Present Referents—Does Iconicity Help?

As discussed in chapter 2, ASL contains a class of agreeing verbs with properties unique to signed languages: The phonological form of these verbs depends on the physical location of the referents associated with the verb. Thus, there is a transparent iconic relationship between the form of the verb and its meaning. For example, to indicate "I give it to you," the signer moves the verb GIVE toward the addressee and to indicate "You give it to me," the signer moves the verb GIVE from the location of the addressee toward the signer's own chest. Meier (1982, 1987) investigated whether children attend to this iconic mapping between form and meaning or whether children ignore these features and are more sensitive to linguistic properties of the verbs. Data from both a longitudinal study and from an imitation task (Meier, 1982, 1987), as well as more recent data from Casey (1999, in press) and Lillo-Martin, Mueller de Quadros, and Mathur (1998), indicate that the acquisition of these verbs follows morphological rather than iconic principles.

Initially (prior to age 2 or so), Deaf children produce prelinguistic action gestures that are spatially displaced toward their associated referents (Casey, 1999, in press). For example, raising the arms toward an agent to indicate a desire to be picked up (by that agent) or an open-handed "give" gesture (typical of hearing children as well) from a desired toy toward the child. This finding indicates that children are aware of the relationship between directionality and referential function. However, despite the fact that action gestures tend to be directed toward present referents, signs produced at this age are most often uninflected (Casey, 1999; Meier, 1982). Furthermore, the first productions of ASL verbs are not more likely to be directed toward present referents, as would be predicted if children were following iconic principles (Meier, 1982). Just as with ASL pronouns, the form-meaning transparency of action gestures (i.e., the fact that they are directed toward associated referents) does not lead to error-free acquisition of ASL agreeing verbs. As children begin to grapple with the ASL verb system (between ages 2 and 3), they may make errors that are actually countericonic, for example, producing the citation form, which is less iconic but grammatically simpler (Meier, 1982) or producing a "reversal error" (e.g., signing "give you" when "give me" was clearly intended; Bellugi & Klima, 1982).

Between 3;0 and 3;6, children begin to consistently and correctly direct verbs toward present referents and may even overgeneralize this morphological pattern to verbs that do not allow it, as shown in Fig. 5.4. Three and a half is relatively late compared to when hearing children acquire the verb system of English—more evidence that iconicity does not facilitate acquisition. Rather, the results indicate that grammatical complexity, not iconicity, determines the nature of errors that children make (Meier, 1982, 1987). Deaf children's sign errors reflect a sensitivity to regularities and complexities within the ASL verb system. Grammatical complexity and the resulting late acquisition may arise from several factors: (a) irregularity of the system (not all verbs are agreeing verbs); (b) variation in semantic roles associated with referents (e.g., some verbs are directed to-

FIG. 5.4. Illustration of morphological overgeneralizations by signing children and the correct adult forms. In A), the child intends "I say to you" and directs the verb SAY towards his mother, and in B) the child intends "I like that lollipop" and directs LIKE toward the candy. However, it is ungrammatical to direct these verbs toward present referents (although verbs like TELL and HATE allow such directional morphology). These errors are analogous to English-speaking children's overregularization of the past tense (e.g., errors like "putted" and "holded"). Illustrations copyright © Ursula Bellugi, The Salk Institute.

ward the patient and some toward the recipient); and (c) variation in directionality ("backwards" vs. regular verbs; see chap. 2).

Thus far, we have seen that the iconic mapping between a form and its meaning does not facilitate the acquisition of first signs, personal pronouns, or verb morphology. Thus, Newport and Meier (1985) concluded that iconicity "appears to have virtually no impact on the acquisition of American Sign Language" (p. 929). Recently, Slobin and colleagues have questioned this strong conclusion for the early acquisition of classifier constructions (Slobin et al., in press). Slobin et al. (in press) found that very young Deaf children (before age 3;0) often treat whole entity classifier handshapes as having iconic or "depictive" properties, rather than as unanalyzed morphemes that simply designate object type (see chap. 3 for a description of classifier constructions).[11] Deaf 2-year-olds also produced handling classifier handshapes productively (i.e., the productions were not frozen [lexicalized] signs), although these forms were not always produced correctly. Slobin et al. (in press) argued that iconicity does play a role in the acquisition of classifier forms because the ability to gesturally represent objects by the hand or to represent holding objects is found in both home signers (children not exposed to a conventional language; see chap. 6) and hearing children not exposed to sign language (see Acredolo

---

[11]The Slobin et al. (in press) study included both Deaf children with Deaf parents and those with hearing parents who were learning sign language. Children acquiring both ASL and Sign Language of the Netherlands were studied.

& Goodwyn, 1988, and our earlier discussion of the early communicative advantage of gesture). This gestural ability may allow the Deaf child to bootstrap into the early use of some classifier forms (particularly handling classifiers), and the child must then learn how such forms are phonologically, morphologically, and syntactically constrained by the language. Complete mastery of the classifier system does not occur until late in development (see next section).

LATER DEVELOPMENT

Although much of the structure of both spoken and signed language is acquired by about age 4, some aspects of language, particularly complex morphology and aspects of discourse structure, are acquired later in childhood. For ASL, children must master the use of signing space to maintain referential cohesion across a narrative, that is, remembering "who is where" in signing space and using this knowledge to direct pronominals and verbs toward the appropriate locations. Children must also learn to use referential shift to mark different points of view within a story (see chap. 2 for a description of referential shift). As discussed in chapter 3, classifier constructions are particularly complex, and Deaf children master these structures relatively late. Full mastery of fingerspelling also occurs during the school years, as children acquire English reading and writing skills, but it appears that Deaf children acquire fingerspelling as part of ASL, rather than as a separate unintegrated system. In this section, we describe later language acquisition and focus on some elements that are unique to signed languages.

The Acquisition of Fingerspelling: Learning to Spell or Learning Language?

As discussed in chapter 2, fingerspelling is not simply a way of representing English orthography, rather fingerspelled words form part of the ubiquitous foreign vocabulary of ASL (Padden, 1998). Although fingerspelling is relatively rare in the input to young children (Padden, 1991), Deaf children as young as age 2 attempt to produce fingerspelled forms. In addition, children understand fingerspelled words that they cannot yet read or write (Padden, 1991). Children initially produce forms that share the adult "movement envelope" of a fingerspelled word; for example, producing a characteristic bouncing motion for doubled letters but with no clear sequence of hand configurations (Akamatsu, 1985; Padden & Le Master, 1985). Children also know that fingerspelling is used to "name" people and objects, but until about age 4, they do not realize that there is a unique fixed sequence of hand configurations for different words. For example, Padden (1991) provides the following anecdote: "At age 2;9, SS was asked what the name of her dog was; she produced a sequence of three clearly articulated segments: U-B-A. (The dog's name was Sasha.) She was then asked to name other objects in the room. For the table, she produced E-B-A" (p. 201). This young child was happy to oblige her mother and attempt a fingerspelled name; however, when children are older, they become uncomfortable when asked to fingerspell because they are aware that there is a required handshape sequence that they do not yet know (Padden & LeMaster, 1985).

Early on (2;0 to 3;0), Deaf children are not learning to spell, and they produce fingerspelled forms without reference to their relation to English orthography. But as Deaf children become more exposed to print (4;0 to 5;0), they begin to make associations between written letters and hand configurations. However, Padden (1991) observed that learning to fingerspell does not merely entail learning these associations. Deaf children attempt to generalize across the linguistic system; for example, they notice the prevalence of initialized signs and the phonological salience for the first handshape in fingerspelled signs and thus tend to correctly produce the initial hand configuration but also misanalyze some signs as initialized (e.g., producing the sequence Y-O-B to name an airplane; the sign AIRPLANE is produced with a Y-like hand configuration). Similarly, hearing children form generalizations about sound–letter correspondences and make creative spelling attempts based on these correspondences, for example, spelling "turtle" as T-R-D-L (Read, 1975, cited in Padden, 1991). The difference is that for older Deaf children, these correspondences are orthographically based, rather than sound based, and relate to phonological generalizations within the ASL lexicon, rather than to the English lexicon. Padden (1993) hypothesized that ". . . Deaf children using fingerspelling at early ages are not necessarily acquiring English. It is possible that the children are acquiring fingerspelling, and the relationship between fingerspelling and English must be consciously constructed by the child at a later time" (p. 108).

The Conquest of Space: Learning to Use Pronouns and Verbs for Nonpresent Referents

Although Deaf children have mastered the ability to direct verbs toward referents in the real world by age 3;0 to 3;6, the ability to direct verbs toward locations in signing space exhibits a much longer and more tortuous acquisition route. Early case studies by Loew (1984) and Hoffmeister (1978) indicated that children are not able to correctly direct verbs and pronouns to refer to nonpresent referents until they are nearly 5 years old.

Lillo-Martin (1999) argued that to be successful Deaf children must learn to "(a) associate a referent with a location; (b) use different locations for different referents (except when a group of referents is being referred to or, in some cases, possession); (c) use verb agreement or pronouns with nonpresent referents; and (d) remember the association of referents with locations over a stretch of discourse" (p. 538). Bellugi (1990) termed this process the child's "conquest of space."

By ages 3;0 to 4;0, children understand that referents may be associated with locations in signing space and can even answer metalinguistic questions about these associations, for example, "Who is here (in signing space)? and "Where is the boy (in signing space)?" (Bellugi, van Hoek, Lillo-Martin, & O'Grady, 1988/1993; Lillo-Martin, Bellugi, Struxness, & O'Grady, 1985).[12] However, despite this understanding and the ability to direct verbs toward present referents, children fail to comprehend the use of agreeing verbs when referents are associated with locations in signing space, until age 5 (Lillo-Martin et al., 1985). In production, Deaf children also fail to distinguish referents by using distinct spatial locations within their stories until about age 5. For example, they may use one location for several different referents or use inconsistent locations for a single referent (Bellugi, Lillo-Martin, O'Grady, & van Hoek, 1990; Loew, 1984). Figure 5.5 illustrates a common "stacking" error in which the child uses the same location for several distinct referents. Children may also use a real object (or location) to serve as a substitute for a nonpresent referent; for example, directing a pronoun toward a lamp in the room to refer to another lamp that had been broken (Hoffmeister, 1978, 1987). However, by age 5, all of these error types have disappeared, and by age 6, the cross-sentential use of pronouns and agreeing verbs with nonpresent referents appears to be firmly in place (Bellugi, Lillo-Martin, et al., 1990).

Is such late acquisition due to grammatical complexity or to non-linguistic cognitive factors? Both Newport and Meier (1985) and Lillo-Martin (1999) argued that the errors children make reflect problems in spatial memory (remembering multiple referent–location associations) rather than a difficulty in mastering syntactic and morphological principles. Newport and Meier (1985) pointed out that the error pattern associated with nonpresent referents does not mirror that of present referents. For example, children do not overgeneralize or produce citation forms once they learn to associate referents with locations in signing space. This result indicates that children have already acquired the basic morphology

---

[12] To test comprehension of the association between a referent and a location in signing space, the examiner would sign a sequence such as BOY HERE$_a$, GIRL HERE$_b$, and then ask WHERE BOY? or WHAT HERE$_a$ (sometimes three referents were tested; Bellugi et al., 1988/1993).

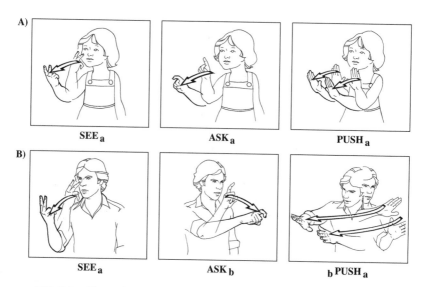

FIG. 5.5. Illustration of a "stacking" error in child discourse (A) and the correct adult model (B). The child uses a single location in signing space for several referents, whereas the adult uses separate spatial locations for the distinct referents associated with the verbs SEE, ASK, and PUSH. Illustrations copyright © Ursula Bellugi, The Salk Institute.

of pronouns and agreeing verbs by 3;0 to 3;6. Furthermore, Lillo-Martin (1991) argued that young children have mastered certain syntactic constraints regarding agreeing verbs and null arguments long before they are able to correctly use signing space to refer to nonpresent referents. Specifically, children respect the syntactic requirement that null arguments must be identified. Null arguments occur when there is no overt subject (or object), as in the Italian sentence "Vengo" meaning "I come" (the verb morphology identifies the subject as first person). Initially, children direct verbs toward real-world referents without lexically specifying the arguments (i.e., they use null arguments that are identified by the verb morphology). Children then go through a stage in which they use overt arguments with unmarked verbs, and their stories contain many repeated nouns and names. Thus, children avoid using unidentified null arguments with unmarked verbs. Finally, between ages 5 and 6, children correctly direct agreeing verbs toward locations in signing space and use null arguments (i.e., they do not lexically specify the arguments of the verb).

These error patterns indicate that children have mastered the relevant morphological and syntactic principles by about age 3, but they have difficulty establishing and remembering unique associations between discourse referents and locations in signing space. Indirect evidence for this explanation comes from the fact that older Deaf children exhibit longer spatial memory spans than their hearing nonsigning peers (see chap. 8), suggesting that signing children must become quite proficient at remembering spatial locations. In addition, children must be able to understand that a location in signing space can serve to represent a referent (and may also represent the referent's spatial location). The research of DeLoache indicates that young children (before age 3) fail to detect the relation between a realistic scale model and the room it represents, despite the highly iconic relationship between the symbols and referents (DeLoache, 1987, 1989, 1991). Older preschoolers also have difficulty understanding the relationship between symbols on very simple maps or aerial photographs and the referents they depict (e.g., Liben & Downs, 1992). It may be that the same cognitive prerequisites for understanding spatial–symbolic representations of pictures, maps, and scale models may be required for understanding the symbolic relation between locations in signing space and nonpresent referents within a discourse.[13] We now turn to a domain that may be even more dependent on these cognitive abilities.

The Acquisition of Complex Morphology: Classifier Constructions

Classifier constructions are used to describe the location, motion, and visual–geometric properties of objects within a scene (see chap. 3 for a detailed description). The movement and location of the hands in signing space can schematically represent the motion and location of objects in the world in an isomorphic fashion. Choice of handshape in a classifier construction is based on semantic and visual–geometric properties of an object and is also affected by aspects of the action to be described. Given the clear iconicity of these forms, researchers have investigated whether children acquire classifier constructions holistically as analogue depictions of events or scenes (Newport, 1981; T. Supalla, 1982). The results overwhelmingly indicate that children do not master classifier constructions early or without error—in fact, full mastery is not achieved until age 8 or 9 (Galvan, 1988; Kantor, 1980; Schick, 1990c). Full mastery of the system requires that children be able to coordinate the two hands to represent figure and ground, to indicate viewpoint appropriately, to express complex path and manner within the predicate, and to choose the appropriate

---

[13]When tested on their ability to understand the relation between a referent and spatial location, 3-year-olds could answer metalinguistic "where" questions ("Where is the boy in signing space?"), but they failed to understand "what" questions ("What is here in signing space?") scoring only 50% correct (Bellugi et al., 1988/1993). Such "where" questions may be construed as deictic (pointing to an actual location) but the "what" questions require a more complex mapping between a location and a referent (i.e., the spatial location itself is not the referent).

scale. Some components of the classifier system may be mastered relatively early, whereas the acquisition of other aspects of the system is more prolonged. As mentioned earlier, Slobin et al. (in press) found that handshapes that represent handling of an object are produced relatively early (at 2 years), and these productions may be based in the child's early gestural competence. Children must then learn how to use such handling classifiers in predicates that involve complex argument structures, serial verb constructions, or figure–ground coordination. Thus, children do not acquire classifier constructions as holistic depictions of actions; rather, they acquire them as part of a morphosyntactic system (Newport & T. Supalla, 1980).

Classifier Handshapes. T. Supalla (1982) studied three Deaf children between 3;6 to 5;11 and asked them to describe short vignettes presented on film. He found that children make several types of errors when attempting to produce classifier handshapes: (a) substitution of a general (unmarked) classifier handshape[14] (e.g., using the B handshape for vehicles, for narrow flat objects, or even for cylindrical objects; see also Kantor, 1980, for other examples); (b) borrowing from the lexicon (e.g., using the H handshape from EGG to refer to a disk-shaped object); and (c) producing a tracing movement to represent the path of motion without specifying the object. These errors decreased with age and indicate attempts to generalize patterns across the ASL lexicon, for example, transferring knowledge from lexical signs to classifier predicates and overgeneralizing relatively unmarked forms.

Schick (1990a, 1990b) studied 24 older Deaf children (4;5 to 9;0) and compared the acquisition of whole entity classifier handshapes (CLASS handshapes in Schick's terminology), size and shape specifiers (SASS classifiers),[15] and handling (or instrument) classifier handshapes. Children were most accurate in producing whole entity classifiers, followed by SASS classifiers, and they were least accurate with handling classifiers. Schick suggests that, like children acquiring classifiers in Thai or Japanese, Deaf children first master superordinate classification (e.g., identifying an object as belonging to the vehicle or human class) before classification based on visual–geometric properties (e.g., its shape or size).

Given the clear iconicity of handling classifiers (the shape of the hand directly represents how a human hand holds or manipulates an object), it is particularly interesting that these handshapes were the most difficult for

---

[14]T. Supalla (1982) called these handshapes "primitive markers."

[15]As discussed in chapter 3, SASS classifiers do not form a coherent category, but Schick's (1990a, 1990c) terminology is retained here to avoid confusion. Most likely, the SASS classifiers in Schick's study involved extension and surface classifier handshapes, but some may have involved whole entity classifiers.

children. Schick hypothesizes that children may be less accurate because the focus of handling classifier predicates is locative transfer and not the specification of object properties; the handling classifier itself is the least relevant aspect of the construction (see also Emmorey & Casey, 1995). In contrast, for SASS classifiers (which can be homonymous with handling classifiers), the handshape itself is the focus of the predicate (e.g., indicating "It's the large cylinder"). Thus, the function of classifier handshapes, rather than their iconicity, appears to determine the order of mastery within Schick's elicited production task. Nonetheless, Slobin et al. (in press) found that handling classifier handshapes, but not SASS handshapes, were produced by very young children in spontaneous signing (prior to age 3;0). The gestural form of handling classifiers may explain their early appearance in child sign, but mastery of these forms requires that the child learn to use these handshapes in contexts that do not involve her own hands (in this respect, the object manipulation task used by Slobin et al., in press, contrasts with the picture description task used by Schick). In addition, children must learn the language-specific constraints on the use of handling classifiers within predicates that specify locative transfer.

Finally, until about age 5, children frequently fail to indicate the ground object within a classifier construction (omitting what T. Supalla, 1982, calls the "secondary object"); for example, in describing a scene in which an object moves toward a telephone pole (the ground object), the child would omit the classifier handshape for the telephone pole. When children first begin to indicate the ground object (at 3;4), it often appears sequentially as a separate lexical item (Newport & Meier, 1985; T. Supalla, 1982). Schick (1990b) found that older children produce the correct classifier handshape for the figure object more often than for the ground object, and this was true even when the two objects required the same classifier handshape (e.g., when indicating one vehicle passed another). Children may omit the ground object in classifier constructions for two reasons: (1) specifying the ground object is often optional, and children acquire optional structures more slowly (Slobin, 1973; T. Supalla, 1982); and (2) children have to determine ordering constraints for specifying figure and ground and learn to coordinate the two hands for simultaneous constructions (Schick, 1990b).

Movement. There has been little systematic investigation of the acquisition of the movement component of classifier constructions. Newport (1981) and Newport and T. Supalla (1980) discussed the acquisition of some movement morphemes in three Deaf children ages 2;6 to 5;0.[16] They report that the youngest child (age 2;6) correctly produced simple

---

[16]These were the same children studied by T. Supalla (1982).

path movements such as linear or arc. The predominant error produced by the children involved omitting a required movement morpheme. For example, when shown a video of a hen jumping from the ground to the roof of a barn, an adult signer would produce a classifier predicate with an upward arc movement, which ends at the spatial location associated with the roof of the barn (the movement pattern shown in Example (2a). T. Supalla (1982) analyzes this motion as a combination of an arc morpheme (2b) and an upward linear morpheme (2c). The youngest child produced only an arc motion, omitting any upward movement. The child who was 4;5 produced a sequencing error, producing a simple arc movement followed by an upward linear movement—thus, separating and sequencing the two movement morphemes. At 5;0, the oldest child produced the correct form.

(2) Illustration of movement patterns:

Slobin et al. (in press) also reported that very young Deaf children correctly produce classifier predicates with simple path movements. However, their spontaneous signing data suggests that the combination of path and manner of movement was not difficult for young children. Much more research is needed to determine the nature and order of acquisition of movement components in classifier constructions. For example, it will be important to determine whether errors like those reported by Newport and T. Supalla (1980) are due to difficulty in combining movement morphemes, to difficulty in depicting complex movement within any system of visual representation (Cogill, 2001), or to difficulty in representing paths that have several meaningful components, such as source, goal, and manner (Slobin et al., in press).

Location.   Schick (1990c) found that children (ages 4;5 to 9;0) were at ceiling when producing "simple" SASS classifier predicates in which only one referent is described and no spatial relationship is specified (e.g., "It's a small round flat object"). Similarly, children were only slightly less accurate when producing simple handling classifier predicates that referred to holding or lifting a referent object (e.g., "The girl is lifting a weight above her head"), scoring about 83% correct for the youngest group (4;5 to 5;11) and 95% for the oldest group (7;5 to 8;11).

However, when the same SASS classifier handshapes were produced in more complex constructions in which a spatial relationship had to be expressed (e.g., "alternating rows of large dots and stripes on a shirt"), the ability to produce the construction with the correct spatial locations dropped to 35% correct for the youngest children and only reached about 60% correct for the oldest group. Similarly, when children had to indicate the spatial relation between two referent objects using whole entity classifiers (e.g., "A monkey sits between two trees"), they had equal difficulty in placing the classifier handshapes in the correct locations. However, when handling classifiers occurred in predicates specifying the transfer of an object from one location to another (e.g., "She took the firewood and carried it to her father"), children made fewer errors in location, compared to whole entity predicates or complex SASS predicates.

The difference in acquisition pattern for indicating location in classifier constructions may be related to the complexity of the mapping between referents and associated spatial locations.[17] The simple SASS predicates were adjectival (providing a description of an object), and no spatial relation had to be specified at all. For simple handling classifier predicates, only one location had to be referenced within signing space (the location or referent toward which an object was moved or transferred), and children produced few errors for these predicates. However, for the more difficult handling predicates elicited by Schick, two locations must be referenced, indicating the initial and final locations of the object transfer. Finally, expression of spatial location was most difficult for whole entity classifier predicates and complex SASS predicates. For these constructions, in addition to specifying distinct locations for each referent, a particular spatial relation between the referents (e.g., *on, next-to, between*) also had to be specified.

In sum, children do not acquire the ASL classifier system easily or without error, despite the clear iconicity of the system. At the youngest ages (2;0 to 3;0), children are able to produce handling classifier handshapes and use whole entity classifier handshapes to designate a moving figure object (Slobin et al., in press). However, the ability to integrate the use of the two hands to express figure and ground relationships is not fully developed until late in childhood. Furthermore, learning the language-specific constraints on the combination of classifier handshapes and movement components occurs throughout childhood. Thus, unlike speaking children, who may produce early gestures that resemble classifier constructions, signing children are acquiring a linguistic system of contrasts in which the phonological, morphological, and semantic–pragmatic properties of classifier forms must be learned.

---

[17]Schick (1990c) proposed that children produce location correctly for handling classifier predicates earlier because these verbs are subcategorized for agreement. However, Padden (1983) provided evidence that verbs such as GIVE-BY-HAND (which can be analyzed as a handling classifier predicate), "agree with" locations, rather than arguments.

Narrative and Conversational Development

Narratives differ from conversation and other types of discourse because they generally involve nonpresent referents. As we have noted, the case study by Loew (1984) and the larger study of Bellugi et al. (1988/1993) both indicated that between 3;6 and 5;0, children may "stack" referents or use inconsistent spatial locations for each referent within a story. Bellugi et al. (1988/1993) argued that each individual sentence is grammatical, but across the narrative, the use of agreeing verbs and pronouns lacks cohesion because each spatial location is not consistently associated with a particular referent.

In addition, children must master *referential shift*, a narrative device that is partially dependent on the association of referents with spatial locations. Referential shift is used extensively in adult narratives to signal point of view and marks either direct quotation or constructed action (see chap. 2). Briefly, referential shift is signaled by a break in eye gaze with the addressee, a shift in head or body position (not obligatory), and a change in facial expression. A referential shift indicates that the ensuing discourse should be understood from the point of view of the referent associated with the shift. As shown in Fig. 2.18 in chapter 2, if the referent "student" is associated with a location on the right, then shifting the shoulders toward the right and gazing left would indicate that the subsequent discourse will be from the student's point of view. This subsequent discourse could be a direct quote (e.g., "I hate that class!") or *constructed action*, a description of an action from the point of view of the referent associated with the shift (e.g., "[the student] slammed her book on the table [in anger]"). The facial expression that accompanies manual signs within a shift is attributed to the referent associated with the shift, and not as the signer's own feeling or evaluation.

Loew (1980, 1984) was the first to study how a Deaf child acquires referential shift in ASL. Early on, at 3;1, the child in her study (Jane) occasionally used affective facial expression to indicate a character's emotions, but it was never clear if the emotions were the child's own or that of a character in the story because there was no indication of a referential shift, as marked by change in eye gaze or body position. At 3;6, Jane marked referential shift with eye gaze away from her addressee, but she did not differentiate between referents. For example, in telling the Rapunzel story, she faced left to quote the witch, but she failed to change eye gaze or body position to quote the father's response, remaining in the same position (she signed FATHER prior to the quote to label the source). In addition, her facial expression did not change markedly at the transition (as it would in adult signing); instead, the witch's angry expression gradually faded during the father's quote. At 4;4, Jane consistently marked referential shift with a change in eye gaze, but because she had not yet mastered the ability to maintain an association between a referent and a location across a narrative, the spatial aspect of the referential shifts was not contrastive or consistent (e.g., eye gaze to the left was associated with three distinct referents).

Finally, at 4;9, Jane often correctly paired her body shift and eye gaze appropriately with the spatial locations she had associated with referents in her narratives. However, she had some difficulty using pronouns correctly within a shift, precisely because of the shifting nature of these forms, that is, a first person pronoun ("I") within a shift does not refer to the signer (Jane) but to the quoted character. In Example (3) below, Jane is describing a conversation between herself (in her story role as a mother) and a woman who has come to Jane's door to take away her children.

(3) Example of a pronominal error within a referential shift (from Loew, 1980):

$$\overline{\qquad\qquad\qquad\text{q}\qquad}$$

[gaze left, as mother]:   FOR-FOR COME?
[gaze neutral, as woman]: WOMAN, FOR PRO$_{1st}$ WANT
POSS$_{1ST}$ . . . POSS$_{slightly\ right}$ . . . JANE+'S CHILDREN
" 'Why have you come?' "
"The woman said, 'For I want my . . . your . . . Jane's children' "

Within the quote, Jane should use a non-first person pronoun ("your") to refer to herself, but she found this difficult, initially using a first person pronoun ("my"), then a non-first person pronoun directed roughly at the location associated with herself in the story; and finally, she resorts to using her name sign. Thus, by 4;9, Jane was able to use referential shift to signal a quotation (although the source of the quote was often also specified lexically as in Example (3).

Reilly and colleagues studied the acquisition of referential shift with a larger group of Deaf children, using *The Three Bears* story to elicit quotation within a narrative (Reilly, 2000; Reilly, McIntire, & Anderson, 1994). Like Loew, Reilly found that 3-year-olds were able to use a break in eye gaze to signal referential shift, most of the time. Three- and four-year-olds also occasionally produced affective facial expressions within a quote, but these expressions were not precisely timed to the manual utterances of the quoted character, and the same expression was sometimes used continuously for distinct characters. It was not until age 6 that the children consistently used affective facial expression when quoting characters. Interestingly, 5-year-olds frequently used the verb SAY to introduce a quote, unlike Deaf adults or Deaf children at other ages. Marking quotations lexically, rather than nonmanually, suggests a linguistic reorganization in which affective facial expressions may be reanalyzed as part of the marking of referential shift, and this pattern follows the general "hands before faces" developmental sequence (Reilly, 2000). Children appear to master the use of referential shift for quotation before they are able to consistently use it for constructed action. Emmorey and Reilly (1998) elicited ASL narratives from children with Mayer's (1969) picture book, *Frog, Where Are You?* When Deaf adults tell this story, the majority of predicates are produced within a referential shift, indicating actions from the point of view of the various characters. Three- and five-year-olds also preferred to use predicates with constructed action, but they were not always able to clearly indicate from whose perspective the action was described. For example, one child (3;7) produced the predicate HOLD-BRANCH with eyegaze away from the addressee and with an angry expression, but it was not clear who was angry. By age 7, Deaf children had completely mastered the use of referential shift for quotation, but not for constructed action. Seven-year-olds still produced some shifted predicates in which the point of view was not clearly marked, and they used constructed action indiscriminately (i.e., without focus on the main character) and much less frequently than adults. Emmorey and Reilly (1998) conjectured that the earlier acquisition of referential shift for quotation may be due to the fact that quotation presents a single and coherent perspective: Both the discourse content (the manual signs) and the nonmanual affective expressions are those of a single referent, the quoted character. In contrast, children may have more difficulty manipulating the "dual" perspectives of constructed action: The discourse content reflects the narrator's perspective, but the affective expressions reflect a character's perspective. That is, the signer as narrator chooses the verbs to describe an action, but the facial expression is not that of the signer, but of the character whose action is described.

Similarly, van Hoek and colleagues found that children acquire the use of referential shift within serial verb constructions very late, between ages 9 and 10 (van Hoek, O'Grady, & Bellugi, 1987; van Hoek, O'Grady-Batch, Norman, & Bellugi, 1989; see also Morgan, 1998, for a study of the acquisition of these constructions in British Sign Language). Figure 5.6A illustrates a type of serial verb construction in adult ASL that is used to describe an agent's action directed toward a location on the patient's body, for example, "The girl paints on the boy's face." Figure 5.6B illustrates a typical attempt at this construction by a child under 5;0. The child's sentence, BOY PAINT-FACE GIRL is ungrammatical for two reasons: (1) referential shift must be invoked in order for PAINT-FACE to refer to another referent's face (i.e., not the child's own face); and (2) PAINT-FACE is intransitive and cannot be followed by the object BOY. Van Hoek found that older 5- and 6-year-olds stop making this error, and instead simply

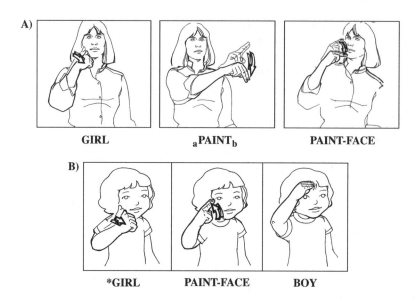

FIG. 5.6.   (A) Illustration of an adult serial verb construction. The boy has been associated with location "b" on the signer's left and the girl with the "a" location on the signer's right. An English translation would be "The girl painted on the boy's face." (B) Illustration of a child's ungrammatical attempt. Illustrations copyright © Ursula Bellugi, The Salk Institute.

omit any mention of the affected body part. Seven- and eight-year-olds begin to use the serial construction, but they almost always omit the required referential shift for the second verb specifying body location. Only 10-year-olds produced the serial verb construction with the shift. Van Hoek et al. (1989) hypothesize that children may naturally view the event described by the serial construction from a single viewpoint—the agent's. It may be difficult to switch from the agent's viewpoint to the experiencer's within a single sentence describing a single event. Hence, the use of referential shift in a serial verb construction appears later than in discourse contexts where the shift occurs between sentences (for either quotation or constructed action).

Finally, Deaf children must learn how to gain and maintain their addressee's attention during conversations. Although Deaf mothers are very adept at ensuring that their Deaf children are watching them before they begin signing, Deaf children must develop the ability to garner their addressee's visual attention before conversing. Siple and colleagues have found that young Deaf children (around age 2) do not initiate conversations with other children or adults, unlike their hearing peers (Richmond-Welty & Siple, 1999; Siple & Akamatsu, 1991; Siple, Richmond-Welty, Howe, Berwanger, & Japser, 1994). At this age, children are generally talking about objects that they are looking at, and signed communication requires that visual attention be directed toward the communicative partner. Hearing children can just start talking and gain another hearing child's attention (without necessarily intending to do so). The heightened demands on visual attention required by sign language may be responsible for the delay in initiation of signed interaction by very young children (Siple, 2000). However, P. M. Prinz and E. A. Prinz (1983) found that by age 3, Deaf children almost always initiated eye contact with their addressee before signing, and as with speaking children, the ability to maintain sustained eye contact with the addressee increased with age. Three- to five-year olds gained their addressee's attention by pulling or tugging on their addressee, but by 7;6, Deaf children were utilizing adult devices such as hand waving, moving toward the addressee, or slight touching of the addressee. By age 5, children were also able to use adult discourse devices for interrupting conversation, such as raising their hands into signing space, averting eye gaze, and increasing the size and frequency of head nodding (P. M. Prinz & E. A. Prinz, 1983). The timing of turn taking was similar to that of speaking children, with more overlapping of utterances for older children (ages 7;0 to 10;0). Thus, although the visual modality may have an effect on very early aspects of conversation for Deaf children, the development of discourse strategies for regulating and maintaining conversations is very similar for both signing and speaking children.

CONCLUSIONS AND IMPLICATIONS

Understanding the nature of language acquisition for a signed language has provided important insight into the nature of human language and the human capacity for language. The developmental course of language acquisition is not tied specifically to speech, even for babbling, a domain in which researchers have proposed explicit links to the mechanisms of speech production. Furthermore, children acquiring ASL do not rely on the iconic and analogue aspects of the language, rather they construct a grammatical system according to linguistic principles. There appears to be an early communicative advantage for gesture, but Deaf children distinguish early on between communicative gestures (either manual or facial) and linguistic gestures (lexical signs and grammatical facial expressions). The study of motherese in ASL has provided insight into what may drive parental modifications of language (i.e., clear and unambiguous communication rather than grammatical simplification). Finally, the visual–spatial aspects of sign language may present some challenges to acquisition, for example, the spatial memory demands of coreference and the visual attention demands of early child-initiated conversations. In general, however, language modality plays a very minor role in how children acquire language, which tells us something very important about ourselves: We are born with the ability to acquire language and when exposed to the appropriate input (either speech or sign), language emerges according to a particular developmental timetable, constrained by linguistic and cognitive principles that are not specific to the visual–manual or aural–oral modalities.

SUGGESTIONS FOR FURTHER READING

Newport, E., & Meier, R. (1985). The acquisition of American Sign Language. In D. Slobin (Ed.), *The cross-linguistic study of language acquisition* (pp. 881–938). Hillsdale, NJ: Lawrence Erlbaum Associates.

This chapter provides an excellent summary of ASL acquisition research up to 1985. Newport and Meier review many early studies that are not described here, and many are dissertations or paper presentations that are difficult to obtain. In particular, the acquisition of ASL morphology is covered in some detail (e.g., aspect morphology, noun compounding, and derivational morphology). The chapter also sets the acquisition of ASL within a broader cross-linguistic context.

Lillo-Martin, D. (1999). Modality effects and modularity in language acquisition: The acquisition of American Sign Language. In W. C. Ritchie & T. K. Bhatia (Eds.), *Handbook of child language acquisition* (pp. 531–567), San Diego, CA: Academic Press.

Lillo-Martin focuses this review on research after 1985. In addition, the chapter contains an important discussion of modality and modularity effects in language acquisition. Lillo-Martin argues that the facts about sign language acquisition support the hypothesis that language is distinct from other cognitive systems, and she suggests that the effects of language modality on acquisition are primarily phonetic in nature.

Chapter **6**

The Critical Period Hypothesis and the Effects of Late Language Acquisition

In 1967, Lenneberg hypothesized that language acquisition may be linked to brain maturation and predicted that the ability to acquire a language would be limited to a period during childhood, before the loss of neural plasticity. In other words, childhood represents an important "window of opportunity" for learning language, and once this developmental period has passed, the ability to acquire language becomes much more difficult. The *critical period hypothesis* has special import for the Deaf population because if a deaf infant is born to hearing parents who do not sign, then exposure to an accessible natural language will be delayed.[1] As discussed in chapter 1, 90% of deaf children are born to hearing parents, and until very recently, there were no programs for early detection of deafness (Yoshinaga-Itano, Sedey, Coulter, & Mehl, 1998) or for early sign language intervention (and more such programs are needed). Thus, some deaf children receive no language input, delayed language input, or inconsistent language input, but unlike other cases of late exposure to language (e.g., the famous case of Genie, who was isolated in her home until age 13; Curtiss, 1977), these deaf children are raised within loving families. The study of such children provide unique insight into the human capacity for language and the limits on language learning imposed by the cognitive and neural maturation that occurs during development.

This chapter reviews the results of investigations that assess the effects of delayed exposure to a first language on linguistic competence, on lan-

---

[1]The term *sensitive period* is sometimes preferred over *critical period* because it implies a more gradual offset.

205

guage processing, on cognition, and on the neural organization for language. We begin, however, with a discussion of the robustness of language, as evidenced by the spontaneous creation of language-like systems by deaf children with no useable language input, and as evidenced by the regularization of a linguistic system by one Deaf child from the inconsistent language input of his Deaf, nonnative signing parents. These studies highlight what capacities the child brings to the language acquisition process.

WHEN LANGUAGE INPUT IS ABSENT
OR INCONSISTENT: THE CONTRIBUTION
OF THE CHILD

Profoundly deaf children who are not exposed to sign language and who do not learn a spoken language spontaneously develop *home sign* gesture systems. Home sign emerges in the situation in which parents, by choice or by circumstance, do not to expose their deaf child to sign language, and profound deafness prevents the child from naturally acquiring spoken language (often the child can only produce a handful of spoken words). Thus, these deaf children have no conventional language model and are exposed only to the spontaneous gestures that their parents make when speaking to them. Goldin-Meadow and colleagues have investigated how home sign systems develop, their structure, and what they tell us about the nature of the child's contribution to the language acquisition process (see Goldin-Meadow, in press; Goldin-Meadow & Mylander, 1990; and Morford, 1996, for reviews).

Surprisingly, home sign systems exhibit a systematic structure that does not vary with individual children and is consistent even across children raised within different cultures, for example, in Taiwan or in the United States (Goldin-Meadow & Mylander, 1998; Wang, Mylander, & Goldin-Meadow, 1995). The children in these studies generally range in age from 3 to 5 years old. Although individual gestures are idiosyncratic for a given child, the gestures are structured at the level of the sentence (in the form of gesture combinations) and at the level of the word (in the form of systematic combinations of meaningful handshapes and movements; Goldin-Meadow & Feldman, 1977; Goldin-Meadow, Mylander, & Butcher, 1995). Unlike the gestures of hearing children, these deaf children combine pointing gestures and iconic "characterizing" gestures to express propositions. Home-signing children produce gestures that indicate agents, patients, recipients, and actions, and they do not order these gestures randomly.

The home-sign pattern of ordering gestures resembles *ergative* systems found in some spoken languages (Goldin-Meadow & Mylander, 1990,

1998). In an ergative system, intransitive actors (*John* in "John danced") and patients (*apple* in "John ate the apple") pattern together and are linguistically distinguished from transitive actors (*John* in "John ate the apple"). Notice that the English examples just given illustrate a nonergative system: intransitive and transitive actors (both examples of *John*) pattern together as subjects, and patients (*apple*) are marked separately as objects within the verb phrase. In contrast, home-sign systems tend to show an ergative pattern; gestures for intransitive actors and for patients are produced before action gestures. Furthermore, gestures representing transitive actors are relatively rare, but when they are produced, they tend to follow action gestures as shown in Fig. 6.1. The following examples illustrate the pattern (from Goldin-Meadow & Mylander, 1990, 1998):

Intransitive actor + action
pointing gesture to a train + a circling gesture
(The child was commenting on a toy train that was circling on a track)

point to Mickey Mouse + a 'swing' gesture
(The child was indicating that Mickey Mouse swings on a trapeze)

Patient + action
point to bubble jar + twisting gesture
(A request to open the jar)

point to cheese + gesture for eat
(The child was commenting on a mouse eating cheese)

Action + transitive actor
clap + point to himself
(The child was indicating that he wanted to break bubbles by clapping them)

gesture for eat + point to addressee (twice)
(The child wanted the addressee to eat some pretzels) See the example in Fig. 6.1.

The ergative pattern of gesture ordering may be motivated by principles of information flow. Du Bois (1985, 1987) studied narratives in Sacapultec, a Mayan language with an ergative system, and found that new participants within a discourse were most often introduced as either intransitive actors or as patients; two noun phrases, one expressing an agent and the other a patient, were very rare. Similar to the home signers, Sacapultec speakers tended to lexically omit transitive actors (i.e., agents) because such actors were already known within the discourse, representing old information (Du Bois, 1987). Thus, the limits on information flow (a tendency for clauses to have only one noun phrase argument) and discourse economy (an avoidance of expressing old information lexically, which often applies to agents) leads to the ergative system in which pa-

FIG. 6.1.   An example of an "action + transitive actor" gesture order in a deaf home signer. The child uses this gesture string to invite his addressee to join him for pretzels. He first indicates the action "eat" and then the transitive actor "you" (the third gesture is a repetition). The child omitted a gesture for the patient (pretzels). Reprinted from *Trends in Cognitive Sciences, 3*(11), S. Goldin-Meadow, "The Role of Gesture in Communication and Thinking," 419–429, copyright © 1999, with permission from Elsevier Science.

tients and intransitive actors pattern together, separately from transitive actors. It is reasonable to hypothesize that home signers operate under the same constraints on information flow and discourse economy (perhaps even more so). Thus, the discourse explanation for the grammaticization of ergativity in spoken languages proposed by Du Bois may help to explain why home-sign systems tend to adopt an ergative pattern for ordering gestures.

Crucially, the children did not learn this gesture order from their mothers. The mothers showed no reliable pattern of gesture order, and the American mothers in particular produced far fewer gesture combinations than their children (Goldin-Meadow & Mylander, 1990, 1998). Such results suggest that children are predisposed to create structures that contain elements with a specific (ergative-type) order, which allow them to distinguish semantic roles (i.e., patients from agents). Thus, ordering constraints may be a "resilient" property of language that does not depend on a consistent or clear language model in order to develop (Goldin-Meadow, 1982).

Home-sign gesture systems also exhibit structure internal to the gesture, that is, a form of morphological structure. Goldin-Meadow et al. (1995) compared the meaning associated with a specific handshape or with a particular movement across a variety of gestures. They found that the children used a limited set of handshapes and movements to represent specific meanings within their gesture systems. For example, one child used a fist hand to represent the handling of small, long, objects and combined this handshape with movements to indicate various types of motion, for example, a short arc (to indicate repositioning), a circular motion, or a back-and-forth motion. These same movements were also combined with other handshapes (e.g., a C handshape was used to represent the handling of objects of any length). The reader will notice that these examples bear a striking resemblance to classifier constructions discussed in chapter 3. The fact that similar (but very simplified) structures appear in home-sign systems attests to the gestural origin of classifier constructions in signed languages and may account in part for their universality (given that all natural sign languages arise from a mixture of home-sign systems; see chap. 1 for discussion).

As with gesture order, the internal structure of gestures was not learned from parental input. The form-meaning mappings developed to account for the children's use of handshapes and movements did not fit their mothers' productions, which were inconsistent. The children generalized beyond the gestures of their mothers by producing novel combinations of handshape and movements that were unattested in their input and by using the gesture components to refer to classes of related events and objects, rather than for specific individual events and objects (Goldin-Meadow et al., 1995). The fact that these deaf children generate language-like structure from very impoverished input suggests that humans have an innate drive to find and create structure within a communicative system (such structure is not spontaneously created by primates).

However, home sign is not a language (see chap. 1) and probably falls somewhere between Protolanguage and Modern language in Jackendoff's (1999) proposed steps in the evolution of language. Although home-sign systems exhibit ordering constraints and an open class of symbols, there is little evidence for hierarchical phrase structure, symbols that expressly encode abstract semantic relationships (e.g., "if," "but"), or a system of inflections to convey semantic relationships. In addition, when home signers are exposed to a signed language, their home sign is almost immediately abandoned, and they quickly begin to replace home sign gestures with lexical signs (Emmorey, Ewan, & Grant, 1994; Morford, 1998). As we see in the next section, home signers also have difficulty mastering a conventional signed language in adulthood.

In fact, the finding that late learners do not acquire competence in ASL provides another opportunity to examine the effects of highly inconsistent input on language acquisition. Singleton and Newport studied one such child (Simon) whose only ASL input came from his nonnative signing parents who both learned ASL shortly after age 15 (Newport, 1999; Singleton, 1989; Singleton & Newport, in press). Simon's parents had been raised in an oral language environment, but they preferred to use ASL as the primary method of communication within their family. Simon's school teachers used Manually Coded English produced simultaneously with speaking, and there were no native signing children who attended his school (a public school with a special classroom for deaf and hard-of-hearing students). Thus, the linguistic input that Simon received was richer than that of home signers, but poorer than native language input because of inconsistencies and errors produced by his nonnative signing parents.

Singleton and Newport (in press) report that Simon's parents produced the movement morphemes of ASL classifier constructions with an accuracy of only about 70%. Their errors consisted primarily of producing a sequence of separate signs to describe a motion event, rather than producing simultaneous combinations of movement morphemes within a classifier construction. In contrast to his parents, Simon (age 7) produced the appropriate movement morphemes with an accuracy of 88%, on a par with Deaf children of the same age who receive native language input. In addition, Simon did not make the periphrastic phrasal responses observed for his parents; rather, when he made an error, he either produced a related morpheme or omitted a required morpheme. Thus, Simon regularized the input of his parents, creating a highly consistent system (Singleton & Newport, in press).[2]

A similar and even more striking pattern was observed for the acquisition of aspect and number inflection (Newport, 1999; Singleton, 1989). Simon's parents have particular difficulty combining and embedding inflections within a verb. For example, they fail to produce verbs with both a dual and a repeated inflection to indicate repetitive actions with two patients (e.g., to describe someone repeatedly blowing out candles [which keep relighting] on two cakes). As with classifier constructions, they produce phrasal descriptions of the events (e.g., signing BLOW-OUT AGAIN or BACK-AND-FORTH). Simon does not acquire these periphrastic descriptions that he observes his parents producing; rather, he correctly embeds number and aspect morphemes within the verb. Not only is Simon regularizing and producing consistent linguistic output from the reduced and inconsistent input of his parents, but he is also imposing a recursive morphological system on this input. That is, Simon somehow "knows" that morphological inflections can be added recursively to a verb and that the order of embedding is semantically important, that is, dual + repeated is distinct from repeated + dual. Simon conserves linguistic domains by combining number and aspect inflections within the morphology, rather than shifting to sentence level syntactic encoding as his parents do (Singleton, 1989).

At the level of syntax, Simon adheres to universal constraints on syntactic form that were never exemplified in the input from his parents. Spe-

---

[2]Interestingly, for handshape morphemes, Simon and his parents all had low accuracy levels (42% for his father, 45% for his mother, and 50% for Simon). Singleton and Newport (in press) hypothesized that this particularly low level of parental consistency may have prevented Simon from regularizing form–meaning mappings, and he may also have never seen the correct ASL form of some classifiers. For example, Simon's parents used a B handshape, rather than a 3 handshape, to describe the motion of cars, and Simon did not "invent" the correct ASL 3 handshape in his productions.

cifically, Simon acquired topicalization as a structurally dependent movement process, but his parents did not (Newport, 1999; Singleton, 1989). That is, Simon's parents produced a consistent SVO word order pattern in ASL, but they only produced *subject* noun phrases with a topic facial expression (see chap. 2). When Simon's parents were presented with sentences in which either a verb phrase or an object noun phrase had been topicalized (see Fig. 2.13 in chap. 2), they consistently misinterpreted the sentence.[3] In contrast, when Simon was given the same comprehension task, he correctly interpreted the topicalized elements as moved constituents—however, he had never seen these sentence types produced by his parents. Simon's performance reveals that he acquired a grammatical system in which constituent structure, rather than the linear order of words, determines how grammatical rules such as topicalization apply. This *structure dependency* is a universal property of human languages, and children do not make errors that violate this constraint, suggesting that children may be predisposed to assume this type of grammar (e.g., Chomsky, 1965).

Thus, at age 7, Simon has been able to do what his parents were not able to do at age 15—acquire a consistent grammatical system. In the remainder of this chapter, we explore in detail the effects of late language acquisition, which may help explain why Simon's parents produced such inconsistent linguistic structures.

THE EFFECTS OF AGE OF ACQUISITION
ON GRAMMATICAL KNOWLEDGE
AND LANGUAGE PROCESSING

Research with other species provides evidence for the existence of innate biological constraints on learning. For example, if song sparrows are only exposed to the song of adult male sparrows *after* a particular period of development (20 to 50 days after hatching), they will not be able to learn the adult song (Marler, 1991). Learning is dependent on the maturational age of the sparrow when first exposed to song. Newport (1990, 1991) investigated the existence of such a critical or sensitive period for the human spe-

---

[3]Newport (1999) reported that "on 8 out of 9 trials, Simon's mother interpreted VN,N sequences as VS,O [underlining indicates topicalization, KE], an order that cannot be derived by any single phrasal movement rule. Simon's father responded in the same way (i.e., incorrectly) on 7 out of 9 trials" (p. 171). It is possible that Simon's parents were using an English-based strategy for interpreting word order patterns (disregarding the ASL topic markers). That is, when English speakers are given VNN sequences, they consistently interpret the first N as the subject, unlike Italian speakers, who do not rely as heavily on word order as a cue to meaning (Bates, McNew, MacWhinney, Devoscovi, & Smith, 1982).

cies by studying Deaf adults who were at different maturational stages of development when they were first exposed to ASL, their primary and preferred language in adulthood.

The subjects in Newport's studies all attended the same residential school and fell into three groups: *Native learners*, exposed to ASL from birth by their Deaf signing parents, *early learners*, first exposed to ASL by Deaf peers when they entered the school between age 4 and 6, and *late learners*, who were not exposed to ASL until after age 12 when they entered the school or later met friends or married spouses from the school. Crucially, all subjects had a minimum of 30 years of daily experience with ASL before they were tested in the study. Thus, the critical factor was the age at which they first began to learn ASL, and not the number of years of "practice" with the language. The subjects were assessed on their ability to produce and comprehend a number of syntactic and morphological structures in ASL.

The results revealed that age of acquisition had no effect on the control of basic word order in ASL, with all three groups of learners performing at ceiling. This finding supports the hypothesis that ordering is a robust or resilient property of language that can be acquired without error after puberty.[4] However, the correlations between scores on tests of ASL morphology and age of acquisition ranged between −.60 and −.70, with subjects exposed to ASL early in childhood consistently outperforming subjects exposed to ASL at later ages (Newport, 1990). Furthermore, like Simon's parents, the late learners in this study exhibited inconsistent control of ASL morphology, despite 30 or more years of exposure to and use of ASL. Newport (1990, 1991) argued that these results demonstrate an effect of the maturational state of the language learner and cannot be explained by differences in linguistic input, social environment, or cognitive abilities.

Late acquisition of language not only affects the ultimate level of grammatical competence, but it also affects language processing. Mayberry and colleagues have found that phonological processing seems to be particularly vulnerable to the effects of late acquisition of language (Mayberry, 1995; Mayberry & Eichen, 1991; Mayberry & Fischer, 1989). In these studies, native and late learners were given both a shadowing task (immediately repeating an ASL sentence as it is seen) and a recall task (immediately repeating an ASL sentence verbatim after watching it). Native learners outperformed both groups of late learners (exposed to ASL between 5 to 8 years or between 9 to 13 years). Again, better performance was linked

---

[4]However, recent data from Mayberry (personal communication, March 2000) indicates that even the acquisition of word order may be vulnerable to the effects of late language acquisition for both spoken and signed languages.

to the age of first exposure to language, rather than to length of practice (subjects had all been signing for an average of 40 years).

For both sign shadowing and recall tasks, late learners made many more phonological substitutions compared to native signers, who tended to produce semantically based errors. For example, if the target sentence was (translated into English), "As a child I always played with my younger brother," a *semantic* error would be substituting OLD for YOUNG. With semantic substitutions, the basic meaning of the sentence is preserved. In contrast, an example of a phonological error would be substituting the sign SLEEP for AND in the target sentence, "I ate too much turkey and potato at Thanksgiving dinner" (see Fig. 6.2). Phonological substitutions indicate that the subject did not fully understand the sentence. The distinct error pattern of native versus late learners was not due to general memory or visual–perceptual differences between the two groups. Rather, late learners appeared to devote much more attention to the phonological structure of signs, which interfered with their ability to quickly access lexical meanings. Native signers, however, were able to automatically access and integrate lexical meaning, and their error patterns indicated they did not focus on decoding the phonology of signs.

Similarly, Emmorey, Corina, and Bellugi (1995) found that late learners took much longer to reject phonologically related probe signs that were foils in the probe recognition task (see chap. 4), for example, late signers were slow to reject ONION as occurring in a target sentence if the sentence actually contained KEY, a phonologically related sign. Late signers may retain more of the phonological representation in working memory, and thus are slower to reject phonologically related probe signs, compared to native signers who have quickly processed (and possibly discarded) the phonological form of the sentence. Native signers tended

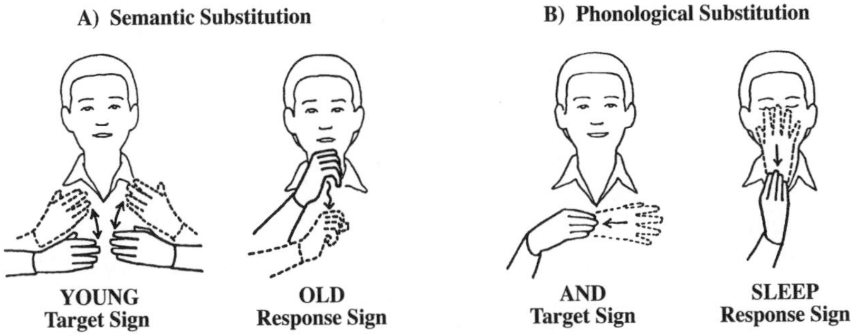

A) **Semantic Substitution**		B) **Phonological Substitution**	

| **YOUNG** | **OLD** | **AND** | **SLEEP** |
| Target Sign | Response Sign | Target Sign | Response Sign |

FIG. 6.2. Example of a semantic substitution and a phonological substitution in the sentence recall task used by Mayberry and Eichen (1991). Illustration by Betty Raskin, copyright © Rachel Mayberry.

to make errors based on semantics for both the probe recognition task and the recall tasks of Mayberry's experiments. Furthermore, in Mayberry's studies, semantic substitutions were positively correlated with comprehension (+ .86). That is, if most recall errors were semantic, subjects showed good comprehension. In contrast, phonological errors were negatively correlated with comprehension (−.84)—subjects who tended to make phonological substitutions exhibited poor comprehension.

Mayberry argued that late learners have a "phonological bottleneck" that causes them to expend additional cognitive effort deciphering phonological patterns, which prevents them from quickly accessing the meanings of lexical signs, thus creating a backlog during online processing (Mayberry, 1994, 1995; Mayberry & Fischer, 1989). Further evidence for such a phonological bottleneck was found by Emmorey and Corina (1990b). Late learners were significantly delayed in identifying ASL signs as measured by the gating task. (A sign is presented repeatedly, with the length of each presentation increased by one videoframe, and subjects attempt to identify the sign after each presentation; see chap. 4). Native signers were able to make use of early phonetic or phonological information to uniquely identify a target sign, whereas late learners needed to see more of the sign before they could identify it. These results suggest that late learners are not able to exploit visual information that is present early in the sign signal.

In addition, Hildebrandt and Corina (2000) found that late learners and native signers differ in which phonological components are perceived as most salient. Native signers judged signs to be most similar if they shared the same movement, whereas both early learners (age of ASL exposure: 1 to 6 years) and late learners (age of exposure: 7 years and older) judged signs as most related if they shared the same handshape. Hearing nonsigners showed yet a third pattern, judging signs that shared either location or movement as equally similar. The saliency of movement for native signers is argued to be due to the critical role that movement plays in defining the syllable in sign language (see chap. 2). It is possible that early and late learners consider movement less salient than native signers because they lack the very early exposure to linguistic movement that gives rise to babbling in native signing children (see chap. 5).

Finally, Boyes-Braem (1999) found that late learners of Swiss German Sign Language do not sign with the same rhythmic structure observed with early learners. Specifically, early learners produce regular "body sways" or side-to-side movements that serve to mark discourse units that visually structure the communication, and these movements are less frequent and less pronounced in late learners. In addition, unlike late learners, early learners frequently produce stretched mouthings that function to mark prosodic units (Boyes-Braem, in press). Like late learners of spoken languages, late learners of sign language appear to sign with an "accent" (see chap. 2 for a discussion of prosody in sign language).

Together, these findings indicate that childhood language acquisition is critical for automatic and effortless phonological processing. Because phonological structure requires additional effort and attention for late learners, lexical, sentential, and discourse structures are harder to construct and maintain. Thus, the effects of the phonological bottleneck are far reaching. For example, a delay in decoding and recognizing signs leads to an increase in working memory load, which creates impairments in memory intensive aspects of language comprehension. Specifically, late learners cannot keep track of the relation between pronominal referents and spatial locations when the number of pronouns is more than two (Mayberry, 1995).

Late learners are also impaired in their ability to rapidly interpret and integrate morphological information. For example, late learners are more likely than native signers to delete bound morphemes during sentence recall tasks (Mayberry & Eichen, 1991), and they may fail to exhibit morphological priming (Emmorey, 1991). Furthermore, even if late learners have a conscious knowledge of ASL morphology, they may not be able to use it during online sentence comprehension. Emmorey, Bellugi, Friederici, and Horn (1995) found that although early and late learners were able to detect violations involving agreeing verbs in an offline grammaticality judgment task, they were not sensitive to these errors in an online task. Subjects were asked to monitor an ASL sentence for a particular target sign and press a button as soon as they detected the sign. Unlike native signers, late learners showed no evidence of a disruption in processing when the target sign followed an error in verb agreement. Thus, even though the late signers had knowledge of the correct morphological form, they had difficulty detecting and interpreting these morphemes online.[5] Similar results were found by Emmorey and Corina (1992) for morphological violations within classifier constructions (reported in Emmorey, 1993).

However, late acquisition of language does not appear to affect some aspects of language processing. Specifically, the mechanisms underlying referential processing appear to be spared, unless working memory is overburdened. For example, late learners exhibit antecedent activation and nonantecedent suppression for both overt and null ASL pronouns

---

[5]Interestingly, Emmorey et al. (1995) found that late learners showed evidence of a processing disruption when errors in aspect morphology were encountered online. There are two possible explanations for this finding: (1) the temporal extension of aspect morphology allowed late signers enough time to process these morphemes, or (2) the greater semantic anomaly created by aspect violations accounted for the greater sensitivity.

(see chap. 4; Emmorey, Falgier, & Gernsbacher, 1998; Emmorey & Lillo-Martin, 1995; Emmorey et al., 1991). Thus, like knowledge of basic word order, the mechanisms underlying coreference processing may be relatively robust and unaffected by late language acquisition. In contrast, phonological processing and an understanding of morphological systems appear to be particularly vulnerable to late exposure to language.

DELAYED FIRST LANGUAGE ACQUISITION DIFFERS FROM SECOND LANGUAGE ACQUISITION

Are the effects of late exposure to sign language the same as the effects observed when speakers learn a second language? Speakers who begin to learn a second language late in childhood also show poorer performance on a variety of measures compared to native speakers (see Birdsong, 1999, for review and discussion). For example, the age at which speakers began to acquire their second language is strongly correlated with their ability to produce speech without an accent and to make correct grammaticality judgments (Flege, Munro, & MacKay, 1995; Johnson & Newport, 1989). However, there is a crucial difference between second language learners and late learners of ASL. Spoken language users have been exposed to a first language from birth, but Deaf, ASL late learners have no early language input and are drilled and trained in spoken English within oral language classrooms, often with very little success (Lane, 1992).[6]

To examine the effects of delayed first versus second language acquisition, Mayberry (1993) compared ASL late learners who were born deaf with ASL late learners who lost their hearing late in childhood and acquired ASL as their second language (because they had acquired spoken English as a first language in early childhood). Mayberry (1993) found that subjects who acquired ASL as a second language outperformed those who acquired it as a first language at exactly the same age (average age of acquisition was 11 years). In the sentence recall task, late first language learners again exhibited a greater proportion of phonological substitutions compared to native learners, indicating abnormal attention to surface form and poorer comprehension. The second language learners performed similarly to the early and native learners, producing a greater proportion of semantic substitutions.

---

[6]Although some deaf children do acquire spoken language in this environment ("oral language successes"), these were not the subjects studied by Mayberry (1993). The late first language learners in this study were transferred to a residential school because of their poor spoken language skills.

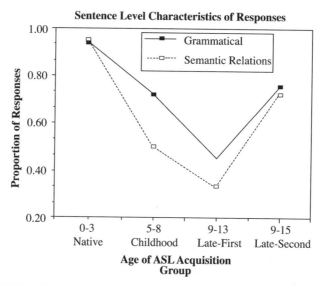

FIG. 6.3.   The mean proportion of subjects total responses that were gram-matically acceptable and semantically parallel to the stimulus sentence. Sub-jects are grouped by age of ASL acquisition and first versus second language acquisition. From Mayberry, 1993; copyright © 1993 by American Speech and Hearing Association. Reprinted with permission.

In addition, sentence repetitions were scored for *grammaticality* (wheth-er the sentence produced was grammatical or not) and for *semantic rela-tions* (whether the sentence produced preserved the meaning of the target sentence). On these measures, late learners who acquired ASL as a first language performed most poorly (see Fig. 6.3). Late learners who ac-quired ASL as a second language performed similarly to the early learners (who were exposed to ASL between 5 to 8 years). However, it was the na-tive signers who were best able to maintain the general meaning of the tar-get sentence and produce completely grammatical responses.

The long-term effects of a delay in first language acquisition appear to be much more detrimental than the effects of acquiring a second language late in childhood. The second language learner can draw on a general knowledge of linguistic systems that was acquired with the first language. In contrast, the deaf child exposed to ASL as a first language begins the acquisition process with little understanding of syntactic principles or knowledge of how morphological and phonological systems are orga-nized. These findings have important educational implications for deaf children. Because signed languages are acquired naturally without explicit training, one is led to the conclusion that deaf children should be exposed to a signed language as early as possible. The results of Singleton (1989; Singleton & Newport, in press) suggested that even impoverished signing of nonnative parents nonetheless leads to nativelike ability if the child is exposed early enough. With a first language in place, it may be much easier to acquire English as a second language. In fact, several studies have shown that native ASL signers have superior reading and literacy skills in English, compared to late learners of ASL (see Chamberlain & Mayberry, 2000, for a review).

In sum, the evidence from Deaf children acquiring ASL at different points during development provides strong evidence for a critical period for language acquisition in humans. Skilled comprehension and production of language in adulthood is dependent on the age of exposure during development—the earlier the acquisition, the better the performance, even after 30 years of experience.

We can now ask what is altered during this developmental period that prevents older learners from acquiring language with the same automaticity of processing and degree of grammatical knowledge as native learners. One possibility is that the decline in neural plasticity during childhood makes it difficult to create and maintain the new neural connections needed to support language learning (e.g., Lenneberg, 1967). Neural plasticity may come to an end due to a genetically determined change in learning capacity, or neural plasticity may decline due the process of learning itself—that is, neural circuits become committed to a particular configuration, which limits learning capacity after a certain point (e.g., Neville, 1991a).

A related hypothesis is that the critical period for language acquisition arises from changes in cognitive maturation. Newport (1990, 1991) hypothesized that because young children have limited short-term memory capacity, they can initially extract only a few morphemes from the linguistic input. In contrast, older learners, with their greater memory capacity, are "faced with the more difficult task of analyzing everything at once" (Newport, 1991, p. 126). Although it may seem paradoxical that less memory is better (the "less is more" hypothesis), Elman (1993) demonstrated the advantage of limited memory capacity with a connectionist model of language learning. When the model started with limited memory and then underwent incremental changes in memory capacity (akin to cognitive maturation), the model was able to learn complex sentences. However, when the starting point was full (adultlike) memory capacity, complex sentences were not successfully learned. Again, these findings indicate that exposure to language at just the right time during development leads to successful acquisition; if such exposure is delayed, language acquisition is incomplete, with effortful processing throughout adulthood.

THE COGNITIVE EFFECTS OF DELAYED FIRST LANGUAGE ACQUISITION

Until recently, much of the research concerning the effect of deficient language experience on cognition in Deaf children was compromised by a failure to recognize sign language as a language. It was assumed that because Deaf children often fail to acquire English competence, they therefore lack *any* language competence. The relevant evidence that does exist suggests that delayed language exposure has no long-lasting effects on general cognitive abilities. For example, a large study by Vernon (1969) found that the deaf and hard-of-hearing populations exhibit essentially the same distribution of intelligence as the general population. Another large study from the Gallaudet Office of Demographic Studies in Washington, DC, reports a similar finding for the distribution of nonverbal intelligence in deaf children who had no additional handicaps (Schildroth, 1976). Finally, a meta-analysis of over 300 studies of IQ and deafness led Braden (1994) to conclude "the distribution of IQ in deaf people is nearly identical to the IQ distribution of normal-hearing people" (p. 103).

However, when Deaf children with Deaf families are specifically compared to Deaf children from hearing families, there is some evidence that delayed exposure to a signed language is associated with cognitive delays during development. Deaf children raised in hearing families with no sign language exposure have been found to score slightly lower on nonverbal intelligence tests compared to Deaf children from Deaf families (Kusché, Greenberg, & Garfield, 1983; Sisco & R. J. Anderson, 1980; Zwiebel, 1987). There have been several interpretations of this finding. Kusché et al. (1983) proposed a genetic explanation, hypothesizing that because Deaf children from Deaf families actually score slightly higher than the general hearing population, these children have inherited genes for superior intelligence along with their deafness. The problem with this explanation, as pointed out by Mayberry (1992), is that there are a myriad of genetic causes for deafness (at least 100), and it is unlikely that all would be associated with intelligence. In contrast, Zwiebel (1987) found no effect of genetic deafness and argued that the superior performance of Deaf children with Deaf parents is due to their rich linguistic home environment, which provides increased social interaction and access to information obtained by observing parental conversations and interactions. However, the specific link between sign language acquisition and nonverbal intelligence remains unclear and controversial (see Marschark, Siple, Lillo-Martin, Campbell, & Everhart, 1997, for a discussion).

In addition, several recent studies with adults indicate that experience with sign language can actually enhance certain nonlinguistic cognitive abilities in both hearing and Deaf signers, compared to hearing adults who did not know sign language (see chap. 8 for a review). However, most of these studies found little difference in performance between adult native signers and those with delayed exposure to ASL. Furthermore, Deaf children with Deaf parents may *initially* outperform Deaf children with hearing parents, but the difference disappears by adulthood. For example, on a face-processing task (the *Benton Faces test*; see chap. 8), Bettger, Emmorey, McCullough, and Bellugi (1997) found that Deaf children with delayed exposure to ASL did not show the same performance enhancement as did native signing children (6 to 9 years of age). However, Deaf adults who acquired ASL late in childhood (or early adulthood) performed similarly to Deaf adults who were native signers, with both groups outperforming hearing nonsigners.

Similarly, a lack of early language experience can affect short-term memory capacity, but the effect is observed only in children and resolves in adulthood. Wilson, Bettger, Niculae, and Klima (1997) found that Deaf children (8 to 10 years of age) who were native ASL signers had longer digit spans than Deaf children who were nonnative signers (these children had no Deaf family members and were exposed to ASL prior to age 6). Similar to many previous studies, both groups of Deaf children had shorter digit spans than their hearing peers, which may be due to several factors including length of articulation differences between sign and speech (see chap. 7 for discussion). Wilson et al. (1997) speculated that their results may reflect the effects of delayed acquisition of ASL, and a series of studies by Bebko and colleagues provides support for this hypothesis (Bebko, 1984; Bebko, Bell, Metcalfe-Haggert, & McKinnon, 1998; Bebko & McKinnon, 1990). Deaf children who had more sign language experience, more automated signing skills, and greater linguistic proficiency were much more likely to exhibit spontaneous rehearsal during serial recall tasks.[7] Linguistic rehearsal (e.g., naming pictures to be remembered and covertly or overtly repeating the names in order of presentation) significantly improves recall, and children with delayed exposure to a first language exhibit a delay in the development of such rehearsal strategies and thus exhibit poorer memory performance (Bebko & McKinnon, 1990). In addition, rate of rehearsal is related to memory performance, with faster articulators exhibiting better recall (see chap. 7 for details). Children with delayed exposure to sign language exhibit slower and less automatic sign production, which is correlated with poorer serial recall (Bebko et al., 1998; Mayberry & Waters, 1991).

---

[7]Although a few Deaf children in these studies encoded the pictures to be remembered orally (with English), the majority preferred to produce signs for the items to be remembered in the serial recall tasks.

However, studies with Deaf *adults* reveal no differences in serial recall performance based on age of exposure to sign language. Native and late learners exhibit similar digit spans for both forward and backward recall (Mayberry, 1993; Mayberry & Eichen, 1991). Furthermore, Wilson and Emmorey (1997a, 1998) observed no differences between native and non-native signers in any of their memory experiments (see chap. 7), and Krakow and Hanson (1985) reported similar performance on serial recall tasks with ASL for native signers and early learners. It appears that de-layed exposure to a first language may delay the development of effective rehearsal strategies during childhood, but such deficits are eventually overcome. Thus, unlike linguistic effects, the cognitive effects of late lan-guage exposure may not continue into adulthood.

Similarly, delayed language acquisition leads to a delay in the develop-ment of *theory of mind* in Deaf children, which appears to resolve by adult-hood (M. D. Clark, Schwanenflugel, Everhart, & Bartini, 1996; Russell, Hosie, Gray, Scott, & Hunter, 1998). Theory of mind broadly refers to the ability to attribute beliefs, intentions, and emotions to people (see Wellman, 1990, for a review). Theory of mind emerges around age 4 when the child exhibits an understanding that people possess minds capable of mental states such as knowing, believing, or wanting, and that people's be-havior can be predicted on the basis of such mental states, which may be at odds with the child's own beliefs or knowledge. Such understanding is of-ten assessed by a *false belief task* that has come to be known as the *Sally–Anne* test (Baron-Cohen, Leslie, & Frith, 1985). In this test, Sally (ei-ther a doll or a person) hides a marble (or other object) in a container, such as a basket, and then leaves. Anne then moves the marble to another location (e.g., a box or the experimenter's pocket). When Sally returns, the child is asked, "Where will Sally look for the marble?" If the child indi-cates the basket (the original location), he or she understands the concept of false belief and is said to have demonstrated theory of mind.

Many studies have shown that Deaf children from hearing families who have delayed exposure to sign language exhibit a marked delay in the de-velopment of theory of mind, but native signing children from Deaf fami-lies exhibit theory of mind at the same age as hearing children (Courtin, 2000; Courtin & Melot, 1998; J. G. de Villiers & P. A. de Villiers, 1999; Pe-terson & Siegal, 1995, 1999; Remmel, Bettger, & Weinberg, 1998; Russell et al., 1998; Steeds, Rowe, & Dowker, 1997). Some researchers have hy-pothesized that a lack of access to conversations about mental states leads to the delay in theory of mind development (Figueras-Costa & Harris, 2001; Peterson & Siegal, 1995; Rhys-Jones & Ellis, 2000). Other research suggests that the acquisition of syntax promotes theory of mind because the structural properties of language allow the child to symbolically repre-sent knowledge that conflicts with directly observable information (i.e., where the marble actually is vs. a representation of another's knowledge of the marble's location; Astington & Jenkins, 1999). More specifically, J. G. de Villiers and P. A. de Villiers (1999) hypothesized that the acquisition of sentential complements provides a means for representing false beliefs. Sentences containing complements, such as "Sally thinks that the marble is in the basket," allow a false belief to be embedded within a true report. Such constructions provide a format for representing false beliefs and may be acquired late when exposure to language is delayed or impeded by hearing loss. In fact, J. G. de Villiers and P. A. de Villiers (1999) found that oral deaf children's performance on false belief tasks was best predicted by their ability to produce sentential complements, and this ability was delayed compared to hearing children. Thus, delays in the development of theory of mind can be tied directly to delays in exposure and acquisition of language. However, the deficit is not permanent, and deaf adults and adolescents appear to exhibit theory of mind abilities (e.g., M. D. Clark et al., 1996; Marschark, Green, Hindmarsh, & Walker, 2000).

In sum, late acquisition of language results in *delays* within certain cognitive domains, but it does not appear to result in deficits that continue throughout adulthood. Studies that compare the cognitive abilities of Deaf adults who are native signers and those with delayed exposure to ASL find no clear differences between these groups (e.g., Parasnis, 1983). Such findings contrast sharply with the detrimental effects of delayed first language acquisition on language processing that continue to be observed in adulthood.

Nevertheless, these negative findings should not be taken as proof that a delay in language acquisition has *no* cognitive or social consequences in adulthood. The relevant research has simply not been done. For example, there are many reports that children with Deaf signing parents academically outperform children with hearing nonsigning parents, but whether poorer academic performance can be specifically tied to linguistic factors, social factors, or other factors has not been clearly determined. Poor academic achievement is likely to have cognitive and social consequences in adulthood. Furthermore, the poor language processing skills of adult late learners is likely to impact their intellectual and professional abilities as adults, but studies investigating this specific hypothesis have not yet been conducted.

THE EFFECTS OF LATE ACQUISITION ON THE NEURAL ORGANIZATION OF LANGUAGE

Critical period effects for language acquisition are hypothesized to arise at least in part from changes in brain maturation that occur throughout development. From birth to 2 years, there is a rapid rise in the number of synapses (neural connections) in the brain, followed by subsequent elimination ("pruning") of these connections, until cortical development finally stabilizes between 15 and 20 years of age (Huttenlocher, 1994). During development, cortical areas may compete for and take over neural sites that do not receive input from other sources, and specific input at specific times is necessary for the normal development of both sensory and motor cortical areas (e.g., Rauschecker, 1995). It is reasonable to suppose that neural substrates for language are also constrained by maturational principles of cortical development and that the timing and nature of linguistic input affects neural organization.

Neville and colleagues have investigated how variations in early linguistic input modify the neural organization for language in adulthood. These studies utilized event-related brain potentials (ERPs), which measure neural activity as a function of voltage fluctuations in the electroencephalogram (EEG; see chap. 9 for more details). Weber-Fox and Neville (1996) examined the effects of age of acquisition for a second language by studying hearing Chinese–English bilinguals who became immersed in English at different ages. Weber-Fox and Neville (1996) investigated (a) *semantic processing*, as measured by the nature of the neural response (the "N400") to semantic violations; and (b) *syntactic processing*, as measured by the neural response (the "syntactic positive shift," or SPS) to syntactic violations. An example sentence with a semantic violation is, "The boys heard Joe's orange about Africa," and an example sentence with a phrase structure (syntactic) violation is, "The boys heard Joe's about stories Africa." The size (amplitude) and the neural distribution of the N400 response to semantic anomolies were not affected by the timing of second language acquisition. In contrast, the SPS response to syntactic violations was absent within the expected time frame for late learners (those exposed after age 11). Other ERP responses to syntactic violations showed changes in the amplitude and distribution of the neural response that were directly related to increased age of acquisition. Specifically, increasing delay in age of acquisition was associated with more symmetrical (bilateral) neural activity.

In a second study, Weber-Fox and Neville (1999) reported similar effects for the neural subsystems for processing open and closed class words. Open class words include nouns, verbs, and adjectives, and primarily convey semantic information, whereas closed class words include determiners, pronouns, and conjunctions, and primarily convey structural or grammatical information within a sentence. The ERP response to open class words in monolingual native speakers is characterized by a negative component that peaks 350 msec after the onset of the word (N350) and is distributed over both the left and right hemispheres. In contrast, the ERP response to closed class words occurs earlier (280 msec post word onset) and is lateralized to the left hemisphere. Like the neural response to semantic anomalies, the neural response to open class words was unaffected by age of second language acquisition. However, delays in language acquisition (after age 7) were associated with an increase in the size (peak amplitude) and with a delay in the neural response to closed class words. The results of Weber-Fox and Neville indicate that late learners utilize altered neural systems for processing English syntax.

Similarly, Deaf adults who acquired ASL as a first language and learned English later as a second language also display alterations in the neural systems for processing English (Neville, 1995). Like the Chinese–English hearing bilinguals, Deaf bilinguals displayed neural responses to open class words that were indistinguishable from those observed in native English speakers. However, the Deaf subjects did not exhibit a left-hemisphere N280 ERP response to closed class grammatical words nor any asymmetries in the size of the neural response to these words. Interestingly, the few Deaf subjects who scored above 95% correct on a complex test of English grammar exhibited the N280 response to closed class words, which was strongly lateralized to the left hemisphere (Neville, 1991a). This finding supports the hypothesis that grammatical competence is a crucial factor in the stabilization of left-hemisphere specialization for language (see also chap. 9).

Finally, Neville et al. (1997) examined the ERP responses to open and closed class signs in ASL, comparing Deaf and hearing native signers and hearing late signers (hearing English speakers who acquired ASL after age 17). Closed class signs included pronouns, conjunctions and auxiliaries. Both native and late learners of ASL (like native and late learners of English) exhibited the same neural response (the N400) to semantic anomalies. In addition, Deaf and hearing native signers displayed differential neural responses to open and closed class signs that generally resembled the pattern observed for hearing subjects reading English words. However, the hearing late learners did not exhibit the differential neural response to open and closed class signs observed for the native signers. Specifically, hearing and Deaf native signers showed evidence of both left- and right-hemisphere activity for closed class signs, but the hearing late learners of ASL did not exhibit any right-hemisphere involvement. This finding suggests that early exposure to ASL results in the recruitment of the right hemisphere for ASL processing. This result is quite unusual because most research indicates more (not less) right-hemisphere involvement for nonnative late learners, at least when reading written text. In chapter 9, evidence is presented indicating that signed languages are lateralized to the left hemisphere to the same degree as spoken languages. However, the right hemisphere may be more involved in processing both signed and spoken language, compared to reading written language. Further studies may reveal that when hearing people listen to speech, rather than read text, the right hemisphere is more engaged for native speakers than for late learners. However, it may turn out that the right hemisphere plays a unique role in sign language processing and that early exposure to ASL engages right-hemisphere structures. In sum, the general results of Neville and colleagues (Neville et al., 1997; Weber-Fox & Neville, 1999) indicate that the neural systems that mediate grammatical processing (closed class items) are more vulnerable to alterations in the nature and timing of early language input than those linked to semantic processing (open class words or signs).

No study (that I know of) has investigated the neural systems underlying ASL processing in Deaf late learners of ASL. However, Wolff and Thatcher (1990) conducted an EEG study with a large group of Deaf signing children (aged 6 to 16 years) from various backgrounds. The EEG results indicated that Deaf children with Deaf parents displayed evidence of greater neural differentiation (an index of functional specialization) within the left hemisphere compared to Deaf children with hearing parents. That is, Deaf children with early exposure to a primary language exhibit an EEG response that suggests a greater degree of specialized function within the left hemisphere compared to Deaf children who have delayed linguistic exposure. However, the behavioral significance of these EEG findings requires further research.

To conclude, studies of Deaf children and adults have provided important insight into the nature of the critical period for language acquisition and into the effects of late language acquisition. The results indicate that the window of opportunity for language acquisition slowly closes during childhood and that late acquisition results in incomplete grammatical knowledge and inefficient language processing that do not improve during adulthood, even with years of experience. Late language acquisition does not appear to exert specific effects on cognitive abilities in adulthood, but it may lead to delays within certain cognitive domains during childhood. Finally, studies of home signers and Deaf children with nonnative input provide evidence for the human drive to find and create structure in language systems and suggest that this ability is most evident in children—just as we observed in chapter 1 with the emergence of Nicaraguan Sign Language.

SUGGESTIONS FOR FURTHER READING

Birdsong, D. (Ed.). (1999). *Second language acquisition and the critical period hypothesis.* Mahwah, NJ: Lawrence Erlbaum Associates.

The chapters in this book present a balanced discussion of the critical period hypothesis, with some chapters arguing in favor and some against the hypothesis. Although most of the chapters focus on second language acquisition, there is some discussion of the critical period for first language acquisition. In addition, the book provides in-depth discussions of the mechanisms that might be responsible for critical period effects.

Chapter 7

Memory for Sign Language: Implications for the Structure of Working Memory

A tremendous amount of past research has investigated how Deaf people remember verbal material (e.g., Conrad, 1970; Furth, 1966; O'Connor & Hermelin, 1973; see Marschark, 1993, for a review). However, the focus of this research was primarily on memory for spoken or written English, with little regard to whether Deaf people might encode information using a sign-based representation. In this chapter, we explore the possibility of sign-based memory and what it can tell us about the architecture and nature of human memory systems. Specifically, we examine *working memory*—the short-term memory system involved in the processing and temporary storage of information.

Models of working memory typically contain two major components, one used for verbal material, the other used for visuospatial material (e.g., Baddeley, 1986; Logie, 1995). Figure 7.1 provides a simplified representation of the model of working memory developed by Baddeley and colleagues (e.g., Baddeley, 1986; Baddeley & Hitch, 1974). Although other accounts have been proposed, the basic architecture of the Baddeley model is still the most parsimonious (see Wilson, 2001a), and it has provided a useful framework for investigating working memory for sign language.

The central executive component shown in Fig. 7.1 regulates information flow within working memory, and it is supplemented by two subcomponents, which Gathercole and Baddeley (1993) characterized as follows: "The *phonological loop* maintains verbally coded information, whereas the *visuo-spatial sketchpad* is involved in the short-term processing and maintenance of material which has a strong visual or spatial component" (p. 4). Given that sign languages are both "verbal" (i.e., linguistic) and

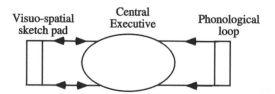

FIG. 7.1. A simplified representation of the Baddeley and Hitch (1974) working memory model. Illustration from A. Baddeley (1986), *Working Memory*. Copyright © 1986 by Alan Baddeley. Reprinted with permission of Oxford University Press.

visuospatial, they pose a challenge for this characterization of working memory. In a series of studies, Wilson and Emmorey took up this challenge by investigating how language modality might shape the architecture of working memory, as well as the nature of the representations that are maintained within working memory (Wilson & Emmorey, 1997a, 1997b, 1998, 2000, 2001).

The division between verbal and visuospatial encoding has been recognized at least since the classic memory studies of Brooks (1967, 1968) and Paivio (e.g., Paivio & Csapo, 1969), and appears to reflect a fundamental division in human cognition. One way to characterize the verbal domain of memory is in terms of language. Thus, printed or lip-read stimuli, although visual, fall primarily within the domain of verbal working memory (Baddeley, 1986; Campbell & Dodd, 1980). On the other hand, the verbal domain can be characterized by its grounding in the auditory and vocal–articulatory properties of speech. Thus, many differences between verbal and visuospatial working memory have been attributed to differences between audition and vision. For example, the visuospatial scratchpad easily maintains spatial information present in visual displays, whereas the phonological loop easily maintains temporal information present in sound. Because of this ambiguity, languages that are not auditory and vocal, namely signed languages, provide a unique window into the factors that shape the structure of working memory.

EARLY EVIDENCE FOR SIGN-BASED WORKING MEMORY

The first question to ask is whether there is any evidence that Deaf signers do in fact remember information in a sign-based form. Bellugi, Klima, and Siple (1975) were the first to find such evidence by studying the types of errors that Deaf people make when they have to remember lists of ASL signs. They found that signers made errors in serial recall based on the phonological properties, not the semantic properties, of the to-be-remembered signs. For example, the sign HORSE was misremembered as UNCLE, a phonologically similar sign sharing the same place of articulation, orientation, and hand configuration. Signers did not make intrusion errors based on the English translation of the ASL signs, even when they were asked to respond using written English (glosses of the ASL signs).

In addition, signers have poorer recall for lists of phonologically similar signs, compared to lists of dissimilar signs (Hanson, 1982; Klima & Bellugi, 1979; Wilson & Emmorey, 1997b; see Fig. 7.2 for examples of phonologically similar and dissimilar signs). This result is parallel to results found with speakers; that is, lists of similarly sounding words, for example, *mad, man, cat, cad,* yield poorer memory performance compared to lists of phonologically dissimilar words, for example, *pit, cow, day, bar,* (Baddeley, 1966; Conrad & Hull, 1964).

This pattern of memory performance is referred to as the *phonological similarity effect* and has been used to argue that information is coded in working memory in some type of phonological (or articulatory) code, rather than in a semantic code. Words or signs that are formationally similar are easily confused in memory, which results in poor immediate recall

PHONOLOGICALLY SIMILAR SIGNS

BOOK   BROOM   BREAD

PHONOLOGICALLY DISSIMILAR SIGNS

EGG   KEY   SOCKS

FIG. 7.2. Example signs used by Wilson and Emmorey (1997a) in a serial recall task. Phonologically similar signs share the same hand configuration, whereas dissimilar signs are produced with varied hand configurations.

performance. The semantic similarity between items stored in working memory appears to have little effect on memory performance for either English words (Baddeley & Levy, 1971) or ASL signs (Poizner, Bellugi, & Tweney, 1981). Furthermore, Poizner, Bellugi, and Tweney (1981) demonstrated that the iconicity of signs also had little effect on recall performance. Together these findings suggest that working memory for signs involves a phonological code based on the visual–gestural properties of signs, rather than a semantic code, an English-based translation (see also Krakow & Hanson, 1985), or a code based on the iconic properties of signs.

EVIDENCE FOR A VISUOSPATIAL PHONOLOGICAL LOOP

For hearing subjects, working memory for language has been argued to consist of a storage buffer that represents information in a phonological form, which decays with time. A process of articulatory rehearsal serves to refresh information within the store and thus maintain items within memory (Baddeley, 1986). The rehearsal process also serves to recode nonphonological inputs, such as written words or pictures, into a phonological form so that they can be held in the phonological store. Baddeley (1986) proposed that speech has direct access to the phonological store and can thus bypass articulatory recoding. This architecture is schematized in Fig. 7.3.

It is possible that this architecture is based on inherent properties of the auditory system and vocal articulatory mechanisms specific to speech. The architecture could arise because of the relationship of these modalities to language in our evolutionary history, or because auditory processing might lend itself to information maintenance in ways that visual processing does not. On either of these accounts, the separation of phonological working memory and visuospatial working memory is built into the system (see Fig. 7.1). An alternative possibility is that the phonological loop owes its structure, at least in part, to the impact of spoken language on the development of the individual. On this account, the phonological loop is shaped by a particular form of expertise.

To address this issue, Wilson and Emmorey (1997a, 1998, 2000, 2001) investigated whether the visuospatial domain of working memory is able to support a language-based rehearsal loop similar to the phonological loop. That is: Do ASL signers possess a visuospatial rehearsal loop that exhibits some or all of the structural properties of the speech-based phonological loop? Addressing this question allows us to investigate which properties of working memory subsystems are dependent on the subsystem's relationship to language, and which are more fundamental properties of the sensorimotor modalities involved.

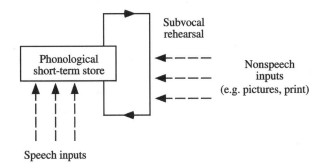

FIG. 7.3. Illustration of the phonological loop model of speech-based working memory (based on S. Gathercole and A. Baddeley, 1993, *Working Memory and Language*. Copyright © 1993. Reprinted by permission of Psychology Press Limited, Hove, UK).

Evidence for the architecture of the phonological loop model shown in Fig. 7.3 comes from a variety of experimental effects and their interactions: the *phonological similarity effect*, as just described, *the word length effect*, and the *articulatory suppression effect*. The word length effect refers to the finding that lists of short words, for example, *sum, wit, hate*, yield better memory performance than lists of long words, for example, *opportunity, university, aluminum* (Baddeley, Thomson, & Buchanan, 1975). The effect appears to be due to word duration (i.e., the time it takes to articulate each word) rather than to the number of syllables, phonemes, or morphemes (Baddeley, 1986). The articulatory suppression effect refers to the finding that memory span is reduced when subjects must perform irrelevant mouth movements, such as repeating "ta, ta, ta," during presentation of a list of words to be remembered (Murray, 1968). The effect does not appear to be due to a general distraction or attention load effect, but is instead a specific form of interference in the verbal domain (e.g., J. D. Smith, Reisberg, & Wilson, 1992). The decrement in memory span found with articulatory suppression suggests that some type of *articulatory* rehearsal is involved in working memory for speech. The phonological similarity effect and the word length effect both indicate that the surface form of language, with its phonological and articulatory properties, is important to the verbal component of working memory.

However, it is the interaction of these various effects that reveals the structure of speech-based working memory. For example, articulatory suppression and the phonological similarity effect interact in different ways depending on how stimuli are presented. When English words are presented auditorily, the phonological similarity effect is not affected by articulatory suppression. However, when stimuli are presented visually as print or pictures, the phonological similarity effect is eliminated under articulatory suppression (Baddeley, Lewis, & Vallar, 1984; Murray, 1968). This pattern indicates that an articulatory mechanism is required to translate visual materials into a phonological code and that the phonological similarity effect is a product of the phonological store to which spoken materials have direct access. In contrast, the word length effect is abolished under suppression, regardless of whether words are presented auditorily or visually (Baddeley et al., 1984). This result suggests that the word length effect arises from the articulatory rehearsal processes itself, unlike the phonological similarity effect, which is tied to the phonological store.

Wilson and Emmorey (1997a) examined these effects in ASL using an immediate serial recall task. First, we replicated the phonological similarity effect observed by other researchers: Deaf signers exhibited poorer recall for lists of phonologically similar signs than dissimilar signs (see Fig. 7.2). In addition, we found that producing meaningless movements of the hands during presentation yielded poorer memory performance. This demonstrates a manual analogue to the articulatory suppression effect, and suggests an articulatory rehearsal mechanism for sign. Crucially, the manual suppression effect did not interact with the phonological similarity effect, indicating that the two effects are independent, arising from separate components of working memory.

We next examined these effects for stimuli that had to be recoded in order to be stored in a sign-based form. Deaf signers were presented with nameable pictures and asked for the ASL sign for each picture at the time of recall. The results paralleled those with hearing subjects. That is, we found an ASL phonological similarity effect when there was no hand motion (no suppression) during encoding, but the effect disappeared under suppression. Thus, an articulatory process is required to translate materials into an ASL code for working memory. When this process is removed through competing movements of the hands, then evidence for sign-based memory disappears. This pattern of results supports a working memory system for sign language that includes a phonological buffer and an articulatory rehearsal loop.

Further evidence for this architecture stems from the finding of a sign length effect, parallel to the word length effect (Wilson & Emmorey, 1998). We found that Deaf signers exhibited poorer memory for lists of long signs (e.g., PIANO, BICYCLE, CROSS, LANGUAGE) compared to lists of matched short signs (e.g., TYPEWRITER, MILK, CHURCH, LICENSE). Long signs contained circular or path movements, whereas short signs involved short repeated movements. Unlike the ASL phonological similarity effect, the sign length effect was eliminated under articulatory suppression, suggesting that the length effect is a direct consequence of the articulatory rehearsal process, which is unavailable under suppression.

The fact that a phonological loop exists for a visuospatial language suggests that the architecture of working memory is not fixed but responds flexibly to experience with either visual or auditory linguistic information during development. Wilson and Emmorey (1997b) suggested that the phonological loop should be conceived of as a configuration of mechanisms that arise in response to appropriate linguistic input—regardless of the modality of that input. The data presented thus far indicate that the structural properties of working memory are the same for both signed and spoken languages and are unaffected by the many motoric and perceptual distinctions between these two language types. Further, the data suggest that linguistic working memory is organized by abstract principles of storage and rehearsal that are not bound to or governed by a particular modality.

WORKING MEMORY CAPACITY: EFFECTS ON MEMORY SPAN FOR SIGN AND SPEECH

The capacity for immediate recall storage for speech-based material is limited by the duration of the articulatory loop, which is estimated to be approximately two seconds and appears to be a universal constant (Baddeley & Hitch, 1974; Baddeley et al., 1984). Furthermore, because speech-based working memory appears to involve some type of subvocal rehearsal, the speed at which people articulate can influence their rate of rehearsal and thus their memory performance, that is, faster articulators exhibit better memory performance (Baddeley, 1986). Is the limit on rehearsal capacity within working memory truly universal, or is it based on the properties of speech? If the articulatory loop for sign has the same limits as speech, there should be a correlation between rate of articulation and number of items recalled correctly. In addition, if immediate recall capacity is a universal constant, which holds for both signed and spoken languages, the number of signs remembered should be related to the number of signs that can be articulated within two seconds.

In fact, Marschark (1996) found a relation between sign articulation rate and memory performance, with faster signers exhibiting better memory performance for serial recall of ASL digits. Furthermore, Marschark (1996) found that the articulatory loop was about two seconds in duration for both sign-based rehearsal and speech-based rehearsal (comparing Deaf signers and hearing speakers on serial recall performance in ASL and spoken English, respectively). Thus, the limited capacity of the articulatory loop does not derive specifically from the limitations of oral articulation or from acoustic properties of speech.

However, this limited capacity results in a difference in memory span for sign and speech. Many studies have found that Deaf signers exhibit a shorter working memory span for signs compared to the working memory span exhibited by hearing subjects for words (e.g., Klima & Bellugi, 1979; Krakow & Hanson, 1985; Wilson and Emmorey 1997b). This difference in memory span may arise simply because signs take longer to articulate than words (see chap. 4). Ellis and Hennelley (1980) and Naveh-Benjamin and Ayres (1986) found that digit span for speakers of different languages is affected by the duration of the words for numbers in their language. That is, speakers of languages with long number words (e.g., Welsh) have shorter digit spans than speakers of languages with short number words (e.g., Chinese). Thus, the motoric requirements of sign language critically impact working memory capacity, resulting in shorter memory span for signs. These facts may also explain in part the rarity of linear prefixation and suffixation in sign languages and the failure of children to acquire Manually Coded English (MCE; see chap. 4 for further discussion). Both MCE and linear affixation may strain working memory capacity by creating sign forms that take a long time to articulate.

EFFECTS OF THE VISUOSPATIAL MODALITY
ON SIGN-BASED WORKING MEMORY

Although the architecture of working memory for sign and for speech is generally parallel, there are some important variations in working memory that appear to be due to distinct processing constraints and capacities of vision and audition. Specifically, spatiotemporal coding is a domain in which audition and vision differ, with audition showing relative superiority in temporal coding (e.g., Lechelt, 1975) and vision showing relative superiority in spatial coding (e.g., Kubovy, 1988). A recent experiment by Wilson and Emmorey (2001) suggested that working memory for ASL may involve a type of spatial coding that is unavailable for spoken language. We were led to this hypothesis by noticing that during serial recall, some Deaf signers spontaneously responded by producing each sign at a separate spatial location. This type of response was not merely an artifact or stylistic preference, but instead appeared to play a functional role—for example, the Deaf signers would refer back to a location to make corrections. This response pattern suggests that introducing a spatial component into the memory representation may assist performance, and that some people spontaneously discovered a strategy of coding in this manner. Although the strategy of memorizing items by localizing them in space is quite old (e.g., the method of loci; see Yates, 1966), spatial coding for order does not appear to be available for speech-based *working* memory. When asked to immediately recall spoken words (in serial order),

English speakers do not benefit from an arbitrary association between words and locations in space (Li & Lewandowsky, 1995).

To investigate the hypothesis that sign-based working memory can co-opt signing space as an additional resource for coding serial order, Wilson and Emmorey (2001) presented Deaf signers with a serial recall task comparing memory for signs with a movable place of articulation (neutral space signs like MILK, LIBRARY, BATHROOM, ONE-DOLLAR) to signs with a fixed place of articulation on the body (body-anchored signs like BAR, LEMON, TWINS, CANDY). Figure 7.4 provides an example of the signs used in this experiment. We also examined whether presenting signs at varied locations on the videoscreen (i.e., in the four quadrants) aided memory compared to presenting all signs to be remembered in the center of the screen. We hypothesized that Deaf signers would be able to use spatial coding only for the signs with a movable place of articulation because only these signs could be mentally "rehearsed" in diverse spatial locations, and also that presenting stimuli at varied locations on the videoscreen might cue them to use a spatial coding strategy.

The results supported one aspect of this hypothesis: Signs with a neutral space place of articulation were remembered more accurately than signs with a body-anchored place of articulation. In addition, several sign-

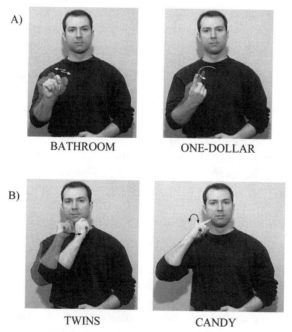

A)

BATHROOM   ONE-DOLLAR

B)

TWINS   CANDY

FIG. 7.4.   Illustration of A) signs with a movable place of articulation (neutral space signs) and B) signs with a fixed place of articulation on the body.

ers were observed to articulate the neutral space signs in a sequence of distinct spatial locations that mirrored the videoscreen locations (i.e., upper left, right; lower left, right quadrants of space). These results demonstrate that spatial coding can be used as a memory device over and above mere repetition of the to-be-remembered signs. However, we found that when signs were presented at distinct locations on the videoscreen serial recall was not improved compared to central presentation. This finding suggests that when the spatial information in the stimulus is nonlinguistic (i.e., the locations on the videoscreen are not part of ASL phonology), signers do not incorporate the spatial information into their rehearsal. However, another possible explanation is that signers spontaneously engage in a spatial rehearsal strategy whenever the structure of the signs allows it, and hence the "suggestion" of a spatial strategy provided by the videoscreen locations produces no increase in use of this strategy. In either case, the difference between the body-anchored and the neutral space signs seems to indicate that performance is enhanced when a spatial rehearsal strategy is available. Because the spatial coding that appears to be used by ASL signers is unavailable to speech-based working memory, these findings suggest that language modality can alter the nature of representations maintained within working memory.

Wilson et al. (1997) presented further support for the hypothesis that ASL working memory involves some type of spatial coding for serial order. Wilson et al. (1997) examined Deaf and hearing children's ability to recall lists of digits (signed or spoken) in either forward or backward order. Many studies have shown that recalling a list of auditory words in reverse order is more difficult than recalling a list in the order presented, suggesting a unidirectional form of coding, much as time is unidirectional. However, spatial coding does not entail a necessary directionality. Thus, if sign-based working memory can capture serial order in a spatial form rather than a temporal form, there may be little difference between backward and forward recall. This is exactly the result observed by both Wilson et al. (1997) for children and Mayberry and Eichen (1991) for adults. Deaf children who were native ASL signers performed equally well on forward and backward recall of signed numbers, exhibiting essentially no cost for the requirement to reverse the order of stimulus input. In contrast, hearing children were substantially worse on backward than forward recall—the standard finding for spoken language materials. Furthermore, Mayberry and Eichen (1991) found that adult native, early, and late learners all did not differ on forward and backward ASL digit span.

These data suggest that sign-based rehearsal mechanisms are not entirely parallel to speech-based mechanisms in working memory (Wilson et al., 1997). The speech loop appears to be specialized for exact repetition of a sequence of items in the order given, an attribute that may be due to the temporal processing abilities of audition; whereas the sign loop appears to be less proficient at exact retention but more flexible with respect to ordering, an attribute that may be due to the spatial processing abilities of vision. The form of representation in the sign loop that makes this possible need not be literally visual imagery—it need only be a form of representation that retains at least some of the informational properties of the visual system. The results of these studies point to a domain (serial order coding) in which the processing requirements of a particular sensory modality place constraints on the structure of working memory for a language within that modality (see also Hanson, 1982, for a discussion of serial order coding in sign vs. speech).

Thus far, we have been primarily concerned with the "rehearsal" aspect of ASL working memory—effects based generally on articulatory processes. Up to this point, however, there has been little evidence concerning the nature of the phonological store. In particular, it has been unclear whether there is any involvement of visual coding, as opposed to a more abstract phonological code. Processing differences between audition and vision—for example, the much greater duration of sensory storage for audition than for vision, and the apparent superiority of audition for time-based coding—suggest that working memory for signs may not make use of any perceptually based representation.

Wilson and Emmorey (2000) investigated this possibility by looking for an *irrelevant sign effect* parallel to the *irrelevant speech effect*. This effect refers to reduced memory performance when subjects are presented with meaningless speech or other structured auditory input irrelevant to the memory task (e.g., Baddeley, 1986; Jones & Macken, 1993). We investigated whether memory for signs would be disrupted by presentation of meaningless sign forms or other structured visual input. The question here is whether there is a single amodal input store for working memory (as proposed by Jones, Beaman, & Macken, 1996) or whether the input store is modality specific and sensitive only to disruption within the relevant modality.

To investigate this question, we presented Deaf signers and hearing nonsigners with an immediate serial recall task. Deaf subjects were presented with ASL signs on videotape, and hearing subjects were presented with printed English words (glosses of the ASL signs) also on videotape. We tested two types of irrelevant visual material for both groups. The first consisted of pseudosigns, which are phonologically possible but nonoccurring ASL signs (see Fig. 4.3 in chap. 4), and the second consisted of moving nonnameable jagged shapes ("Atteneave" figures; from Atteneave, 1957). The irrelevant visual material was presented during a retention interval (after subjects had seen the to-be-remembered list of words or signs but before they responded). For the baseline condition, each group watched a uniform grey screen alternating with dark grey during the retention interval.

The results indicated that irrelevant visual material only disrupted memory for Deaf signers viewing ASL signs and not for hearing people reading English words. Based on the body of evidence on speech-based working memory, hearing people almost certainly translated the printed words into phonological or quasiauditory form for the purposes of rehearsal. Once in this recast form, hearing people were not vulnerable to disruption from incoming visual material. In contrast, when Deaf signers were required to watch either pseudosigns or moving shapes while trying to retain a list of ASL signs, they performed quite poorly compared to the baseline grey-field condition. This finding suggests some type of visual coding of ASL signs within working memory.

More generally, this pattern of results argues for modality specific representations within working memory, because visual and auditory input each have selective disruptive effects on language based in the relevant modality. However, we need to clarify what is meant by *modality specific* because irrelevant visual input produced significant disruption only for the retention of ASL signs, and not for printed words. Wilson and Emmorey (2000) therefore suggested that the disruption to memory is specific, not to the modality of the stimulus itself, but to the modality of the primary, expressive form of the language whose phonological code will be used for memory maintenance.

A MODALITY EFFECT FOR SIGN LANGUAGE?
IMPLICATIONS FOR MODELS OF WORKING
MEMORY

The *modality effect* refers to the finding that hearing people almost always remember the last word on a list of spoken words (the *recency effect*), but this effect is much weaker for visually presented word lists (Conrad & Hull, 1968). Crowder and Morton (1969) interpreted the modality effect in serial recall as a reflection of an auditory input buffer (the "precategorical acoustic store" or PAS). The basic idea is that as each word in a list is heard, it enters an acoustic store and "overwrites" any existing acoustic traces in the store. Auditory recency is explained as a recall advantage for the remaining item in the acoustic store. An auditory input buffer has also been used to explain the *suffix effect*: the finding that the recency effect is eliminated or greatly reduced if the list of to-be-remembered items is immediately followed by a single word that subjects are instructed to ignore (Crowder, 1967); for example, the word "end" occurs at the end of each list, but subjects are instructed not to report this word. Because access to the acoustic input buffer is hypothesized to be obligatory, the "suffix" word automatically overwrites traces of the final list item that would normally give rise to the recency effect. If these effects are due solely to an auditory input buffer, we should not find them with sign language.

However, Shand (1980) observed a recency advantage for Deaf native signers for ordered recall of ASL signs (see also Bellugi et al., 1975), but not for printed English words. That is, even though both lists were visual, signers more easily recalled the last few signs on the ASL lists, but did not show this advantage for the last few English words on the written lists. Furthermore, Shand and Klima (1981) found a suffix effect when an ASL sign was added to a list of signs and when a line drawing of an ASL sign was added to a list of line drawings of signs. Krakow and Hanson (1985) also observed a strong recency effect for lists of ASL signs and lists of finger-spelled words, but not for lists of written English words. These findings argue against the "modality" explanation of the recency and suffix effects. That is, the ease of recall for the last item(s) on a spoken list and the elimination of this advantage by adding redundant word to the list are facts that are not best explained by the properties of an auditory input buffer.

Instead, some researchers have attributed these effects to an advantage in remembering changing-state (or dynamic) information over remembering static information (Campbell & Dodd, 1980; Krakow & Hanson, 1985). Such an hypothesis would explain Campbell and Dodd's (1980) finding that silent lip-read stimuli (mouthed English words), although visual, produce both recency and suffix effects. However, the changing-state hypothesis does not account for Shand and Klima's (1981) finding that line drawings (static images) of ASL signs also give rise to these effects.

Therefore, Shand and Klima (1981) proposed that the explanation for these various effects lies in the distinction between primary and derived language codes. Written English is "derived" in the sense that it is not naturally acquired (it must be taught), and there is a relatively abstract relation between orthography and sound. In contrast, spoken language is a primary linguistic code, and understanding speech is directly affected by visual perception of articulatory gestures (e.g., the "McGurk" effect; McDonald & McGurk, 1978), indicating that lip reading is integral to speech perception (see also Massaro, 1998). Like speech, sign language is also a primary language code, and static drawings of signs, although not natural language input, transparently represent actual signs—only the movement of the sign is missing from the representation. It may be that stimuli presented in a primary language code, whether auditory or visual, have direct and immediate access to a storage buffer within working memory.[1]

---

[1]Krakow and Hanson (1985) argued against the primary language hypothesis because they found that fingerspelled words gave rise to a strong recency effect, compared to printed words. However, fingerspelling can be considered part of a primary language (ASL) because fingerspelled words are included in the ASL lexicon (see chap. 2), are acquired in early childhood without instruction (see chap. 5), and although sentences are not naturally fingerspelled, word lists may be.

THE ARCHITECTURE OF WORKING MEMORY FOR
SIGN LANGUAGE: SUMMARY AND CONCLUSIONS

Taken together, the findings discussed in this chapter indicate that both the universal structural properties of language and the specific processing constraints of sensory modality interact to determine the architecture of working memory. The pattern of data for memory for signs parallels that of memory for *speech*, and not memory for *print*. Thus, despite shared modality between sign and print, it appears that properties common to speech and sign are critical in determining the structure of sign-based working memory. The pattern of results indicates that the basic configuration of components and how they interact within working memory is the same for speech and sign, as illustrated in Fig. 7.5. The striking similarities observed between the sign-based and speech-based mechanisms suggest that properties of language such as dynamic, temporally structured, sensory input and a close relationship between receptive and productive forms are sufficient to generate a rehearsal mechanism in working memory.

The pattern of results reviewed in this chapter also reveals that the visual–gestural nature of sign language plays a critical role in the representation of signed material within working memory. Sign-based and speech-based working memory each take advantage of the distinctive capacities of their respective sensory modalities. Audition appears to be particularly well suited for retaining information about sequences of stimuli over time, whereas vision excels at processing stimuli distinguished by spatial location. Similarly, speech-based working memory appears to excel at using time to code serial order, whereas sign-based working memory is able to use space to code serial order. In addition, the distinct articulatory properties of sign and speech lead to differences in memory span, apparently due to a universal limit on the articulatory loop.

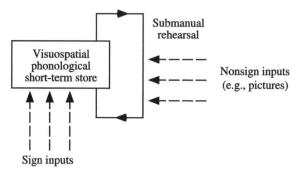

FIG. 7.5.   Illustration of the phonological loop model of sign-based working memory, based on Wilson and Emmorey (1997b).

Finally, the model depicted in Fig. 7.5 has implications for our understanding of how working memory develops. The structure of the phonological loop appears not to be predetermined by the evolutionary relationship between language and the auditory/vocal modality. Instead it appears to develop in response to language experience, regardless of sensorimotor modality.

SUGGESTIONS FOR FURTHER READING

Gathercole, S. (Ed.). (1996). *Models of short-term memory*. Hove, UK: Psychology Press.

The chapters in this volume represent a broad perspective on working memory, drawing on empirical data from laboratory studies, computational modeling, and neuropsychological evidence. The chapter by Baddeley ("The Concept of Working Memory") is particularly relevant to the research described within this chapter.

Marschark, M. (1993). *Psychological development of deaf children*. New York: Oxford University Press.

Chapter 8 ("Short-Term Memory: Development of Memory Codes," pp. 150–166) reviews much of the early research on working memory in Deaf children, which focused primarily on memory coding for written English and on memory for nonverbal stimuli.

The Impact of Sign Language Use on Visuospatial Cognition

Online comprehension of sign language involves many visuospatial processes, such as recognition of hand configuration, motion discrimination, identification of facial expressions, and recognition of linguistically relevant spatial contrasts (see chap. 4). Production of sign language also involves visuospatial processes linked to motor processes, for example, production of distinct motion patterns, memory for spatial locations, and integration of mental images with signing space. In this chapter, we review several studies that suggest the habitual use of a signed language has an impact on nonlinguistic aspects of spatial cognition.[1]

Many studies have investigated the visuospatial skills of deaf people; however, most of these studies are not applicable to the question addressed here because the language background of subjects was not examined. Attention to language background is critical because as we saw in chapter 6, deaf people have varying degrees of exposure to ASL, and some may never learn to sign. Thus, only those studies are reviewed that selected subjects for language background (studying fluent ASL signers), and those studies that addressed the question of how experience with sign language might affect nonlinguistic visuospatial abilities.

We examine three domains of visuospatial cognition: motion processing, face processing, and mental imagery. Within each of these domains, there is strong evidence that experience with sign language enhances specific cognitive processes. These findings have important implications for

---

[1]An earlier version of this chapter appeared in Emmorey (1998).

the relationship between language and thought and for cognitive modularity, which are discussed at the end of the chapter.

MOTION PROCESSING

Interpreting movement is critical to online comprehension of sign language. For example, as discussed in chapter 4, movement identification coincides with lexical identification—when the movement of a sign is recognized, the sign itself is also identified. Variations in movement patterns signal differences in aspect and agreement morphology, and movement has been identified as central to identifying syllables in sign (see chap. 2). Given the significant role of movement in conveying phonological, morphological, and lexical contrasts in ASL, there is reason to expect that experience with processing motion within the linguistic domain might influence nonlinguistic motion processing. The studies reviewed here all find an influence of sign language use on different aspects of motion processing: motion detection, motion categorization, and the perception of apparent motion.

Detection of Motion in Peripheral Vision

Neville and Lawson (1987a, 1987b, 1987c) conducted a series of experiments that investigated the ability of Deaf and hearing subjects to detect the direction of motion in the periphery of vision. Identification of movement in the periphery is important for sign perception because signers look at the face, rather than track the hands, when they are conversing or watching a sign narrative (Siple, 1978). Thus, lexical identification depends on peripheral vision when signs are produced away from the face. Identification of motion direction appears to be a selective function of peripheral vision (Bonnet, 1977).

Neville and Lawson used event-related brain potentials (ERPs) to study the neural activity associated with motion perception for Deaf and hearing subjects. The subjects' task was to detect the direction of motion of a small, white square presented in either the left or right visual field (18° lateral of central fixation). The motion was very quick and could occur in eight possible directions. The following subject groups were studied: native Deaf signers (Deaf subjects exposed to ASL from birth by their Deaf parents), hearing native signers (hearing subjects with Deaf parents exposed to ASL from birth), and hearing nonsigners (hearing subjects with no knowledge of a signed language).

Deaf signers were significantly faster than hearing nonsigners in detecting the direction of motion of the square. However, this enhanced detection ability appears to be an effect of auditory deprivation rather than an effect of the use of sign language because Deaf native signers were also much faster than hearing native signers, who performed similarly to hearing nonsigners. Several other studies have found that Deaf subjects are able to detect information in the periphery of vision much more quickly than hearing subjects (Loke & Song, 1991; Parasnis & Samar, 1985; Reynolds, 1993). It is unclear whether Deaf subjects simply have enhanced perceptual sensitivity within peripheral vision or whether they are more efficient at allocating attention to the periphery. Some evidence that auditory deprivation can alter visual attention processes comes from a study by Stivalet, Moreno, Richard, Barraud, and Raphel (1998) who found that Deaf subjects process some information (letter arrays) presented in central vision in parallel with no attentional shifts, whereas hearing subjects had to shift attention and serially search the array. Similarly, Smith, Quittner, Osberger, and Miyamoto (1998) found that lack of auditory input may lead to less selective (and perhaps more distributed) visual attention in deaf children. Stivalet et al. (1998), along with Neville (1990), argued that more efficient visual processing is due to intermodal sensory compensation, that is, the increased allocation of visual attention may arise from neural reorganization caused by auditory deprivation from birth. Recent functional Magnetic Resonance Imaging (fMRI) evidence from Bavelier et al. (2000) supports this hypothesis: when attention was required, deaf subjects showed greater activation in movement sensitive cortical areas, middle temporal area (MT) and middle superior temporal area (MST), along with the recruitment of additional cortical areas (posterior parietal cortex; see chap. 9 for a description of brain imaging with fMRI). Furthermore, Bavelier, Tomann, Brozinsky, Mitchell, Neville, and Lui (2001) report that enhanced neural activation in MT/MST when perceiving movement in the periphery occurred only for deaf signers and was not found for hearing native signers, suggesting that auditory deprivation leads to enhanced attention to motion in the visual periphery (deaf individuals may rely extensively on attention to and visual monitoring of their peripersonal space).

In the Neville and Lawson (1987c) study, the effect of sign language use was not found in absolute performance level, but rather in the pattern of responses within the left and right visual fields. Both Deaf and hearing ASL signers were more accurate in detecting motion in the right visual field (left hemisphere) compared to hearing nonsigners. In addition, the electrophysiological results showed that both groups of signers showed increased left hemisphere activation during the motion detection task compared to hearing nonsigners. Bosworth and Dobkins (1999) replicated these results using a motion discrimination task that eliminated the confound between position and motion cues in the task used by Neville and

Lawson. They found that hearing and Deaf groups did not differ in absolute performance (motion discrimination thresholds), but Deaf subjects were much faster at discriminating motion direction when the stimuli were first presented to the left hemisphere; in contrast, hearing subjects showed a slight advantage for *right* hemisphere processing of motion. Data from Finney and Dobkins (2001) indicated that the left-hemisphere advantage for discriminating motion direction did not generalize to contrast sensitivity to moving stimuli. That is, Deaf and hearing subjects did not exhibit behavioral or laterality differences in the amount of contrast required to see a moving black/white grating against a grey background. Finally, the neuroimaging data from Bavelier et al. (2000) and Bavelier et al. (2001) also supports a greater role of the left hemisphere in processing motion in peripheral vision for Deaf and hearing signers. They report greater activation in area MT (a motion sensitive neural structure) in the left hemisphere for ASL signers when they were attending to motion in the periphery (activation tended to be greater in the right hemisphere for hearing nonsigners).

Neville (1991b) hypothesized that the increased role of the left hemisphere may arise from the temporal coincidence of motion perception and the acquisition of ASL. That is, the acquisition of ASL requires the child to make linguistically significant distinctions based on movement. If the left hemisphere plays a greater role in acquiring ASL, the left hemisphere may come to mediate the perception of temporal sequences of nonlanguage material as well as linguistically relevant motion. These results suggest that the acquisition of a signed language can alter the brain areas responsible for certain aspects of (nonlinguistic) motion perception.

Perceptual Categorization of Motion

Just as the acquisition of a particular spoken language can alter the nature of perceptual categorization of speech sounds, the acquisition of a signed language may alter the perceptual categorization of motion (and perhaps hand configuration; see the discussion of categorical perception in chap. 4). As discussed in chapter 5, experience with a particular spoken language causes a perceptual reorganization that fine-tunes the ability to perceive linguistically relevant distinctions. For example, Swedish and American infants develop distinct prototypes for the vowel categories of their native language, and both infants and adults categorize the vowel sounds of their native language differently from the vowel sounds of a foreign language (Kuhl, 1993). Similarly, Poizner and colleagues discovered that experience with sign language can influence the perceptual categorization of linguistic movements (Poizner, 1981, 1983; Poizner et al., 1989).

In Poizner's experiments, Deaf native signers and hearing nonsigners were asked to make triadic comparisons of motion displays, deciding which two of three movements were most similar. Johansson's (1973) technique for presenting biological motion as patterns of moving lights was used to create the motion displays. A signer was filmed in a darkened room with lights attached to the head, shoulder, joints of the arm, and the index fingertip. Thus, subjects did not see the signer's face or hand configuration. Motion similarity judgments were based on the pattern of the movement alone. Poizner (1981, 1983) found that Deaf and hearing subjects differed in their motion similarity judgments. Using multidimensional scaling techniques, Poizner found that certain linguistically relevant dimensions of movement were more salient for native ASL signers compared to hearing subjects with no knowledge of ASL. In particular, movement repetition and cyclicity were much more salient for the Deaf signers, and repetition and cyclicity are both phonologically distinctive in ASL. These results suggest that the acquisition of ASL can modify the perceptual categorization of linguistically relevant motion. ASL signers categorize such motion patterns differently than nonsigners for whom the patterns carry no linguistic information. However, the extent to which differences in motion categorization are due to differences in motion perception itself versus the cognitive process of categorization has yet to be determined.

Poizner et al. (1989) also found that the nature of motion categorization may depend on the particular sign language acquired, just as the categorization of speech sounds depends on the particular spoken language acquired. Using the same motion similarity judgment task, Poizner et al. (1989) found that Deaf subjects from Hong Kong who acquired Chinese Sign Language as their first language exhibited a slightly different pattern of motion salience compared to native ASL signers. Both ASL and CSL signers found motion repetition to be particularly salient—in contrast to both the hearing English and hearing Chinese speakers. Repetition is phonologically significant for CSL, as it is for ASL (van Hoek, Bellugi, & Fok, 1986). However, the CSL signers weighted the "arcness" of motion as less salient than did the ASL signers. A straight versus arced movement is phonologically distinctive in ASL, but Poizner et al. (1989) speculated that arcness may not be distinctive in CSL. However, Yau (1987) and van Hoek et al. (1986) provided evidence that CSL distinguishes between several movement paths on the basis of arcness (e.g., distinguishing circular from straight paths). It is possible that arcness of motion is a more prevalent lexical contrast in ASL than in CSL, but until more comparative linguistic analysis is done, the interpretation of the differential sensitivity of ASL and CSL signers to this parameter of motion must remain open.

These studies indicate that acquisition of a signed language can alter the categorization of linguistically relevant movement. The observed perceptual fine-tuning might be limited to motion that is clearly linguistic because these experiments presented the movements of actual signs rather than nonlinguistic motion. Further, ASL signers are able to recognize such dynamic point light displays as signs (Poizner, Bellugi, & Lutes-Driscoll, 1981).

However, results from Klima, Tzeng, Fok, Bellugi, and Corina (1996) and Bettger (1992) suggested that sign language acquisition can affect the categorization of movement that is not linguistic, that is, not derived from signs. Klima et al. (1996) presented dynamic point light displays of Chinese pseudocharacters to Deaf and hearing Americans (see Fig. 8.1). The subjects' task was to draw the Chinese character that had been "written in the air." Because neither group was familiar with Chinese, no linguistic knowledge could be used to determine the underlying stroke pattern. Thus, the movement patterns were nonlinguistic for these subjects. Klima et al. found that the Deaf ASL signers were significantly better at segmenting the continuous light image into discrete movement strokes. Deaf signers were better able to distinguish between transition and stroke components of the movement and were less likely to include transitional movements in their drawings compared to the hearing subjects.

Klima et al. (1996) hypothesized that this enhanced ability to analyze movement may arise from the processing requirements of ASL. Signers must separate out phonologically significant and transitional movement online during sign perception. This linguistic processing skill may make signers more sensitive to the distinction between purposeful movement and transition. Bettger (1992) provided support for this hypothesis. Using the same experimental paradigm, Bettger found that hearing native ASL signers were also better able to segment the movement pattern into strokes and transitions compared to hearing nonsigners, suggesting that this skill is linked to language experience rather than to deafness.

In summary, the acquisition of a signed language can influence how motion is categorized. Signers not only categorize linguistic motion differently than nonsigners, but they may also have a heightened sensitivity to certain perceptual qualities of nonlinguistic motion.

Perception of Apparent Motion

Apparent motion is the perception of a single moving object when a static object occurs at one location, followed rapidly by a static object at another location. The object does not actually move, but it is perceived as moving from one location to another. For example, apparent motion accounts for the perception of Christmas lights "moving" along a string. In reality, each light bulb simply blinks on and off—there is no real motion. It turns out that object identity usually does not alter how we perceive apparent motion. In general, we perceive objects taking the shortest path between

Point Light Motion

Target Structure

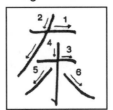

Hearing American Adults

Deaf American Adults

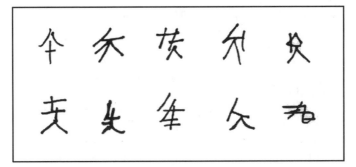

FIG. 8.1. Example of a point light motion stimulus, its target structure, and representative drawings from Deaf ASL signers and hearing nonsigners. Adapted from Klima et al. (1996) with permission. Illustration copyright © Ursula Bellugi, The Salk Institute.

two locations, even when such a path is not plausible in the real world (e.g., a solid object would have to pass through another solid object to get to the second location).

However, Shiffrar and colleagues found object identity does affect how we perceive the path of motion when the object is a human figure (Chatterjee, Freyd, & Shiffrar, 1996; Shiffrar & Freyd, 1993). Shiffrar and Freyd (1990) found that apparent motion for the human body sometimes appears to take a longer, indirect path, when the shortest path would require it to pass through the body. For example, if the hand is shown first in front of the torso and then behind the torso, the shortest path would require it to go through the body. In fact, subjects report seeing this direct path at fast presentation rates (e.g., 150 msec between presentation of the two pictures). However, as presentation rate is slowed, subjects increasingly report seeing the longer, but physically possible path, in which the hand moves around the body.

When the two objects are not part of the human body, subjects continue to see one object moving through another at longer presentation rates, despite the physical impossibility of such motion. Thus, the visual system appears to utilize constraints on the perception of motion that are specific to biological motion. Furthermore, sensitivity to constraints on biological motion appears in young infants, suggesting that knowledge about the properties of biological motion may be innate (Bertenthal, 1993; Bertenthal, Proffitt, Kramer, & Spetner, 1987). However, it is possible that infants have sufficient visual exposure to the human body during the first few months of life to alter the sensitivity of the visual system for biological motion.

Recently, Wilson (2001b) asked the following question: If the constraints on motion perception for the human body are acquired through experience, could experience with a rule-governed motion system (such as sign language) create additional constraints on the perception of biological motion? Wilson presented Deaf and hearing subjects with apparent motion stimuli derived from ASL signs. Subjects were presented with the beginning and endpoints of a sign—they were not shown the actual motion of the sign. Two sets of signs were used: those that have an arc motion between two locations (e.g., BRIDGE, IMPROVE, MILLION), and signs that have a straight path between two locations (e.g., BUSY, CREDIT-CARD, FEVER). In the absence of other constraints, all subjects should be biased to see a straight path motion between the endpoints of both sets of signs because this is the shortest path between locations. However, Wilson (2001b) reasoned that if acquired knowledge of ASL can influence perceived biological motion, then Deaf ASL signers (but not hearing nonsigners) should report seeing arced motion for those signs that lexically contain an arced movement.

Wilson (2001b) found that for signs that used a straight path, both hearing and Deaf subjects primarily reported seeing a direct path between locations. However, for signs that used an arced path, Deaf subjects were significantly more likely to report an arced motion than hearing subjects. Furthermore, as presentation rate slowed, the tendency to report arced movement increased dramatically for the Deaf subjects but the increase was minimal for the hearing subjects. Wilson concluded that experience with ASL alters the probability of perceiving an indirect (arced) path of motion when that motion path yields an ASL sign. Wilson proposed a *lexicality constraint*, which influences the visual system through exposure to ASL. Wilson's results demonstrate that constraints on the perception of biological motion can be acquired. Furthermore, her results are the first to directly show that knowledge of ASL can alter motion *perception*. Deaf signers perceived the hand moving with an arc motion, whereas hearing nonsigners perceived a straight path motion for the same stimuli.

FACE PROCESSING

As described in chapter 2, certain facial expressions play a significant role in the syntax and morphology of ASL, and signers must be able to rapidly discriminate among many different expressions during language comprehension. In addition, as noted earlier in this chapter, signers fixate on the face of their addressee rather than track the hands. The fact that signers focus on the face during sign perception and the fact that facial expressions convey grammatical and lexical distinctions may lead to the enhancement of certain aspects of face processing.

Face Discrimination: The Benton Faces Test

Several studies have shown that ASL signers exhibit superior performance on the Benton Test of Face Recognition (Benton, Hamsher, Varney, & Spreen, 1983). In the Benton Faces test, subjects match the canonical view of a target face with other views of the same person (see Fig. 8.2). The target faces and distractor faces are presented under different orientation conditions, lighting conditions, or both. Bellugi, O'Grady, et al. (1990) found that Deaf signing children between the ages of 6 and 9 performed significantly better at every age level than hearing children on this test. Bettger (1992) replicated this result with adult signers, finding that both Deaf and hearing ASL signers outperformed hearing nonsigners, suggesting this effect is language linked. Furthermore, Parasnis, Samar, Bettger, and Sathe (1996) found that oral deaf (deaf people who do not know sign language) do not exhibit superior performance on the Benton Faces test

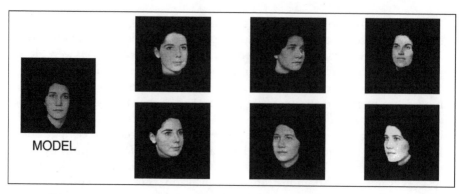

FIG. 8.2.   Example stimulus from the Benton Faces test. The model face is the same face as the top middle, bottom middle, and bottom right face.

compared to hearing subjects. Because these subjects were deaf, but had no experience with sign language, Parasnis et al.'s (1996) finding again suggested that the superior performance of the Deaf subjects is due to their signing experience rather than to effects of deafness. Finally, results from Bettger (1992) indicated that exposure to ASL from birth is not required to improve performance. Bettger tested Deaf signers who were very late learners of ASL and found that these signers were also more accurate on the Benton Faces test than hearing nonsigners, and their performance did not differ significantly from that of native Deaf and hearing signers. Thus, it appears that life-long experience with ASL is not required to enhance face processing skills.

Inverted Faces: Evidence for a Specific Enhancement of Face Processing

Bettger et al. (1997) found evidence suggesting this enhancement is linked to processes specifically involved in face perception, rather than a general enhancement of visual discrimination or object recognition. Deaf and hearing subjects (both children and adults) were presented with a version of the Benton Faces test in which the faces were turned upside down. It has been found that inversion disproportionally impairs face recognition compared to the recognition of other objects, such as houses (Yin, 1969). This "inversion effect" has been interpreted as indicating that there are unique mechanisms underlying face processing. Farah, Wilson, Drain, and Tanaka (1995) suggested that these specialized mechanisms are not utilized when faces are turned upside down and that face perception systems are specific to upright faces. Bettger et al. (1997) found that Deaf signers (both adults and children) were more accurate than hearing nonsigners when the Benton Faces were presented in their canonical upright orientation. However, Deaf signers and hearing nonsigners (both adults and children) did not differ in performance when the faces were inverted. This result suggests that experience with sign language affects mechanisms specific to face processing and does not produce a general enhancement of discrimination abilities (even when the stimuli are faces).

Face Recognition

McCullough and Emmorey (1997) conducted a series of experiments that investigated whether enhanced performance extended to other aspects of face processing. Although the Benton Faces test is called a test of face recognition, it actually taps face *discrimination* by asking subjects to distinguish among faces that differ in lighting and profile. There is no memory component, as the target and the response choices are presented simultaneously. The first study conducted by McCullough and Emmorey (1997), therefore, investigated whether the enhanced face discrimination abilities of ASL signers extended to face *recognition* as well.

Deaf signers and hearing nonsigners were presented with the Warrington (1984) Recognition Memory Test for Faces. In this test, subjects are first given a foil task in which they rate 50 individual faces as "pleasant" or "unpleasant." Subjects are then given a surprise recognition test. They are presented with two faces and must decide which face they saw previously during the rating task. McCullough and Emmorey (1997) found that Deaf signers were not more accurate on this task than hearing nonsigners. In another experiment, Deaf and hearing subjects were given the same face recognition test but the stimuli were presented on the computer, and subjects were asked to respond as quickly as they could. Again, the subject groups did not differ in accuracy, and they had similar response times. These findings suggest that experience with ASL does not lead to an enhanced ability to recognize unfamiliar faces from memory. This result is actually not that surprising given that the face-processing skills required for ASL do not involve recognition of the faces of individual people—just the opposite, in fact. Signers must be able to generalize facial expressions across individuals, disregarding aspects of a face that are unique to an individual.

Using the same faces from the Warrington (1984) test, Arnold and Murray (1998) found that Deaf and hearing signers (users of British Sign Language) were more accurate than hearing nonsigners in remembering the location of faces in the game *Concentration* (also known as *Matching Pairs* or *Pelmanism*).[2] Critically, the performance of the Deaf and hearing

---

[2]In this game, cards are placed face down in a matrix, and the player tries to find the matching pairs by turning over two cards on each attempt. If the cards match (show the same object/face), the player removes them from the board. If the cards do not match, the cards

groups did not differ when the stimuli were pictures of nameable objects. In addition, memory performance for faces (but not for objects) was correlated with number of years of signing experience for the hearing signers (the longer the exposure to signing, the better the memory performance). Unlike the McCullough and Emmorey (1997) study, subjects did not have to decide whether they had seen a particular face before; rather, they had to correctly remember the association between a spatial location and a particular face. In addition, faces could be seen more than once during the game. Thus, signing experience may enhance the discrimination among faces within memory such that a particular face can be more accurately paired with a location. That is, signers may be less likely to confuse similar faces than nonsigners, but this ease of discrimination does not extend to nameable objects, which may be recoded as words or signs.

Gestalt Face Processing

McCullough and Emmorey (1997) explored other aspects of face processing, using the Mooney Faces Closure test (Mooney, 1957), which taps gestalt face processing ability. This test consists of high-contrast pictures of human faces of various ages and different genders (see Fig. 8.3). Deaf and hearing subjects were asked to sort the pictures into different groups (boy, girl, adult man, adult woman, old man, old woman). Because few local facial features are shown in these high contrast images, subjects must rely on global information derived from the faces to identify and categorize the stimuli into different age and gender groups. Before individual features can be identified, recognition of the face must be achieved through the gestalt process of visual closure. McCullough and Emmorey (1997) found that Deaf and hearing subjects did not differ on this task (in fact, Deaf signers were slightly less accurate than hearing nonsigners). This result suggests that when a configurational analysis with a gestalt closure process is required for face identification, Deaf signers perform on a par with hearing subjects. The fact that Deaf signers were not superior to hearing subjects on the Mooney Faces Closure task suggests that the mechanism(s) responsible for their superior performance on the Benton Faces test may involve processes related to local facial features rather than to global facial features. Such a hypothesis is reasonable given that signers must discriminate among facial expressions that involve individual facial features (e.g., eyebrows) rather than global features (e.g., the overall configuration of features within the face).

---

are turned back over. When the player finds all of the pairs, the game is over. The dependent measure for the Arnold and Murray (1998) study was the number of attempts within the face or object game.

FIG. 8.3. Example stimuli from Mooney Faces test. The faces are those of an adult woman and young boy.

Discrimination of Facial Features

McCullough and Emmorey (1997) conducted a third experiment that investigated whether ASL signers exhibit a superior ability to discriminate subtle differences in local facial features. Deaf and hearing subjects' abilities to detect changes in facial features within the *same* face were compared. It was hypothesized that because ASL signers must attend to facial features in order to interpret signed sentences, they may perform better than nonsigners in detecting differences in facial features. In this experiment, subjects were first presented with a target face in the center of a computer screen. After several seconds, two response faces were presented side by side; one was exactly the same as the target face and the other was also the same face, but one facial feature had been replaced by a feature from a different face (either the eyes, nose, or mouth). Subjects had to indicate which face was the same as the target face (see Fig. 8.4).

McCullough and Emmorey (1997) found that Deaf signers were significantly more accurate than hearing nonsigners in discriminating between faces that were identical except for a change in a single facial feature. When the performance of hearing signers was compared to both Deaf signers and hearing nonsigners, the pattern that emerged suggested that both experience with ASL and experience with lipreading can lead to an enhanced ability to identify differences in facial features. Specifically, experience with ASL may lead to an enhanced ability to detect differences in eye configuration. Both Deaf and hearing ASL signers were more accurate in detecting a difference in the eyes than hearing nonsigners. In ASL, changes in eye configuration (e.g., raised eyebrows, squinted eyes, fur-

Target stimulus

Original

Altered

FIG. 8.4.   Example stimuli set. The altered face has different eyes than the target face. From S. McCullough and K. Emmorey, 1997, "Face Processing by Deaf ASL Signers," in *Journal of Deaf Studies and Deaf Education, 2*(4), 212–222. Copyright © 1997 by Oxford University Press. Reprinted by permission.

rowed brows) convey various syntactic distinctions, which may lead to the observed enhancement. In contrast, Deaf signers were more accurate than both hearing signers and nonsigners in detecting differences in the mouth feature. This result suggests that experience with lipreading may lead to a superior ability to detect differences in mouth shape. Deaf signers receive extensive training in lipreading, unlike hearing signers. Finally, Deaf and hearing subjects did not differ in their ability to detect alterations of the nose. This result was expected because ASL grammatical facial expressions do not involve the nose, and the nose is also not relevant for lipreading skills. Thus, Deaf signers were best able to remember and discriminate between just those facial features that are relevant for lipreading and ASL linguistic facial expressions.

Recognition of Emotional Facial Expressions

N. Goldstein and Feldman (1996) explored the hypothesis that ASL signers might exhibit a heightened proficiency in the identification of emotional facial expressions. They reasoned that because signers must attend to linguistic facial expressions, they may also have heightened attention to emotional facial expressions. This hypothesis is even more plausible given the role of affective facial expressions in ASL narratives described in chapter 2. Heightened attention to facial expressions (both linguistic and affective) when comprehending ASL discourse might lead to a strengthened ability to identify emotional expressions.

N. Goldstein and Feldman (1996) presented a silent videotape of people expressing spontaneous emotions to hearing subjects who either had no knowledge of ASL or who had studied ASL for an average of 2 years (range: 10 months to 5 years). Subjects had to identify each facial expression as showing happiness, sadness, fear-surprise, anger, or disgust. Overall, ASL signers were significantly more accurate than nonsigners in identifying these emotional facial expressions. All subjects were equally good at identifying happy facial expressions. However, signers were more accurate in identifying disgusted and angry facial expressions. These are the emotions that are typically most difficult to distinguish (Coats & Feldman, 1995), and angry facial expressions resemble the linguistic expression marking WH clauses (see chaps. 2 and 5). N. Goldstein and Feldman (1996) suggested that the heightened saliency of facial expression for signers may lead to an increase in experience decoding facial expressions and thus improve their ability to identify facial expressions of affect.

In addition, Goldstein, Sexton, and Feldman (2000) found that hearing ASL signers were more adept at producing emotional facial expressions, compared to hearing nonsigners. The subjects in this experiment were asked to produce affective facial expressions that conveyed happiness, sadness, fear, surprise, anger, and disgust, and their expressions were videotaped and shown to untrained (nonsigning) judges for identification. The judges were better able to identify the emotional facial expressions produced by the signers, suggesting that experience with ASL can also enhance the ability to consciously produce affective facial expressions.

In summary, the combined results of these studies suggest that ASL signers are not enhanced in all aspects of face processing. Specifically, Deaf signers and hearing nonsigners do not differ in their ability to recognize faces from memory or in their gestalt face-processing abilities. Enhancement of face-processing skills appears to be most strongly tied to the ability to discriminate among faces that are very similar (as in the Benton Faces test) and to recognize subtle changes in specific facial features. These skills are most closely tied to recognizing and interpreting linguistic facial expression in ASL. To identify and categorize ASL facial expressions, signers need not recognize the person. Rather, signers must rely on featural processing of the face in order to identify specific facial expressions. The gestalt aspect of the face does not change with different facial expressions. Ability to generalize over individual faces and to focus on specific local features rather than on the global configuration of the face are characteristic of lipreading as well. Finally, experience with ASL appears to enhance the ability to identify emotional facial expressions. These expressions, like linguistic facial expressions, are generalized over individual faces and rely on changes in individual features. Thus, it appears that sign language experience enhances face-processing skills that are relevant to interpreting subtle differences in local feature configurations and that must be generalized over individual faces.

MENTAL IMAGERY

Several studies have examined the relation between processing ASL and the use of visual mental imagery (Chamberlain & Mayberry, 1994; Emmorey, Klima, et al., 1998; Emmorey & Kosslyn, 1996; Emmorey, Kosslyn, & Bellugi, 1993; Talbot & Haude, 1993). Specifically, these studies examined the ability of Deaf and hearing subjects to mentally transform images (e.g., by rotation) and to generate mental images. Emmorey and colleagues hypothesized that these imagery abilities are integral to the production and comprehension of ASL and that their constant use may lead to an enhancement of imagery skills within the nonlinguistic domain for ASL signers.

Mental Rotation and Mirror Reversals

McKee (1987) was one of the first to investigate mental rotation skills in Deaf and hearing subjects. McKee used a task similar to the one devised by Shepard and Metzler (1971) in which subjects were shown three forms created by juxtaposing cubes to form angular shapes. The constructions were rotated in space around a vertical axis. One of the three shapes was a mirror image of the other two, and subjects were asked to indicate on an answer sheet which of the two constructions were exactly alike. Deaf signers were significantly more accurate on this task than hearing nonsigners.

Emmorey et al. (1993) used a similar task in which subjects were shown two separate two-dimensional shapes and were asked to decide as quickly as possible whether the two shapes were the same or mirror images, regardless of orientation (see Fig. 8.5). Both Deaf and hearing signers had faster reaction times than nonsigners at all degrees of rotation. Emmorey et al. (1993) suggested originally that ASL signers may be faster in detecting mirror reversals rather than in rotation per se because they were faster even when no rotation was required (i.e., at 0°). However, research by Ilan and Miller (1994) indicated that different processes may be involved when mirror/same judgments are made at 0° within a mental rotation experi-

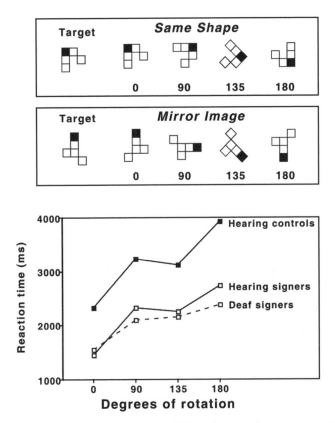

FIG. 8.5.   Results and example stimuli from the mental rotation experiment conducted by Emmorey et al. (1993).

ment, compared to when mental rotation was not required on any of the trials. In addition, results from Emmorey and Bettger (1995) indicated that when native ASL signers and hearing nonsigners were asked to make mirror/same judgments in a comparison task that did not involve mental rotation, these groups did not differ in accuracy or reaction time. This result suggested that signers' enhanced performance stemmed from processes critical to mental rotation tasks, rather than from processes that are specific to mirror-reversal detection.

The fact that Deaf and hearing signers were both faster than hearing nonsigners suggests that the enhanced performance on mental rotation tasks is a result of experience with ASL. Further support for this hypothesis was found by Talbot and Haude (1993), who showed that mental rotation performance depended on ASL skill level. Using a variation of the mental rotation task developed by Vandenberg and Kuse (1978), Talbot and Haude (1993) found that hearing subjects who were student interpreters with 6 years of ASL experience performed significantly better than hearing subjects who had less than 1 year of experience or no experience with ASL. These results suggest that a lifetime of ASL experience or exposure to ASL at an early age are not required for an effect on nonlinguistic mental rotation tasks to be observed. Finally, Chamberlain and Mayberry (1994) found that deaf subjects who do not know sign language (oral deaf) do not exhibit enhanced performance on mental rotation tasks—their performance did not differ from hearing nonsigners. Together these results support the hypothesis that use of ASL can enhance mental rotation skills. But why? What is it about processing ASL that might lead to such an effect within a nonlinguistic domain of spatial cognition?

Emmorey et al. (1993) and Emmorey, Klima, et al. (1998) hypothesized that mental rotation may play a crucial role in sign language processing because of the mental transformations that the sign perceiver (i.e., the addressee) must perform while comprehending certain types of discourse. As discussed in chapter 3, spatial scenes are most often described from the perspective of the narrator (the person signing), such that the addressee, if facing the signer, must perform what amounts to a 180° mental rotation to correctly comprehend the description (see Fig. 3.12A in chap. 3). We hypothesized that this habitual transformation during discourse comprehension may lead to enhanced mental rotation skills within the nonlinguistic domain.

Emmorey, Klima, et al. (1998) investigated whether mental rotation during sign language processing was difficult for ASL signers and whether there are differences between linguistic and nonlinguistic mental rotation. The first experiment required subjects to decide whether a signed description matched a room presented on videotape. Deaf ASL signers were more accurate when viewing scenes described from the "speaker's" perspective (even though rotation was required) than from the addressee's perspective (no rotation required).[3] In a second experiment, Deaf signers and hearing nonsigners viewed videotapes of objects appearing briefly and sequentially on a board marked with an entrance. This board either matched an identical board in front of the subject or was rotated 180°. Subjects were asked to place objects on their board in the orientation and location shown on the video, making the appropriate rotation when required. All subjects were significantly less accurate when rotation was required, but ASL signers performed significantly better than hearing nonsigners under rotation. ASL signers were also more accurate in remembering object orien-

---

[3] To indicate that the scene was being described from the addressee's perspective, the speaker signed YOU-ENTER at the beginning of the description, and then signed the location of objects with respect to how the addressee would view the room from the entrance (thus reversing the space for the addressee; see chap. 3).

tation. Signers then viewed a video in which the same scenes were *signed* from the two perspectives (i.e., rotation required or no rotation required). In contrast to their performance with real objects, signers did *not* show the typical mental rotation effect. Interestingly, males outperformed females on the rotation task with objects, but the superiority disappeared in the linguistic condition. These findings suggest that experience with rotation in the linguistic domain may eliminate the rotation effect within that domain, but such experience only reduces rather than eliminates rotation difficulty within the nonlinguistic domain.

However, another possible interpretation of the lack of mental rotation effect within sign language is that signers do not actually mentally *rotate* locations within signing space when they are the addressee (the viewer). In fact, the intuitions of native signers suggest that they may not. Signers report that they instantly know how to interpret the narrator's description (Emmorey, Klima, et al., 1998). They do not experience a sensation of rotating a mental image of a scene or of objects within a scene. Signers may transform signing space not by mental rotation but by a transformation in which an image is reversed or instantly repositioned in an opposite position within a horizontal plane. If sign language processing involves mental reversal rather than mental rotation, then we must reexamine our explanation of enhanced mental rotation skills in ASL signers. One possibility is that experience with ASL enhances other processes that are involved in mental rotation tasks. To perform mental rotation, subjects must generate an image, maintain that image, and then transform it (Kosslyn, 1980). Emmorey et al. (1993) and Emmorey and Kosslyn (1996) found that Deaf and hearing ASL signers were faster at generating mental images than hearing nonsigners. Thus, signers may also be faster at mental rotation tasks because they are able to generate mental images quickly prior to manipulating them. We turn to studies that investigated image generation skills in ASL signers in the next section.

Another clue to the mechanism that may underlie signers' superior performance on mental rotation tasks is the finding by Masataka (1995) that native signing Japanese children exhibit an enhanced ability to conduct perception-to-production transformations involving mirror reversals. A critical characteristic of sign language processing is the fact that signers perceive the reverse of what they themselves would actually produce (assuming that both signers are right-handed.) For example, a sign produced with left-to-right motion (e.g., SUMMER) would be visually perceived during face-to-face signing as moving from right-to-left. This subtle and complex transformation of perceived articulation into a reversed representation for motor production is required for the acquisition of lexical signs during development and is also notoriously difficult for adult learners of ASL.

Masataka's (1995) study was based on the common finding that a figure (such as a letter) drawn on the forehead or back of the hand is perceived tactilely by subjects as a mirror reversal of the experimenter-defined stimulus (e.g., Corcoran, 1977; Natsoulas & Dubanoski, 1964). However, Masataka (1995) found that Deaf signing Japanese children did not show such a mirror-reversal tendency, unlike their hearing peers. That is, when a "p" was written on a particular body surface, signing children overwhelmingly chose "p" as a matching response, whereas hearing children were three times more likely to choose the mirror-reversed "q" response. The signing children were apparently more skilled at mentally transforming a tactilely perceived pattern into the movement pattern that was used to create it ("analysis-by-synthesis"; Corcoran, 1977). Evidence that this ability is language-linked stems from the fact that signing vocabulary correlated negatively with mirror-reversal tendency: the larger the child's sign vocabulary, the less likely he or she was to make mirror-reversal matches. To the extent that motor processes are recruited during mental rotation (see Kosslyn, 1994), the enhanced perception-to-production mapping suggested by the results of Masataka (1995) might improve the rotation performance of signers.

Image Generation and Maintenance

Image generation is the process whereby an image (i.e., a short-term visual memory representation) is created on the basis of information stored in long-term memory (see Kosslyn, Brunn, Cave, & Wallach, 1985). In ASL, image generation and maintenance may be an important process underlying aspects of referential shift. As discussed in chapter 2, Liddell (1990) argued that under referential shift, signers may imagine referents as physically present, and these visualized referents are relevant to the expression of verb morphology. Liddell (1990) gave the following example involving the verb ASK, which is lexically specified to be directed at chin height:

> To direct the verb ASK toward an imagined referent, the signer must conceive of the location of the imaginary referent's head. For example, if the signer and addressee were to imagine that Wilt Chamberlain was standing beside them ready to give them advice on playing basketball, the sign ASK would be directed upward toward the imaged height of Wilt Chamberlain's head. . . . It would be incorrect to sign the verb at the height of the signer's chin . . . This is exactly the way agreement works when a referent is present. Naturally, if the referent is imagined as lying down, standing on a chair, etc., the height and direction of the agreement verb reflects this. Since the signer must conceptualize the location of body parts of the referent imagined to be present, there is a sense in which an invisible body is present. The signer

must conceptualize such a body in order to properly direct agreement verbs. (p. 184)

In addition, ASL classifier verbs of location and motion often require relatively precise representation of visuospatial relations within a scene (see chap. 3), and such explicit encoding may require one to generate detailed visual images. Some spoken languages, such as Navajo (Pinxten, van Dooren, & Harvey, 1983) or Tzeltal (P. Brown, 1991), require similar explicit linguistic marking of spatial relations on predicates of location and position. What is unique about ASL is that space itself is used to express spatial relationships. Thus, not only does ASL have a very rich linguistic system for expressing complex spatial relations, but these relations are also directly encoded in physical space. Emmorey et al. (1993) and Emmorey and Kosslyn (1996) hypothesized that ASL signers generate images frequently because of the interaction between what must be encoded from a referent object and how it is expressed in ASL.

If Deaf subjects are in fact generating visual images prior to or during sign production, the speed of forming these images would be important, and signers might develop enhanced abilities to generate images. The image-generation task used by Emmorey et al. (1993) required subjects to first memorize uppercase block letters. Subjects were then shown a series of grids (or sets of brackets) that contained an X mark (see Fig. 8.6). A lowercase letter preceded each grid, and subjects were asked to decide as quickly as possible whether the corresponding uppercase block letter would cover the X if it were in the grid. The crucial aspect of the experiment was that the probe mark appeared in the grid only 500 msec after the lowercase cue letter was presented. This was not enough time for the subjects to complete forming the letter image. Thus, response times reflect, in part, the time to generate the image. Kosslyn and colleagues used this task to show that visual mental images are constructed serially from parts (e.g., Kosslyn, Cave, Provost, & Von Gierke, 1988; Roth & Kosslyn, 1988). Subjects tend to generate letter images segment by segment in the same order that the letter is drawn. Therefore, when the probe X is covered by a segment that is generated early (e.g., on the first stroke of the letter F), subjects have faster reaction times, compared to when the probe is located under a late-imaged segment. Crucially, this difference in response time based on probe location is not found when image generation is not involved, that is, in a baseline condition where both the probe X and letter (shaded gray) were physically present.

Using this task, Emmorey et al. (1993) found that both Deaf and hearing signers formed images significantly faster than nonsigners. This finding suggests that experience with ASL can affect the ability to mentally generate visual images. Results from the perceptual baseline task indi-

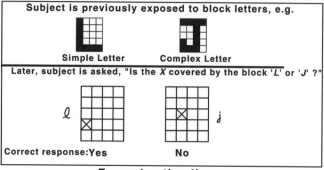

Example stimuli

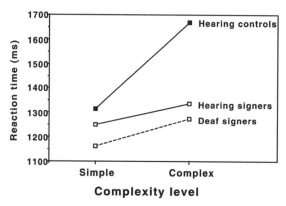

Complexity level

FIG. 8.6.   Results and example stimuli from the image generation experiment conducted by Emmorey et al. (1993).

cated that this enhancement was due to a difference in image generation ability, rather than to differences in scanning or inspection. The signing and nonsigning subjects were equally accurate on the image generation task, which suggests that although signers create complex images faster than nonsigners, they generate equally good images. Furthermore, Deaf and hearing subjects appeared to image letters in the same way: Both groups of subjects required more time and made more errors for probes located on late-imaged segments, and these effects were of comparable magnitude in the two groups. This result indicates that neither group of subjects generated images of letters as complete wholes, and both groups imaged segments in the same order. Again, the fact that hearing signers performed similarly to Deaf signers suggests that the enhanced image generation ability is due to experience with ASL, rather than to auditory deprivation.

Emmorey and Kosslyn (1996) also investigated whether the processes underlying image generation were lateralized within the brain in the same way for Deaf signers and hearing nonsigners. Kosslyn and colleagues argue that each cerebral hemisphere can generate mental images, but the images are constructed using two different types of spatial relations representations (Kosslyn, 1987, 1994; Kosslyn et al., 1988; Kosslyn, Maljkovic, Hamilton, Horwitz, & Thompson, 1995). This hypothesis is based in part on the finding that the hemispheres apparently encode different types of spatial relations, which subsequently may be differentially available for use in juxtaposing parts of an object in a visual mental image. Specifically, several research groups found that the left hemisphere encodes *categorical* spatial relations more efficiently than the right; such relations specify an equivalence class, such as "connected to" or "above." In contrast, the right hemisphere processes *coordinate* spatial relations more efficiently than the left; these relations specify metric spatial properties, such as precise distance. Representations of categorical spatial relations are used when the precise arrangement among parts of an object can vary, but the general category of the relation remains constant. This type of spatial categorization has parallels to the categorical and symbolic nature of language. In contrast, coordinate spatial relations representations are used primarily to guide movements; for example, in navigation, one must be aware of precise distances in order to avoid collisions with objects.

Emmorey and Kosslyn (1996) used the same image generation task as Emmorey et al. (1993), but the stimuli were presented to either the right visual field (left hemisphere) or the left visual field (right hemisphere; see chap. 9 for further explanation of this technique). Stimuli presented within grids were used to tap use of categorical spatial relations representations, and stimuli presented within brackets were used to tap use of coordinate spatial relations representations. Deaf signers were found to generate images more quickly when stimuli were presented to the right hemisphere, and generally were faster than hearing subjects. Furthermore, Deaf signers exhibited a strong right-hemisphere advantage for image generation using *either* categorical or coordinate spatial relations representations. In contrast, hearing subjects showed evidence of left-hemisphere processing for categorical spatial relations representations, and no hemispheric asymmetry for coordinate spatial relations representations. These findings suggest that the enhanced image-generation abilities in Deaf ASL signers may be linked to right-hemisphere processing.

However, it is clear that this enhanced image generation ability of the right hemisphere is not a consequence of a right-hemisphere dominance for processing sign language (see chap. 9). Nonetheless, Emmorey and Corina (1993) found that Deaf signers had a right-hemisphere advantage for imageable ASL signs in a lateralized lexical decision task, whereas English speakers simply showed a weaker left-hemisphere advantage for imageable words. Thus, it is possible that the right hemisphere of Deaf signers is more proficient in using categorical spatial relations representations during image generation because it has a greater role in processing aspects of ASL that involve image-generation processes.

Emmorey et al. (1993) also investigated signers' ability to maintain an image in short-term memory. In this experiment, subjects first studied a pattern within a grid or set of brackets. The patterns were created by blackening several contiguous cells within a 4 × 5 grid. After subjects memorized the pattern, it was removed and an X probe appeared within the empty grid or brackets after a delay of either ½ second or 2½ seconds. Subjects indicated whether the X would have fallen on the pattern, were it still present. Thus, subjects did not need to retrieve information from long-term memory or generate the image; they simply needed to retain an image of the pattern in visual short-term memory. The results indicated experience with ASL did not enhance the ability to maintain a pattern in a visual image—at least not as tested by this task.

Although signers may not differ from nonsigners in their ability to maintain *visual* images, signers may have an enhanced ability to maintain *spatial* images. Farah, Hammond, Levine, and Calvanio (1988) argued that visual images are specifically *visual* and encode the appearance of objects, including perspective and color information, whereas spatial images are relatively abstract, amodal, or multimodal representations of the layout of objects in space with respect to the viewer and each other. As will be discussed, Wilson et al. (1997) provided data suggesting that signers may have a superior ability to maintain information spatially in short-term memory (see also chap. 7).

In sum, Deaf signers exhibit an enhanced ability to generate mental images, and this ability appears to be linked to their use of ASL. Linguistic requirements may promote image generation during certain types of discourse, that is, referent visualization during referential shift and the generation of object images that may be necessary to encode object shape, orientation, and location when producing certain classifier constructions. Image generation processes appear to be more strongly tied to the right hemisphere for Deaf signers, which again suggests that experience with ASL can alter the neural organization for nonlinguistic visuospatial processes.

Spatial Imagery

Wilson et al. (1997) examined spatial working memory in children ages 8 to 10 who were either native Deaf signers or hearing English speakers. Subjects were given the Corsi blocks task (Milner, 1971), in which they had to remember and reproduce a sequence of identically marked spatial locations. The Deaf signers had a significantly longer spatial memory span than the hearing nonsigners. This result is complemented by the finding of Parasnis et al. (1996), who showed that deaf children who had no exposure to sign language performed as well as hearing children on the Corsi blocks task. In addition, Capirci, Cattani, Rossini, and Volterra (1998) found that Italian hearing children (age 6) who attended a year-long course in Italian Sign Language exhibited increased spatial memory span (as measured by the Corsi blocks task) compared to children who attended an English course or who did not attend a language course. Thus, the spatial memory advantage observed by Wilson et al. (1997) appears to be due to experience with a signed language. One possible source of this advantage is an enhanced ability to maintain spatial images of locations. However, some other possible explanations are that there is a stronger relationship between motoric and spatial representations for signers (cf. Masataka, 1995) or that signers co-opt linguistic representations to encode nonlinguistic spatial information. More research is needed to tease apart these potential sources of explanation.

In summary, several studies have shown that Deaf and hearing ASL signers exhibit superior performance on mental imagery tasks compared to deaf and hearing nonsigners. The evidence suggests that signers do not actually *rotate* images faster (e.g., the slopes for mental rotation do not differ for signers and nonsigners). Rather, ASL signers generate images faster, may be more skilled at reversal transformations, and have longer spatial memory spans. Emmorey and colleagues (Emmorey et al., 1993; Emmorey, Klima, et al., 1998) argued that image generation and reversal transformation processes may occur much more frequently during the production and comprehension of ASL compared to spoken languages like English.

DOMAINS UNAFFECTED BY SIGN LANGUAGE USE

It is important to point out that there are several visuospatial cognitive processes that do not appear to be influenced by sign language use. We have already seen that Deaf signers and hearing nonsigners do not differ with respect to motion discrimination thresholds (Bosworth & Dobkins, 1999), face recognition ability (McCullough & Emmorey, 1997), and the maintenance of visual images (Emmorey et al., 1993). In addition, Poizner and Tallal (1987) found no differences between Deaf and hearing subjects in critical flicker-fusion thresholds and two-point thresholds to a flashing light. That is, both Deaf and hearing subjects exhibited an equal ability to distinguish rapidly presented visual flashes. Bellugi, O'Grady, et al. (1990) reported little difference between Deaf and hearing children in visuospatial constructive abilities, that is, drawing, copying, and block construction. McKee (1987) found no difference between Deaf signers and hearing nonsigners in "localization skill" (the ability to remember the location of an X within a frame after a short delay). Parasnis (1983) found no difference between signers and nonsigners on the Embedded Figures test (taps

TABLE 8.1
Summary of the Impact of Sign Language
Use on Visuospatial Cognition

Affected Domains	Unaffected domains
• Mental rotation and image generation • Face discrimination and processing of facial features • Motion categorization and parsing • Neural organization for motion processing • Memory for spatial locations	• Visuoconstructive abilities • Face recognition and gestalt face processing • Flicker-fusion thresholds • Motion detection and contrast sensitivity thresholds • Memory for visual images

the ability to perceive a visual form embedded within a surrounding context), on an abstract reasoning task (concerns nonverbal conceptual sequences), or on a spatial-relations test (taps the ability to transform two-dimensional designs to three-dimensional figures). These studies cover the gamut from low-level perceptual processes (e.g., visual fusion and motion detection thresholds) to high-level cognitive functions (e.g., abstract reasoning). In particular, however, we find little effect of sign language use on low-level visual processing, memory for visual images, or visual constructive abilities like drawing. Table 8.1 summarizes the findings.

Thus, sign language use does not create a general enhancement of visuospatial cognitive processes; rather, there appears to be a selective effect on certain processes argued to be involved in sign language production and comprehension. In particular, motion analysis and categorization, spatial memory, mental image transformations, and facial feature discrimination are enhanced or altered by experience with sign language. However, much more research is needed to determine the extent and nature of these patterns of performance. For example, are there any low-level perceptual processes that are affected? Are there processes that might actually be impaired due to interference from sign language processing? How similar does a nonlinguistic visuospatial process have to be to the sign language process in order to be affected? Answers to these questions will help us to understand what factors determine whether a given visuospatial ability will be affected by exposure to sign language.

IMPLICATIONS: DOES LANGUAGE AFFECT COGNITION?

One result that emerges from the studies reviewed here is that life-long experience with ASL is not needed to enhance performance on certain cognitive tasks (e.g., face discrimination, facial expression identification, and mental rotation). Thus far, there is little evidence that early exposure to ASL is necessary to enhance performance. However, the requisite research in most domains has not been conducted. For example, Neville (1991b) suggested that early exposure to ASL may result in a reorganization during development, in which the left hemisphere comes to mediate aspects of motion perception. However, until subjects who acquire ASL later in life are studied, the extent of neural plasticity will not be clear. For example, can exposure to ASL shift motion detection processes from the right hemisphere to the left in late childhood or in adulthood? The fact that only a few years of experience with a signed language can influence at least some nonlinguistic cognitive processes suggests that there is a malleable and sensitive relation between linguistic and nonlinguistic visuospatial domains beyond childhood.

Is this influence of sign language use and knowledge on nonlinguistic cognition a *Whorfian effect*? That is, do these findings provide support for the linguistic relativity hypothesis? The answer depends on how one defines this hypothesis (for excellent discussions of linguistic relativity, see Gumperz & Levinson, 1996; and Lucy, 1992b). The results of studies with ASL signers do not provide evidence for the hypothesis that the language one uses can qualitatively alter the very nature of cognitive processes or representations. However, the evidence does suggest that the language one uses can enhance certain cognitive processes through practice. Through habitual use within the language domain, cognitive processes can be faster (as with image generation), more fine tuned (as with face discrimination and aspects of motion processing), or more adept at coding certain types of information (as with memory for spatial sequences). These effects of language use on cognitive behavior go beyond the "thinking for speaking" relativity hypothesis put forth by Slobin (1991, 1996). Slobin's hypothesis is that the nature of one's language (in particular, the grammatical categories of one's language) affect cognitive processes *at the moment of speaking*. The results with users of American Sign Language, as well as recent work by Levinson (1996) and Pederson (1995) with users of different spoken languages (Tzeltal, Tamil, and Dutch), indicate that the language one uses can influence cognitive processes even when speaking/signing is not required.

But are these effects of language on cognition just practice effects? In some sense, the answer must be *yes*. Language does not appear to introduce *new* conceptual categories or processes—rather languages differ with regard to whether and how certain cognitive distinctions are grammatically encoded (e.g., number distinctions) and with regard to whether certain processes are utilized during their interpretation (e.g., imagery processes). It may be the habitual attention to or use of specific conceptual categorizations and processes that leads to varied patterns of cognitive behavior (see Lucy, 1992b). Differences in cognitive behavior may take the form of improved performance on nonlinguistic tasks that utilize processes habitually required for either language production or comprehension (as in most of the sign language studies), or these differences may take the form of preferential attention to conceptual concepts that are obligatorily (i.e., habitually) encoded by a particular language (e.g., differential attention to the number of objects by English vs. Yucatec speakers; Lucy, 1992a).

Finally, the findings discussed in this chapter bear on the relation between language and other cognitive systems. The results indicate that the visuospatial processing required by ASL can impact nonlinguistic visuospatial processing. One could also investigate whether auditory language processing affects nonlinguistic auditory processing. However, this question is difficult to study because auditory processing cannot be observed in the absence of experience with speech. The visual domain, in contrast, provides an ideal means of studying these questions because visuospatial processes can be observed with and without the influence of a visuospatial language. By comparing visuospatial functions in Deaf and hearing subjects, we gain a window into the nature of cognitive modularity and interactivity. The research described here suggests that aspects of higher level ASL visuospatial processing interact with and influence other types of visuospatial processing.

SUGGESTIONS FOR FURTHER READING

Gumperz, J., & Levinson, S. (Eds.). (1996). *Rethinking linguistic relativity.* Cambridge, England: Cambridge University Press.

Part I of this volume ("Linguistic Determinism: The Interface Between Language and Thought"), and Part II ("Universals and Variation in Language and Culture") are most relevant to the issues discussed in this chapter. The papers in Part I describe important language-specific effects on cognitive processing, whereas the papers in Part II explore the nature of linguistic versus cognitive universals in various domains (e.g., spatial language and spatial cognition).

Marschark, M., Siple, P., Lillo-Martin, D., Campbell, R., Everhart, V. S. (1997). *Relations of language and thought: The view from sign language and deaf children.* New York: Oxford University Press.

This volume presents a wide-ranging discussion that begins with the question: "Does growing up deaf or having a sign language as a first language affect children's cognitive development?" The chapters discuss some of the same issues discussed here, but from a developmental perspective.

Chapter 9

Sign Language and the Brain

A major theme of this book is the extent to which there are biological constraints on the nature of language. We have examined whether the visual–gestural nature of signed languages has an impact on linguistic form, on language processing, on language acquisition, or on other cognitive domains. We now turn to the question of whether the contrasting sensorimotor properties of sign and speech constrain the underlying neural systems for language. Is the functional neuroanatomy of language dependent on the sensory and motor modalities through which it is perceived and produced? Detailed studies are beginning to reveal the neural systems that are involved in language comprehension and production in users of signed languages. Figure 9.1 provides a very basic road map for the major structures of the human brain that will help the reader follow the discussions in this chapter.

WHAT DETERMINES THE LEFT-HEMISPHERIC SPECIALIZATION FOR LANGUAGE?

For more than a century (since the time of Broca and Wernicke), we have known that the left hemisphere of the human brain is critical for producing and comprehending speech. Damage to perisylvian areas within the left hemisphere (the language zone; see Fig. 9.2) produces various types of *aphasia*, language disorders caused by brain injury. Damage to equivalent areas within the right hemisphere does not produce aphasic symptoms, such as effortful speech, phonological and morphological errors, or difficulty understanding words or sentences. Why does the brain exhibit this asymmetry in specialization for linguistic functions? One hypothesis is

A)

Superior

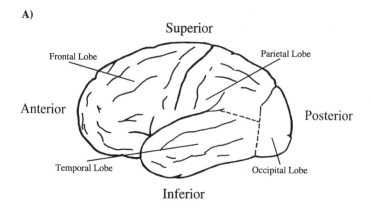

Inferior

B)

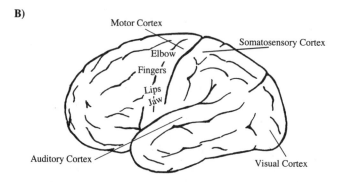

FIG. 9.1.   A) Lobes of the left hemisphere of the brain and terms of relationship in neuroanatomy. B) The major sensory and motor areas of the
brain.

that the temporal processing demands for auditory speech processing determine the lateralization pattern for language (Fitch, Miller, & Tallal,
1997). Speech perception relies on very fast temporal changes (on the order of 30 to 40 msec), and the left hemisphere has been argued to be specialized for processing rapidly changing sensory events (Tallal et al.,
1993). Another possibility is that the left hemisphere is specialized for
general symbolic functions, including mathematics and other symbol systems (J. W. Brown, 1977; K. Goldstein, 1948). A further possibility is that
the left hemisphere is specialized for the control of complex motor movements, regardless of whether they are linguistic (Kimura, 1993). Yet another possibility is that the basis for left-hemispheric specialization for language lies in the nature of *linguistic* systems rather than in the sensory
characteristics of the linguistic signal or in the motor aspects of language
production (Hickok, Klima, & Bellugi, 1996). Understanding the neural

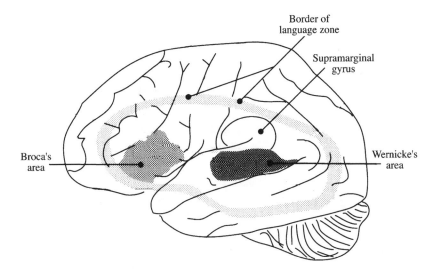

FIG. 9.2.   The perisylvian areas that make up the language zone within the left hemisphere. From *Understanding Aphasia* by H. Goodglass, 1993. Copyright © 1993 by Academic Press. Reprinted with permission.

systems involved in signed language processing can help to decide among these alternatives because sign languages are not based on auditory processing, are distinct from pantomime (symbolic gesture), involve complex motoric activity, and are clearly linguistic systems.

Evidence From Neurological Patient Studies

Lesion Studies: Sign Aphasia.   Injury to the brain can occur from a variety of causes, for example, stroke, infection, trauma, or tumor. The data from adult signers who have suffered some type of brain injury clearly show that damage to perisylvian areas of the *left* hemisphere (the language zone) can cause frank sign language aphasias (Poizner et al., 1987). A historical review of 16 cases of signers who sustained left-hemisphere damage (LHD) and 5 cases of signers with right-hemisphere damage (RHD) reveals that only damage to critical left-hemisphere structures leads to sign language impairments (Corina, 1998a, 1998b). In addition, Hickok, Klima, and Bellugi (1996) conducted a group study comparing 13 LHD and 10 RHD signers on a range of standard language tests from the Boston Diagnostic Aphasia Examination (BDAE; Goodglass & Kaplan, 1983) that had been adapted for ASL. The LHD signers performed significantly worse than the RHD signers on all measures. Figure 9.3 provides a summary of the performance of LHD, RHD, and normal control signers on BDAE measures of sign production and comprehension.

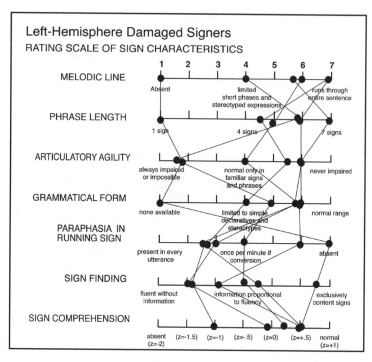

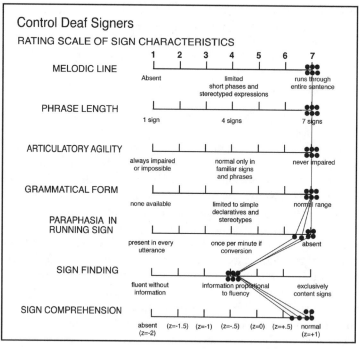

FIG. 9.3. *(Continued)*

274

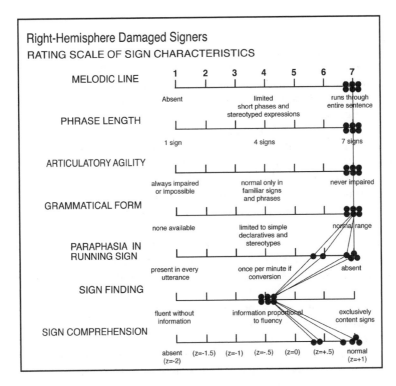

FIG. 9.3.   BDAE sign language profiles of left-lesioned signers, normal control signers, and right-lesioned signers. From Bellugi and Hickok, 1995; copyright © Ursula Bellugi, The Salk Institute.

The poorer performance of the LHD signers cannot be attributed to group differences in (a) onset of deafness, (b) age of language acquisition, or (c) age at test (Hickok, Klima, & Bellugi, 1996). These variables did not correlate with scores on the BDAE. Although these factors (particularly age of acquisition) affect sign language competence and aspects of the neural organization for language (see chap. 6), they were not the dominant factors that predicted performance on the basic language assessment tasks of the BDAE (e.g., understanding simple commands, naming pictures, number of phonological or semantic errors in spontaneous production). Thus, data from right-handed signers with brain injury indicate that structures within the left hemisphere of the brain are critical to sign language comprehension and production, such that if they are damaged, sign language impairments result.[1]

---

[1]Some left-handed signers, like some left-handed speakers, may show reverse dominance for language (K. Clark, Hickok, Love, Klima, & Bellugi, 1997; Kegl et al., 1996).

Cortical Stimulation Mapping of the Brain.   A few rare cases have been reported in which a Deaf or hearing signer has needed surgical treatment for seizures. During the surgical operation under local anesthesia, electrical stimulation of the brain can identify areas that are essential to language processing by activating or blocking neuronal function at very local regions of the cortex. Studying a hearing ASL signer, Haglund, Ojemann, Lettich, Bellugi, and Corina (1993) reported that cortical stimulation of areas within the left temporal lobe evoked many handshape errors while the signer labeled objects with ASL signs. Corina, McBurney, et al. (1999) studied a Deaf signer undergoing cortical stimulation mapping, and they also reported that stimulation within the left hemisphere evoked handshape errors during sign production (specifically with electrical stimulation to Broca's area and the supramarginal gyrus, see next section).

The Wada Test (Sodium Amytal Injection).   Prior to the surgical treatment of seizure disorders, patients may undergo the Wada test in which a barbiturate is injected into the left- or right-carotid artery, and either the left or right hemisphere is temporarily incapacitated. The purpose of this test is to determine which hemisphere is dominant for memory and language functions before removing part of the patient's temporal lobe to relieve the seizures, and thus to avoid serious language and memory impairments for the patient. A. Damasio, Bellugi, H. Damasio, Poizner, and Van Gilder (1986) studied a hearing ASL signer and found that when her left hemisphere was rendered inoperative by the Wada test, both sign and speech were impaired. When this patient subsequently underwent surgical removal of the anterior portion of the *right* temporal lobe, no impairments in either English or ASL were observed. Furthermore, Corina, McBurney, et al. (1999) studied a Deaf signer and found only left-hemisphere injection resulted in sign blockage and object naming errors—no language errors were observed with injections to the right hemisphere. Wolff, Sass, and Keiden (1994) reported similar findings with another Deaf signer. These results indicate that the left but not the right hemisphere is sufficient to support sign language production.

Evidence From Studies With Neurologically Intact Signers

Data from studies with normal Deaf signers also indicate left-hemispheric specialization for sign language processing. Various techniques can be used to measure neural function and lateralization in normal signers. The methodology and laterality findings for each technique are summarized next, and we return to some of these studies in more detail when we discuss specific aspects of the neural representation of sign language.

Visual Hemifield Presentation. This technique takes advantage of the crossed nature of the visual pathways within the brain. For example, words presented in the *right* visual field (RVF) initially stimulate the *left* hemisphere, and words presented in the *left* visual field (LVF) initially stimulate the *right* hemisphere. Many studies have found that written words presented to the RVF (left hemisphere) are recognized faster and more accurately than words presented to the LVF (right hemisphere; see Bryden, 1982). These results indicate that the left hemisphere exhibits a processing advantage for linguistic stimuli compared to the right hemisphere.

Results with Deaf signers also show a left hemisphere advantage for sign language when the appropriate methodological controls are in place. If static images of signs (e.g., line drawings) are presented with the hemifield technique, investigators generally find either a right-hemisphere advantage or no hemispheric asymmetry for sign recognition (McKeever, Hoemann, Florian, & Van Deventer, 1976; Poizner & Lane, 1979; Sanders, Wright, & Ellis, 1989). However, a left-hemisphere advantage is observed when the presentation of signs includes their movement (Emmorey & Corina, 1993; Neville, 1991a, 1991b; Poizner & Bellugi, 1984, described in Poizner & Kegl, 1992) or when signers are asked to make a semantic judgment, rather than simply recognize the sign (Grossi, Semenza, Corazza, & Volterra, 1996, studying Italian Sign Language; Vaid & Corina, 1989). These results suggest that to principally engage the left hemisphere in language processing, identifying static pictorial representations of signs is not enough, unless signers are also required to make a decision about meaning. Moreover, movement is critical to engaging the left hemisphere in sign recognition (see also Poizner, Battison, & Lane, 1979). This is not surprising, given that sign language processing involves recognizing moving signs, not static line drawings (see chap. 4 for further discussion of the importance of movement for lexical processing in ASL). When hearing subjects who do not know ASL are asked to process ASL sign forms (e.g., by making matching judgments), they never show a left-hemisphere advantage (either no asymmetry or more often, a right-hemisphere advantage is found). This result indicates that the left-hemisphere advantage for signers arises from the linguistic status of the ASL signs.

Dual Task Paradigm. This procedure assesses hemispheric asymmetries by measuring the disruption that occurs for one activity when another activity is performed at the same time, and it relies on the fact that the left hemisphere controls the right hand, and the right hemisphere controls the left hand. For example, speakers exhibit a slower rate of finger tapping with the right hand when simultaneously repeating words, compared with the left hand. The pattern of interference is interpreted as an index of "intrahemispheric resource competition" (Kinsbourne & Hicks, 1978).

That is, the left hemisphere must execute both the rapid finger tapping of the right hand and speech. Thus we observe a greater decrement in tapping for the right hand compared to the left because left-hand tapping is controlled by the right hemisphere, and therefore within hemispheric competition does not occur.

Using this paradigm, Corina, Vaid, and Bellugi (1992) tested hearing and Deaf native signers and found a decrement in right-hand tapping while the subjects were repeating ASL signs and while repeating English words (for the hearing signers), indicating left-hemisphere dominance for both spoken and signed language production. Furthermore, unpublished research by Emmorey and Corina (1990a) observed significantly slower right-hand tapping rates when Deaf signers were asked to simultaneously watch ASL stories for comprehension, indicating that the left hemisphere plays a greater role in sign language comprehension as well.

Event-Related Brain Potentials (ERPs).   For this technique, electrodes are placed on the scalp to record the electrical potentials (the voltage) of large populations of neurons within the brain. The resulting trace of voltage across time is known as an electroencephalogram (EEG), and event-related potentials (ERPs) are extracted from EEG recordings by time-locking the presentation of a stimulus with the EEG and then averaging across repeated presentations. In a study with native Deaf signers, Neville (1991a, 1991b) presented moving ASL signs to either the right or left visual hemifield, and subjects had to identify the signs. All subjects reported signs more accurately when they were presented initially to the left hemisphere (RVF). Furthermore, the ERP data showed a strong left-hemisphere asymmetry for processing ASL signs (specifically, there was a larger negative–positive shift from the left hemisphere 300 to 600 msec after the onset of sign presentation to either hemifield).

Neville et al. (1997) examined ERPs to ASL sentences presented to Deaf and hearing signers who were asked to decide whether the sentences were correct or semantically anomalous. The results indicated that the early left-hemisphere asymmetries that Neville, Mills, and Lawson (1992) previously observed when hearing subjects read English were not found for ASL comprehension. That is, when hearing subjects read English, there was an early negativity over the left hemisphere (between 150 to 280 msec), whereas when Deaf or hearing native signers were processing ASL, these early components were symmetrical across the left and right hemispheres. Later processing of ASL (550 msec after sign onset) was asymmetrical with a positivity that was larger from the left hemisphere. Neville et al. (1997) speculated that the early bilateral processing of ASL stimuli may result from "the recruitment of specialized areas within the right hemisphere in the analysis of shape, motion, and location information that is central to ASL" (p. 304). However, ERP studies of *auditory* language processing, rather than word-by-word reading, indicate less asymmetric and more bilateral processing for spoken language comprehension (e.g., Müller, King, & Kutas, 1997). The right hemisphere may play a greater role in both sign and speech comprehension, compared to reading written English (see also Hickok, Bellugi, & Klima, 1998b).

Positron Emission Tomography (PET).   The PET technique measures regional cerebral blood flow and relies on the link between blood flow and neuronal metabolism. When neurons become activated, they require an immediate increase in glucose and oxygen, and thus blood flow is increased to regions surrounding these neurons. Blood flow within the brain is measured by injecting a short-lived radioactive tracer into the blood stream (the amount of radiation is very small, about two times the natural background radiation one receives annually living in Denver, Colorado). The tracer preferentially flows toward areas of high blood flow. Thus, neuronal activation can be imaged by recording emissions from the tracer to localize those regions of the brain that exhibit higher rates of cellular metabolism and increased blood flow.

Using the PET technique, McGuire et al. (1997) found left-hemisphere activation when Deaf signers were asked to mentally recite sentences in British Sign Language. The activated regions (left inferior frontal cortex) corresponded to the same areas that are engaged during silent articulation of English sentences by hearing subjects. Visuospatial areas within the right hemisphere did not show significant activation for "inner signing" (or for "inner speech"). Similarly, Petitto et al. (2000) observed left-hemisphere activation when Deaf ASL signers and signers of Langue des Signes Québécoise (LSQ) were asked to overtly produce signs (subjects saw signed nouns and produced associated verbs). San Jose, Corina, Ackerman, Guillemin, and Braun (2000) also found activation within the left hemisphere in a verb generation task (left operculum and prefrontal cortex); crucially, this activation was observed whether signers produced verbs with their dominant right hand, with their left hand, or with both hands. This result suggests that the left hemisphere lateralization for sign language production is not simply due to contralateral motor control of the dominant right hand in signing.

Söderfeldt et al. (1997) studied the comprehension of continuous signing by hearing native signers of Swedish Sign Language (see also Söderfeldt, Rönnberg, & Risberg, 1994). During PET scanning, these bilingual subjects either watched signed stories or watched and listened to a speaker telling stories. The results showed bilateral activation for both spoken and sign language processing. During sign language comprehension, there was more activation in bilateral visual association areas (compared to watching and listening to a speaker), and there was more activation in bilateral perisylvian areas, which include auditory cortex, during spoken language comprehension (compared to watching a signed story). Although these results suggest differences in the neural areas responsible for speech and sign perception that are tied to sensory modality, the differences were not lateralized. That is, both hemispheres appeared to be engaged when processing complex language when it is in a primary code (speech or sign), as opposed to a derived code (written language; see chap. 7 for a discussion of written language as a derived code and the implications of primary vs. derived codes for working-memory processes).

Functional Magnetic Resonance Imaging (fMRI).   Traditionally, magnetic resonance imaging (MRI) has been used to provide high resolution images of internal anatomy, from knees to hearts to brains. Within recent years, however, the technique has been adapted to provide *functional* images of brain activity. It turns out that the magnetic resonance (MR) signal is sensitive to changes in the metabolic state of the brain. Small changes in the MR signal arise from changes in the magnetic state of hemoglobin, which carries oxygen in the blood. To be specific, deoxygenated hemoglobin is paramagnetic (responds to an induced magnetic field), whereas oxygenated hemoglobin is not. Thus, the fMRI technique measures the changes in blood oxygenation that accompany neural activity.

In a large fMRI study, Neville and colleagues investigated neural activity that occurred while Deaf and hearing subjects processed sentences in ASL and written English (Bavelier et al., 1998; Neville et al., 1998). The English stimuli were written sentences presented in 30-second blocks, which alternated with 30-second blocks of consonant strings. The ASL stimuli were ASL sentences, which alternated with strings of nonsign gestures. At the end of each run, subjects had to decide whether or not specific sentences and nonsense strings had been presented. For each subject group, statistical analysis of the MR signal determined which areas of the brain were more active during the language processing blocks, compared to the blocks with nonsense stimuli (consonant strings or nonsign gesture strings).

For both hearing and Deaf native ASL signers, fMRI revealed activation within left-hemisphere structures that are classically linked to language processing (Broca's and Wernicke's areas, see Figs. 9.2 and 9.4). These same left-hemisphere areas were also active when native speakers read English sentences. In addition, both Deaf and hearing signers exhibited a comparable increase in neural activation in the equivalent areas within the right hemisphere, but such right-hemisphere activation was not observed when native speakers read English sentences. Neville et al. (1998) interpret these findings as indicating that "the specific nature and structure of ASL results in the recruitment of the right hemisphere into the language system" (p. 928). However, Hickok, Bellugi, and Klima (1998b) took issue

English

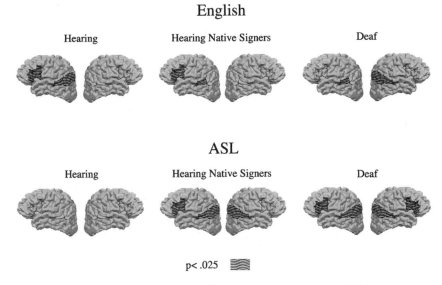

p<.025

FIG. 9.4. Representation of brain activation measured by fMRI in response to viewing ASL or reading English in three subject groups (hearing nonsigners, hearing native ASL signers, and Deaf native signers). From D. P. Corina, 1998c, "Neuronal Processing in Deaf Signers: Toward a Neurocognitive Model of Language Processing in the Deaf," in *Journal of Deaf Studies and Deaf Education, 3*(1), 35–48. Copyright © 1998 by Oxford University Press. Reprinted with permission.

with this interpretation, arguing that matching ASL processing with reading written English is not the appropriate comparison to investigate hemispheric laterality. They argue that reading may be much more lateralized to the left hemisphere than auditory language processing and that both lesion studies and brain imaging studies indicate a clear role for the right hemisphere in spoken language comprehension. In addition, recent fMRI results comparing reading and listening support stronger left-lateralization for reading (Michael, Keller, Carpenter, & Just, 1999). Nonetheless, the amount of right-hemisphere activity observed in the Neville et al. (1998) study for sign language comprehension is intriguing and deserves further investigation.

Conclusion: Left-Hemisphere Specialization for Language Is Not Due to the Rapid Temporal Sequencing Requirements of Speech

All of the studies investigating hemispheric specialization for sign language, from lesion studies to neural imaging, have found that language areas within the left hemisphere are recruited for sign language processing. Such findings imply that these particular brain areas are well de-signed to process linguistic information independent of language modal-ity. The data thus allow us to reject the rapid temporal processing account of left-hemispheric specialization for language. As discussed in chapter 4, the rate of sign production is much slower than speech production due to the larger articulators, and these production constraints create a segment transmission rate of about 7 to 11 segments per second, compared to the 10 to 15 segments per second for speech. Furthermore, transitions be-tween handshapes within a sign have been estimated as 200 msec in dura-tion (Corina, 1993), whereas consonant–vowel transitions within spoken words have a duration of only about 40 msec. Given these data, Hickok, Klima, and Bellugi (1996) concluded that "left-hemisphere dominance for language is not solely determined by a general proclivity for processing fast temporal information" (p. 702).[2] Thus, left-hemisphere specialization for language does not appear to arise from the particular demands of au-ditory speech perception.

**Dissociating Left-Hemispheric Specialization
for Language From Symbolic Gesture
and Complex Motor Control**

The findings discussed thus far do not allow us to determine whether left-hemisphere specialization may arise from a domain-general specialization in symbolic processing or from the motoric properties of linguistic expres-sion because both signed and spoken language are symbolic and involve complex motor activity. We now turn to investigations that address these issues.

Dissociating Sign Language and Symbolic Gesture. Several studies provide convincing evidence of a dissociation between the neural systems involved in sign language versus conventionalized gesture and panto-mime. Using the dual-task paradigm, Corina, Vaid, et al. (1992) reported left-hemisphere dominance for producing ASL signs, but no laterality ef-fect when subjects had to produce symbolic gestures (e.g., waving good-bye or thumbs-up). In addition, several studies report LHD patients who exhibited sign language impairments but well-preserved conventional

---

[2]Corina (1999b) took issue with this conclusion, suggesting that "the integration of a highly parallel articulatory signal may place quite serious demands on temporal processing systems which are keeping track of relations between parallel dimensions, just as is found for speech" (p. 234). However, the claim has been that the left hemisphere is specialized for rapid *sequential* processing of temporal information (Tallal et al., 1993), and all evidence in-dicates that sequential information within the signed signal is nowhere near the 30 to 40 msec distinctions found for speech.

gesture and pantomime (Corina, Poizner, et al., 1992; Kegl & Poizner, 1997; Poizner et al., 1987).

In a detailed case study, Corina, Poizner, et al. (1992) described patient WL who sustained damage to perisylvian regions in the left hemisphere and was aphasic for sign language. He exhibited poor sign language comprehension, and his sign production was characterized by phonological and semantic errors with reduced grammatical structure. Nonetheless, WL was able to produce stretches of pantomime and tended to substitute pantomimes for signs, even when the pantomime required more complex movements (this tendency to pantomime was not present prior to his stroke). Furthermore, WL showed a similar dissociation in his ability to *comprehend* ASL signs versus pantomimed gestures. When shown single ASL signs (e.g., APPLE), he was impaired in his ability to select the matching picture, but when shown pantomime (e.g., someone pretending to eat an apple), WL's comprehension was normal. Corina, Poizner, et al. (1992) concluded that such cases indicate that sign language impairments arising from left-hemisphere damage cannot be attributed to general symbolic impairments. In addition, these data provide neurological evidence that signed languages consist of *linguistic* gestures and not simply elaborate pantomimes.

Dissociating Neural Control for Motoric Versus Linguistic Processes. The case of WL and other LHD signers indicate that the neural systems underlying sign production and pantomime are separable (at least at some level). However, it is possible that impairments in sign language production (and spoken language production for that matter) may arise from an underlying disorder in motor movement selection and sequencing (Kimura, 1993). A motor-programming deficit might affect sign language production, but not pantomime, because sign language (like speech) requires the programming of novel combinations of movements, whereas pantomime can rely on familiar stereotypic movements (such as hammering or combing the hair). To assess the ability to produce nonsymbolic motor movements, patients with aphasia are often given a diagnostic test in which they are asked to copy meaningless movement sequences of the hand and arm (Kimura & Archibald, 1974). Corina, Poizner, et al. (1992) reported that WL performed within normal limits on this task, as did other aphasic signers described by Poizner et al. (1987). Furthermore, in a group study, Hickok, Klima, and Bellugi (1996) found that scores on this movement copy task did not correlate with linguistic impairments as measured by the BDAE.

However, it is unlikely that motor planning for signing is completely autonomous and independent of the motor systems involved in producing nonlinguistic movements. In fact, Corina (1999b) argued that the relation between linguistic processes and motor programming has not been adequately evaluated, citing the small population of aphasic signers that have been assessed and the inadequacies of measuring voluntary motor control with a test that contains only a few items. Furthermore, Corina and colleagues have recently shown in a series of PET studies that cortical regions engaged in the everyday perception of human actions appear to also be recruited for linguistic processing in native Deaf signers (Corina et al., 2000; Knapp et al., 2001). Specifically, neural areas implicated in the processing of biological motion and neural sites within left inferior frontal cortex implicated in recognizing meaningful actions (e.g., Decety et al., 1997) were engaged when Deaf signers watched either ASL signs or meaningful human actions (e.g., "self-grooming" behaviors or human actions performed with an object).

Nonetheless, the findings to date suggest that sign language impairment arising from left-hemisphere damage cannot be attributed solely to a simple disruption of motor control. For example, some aphasic error types are more easily explained as phonological substitutions, rather than as phonetic or motoric deficits (Corina 1999a, 2000b). In addition, using the dual-task paradigm with neurologically intact signers, Corina, Vaid, et al. (1992) found no hemispheric asymmetry for producing arbitrary (non-symbolic) gestures, but a clear left-hemisphere asymmetry for producing ASL signs.

Dissociating Sign Language Ability and Nonlinguistic Spatial Cognitive Ability

As already noted, single case studies and larger group studies indicate that damage to the right hemisphere does not result in sign language aphasia (Corina, 1998a, 1998b; Hickok, Klima, & Bellugi, 1996; Poizner et al., 1987). These same studies have also shown that right hemisphere damage does result in various types of nonlinguistic spatial cognitive deficits. Like RHD speakers, signers with right-hemisphere damage exhibit impairments of visuospatial abilities, such as perceiving spatial orientation, creating perspective within a drawing, or interpreting spatial configurations. Figure 9.5 provides an illustration of the performance of LHD aphasic signers and RHD nonaphasic signers on standard spatial cognitive tasks. The pattern of linguistic deficits observed with left-hemisphere damage does not appear to simply be a function of deficits in general spatial cognitive ability. In fact, we see a double dissociation between sign language abilities and basic visuospatial cognitive functions: Sign language aphasia can occur without accompanying nonlanguage visuospatial impairment, whereas severe deficits in visual spatial constructive abilities can occur without an accompanying sign language aphasia.

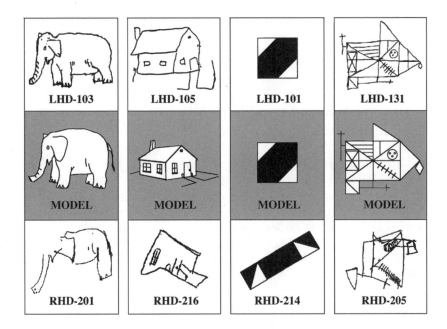

FIG. 9.5.   Comparison of spatial cognitive abilities in signers with LHD (top) or RHD (bottom). A) The BDAE Drawing to Copy subtest (subjects are asked to draw the model picture); B) The WAIS Block Design test (subjects are asked to recreate the model using red and white colored blocks); C) The Rey Osterrieth Complex Figure (subjects are asked to copy the model figure). Illustrations copyright © Ursula Bellugi, The Salk Institute.

However, it is not the case that the left hemisphere is aspatial with no associated visuospatial functions. In fact, the left hemisphere has been shown to be more accurate in processing *local level* visuospatial information, whereas the right hemisphere is more accurate in processing *global level* visuospatial information (Delis, Robertson, & Efron, 1986; Martin, 1979). For example, when drawing, LHD patients tend to omit the details of a figure while maintaining its overall global configuration; in contrast, RHD patients may correctly reproduce the local details of the figure, while failing to accurately reproduce the global configuration (Kritchevsky, 1988). Hickok, Kirk, and Bellugi (1998) investigated whether this pattern of hemispheric specialization holds for Deaf signers and whether the sign language deficits observed with left-hemisphere damage can be explained in terms of a more general deficit in local level visuospatial processing. Their results paralleled those with hearing patients: LHD signers were significantly worse at reproducing local-level features (e.g., drawing the window panes on a house; see Fig. 9.5), whereas RHD signers were significantly worse at reproducing global level features (e.g., omitting the side or roof

of the house; see Fig. 9.5). In addition, the local level performance of the
LHD signers did not correlate with their performance on sign language
tasks, which indicates that their language deficits do not arise from an underlying general deficit in processing local level visuospatial information.

WITHIN HEMISPHERE ORGANIZATION
OF SIGN LANGUAGE

The left hemisphere is clearly dominant for both signed and spoken language. This neural asymmetry suggests that neither perceptual mechanisms
(audition or visuospatial processing) nor motoric systems drive brain organization for language. Indeed, the evidence suggests that the brain respects
distinctions in *function*, rather than form. We now further explore this hypothesis by examining whether neural systems *within* the left hemisphere
are influenced by the visual input pathways and the manual output pathways required for sign language comprehension and production.

Aphasic Syndromes

The left hemisphere is not homogenous; damage to different perisylvian
areas causes distinct types of language impairment for both signers and
speakers, and damage outside of this region does not give rise to aphasic
deficits. The patterns of impairment that have been reported for sign
aphasia are similar to what has been found for spoken language aphasia,
indicating that there is a common functional organization for the two
forms of language. Specifically, damage to anterior language regions
causes nonfluent aphasias (e.g., Broca's aphasia), whereas fluent aphasias
(e.g., Wernicke's aphasia) arise from lesions involving posterior language
regions (Hickok et al., 1998b). A common feature of nonfluent aphasia is a
tendency to omit grammatical morphology and to produce effortful and
halting speech or sign. The following English example of nonfluent
agrammatic production is from Goodglass (1993, p. 81) and the ASL example is from Poizner et al. (1987, p. 120):

English
Examiner: What brought you to the hospital?
Patient: Yeah . . . Wednesday, . . . Paul and dad . . . . Hospital . . . yeah . . .
doctors, two . . an' teeth

ASL
For presentation purposes the Examiner's questions are given in English.
Examiner: What else happened?
Patient GD: CAR . . . DRIVE . . . BROTHER . . . DRIVE . . . I . . . S-T-A-D

[Attempts to gesture "stand up"]
Examiner: You stood up?
Patient: YES . . . BROTHER . . . . DRIVE . . . DUNNO . . [Attempts to gesture "wave goodbye"]
Examiner: Your brother was driving?
Patient: YES . . . BACK . . . DRIVE . . . BROTHER . . MAN . . MAMA . . STAY . . . BROTHER . . . . DRIVE

In contrast to these production deficits, signers and speakers with anterior lesions often have relatively spared language comprehension (Goodglass, 1993; Hickok et al., 1998a). The reverse is true for posterior lesions, which often result in language comprehension deficits.

Posterior perisylvian lesions generally result in fluent aphasia, in which signing or speaking is fluent but often ungrammatical, and there is a tendency to select inappropriate words or to produce jargon (nonsense words). The following are examples of fluent aphasic production in English (from Goodglass, 1993; p. 86) and in ASL (from Poizner et al., 1987; p. 98):

English (in response to "How are you today?")
I feel very well. My hearing, writing have been doing well. Things that I couldn't hear from. In other words, I used to be able to work cigarettes I didn't know how. . . . Chesterfeela, for 20 years I can write it.

ASL (asterisks indicate errors)
AND HAVE ONE *WAY-DOWN-THERE (unintelligible). MAN WALK, MAN SEE THAT *DISCONNECT E-X-T-E-N-T-I-O-N O-F *EARTH ROOM. HAVE FOR MAN CAN *LIVE ROOF, LIGHT, SHADE[seriated plural] *PULL-DOWN[[+dual]+habitual]

English translation: "And there's one way down at the end [unintelligible]. The man walked over to see the disconnected, an extension of the earth room. It's there for the man can live a roof and light with shades to keep pulling down."

The ASL example is from patient PD who was somewhat unusual because although his output was similar to a Wernicke's aphasic, his ASL comprehension was relatively spared.

The findings thus far indicate that the pattern of within hemispheric organization for sign language broadly mirrors that for spoken language. The general dichotomy between anterior–posterior lesions and nonfluent–fluent aphasia holds for sign language as well. We now assess the specific neural systems involved in sign language production and comprehension and explore whether there is evidence for within hemisphere reorganization for language in Deaf signers.

The Functional Neuroanatomy of Sign Language Production

Damage to the left hemisphere can cause not only aphasia but hemiparesis (weakness) in the right hand, and, thus, some right-handed aphasic signers must use their left hand as the dominant hand for signing after their stroke. However, the signing errors produced by these patients do not arise from a lack of agility with their left hand. For example, when right-handed signers without brain injury are asked to sign with the left hand, they do not produce the phonological errors observed with aphasic signers (Vaid, Bellugi, & Poizner, 1989). For speakers, the vocal tract and tongue are midline structures innervated bilaterally (i.e., by both hemispheres), but it is the left hemisphere that unilaterally controls speech production. One might hypothesize that because the two hands are independent articulators controlled to a large extent by opposite hemispheres, there might be less unilateral control over sign language production. However, the evidence strongly indicates left hemisphere control for the production of linguistic movements in sign language.

Broca's area has long been thought to play an important role in speech production. As can be seen in Figs. 9.1 and 9.2, Broca's area is just anterior to the primary motor areas for the lips and tongue, and it is logical that an area involved in the control of speech would be anatomically located near the speech articulators. Is this same area involved in sign language production? Or is the functional equivalent of Broca's area shifted superiorly so that it is next to the motor representation for the hand and arm? To answer these questions, Hickok, Kritchevsky, Bellugi, and Klima (1996) studied a native Deaf signer (RS) who had a left hemisphere lesion principally involving Broca's area (specifically, the left frontal operculum and inferior portion of the primary motor cortex). RS exhibited good comprehension but deficits in sign production. Specifically, she tended to "shadow" one-handed signs with her nondominant (left) hand, and she had difficulty coordinating the two hands in two-handed signs, as illustrated in Fig. 9.6. The deficits in bimanual coordination were specific to sign language production and were not present when RS produced nonlinguistic hand movements. Such deficits in coordinating the two hands may be similar to the phonetic deficits observed for speakers with nonfluent aphasia who have difficulty coordinating independent speech articulators, for example, the larynx, tongue, and lips (see Blumstein, 1998). The case of RS suggests that Broca's area plays a similar role in language production for both speech and sign.

Further evidence for the role of Broca's area in sign language production comes from a cortical stimulation mapping study by Corina, McBurney, et al. (1999). Stimulation of Broca's area resulted in sign execution er-

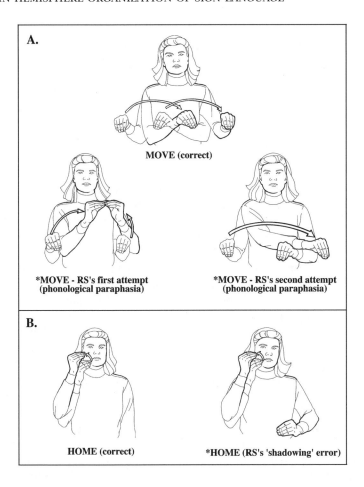

FIG. 9.6.   A) Examples of phonemic paraphasias involving bimanual coordination. The correct form is shown at the top. In the first example, both hands incorrectly articulate mirror movements (bottom left). In the second example, one hand fails to move at all. B) Example of 'shadowing' during sign production. The correct (nonshadowed) form is on the left. Illustrations from Hickok, Kritchevsky, Bellugi, and Klima (1996); copyright © Ursula Bellugi, The Salk Institute.

rors, even though this area was just anterior to the motor representation of the lips for this Deaf signer. The errors produced by stimulation to Broca's area were characterized by a lax articulation of the intended sign. For example, handshapes were reduced (e.g., a loose fist, rather than the intended Y handshape of the sign COW), and movement was nonspecific (e.g., repeated tapping or rubbing, rather than the intended twisting movement). In general, stimulation of Broca's area resulted in a disruption of the global articulatory integrity of sign production. This finding is consistent with the hypothesis that Broca's area participates in the motoric execution of language output, particularly at the level of phonetic implementation.

In contrast, stimulation of the supramarginal gyrus (see Fig. 9.2) produced both phonological and semantic errors, rather than the reduced articulations that characterized signing under stimulation to Broca's area (Corina, McBurney, et al., 1999). The phonological errors involved misselections of phonological components; for example, the signer produced a clearly articulated X handshape for the open-A handshape of the intended sign PEANUT and a 3 handshape for the B handshape in PIG. The semantic errors were generally formationally similar to the intended targets. For example, when shown a picture of a horse, the signer produced the sign COW, which differs only in handshape from the sign HORSE. Furthermore, when asked to repeat a sign presented on videotape, stimulation to the supramarginal gyrus (SMG) did not result in production errors, but stimulation to Broca's area again resulted in imprecise sign articulation. Thus, the SMG may be involved in sign production when semantic information (as required for picture naming) and phonology interact. Signers with lesions to this area also produce errors, which are semantic–phonological blends (Corina et al., 1992). Corina, McBurney, et al. (1999) hypothesized that the SMG plays a critical role in the selection of phonological feature information and the association of this information with semantic representations during language production. Support for this hypothesis comes from a PET study by Emmorey, Grabowski, McCullough, Damasio, and Bellugi (2000). We found that the SMG was more engaged when signers produced native ASL signs compared to fingerspelled signs in a picture naming task. Native signs engage phonological processes that are violated by fingerspelled signs (see chap. 2), suggesting that the SMG is indeed involved in the selection of phonological features of ASL signs.

Corina, McBurney, et al. (1999) also found sporadic semantic and phonological errors with stimulation to other areas within the left temporal lobe. Some semantic and phonological errors, or paraphasias, occur with almost all forms of aphasia, and this is true for sign language aphasia as well (Hickok et al., 1998a). Examples of a phonological and a semantic paraphasia from English speaking aphasics would be saying "paker" for "paper" and "atlas" for "globe" (Goodglass, 1993). Sign aphasics also produce semantic paraphasias, for example signing YEAR for HOUR, BED for CHAIR, GRANDMOTHER for GRAND-DAUGHTER, or FOX for WOLF (Brentari, Poizner, & Kegl, 1995; Poizner et al., 1987). Figure 9.7 provides examples of phonological errors made by signers with left-hemisphere damage.

Corina (2000b) recently pointed out that a priori one would expect the major phonological components of sign language to be equally vulnerable

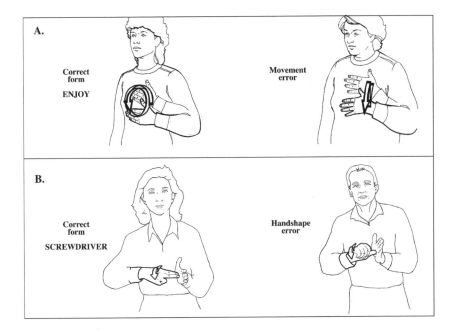

FIG. 9.7. Examples of phonemic paraphasias from LHD signers. A) Handshape and movement substitution errors made by LHD signer KL (from Poizner, Klima, & Bellugi, 1987). B) Handshape substitutions errors made by LHD signer WL (from Corina, Poizner, Bellugi, Feinberg, Dowd, & O'Grady-Batch, 1992). Illustrations copyright © Ursula Bellugi, The Salk Institute.

to disruption; however, it appears that phonological paraphasias disproportionately involve handshape. Corina suggests that this pattern of disruption supports the special status of handshape as a separate and independent autosegment (see chap. 2) and the analogy between handshape and consonants in spoken language. In spoken language, phonological paraphasias disproportionally affect consonants compared to vowels. In addition, phonological substitutions in spoken language tend to result in more unmarked (more basic) forms (Goodglass, 1993). Similarly, Corina (2000b) argued that phonological paraphasias in ASL tend to arise from the substitution of an unmarked handshape for a marked handshape (assuming Brentari's, 1990, analysis of markedness, rather than Battison's, 1978, analysis). Finally, spoken-language paraphasias tend to maintain the syllabic structure of the intended word, and the rarity of movement errors in signed paraphasias may arise from the prosodic status of movement within the sign syllable (see chap. 2).

In sum, the data from sign language suggest that there are invariant principals for the organization of neural systems underlying language production. Neural reorganization for language production systems does not occur for Deaf signers, despite the considerable differences between the vocal tract and the hands as articulators. Thus, the functional specialization of neural systems is not dependent on the nature of the motor systems involved in language production. Rather, the abstract nature of phonology as a level of linguistic representation and the interface between phonology and semantics may drive the organization of neural systems within the brain.

The Functional Neuroanatomy of Sign Language Comprehension

Impairments in auditory language comprehension occur with damage to the left-temporal lobe in regions bordering primary auditory cortex (Goodglass, 1993). Given that linguistic input is visual for Deaf signers, we can ask whether the temporal lobe plays the same role in sign language comprehension as it does for spoken language. Love, Bellugi, Klima, and Hickok (1999) conducted a large group study with nineteen LHD and RHD signers, comparing performance on sign language comprehension tasks with respect to whether the signers' lesions involved the temporal lobe. Only the signers with left-temporal lobe lesions performed poorly on all sign comprehension tasks—signers with lesions outside the temporal lobe performed quite well, particularly on single-sign and simple-sentence comprehension tasks. Thus, language comprehension depends on intact left-temporal lobe structures, regardless of whether language is perceived auditorily or visually.

What about the role of auditory cortex within the temporal lobe? As diagrammed in Fig. 9.1, auditory cortex lies in the posterior portion of the superior temporal gyrus (STG). Primary auditory cortex (the first cortical area to receive input from the cochlea or *Heschl's gyrus*) is buried within the STG, and the area posterior to Heschl's gyrus is called the *planum temporale* (PT) and contains secondary auditory association cortex. Several recent PET and fMRI studies have found activation in posterior STG (and the planum temporale) for Deaf signers when they were watching signed language (MacSweeney et al., 2001, for British Sign Language; Nishimura et al., 1999, for Japanese Sign Language; Petitto et al., 2000, for ASL and Langue des Signes Québécoise). This neural area has long been known to respond to spoken language input (either internally or externally generated), but the language input was completely visual in the sign language studies. In the MacSweeney et al. (2001) fMRI study, subjects watched signed sentences and pressed a button when they detected a semantically anomalous sentence; in the Nishimura et al. (1999) PET study, the subject passively viewed single signs, and in the Petitto et al. (2000) PET study subjects passively viewed signs or nonsigns. Petitto et al. (2000) suggested that "the PT can be activated either by sight or sound because this tissue may be dedicated to processing specific distributions of complex, low-level units in rapid temporal alternation, rather than to sound, *per se*. Alternatively, the cortical tissue in the STG may be specialized for auditory processing, but may undergo functional reorganization in the presence of visual input when neural input from the auditory periphery is absent" (p. 8). As we have already discussed, the rapid temporal alternations of sign do not approach the 40 msec rate found for the sound alternations of speech, arguing against Petitto et al.'s initial hypothesis. Support for their alternative hypothesis can be found in the study by MacSweeney et al. (2001). MacSweeney et al. (2001) found that the activation in left STG during sign language comprehension was significantly *less* in hearing native signers compared to deaf native signers, suggesting that auditory association cortex is predominantly reserved for processing auditory input for hearing signers, but this neural region is engaged when processing visual signed input for Deaf signers. Thus, the STG may be initially specialized for auditory processing, and this neural region retains its specialization when auditory input is received during development (as for hearing signers), but undergoes functional reorganization to process visual sign language input when no auditory input is received (see also Söderfeldt et al., 1997).

Finally, no study thus far has reported clear activation within primary auditory cortex (Heschl's gyrus) for Deaf signers viewing sign language (see also Hickok et al., 1997). Nishimura et al. (1999) reported that primary auditory cortex was not activated when their Deaf subject watched single signs, but after the subject had been given a cochlear implant (an artificial prosthesis inserted into the inner ear that electrically stimulates the cochlear nerve), auditory stimulation (spoken words) delivered via the implant was found to activate primary auditory cortex. Thus, the primary projection area within the cortex for audition may be rigidly specialized, but other auditory related areas within the superior temporal gyrus may be more plastic (or multi-modal) and can process visual linguistic input.

Unlike for spoken language comprehension, visual cortices are critical for sign language comprehension (as one would expect). Hickok, Klima, Kritchevsky, and Bellugi (1995) presented a case of "sign blindness," in which the signer, BC (also referred to as LHD–111) had a lesion that involved all of the left primary visual cortex and affected projections through the posterior part of the corpus callosum (the structure that connects the left and right hemispheres). In essence, this lesion disconnected the language areas of the left hemisphere from visual input. Thus, BC was able to sign fluently and grammatically, but her sign language comprehension was severely impaired. Crucially, her nonlinguistic visual object recognition abilities were unimpaired. BC was essentially blind for sign language as a result of the disconnection between left-language cortices and visual input.[3] This case also demonstrates that the right hemisphere is extremely limited (at best) in its ability to support sign language comprehension.

Other left-hemisphere structures also appear to be involved in both spoken and signed language comprehension. Specifically, the supramarginal gyrus appears to be involved in phonological processing of speech (Caplan, Gow, & Makris, 1995) and of sign (Corina, McBurney, et al., 1999; Love et al., 1997). Signers with lesions involving the SMG performed significantly worse on a test of phonological ability (choosing which two pictures corresponded to rhyming signs), compared to those with no damage to this area (Love et al., 1997). As just discussed, the planum temporale (PT) is another structure thought to be involved in spoken language comprehension because of its proximity to primary auditory cortex and its asymmetry; the PT tends to be larger and have a different shape in the left hemisphere (Geschwind & Levitsky, 1968; Rubens, Mahowald, & Hutton, 1976). Recently, Cismaru et al. (1999) found a similar anatomical left–right asymmetry for the PT in Deaf signers. Furthermore, using PET, Petitto et al. (1998) found bilateral activation in the PT for native Deaf signers when they were asked to make phonological judgments (i.e., deciding whether two signs were the same or different, with the different signs varying by only a single phonological parameter). When hearing nonsigners were asked to make such same–different judgments, no activation was observed in the PT. Because the same–different task was a purely visual task for the hearing nonsigners, but a linguistic task for the Deaf signers, Petitto et al. (1998) hypothesized that the PT is involved in processing sublexical aspects of sign language.

Furthermore, the results of the fMRI study of Neville et al. (1998) indicated that the activation of several critical left-hemisphere structures during sign language processing is not the result of neural reorganization due to a lack of auditory input because these same areas were active when *hearing* native ASL signers processed sign language. Specifically, when either hearing or Deaf native signers were asked to watch ASL sentences for comprehension, neural activation was seen within the following language areas in the left hemisphere (see Fig. 9.4): Broca's area, Wernicke's area, the superior temporal sulcus, and the angular gyrus (implicated in reading processes for hearing people).

Finally, as discussed in chapter 6, results from studies using event-related brain potentials (ERPs) suggest that different neural systems un-

---

[3] This case is analogous to "word blindness" or "pure alexia" that occurs for speakers with a similar type of lesion (A. R. Damasio & H. Damasio, 1983). Because language areas in the left hemisphere are disconnected from visual input, these patients can write, but they cannot read. BC was also alexic and could not read English.

derlie the comprehension of *open class* and *closed class* words for both speakers and signers (Neville et al., 1997; Neville, Mills, & Lawson, 1992). Open class words include nouns, verbs, and adjectives and make reference to specific objects, events, or qualities, whereas closed class words include articles, conjunctions, and auxiliaries and are critical to grammatical processing. Neville et al. (1997) found that Deaf and hearing native signers exhibit distinct patterns of ERPs for open and closed class ASL signs.[4] Specifically, closed class signs elicited an early anterior negativity not observed for open class signs, and open class signs elicited a later posterior negativity. This pattern mirrors that found for speakers reading open and closed class words, except that the ERP response to closed class words was lateralized to the left for English speakers, but it was bilateral for native ASL signers (but not for late learners; see chap. 6). Overall, the ERP results indicate that for both signed and spoken languages, there are distinct neural systems that underlie semantic and grammatical processing.

In sum, although the neural areas surrounding primary auditory cortex within the left hemisphere have received minimal auditory input for congenitally deaf signers, these areas nonetheless come to subserve language functions. In addition, several structures within the left hemisphere that have been shown to be involved in spoken language comprehension are also recruited for sign language processing. These results suggest a great deal of neuronal plasticity, and they also imply that there are biological or developmental constraints that cause specific brain areas within the left hemisphere to be well-suited for processing linguistic information, independent of input modality.

The Functional Neuroanatomy for the Production and Perception of Emotional and Linguistic Facial Expressions

The right hemisphere appears to mediate the production of emotional facial expressions and may also play a greater role in the recognition of emotional expressions (e.g., Borod, Koff, & Caron, 1983; Strauss & Moscovitch, 1981). Is this right hemispheric specialization due to a superiority in processing human faces in general, or is it due to a superiority in processing emotional information? Sign language provides a unique tool for investigating these questions because facial expression is used to signal linguistic distinctions (as was elaborated in chap. 2). Corina (1989) presented linguistic and affective facial expressions to both Deaf signers and hearing nonsigners, using the visual hemifield technique. For hearing

---

[4]Closed class ASL signs included pronouns, conjunctions, and auxiliaries. Verbs with inflectional morphology, classifier signs, and compound signs were excluded from the analysis.

nonsigners, a right-hemisphere advantage was found for both types of facial expressions, suggesting that the right hemisphere is specialized for recognizing all forms of facial expression. In contrast, for Deaf signers, hemispheric processing was influenced by the function of the facial expression,
with more left hemisphere involvement for linguistic expressions.

Similarly, Corina, Bellugi, and Reilly (1999) presented evidence from
two studies that indicated differential neural control of emotional versus
linguistic facial expressions. One study capitalized on the finding that the
left side of the face (controlled by the right hemisphere) exhibits a more
intense expression, which is attributed to a greater role of the right hemisphere in mediating affective behavior (Campbell, 1978). Corina, Bellugi,
and Reilly (1999) found the opposite asymmetry for linguistic facial expressions, with the right side of the face (controlled by the left hemisphere) exhibiting a more intense expression. A second study found a
double dissociation for the control of the production of linguistic and affective facial expressions. Specifically, an aphasic LHD signer, GD, tended
to omit linguistic facial expressions when required, but she was able to
produce affective expressions in expected contexts. Kegl and Poizner
(1997) also described an aphasic signer, NS, who exhibited preserved facial affect but nonetheless omitted syntactic facial expressions. In contrast,
a nonaphasic RHD signer, SM, produced linguistic facial expressions correctly, but her face was blank when expressing her own emotions (either
positive or negative). Similar loss of affective expression has been observed in speakers with right-hemisphere damage (Feyereisen, 1986).

Thus, the neurological evidence joins the developmental evidence presented in chapter 5 to indicate that function rather than form drives the
development of neural systems controlling human facial expression. For
Deaf signers, there appears to be a reorganization of the neural systems
underlying possibly innate behaviors (emotional facial expression) to subserve new functions. The left hemisphere comes to control the production
and recognition of linguistic facial expressions as part of the grammar of
ASL.

THE ROLE OF THE RIGHT HEMISPHERE
IN LANGUAGE PROCESSES

Although aphasia does not result from right hemisphere damage, the
right hemisphere is clearly not alinguistic. The right hemisphere has been
shown to exhibit linguistic abilities at both lexical and discourse levels
(Beeman & Chiarello, 1998; Joanette, Goulet, & Hannequin 1990), and as
already noted, it is becoming clear that the right hemisphere is more engaged when individuals are listening to spoken language than when they

are either reading or speaking, which both appear to be more left-lateralized. In this section, we explore whether the right hemisphere is also similarly involved in sign language comprehension and whether it might also play a unique role in certain aspects of sign language processing.

Lexical Processing

The right hemisphere has been claimed to be much better at processing words with imageable, concrete referents (e.g., bed, flower) compared to words with abstract referents (e.g., truth, rule; Day, 1979; Young & Ellis, 1985). Chiarello, Senehi, and Nuding (1987) hypothesized that this effect is postlexical, occurring after semantic information has been retrieved. They suggest that "once the lexicon has been accessed, and a semantic representation retrieved, subsequent right hemisphere semantic processing is mediated by imagery, while the left hemisphere can utilize either verbal or imaginal codes" (p. 56). As discussed in chapter 8, signers exhibit enhanced imagery abilities that are hypothesized to be tied to certain processing requirements of ASL, and this enhancement seems to be linked to the right hemisphere (Emmorey et al., 1993; Emmorey & Kosslyn, 1996).

Emmorey and Corina (1993) used the visual hemifield technique to investigate the pattern of laterality for imageable and abstract signs, hypothesizing that imagery might play a greater role in processing ASL. The results supported this hypothesis. Deaf signers showed a right-hemisphere advantage for recognizing imageable signs, and a left-hemisphere advantage for abstract signs. In contrast, hearing subjects tend to simply show improved performance for imageable words within the right hemisphere (compared to abstract words), rather than a processing *advantage* of the right over the left hemisphere. Emmorey and Corina (1993) speculated that the superior imagery abilities of ASL signers may enhance some linguistic processes within the right hemisphere when a high degree of imagery is involved.

Classifier Constructions and Topographic Functions of Signing Space

As discussed in chapter 3, signing space can function iconically to represent spatial relations among objects. Signers with right-hemisphere damage have been reported to exhibit impairments in the topographic function of signing space. For example, when a RHD signer, BI,[5] was asked to

---

[5]Lesion information was not published, but BI exhibited neurological symptoms and behavior typical of right-hemisphere damaged patients.

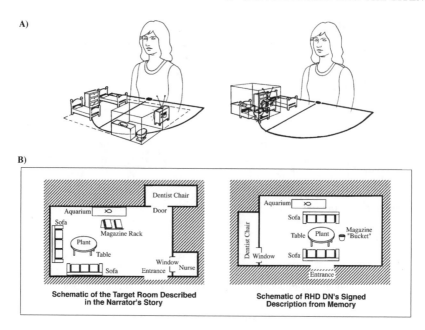

FIG. 9.8.   Illustration of the breakdown in the use of topographic space following right-hemisphere damage. A) A schematic of RHD signer BI's spatially distorted room description (from Poizner, Klima, & Bellugi, 1987). B) Schematic of RHD signer DN's retelling of a spatial description (adapted from Emmorey, Corina, & Bellugi, 1995). Illustrations copyright © Ursula Bellugi, The Salk Institute.

describe her room, she displaced all of the objects to the right in signing space and did not respect spatial relations, haphazardly placing the furniture in one place (see Fig. 9.8A, from Poizner et al., 1987). Emmorey, Corina, et al. (1995) asked another RHD signer, DN,[6] to immediately repeat two types of ASL stories, each 30 seconds long. In one set, signing space functioned topographically (e.g., a description of the layout of a dentist's office), and in the other set, no topographic information was conveyed (e.g., a discussion of favorite foods). The stories were matched for the amount of information they contained (i.e., the number of propositions). The RHD signer, DN, correctly retold the stories that contained no topographic information, remembering even slightly more information than control signers. However, she was quite impaired in her ability to retell the spatial stories. The impairment was not in remembering the items in the stories, but in the correct placement of classifier signs within signing space to indicate the spatial relations among those items. Figure 9.8B pro-

---

[6] This signer was referred to by the initials AS in Poizner and Kegl (1992), and in Loew, Kegl, and Poizner (1997).

vides a schematic of the nature of her errors. Neither of these RHD signers were aphasic for ASL—their descriptions of spatial layouts were fluent and grammatical, but the location and orientation of the objects were described incorrectly.

Poizner et al. (1987) suggested that there is a double dissociation between *spatial mapping* (the topographic function of signing space) and *spatialized syntax* (the use of signing space for coreference and agreeing verbs; see chap. 2). For example, although the RHD signer BI was impaired in her ability to use signing space topographically, she was able to use space for coreference and to correctly use agreeing verbs in other contexts. In contrast to BI, the aphasic signer PD described his apartment with no spatial distortions, but he produced errors in verb agreement (Poizner et al., 1987).

Hickok, Say, et al. (1996) further pursued this apparent dissociation by directly comparing the performance of an aphasic LHD signer, RS, and a nonaphasic RHD signer, SJ, on tests assessing the *comprehension* of signing space when it was used to express subject–object distinctions or to express topographic information. The first test assessed comprehension of verb agreement in simple reversible sentences (e.g., "The cat bit the dog"). The examiner produced a signed description in which two nominals (e.g., CAT, DOG) were first associated with two locations in signing space via indexing (pointing) signs; the examiner then produced an agreeing verb (e.g., BITE) with movement between the two spatial locations indicating the referents associated with the subject and object. Subjects then chose which of two pictures matched this signed description. The LHD signer RS performed significantly worse than control signers on this task, whereas the performance of the RHD signer SJ did not differ from controls. The second test assessed comprehension of the topographic use of space. Subjects first viewed a room layout on videotape, and then a signed description of the room; the task was to determine whether the room layout matched the signed description. On this task, the LHD and RHD signers showed the reverse pattern: RS (LHD) was unimpaired (scoring 100% correct), whereas SJ's performance was no better than chance. Hickok, Say, et al. (1996) concluded that "the linguistic and spatial uses of space in ASL are dissociable" (p. 590).

However, further exploration does not support a strong distinction between syntactic and topographic functions of space. For example, Poizner et al. (1987) reported that *both* LHD and RHD signers performed poorly on the verb agreement comprehension test used by Hickok, Say, et al. (1996). LHD signers PD and KL scored 57% and 53% correct, respectively, whereas RHD signers SM and GG scored 64% and 43% correct, respectively. Furthermore, many of the spatial syntax errors of the LHD signer PD described by Poizner et al. (1987) can be analyzed as errors in

TABLE 9.1
Errors by LHD Signer PD*

Error	Correct Form
ARRIVE$_a$ STAY$_b$ (THERE)$_c$	ARRIVE$_a$ STAY$_a$ (THERE)$_a$
$_a$PARK-OVER-THERE$_b$, WALK, $_c$GO-THERE$_b$	$_a$PARK-OVER-THERE$_b$, WALK, $_b$GO-ELSEWHERE$_c$
GET-OUT-OF$_a$, $_b$PEOPLE-FILE-OVER-TO$_c$	GET-OUT-OF$_a$, $_a$PEOPLE-FILE-OVER-TO$_b$
$_a$GO-HOME$_b$, $_c$DRIVE-AWAY$_d$	$_a$GO-HOME$_b$, $_b$DRIVE-AWAY$_c$
RUN$_a$ $_b$THROW BASKETBALL	RUN$_a$ $_a$THROW BASKETBALL

*Subscripts correspond to locations in signing space.
Note. From H. Poizner, E. S. Klima, and U. Bellugi, *What the Hands Reveal About the Brain*, 1987, Cambridge, MA: MIT Press. Copyright © 1987 by MIT Press. Reprinted with permission.

spatial mapping. These errors are listed in Table 9.1, corresponding to Table 4.1 in Poizner et al. (1987). Notice that in all cases, the spatial location of referents is indicated, for example, *where* someone arrived, parked, walked over to, drove, and ran. These aphasic errors do not involve arbitrary abstract locations in signing space and thus do not support a dissociation between spatialized syntax and topographic functions of space.

In addition, the fMRI study by MacSweeney et al. (2001) directly compared the neural areas engaged when Deaf and hearing users of British Sign Language (BSL) comprehended sentences that used space topographically (e.g., "The cat sat on the bed") versus BSL sentences that did not (e.g., "The man telephoned the woman"). Their results did not show more right hemisphere activation for processing topographic sentences compared to nonlocative sentences. Rather, the results revealed greater activation in *left* inferior parietal cortex when comprehending topographic BSL sentences. This finding is consistent with the results of the previously mentioned dual task experiment of Emmorey and Corina (1990a). We compared the decrement in left- and right-hand tapping when Deaf signers watched stories using topographic space versus stories with minimal or no use of space. The results indicated greater decrement in right-hand tapping (implicating left hemisphere processing) for both types of stories. Interestingly, when MacSweeney et al. (2001) translated their topographic and nontopographic BSL sentences into English and presented them audiovisually to hearing nonsigners, they found no differences in parietal activation in the left hemisphere for the two sentence types. This finding suggests that the comprehension of signed sentences that use space topographically engages parietal structures within the left hemisphere that may be uniquely required for processing signed language.

Another issue to consider when examining locative and nonlocative uses of space is complexity. Room descriptions typically require the establishment and maintenance of an association between several object referents and many distinct spatial locations. However, in nonlocative discourse, only two or three referents are generally associated with locations in signing space, and this was true of the verb agreement comprehension task described earlier. Thus, the RHD signer SJ may have been able to do well on that task, but fail on the room-description task because of the sheer number of spatial locations that must be remembered for room descriptions. Similarly, the RHD signer BI may have been able to correctly maintain an association between two referents and two spatial locations for the purposes of verb agreement, but nonetheless fail to correctly distinguish the several spatial locations required to describe the layout of her room. The data from the RHD signer DN indicates that the relevant aspect of complexity is the number of spatial contrasts—not the number of referents.

In chapter 3, we concluded that there is a continuum between the locative and nonlocative functions of signing space. The data from lesion studies suggest that as the topographic functions of signing space increase in complexity, the right hemisphere may become more engaged. Thus, signers who have suffered right-hemisphere damage exhibit impairments in visuospatial processing within nonlinguistic domains (e.g., visual–constructive abilities; see Fig. 9.5) and also within a circumscribed linguistic domain: when spatial locations in signing space must be understood as representing spatial relations among objects. LHD signers may be relatively unimpaired in the ability to understand the topographic mapping between a location in signing space and the location of an object, hence the perfect performance of LHD signer RS when matching a room layout to a signed description. Aphasic LHD signers may make errors with both agreeing and spatial verbs because of a deficit in the ability to determine the argument structure of these verbs from their movement in space (see also Kegl & Poizner, 1997). Some RHD signers may also make errors on the verb agreement comprehension task used by Poizner et al. (1987) because it involves somewhat unusual discourse, for example, directing an agreeing verb between two locations in signing space is relatively rare. Thus, LHD and RHD signers may make errors on the verb agreement comprehension task for different reasons.[7] Finally, RHD signers do not appear to produce errors in either agreeing or spatial verbs at the sen-

[7]Unpublished data from Hickok (1997) indicated that LHD and RHD signers make different types of errors on the tests of verb agreement comprehension used by Poizner et al. (1987). The order of the introduction of subject and object nouns is irrelevant to the performance of LHD signers, but RHD signers make significantly more errors when the noun that is coreferential with the subject of the agreeing verb is introduced first (Hickok, personal communication, December, 1999).

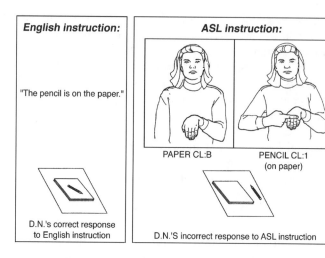

FIG. 9.9.   Illustration of the hearing RHD signer DN's differential performance in comprehending English versus ASL spatial commands. The lexical
signs PAPER and PENCIL are not shown (from Emmorey, 1996). Copyright
© 1996 by MIT Press. Reprinted with permission.

tence level. For example, although the RHD signer DN made errors with
classifier constructions when describing spatial relations, she correctly
produced both agreeing verbs (e.g., SEND) and spatial verbs (e.g.,
DRIVE) in free conversation and in retelling ASL stories that did not contain detailed spatial information (Emmorey et al., 1995).

Evidence that the right hemisphere is involved in comprehending certain aspects of the topographic function of signing space (particularly
when classifier constructions are involved) comes from two additional studies. The first further examined the RHD signer DN who was hearing and bilingual for ASL and English (she was a certified interpreter and learned
ASL at an early age from her Deaf grandmother). When DN was asked to
set up real objects in accordance with spatial descriptions given in either
English or in ASL, she performed relatively well in English (83% correct),
but she performed poorly when the same description was given in ASL
(39% correct) (Corina, Bellugi, Kritchevsky, O'Grady-Batch, & Norman,
1990; Emmorey, 1996). An example of a spatial description in English is
"The pen is on the paper." The ASL version of this description and DN's responses are shown in Fig. 9.9. In English, the spatial relation is encoded by
the preposition *on*, but in ASL the spatial relation must be recovered from
the spatial positioning of the classifier signs within signing space.

A similar dissociation between the comprehension of ASL spatial prepositions and classifier constructions was reported by Emmorey (1997a,
1998). In this study, 2 LHD aphasic signers, RS and KH, and one RHD

signer, AR, were compared in their comprehension of ASL prepositions and classifier constructions using a picture-matching task.[8] The signers were asked to pick which picture best matched a preposition (e.g., IN) or a classifier construction depicting a similar spatial relation (e.g., the classifier for banana (a curved 1 handshape) placed within a C handshape for the bowl). Like many hearing English speakers with left-hemisphere damage, the LHD signers performed poorly on the preposition comprehension task (57% correct for RS and 36% correct for KH). In contrast, the RHD signer AR performed relatively well, scoring 79% correct. The reverse pattern was observed when location was conveyed by the placement of classifier signs in space: the RHD signer, AR, performed poorly (44% correct), whereas the LHD signers performed much better (94% and 81% correct for RS and KH, respectively). Both of these studies suggest that the comprehension of spatial prepositions may be subserved primarily by the left hemisphere, whereas comprehension of the isomorphic mapping between the location of the hands in signing space and the locations of objects in physical space may be subserved primarily by the right hemisphere.

It is important to point out that the tasks in these studies were quite different from the semantic anomaly detection task performed by the BSL signers in the fMRI study conducted by MacSweeney et al. (2001), in which no differential right hemisphere activation was found for comprehending topographic sentences. In the Corina et al. (1990) and Emmorey (1997b) studies, subjects had to translate the spatial relation between the hands in signing space into another spatial representation (i.e., the location of physical objects in nonsigning space). The right hemisphere may be specifically engaged when spatial locations in signing space must be related to another representation of spatial locations either in the form of a mental image (e.g., when describing a room from memory) or in the form of physical objects (e.g., objects in a manipulation task or pictures in a picture-matching task). A reasonable hypothesis suggested by Corina (1998b) is that the difficulties that right hemisphere damaged patients exhibit in producing and comprehending classifier constructions and the topographic functions of signing space may stem from a more general problem with encoding external spatial relations into body-centered manual representations, particularly when two articulators are used. Thus, the right hemisphere may play a unique role in the interpretation of ASL spatial descriptions, a role that is not required for English spatial descriptions.

Evidence to support this hypothesis can be found in a recent PET study by Emmorey et al. (2001). In this study, Deaf native ASL signers viewed line drawings depicting a spatial relation between two objects (e.g., a cup

---

[8] This study was conducted in collaboration with Ursula Bellugi, Edward Klima, Kevin Clark, Antonio Damasio, Daniel Tranel, and Paul German.

on a table) and were asked to produce either a two-handed classifier construction or an ASL preposition that described the spatial relation. In a separate condition, they were asked to name the figure object which was colored red. Compared to naming objects, describing spatial relationships with classifier constructions engaged the supramarginal gyrus bilaterally, with more extensive activation in the right parietal cortex. In contrast, when hearing English speakers were given the same task, H. Damasio et al. (2001) found that naming spatial relations with English prepositions engaged only the *left* SMG. Thus, in addition to the left hemisphere, neural areas within the right hemisphere appear to be recruited when signers describe spatial relationships using classifier constructions. Surprisingly, naming spatial relations with ASL prepositions did not activate left SMG and engaged only the posterior right SMG (perhaps reflecting the marginal status of prepositions in ASL). Finally, compared to ASL prepositions, naming spatial relations with classifier constructions engaged left inferior temporal cortex in a region known to be activated when naming manipulable concrete objects (H. Damasio, Grabowski, Tranel, Hichwa, & A. Damasio, 1996). This pattern of neural activation may reflect the fact that handshape in classifier constructions encodes information about object type.

Overall, these results indicate that both the production and comprehension of classifier constructions that express spatial relationships engage neural areas within both left and right parietal cortex. Parietal regions of the cortex in both hemispheres have long been known to be involved in the attention to and perception of the spatial location of physical objects in the environment (e.g., Posner & Petersen, 1990; Ungerleider & Mishkin, 1982). With respect to language, parietal regions may be uniquely engaged during the production and comprehension of spatial language in signed languages, particularly for locative classifier constructions in which the location of the signer's hands in space specifies the spatial relation between objects.

Discourse Processes

Quite a bit of evidence from spoken language users indicates right-hemisphere engagement in higher level discourse processes, suggesting some degree of dissociation between sentence and discourse levels of language processing (see Joanette et al., 1990; and Brownell, Gardner, Prather, & Martino, 1995, for reviews). Mildly or moderately impaired aphasics exhibit relatively preserved narrative discourse skills; for example, narrative superstructure is preserved (there is a setting, a complicating action, and a resolution), despite grammatical deficits at the sentence level. In contrast, nonaphasic right-hemisphere damaged subjects do not produce grammatical errors but nonetheless show impairments in discourse coherence. They exhibit an overall difficulty maintaining a topic and integrating information, and they produce uninformative details and circumlocutions within a narrative.

Although only a few case studies of discourse in RHD signers have been conducted, the results suggest the same neural organization for signed and spoken language at the discourse level. Two types of discourse-level deficits have been reported with right-hemisphere damage for ASL signers. Hickok et. al (1999) found that the RHD signer AR had difficulty with topic maintenance and frequently produced tangential utterances. Similarly, Corina, Kritchevsky, and Bellugi (1996) reported that the RHD signer JH produced occasional nonsequiturs and exhibited an abnormal attention to detail. They provide the following example from JH's description of the *cookie theft picture* (a standard picture used to elicit a language sample):

JH: ME SEE$_i$KITCHEN LITTLE BOY STEP-UP #L-A-D-D-E-R AND MAYBE HIS MOTHER STAND #B-Y #S-I-N-K, WINDOW WASH #D-I-S-H-E-S. OUTSIDE, LITTLE COLD. SEE$_i$ WINDOW CURTAIN #D-R-A-P-E-S #C-U-R-T-A-I-N-S. MAYBE ASK HIS MOTHER PERMISSION?

"I see a kitchen, a little boy is stepping up a ladder. Perhaps, his mother, is standing by the sink under the kitchen window washing dishes. Outside it appears cold. I see the window curtains, the drapes. Maybe the boy has asked his mother permission [to get the cookies]?" (p. 325)

Another type of discourse deficit that can occur independently of a deficit in topic maintenance is an impairment in spatial coreference across a discourse, which is often accompanied by errors in the use of referential shift (see chap. 2). Two RHD signers, SJ and DN, have been reported to have difficulty maintaining consistent spatial locations for referents within a discourse (Hickok et al., 1999; Poizner & Kegl, 1992). For example, when retelling the "paint story" about a boy and girl painting on each other (see chap. 5), the RHD signer SJ initially associated the referents (the boy and girl) with spatial locations along the midsagittal plane, but then switched the association to the horizontal (left–right) plane, and he switched back and forth between planes without any marking to indicate a referential shift (Hickok et al., 1999). The RHD signer DN appears to compensate for her difficulty in maintaining the association between referents and spatial locations across a discourse by frequently substituting fully specified noun phrases where pronouns would be more suitable; this renders her narratives stylistically awkward, although they are still intelligible (Poizner & Kegl, 1992). Loew et al. (1997) also reported that DN was impaired in her ability to nonmanually signal changes in perspective with appropriate shifts in eye gaze, and she did not produce the affective facial expressions that control signers produced to convey the perspective of a given character within a referential shift.

It is important to reiterate that none of these RHD signers (JH, SJ, AR, or DN) made errors in pronoun use or verb agreement within a sentence or across very short discourses (2 or 3 sentences). Furthermore, the discourse deficits described cannot be accounted for by general deficits in visuospatial processing (Hickok et al., 1999). For example, SJ and AR both exhibited relatively severe visuospatial deficits, but only SJ was impaired in maintaining spatial coreference; in addition, DN suffered only mild visuospatial impairments, but exhibited the same type of discourse impairments observed for SJ. These initial results indicate that the right hemisphere is engaged in similar discourse encoding functions for both spoken and signed languages: topic maintenance, discourse cohesion, and interpreting character mood (Brownell, Carroll, Rehak, & Wingfield, 1992).

Neglect: The Right Hemisphere and Visuospatial Attention

Neglect is a failure to report, respond, or orient to stimuli that are presented to the visual field that is contralateral to (opposite) the hemisphere with the brain lesion (Heilman, Watson, & Valenstein, 1997). For example, patients with *right*-hemisphere damage may fail to draw the *left* half of an object because they fail to attend to the left side of space (visual neglect) or they have a motoric bias against moving toward the left (motor neglect). As shown in the drawings in Figs. 9.5 and 9.10, RHD signers exhibit symptoms of neglect that are generally not observed with the LHD signers. That is, the RHD signers often failed to draw the left half of objects. Although neglect can occur with both right- and left-hemisphere lesions, it is more common and more severe with right-hemisphere damage (for both signers and speakers). One hypothesis is that this asymmetry may be related to the asymmetrical representation of space and the body within the two hemispheres (Heilman et al., 1997). The left hemisphere primarily attends to the right side, but the right hemisphere attends to both sides. Similarly, the left hemisphere prepares for right-side action, whereas the right hemisphere prepares for both (Heilman & Van Den Abell, 1980). An obvious question is whether the left-sided neglect demonstrated by RHD signers impacts sign language comprehension or production.

As discussed in the previous section, the RHD signer BI failed to use the left half of signing space when describing her room, piling all furniture on the right (see Fig. 9.8A), and she also exhibited neglect on nonlinguistic drawing tasks. However, in other nonspatial contexts, BI was reported to use spatial locations on the left half of space for pronominal reference and verb agreement (Poizner et al., 1987). Similarly, Corina et al. (1996) reported that the RHD signer JH exhibited neglect (see Fig. 9.10), but he produced signs using the left half of his body (e.g., LAZY is signed by tapping the left shoulder with an L handshape), and he also directed pronouns and verbs toward the left half of signing space in spontaneous signing. Interestingly, Corina et al. (1996) reported difficulty eliciting spatial descriptions from JH who tended to "avoid using topographic space and simply list[ed] the contents of his room" (p. 338). Poizner and Kegl (1992, 1993) reported that the RHD signer DN (AS in their studies) exhibited mild neglect, which appeared to affect the production of some two-

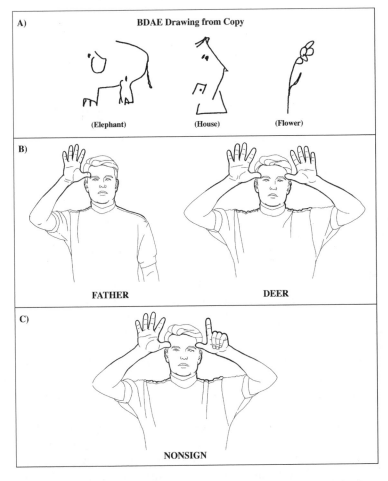

FIG. 9.10. A) Drawing examples that illustrate neglect; B) the minimal pairs FATHER and DEER, C) an (illegal) two-handed nonsign. Illustrations copyright © Ursula Bellugi, The Salk Institute.

handed signs (her left hand lagged slightly), and she also tended to shift her signing rightward, but the shift did not result in ungrammatical signing. Thus, visual or motor neglect appears to have minimal impact on sign language production, except in contexts that rely heavily on the topographic functions of signing space. It appears that left hemispheric control for linguistic production generally compensates for left-sided attention deficits unless the spatial complexity of the discourse requires the use of several locations representing left–right spatial distinctions.

None of these RHD signers exhibited sign comprehension deficits. However, only Corina et al. (1996) explicitly tested for the effect of visual neglect on ASL comprehension. The RHD signer JH was shown ASL minimal pairs, which were distinguished only by a second identical hand articulator. For example, DEER is made with two 5 handshapes at the forehead, whereas FATHER is made with a single hand, as shown in Fig. 9.10. Because the second hand of DEER falls within the viewer's left visual field, the presence of neglect could disrupt the comprehension of this sign, which would be misinterpreted as FATHER. However, JH was unimpaired in the identification of such signs. In contrast, he failed to identify nonlinguistic objects that were moved to the same locations as the hands in the ASL signs, for example, a camera and a pack of cigarettes were raised and held next to the head. JH consistently failed to report objects that fell within his left visual field on bilateral (two-object) trials. At first, these results suggest that linguistic stimuli are impervious to the attentional deficits caused by visuospatial neglect. However, Corina et al. (1996) presented further evidence, which indicates that there is an interaction between attention and the representational properties of linguistic systems that gives rise to the apparent dissociation between sign and object recognition.

Corina et al. (1996) speculated that some degraded information is registered in the unattended visual field and that this information is interpretable for sign comprehension but not for object recognition. The information is only interpretable for linguistic stimuli because of the phonological constraints imposed on sign formation. As noted in chapter 2, the *symmetry condition* of Battison (1978) requires that both hands be specified for the same handshape if they move independently. Thus, if any information is detected within the left visual field, the lexical access system can map the input to the correct lexical entry for bilateral ASL signs like DEER (see chap. 4 for a model of lexical access for sign language). Of course, the object recognition system does not benefit from such systematic constraints. To test this hypothesis, Corina et al. (1996) presented JH with impossible ASL signs in which the two handshapes differed, as shown in Fig. 9.10C. For these stimuli, JH misidentified the impossible signs as true bilateral signs, for example, JH misidentified the stimulus in Figure 9.10c as DEER. Thus, when phonological constraints cannot apply (as with these impossible signs), the effects of visual neglect emerge for sign language stimuli. More importantly, however, these findings indicate that linguistic constraints on sign recognition ameliorate the effects of visuospatial neglect caused by right-hemisphere damage.

THE ROLE OF SUBCORTICAL STRUCTURES IN SIGN LANGUAGE

Subcortical structures lie deep within the brain and have extensive connections with the cerebral cortex. Certain subcortical structures (e.g., the basal ganglia) are known to play a critical role in motor behavior.[9] For example, Parkinson's disease is associated with subcortical cell loss (primarily in the substantia nigra), which results in motor disturbances, including tremor, slowed movements, monotone dysfluent speech, and a "masked" (unexpressive) face. In a series of studies, Poizner and colleagues have systematically studied the effects of Parkinson's disease on the production of sign language in an effort to understand the role of the basal ganglia in language processing (for reviews, see Kegl, Cohen, & Poizner, 1999; Poizner, Brentari, Tyrone & Kegl, 2000). Such studies are somewhat easier to undertake for signers because sign articulators are fully visible, unlike the primary speech articulators (i.e., the tongue and vocal cords).

First of all, signers with Parkinson's disease do not exhibit syntactic, morphological, or discourse-level impairments—they produce complex signing with a full range of sentence types (Loew, Kegl, & Poizner, 1997; Poizner et al., 2000). However, these signers have particular difficulty with sign articulation and minimize motoric effort in a variety of ways. Table 9.2 lists the characteristics of Parkinsonian signing, described by Poizner et al. (2000). As noted in Table 9.2, Parkinson's patients exhibit a dampening of facial expressions (facial masking), which affects both affective and linguistic facial expressions for Deaf signers, unlike unilateral cortical lesions, which can selectively impair the production of either linguistic or affective expressions.

As discussed in chapter 5, children and adults learning sign language tend to proximalize the movement of signs. In contrast, signers with Parkinson's disease show the opposite pattern and distalize sign movement, for example, the path movement of the sign BETTER is normally articulated at the elbow, but the Parkisonian signer RH distalized the movement to the wrist, as illustrated in Fig. 9.11A. An example of the articulation of

---

[9]Recent evidence suggests that the basal ganglia may be involved in some aspects of morphosyntactic processing (e.g., Ullman et al., 1997). Our focus however is on the phonological level of the grammar.

TABLE 9.2
Articulatory and Timing Simplifications Observed in Signers
With Parkinson's Disease (from Poizner et al., 2000)

Simplifications in Sign Articulation	
Facial masking	Distalization of movement
Deletion of contact	Displacement and reduction of signing space
Blending of selected finger features	Shadowing
Laxing of handshape and orientation	

Simplifications in the Timing Properties of Signing	
Flattening of prosodic contrasts in pause durations	Feature unraveling during fingerspelling
Atypical assimilation effects across signs	Segmentation during fingerspelling
Oversynchronization of movement	

Note. From Poizner et al. (2000). Copyright © 2000 by Lawrence Erlbaum Associates. Reprinted with permission.

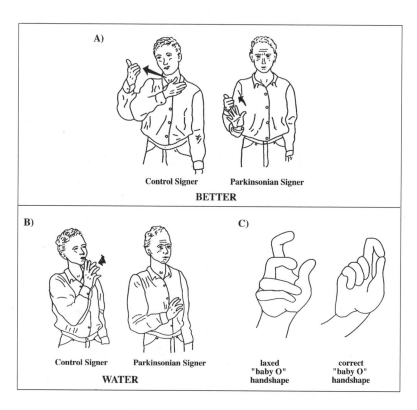

FIG. 9.11. Examples of Parkinsonian signing. From D. Brentari and H. Poizner, 1994, "A Phonological Analysis of a Deaf Parkinsonian Signer." *Language and Cognitive Processes, 9*(1), 69–99. Copyright © 1994 by Academic Press. Reprinted with permission.

the sign WATER in Fig. 9.11B illustrates the deletion of contact (on the chin) and the reduction and displacement of signing space (not unlike whispering; see Fig. 4.11 in chap. 4). Shadowing occurs when the non-dominant hand mirrors the movements of the dominant hand, and these errors may be similar to those observed for the LHD signer RS (see Fig. 9.6B), but the Parkinsonian errors arise from a more general deficit in motor control. Blending of selected finger features is observed more frequently with fingerspelling and refers to the coalescence of two hand-shapes, for example, combining the P and I handshapes in P-I-L-L-S (Tyrone, Kegl, & Poizner, 1999). Finally, Fig. 9.11C illustrates the laxing of handshape articulation that occurred within the sign WRITE[continuative]. All of these alterations reduce the motoric effort involved in sign production, but such alterations nonetheless spare required linguistic distinctions. Parkinsonian signing is still comprehensible, more so even than Parkinsonian speech at the later stages of the disease (Kegl, Cohen, & Poizner, 1999).

Just as the timing of speech is disrupted by Parkinson's disease, signers also exhibit timing impairments. Unlike normal signers, Parkinsonian signers have similar pause durations between words and between phrases, which leads to a perception of monotonous signing (Loew et al., 1997). Parkinsonian signers may also anticipate articulations and produce certain sign components prematurely (atypical assimilation effects). Finally, oversynchronization of movement (see Table 9.2) refers to the abnormal coupling of handshape and movement during transitional movements for Parkinsonian signers (Brentari & Poizner, 1994; Brentari, Poizner, & Kegl, 1995). For normal signers, handshape change within a sign is precisely linked to the duration of the path movement(s) of the sign, but handshape change that occurs during the transition between two signs is not coupled with the transitional movement and is often completed before the end of the movement (see chap. 2). However, Parkinsonian signers reduce the demands of motoric planning by synchronizing handshape change with *both* transitional and lexical path movements, thus (over)regularizing the synchronization of handshape change and movement.

Fingerspelling is much more rapid and sequential than signing, and certain impairments only emerge under its intense motoric demands. Specifically, *feature unraveling* occurs when one feature of a fingerspelled letter is produced either before or after all of the other features (Tyrone et al., 1999). For example, when fingerspelling A-S-L, one Parkinsonian signer, LN, did not begin to move the index finger for 'L' until the thumb was almost fully extended, which made it appear as if an 'A-bar' handshape had been inserted between the 'S' and 'L' (Tyrone et al., 1999; see Appendix A for handshape illustrations). Such feature unraveling of handshape simplifies movement by allowing the signer to execute movements of different joints one at a time. Another strategy for simplifying movement planning is to bypass the requirements of coarticulation by segmentation (Tyrone et al., 1999). Segmentation occurs when the signer separates articulatory gestures temporally so that they are produced independently. Transitions may be relatively normal, but the fingerspelled letters are held for an abnormal amount of time.

The role of subcortical structures in sign language production is quite distinct from the role of cortical language areas. The phonological paraphasias described earlier for LHD aphasic signers do not occur for Parkinsonian signers. Furthermore, Brentari et al. (1995) directly compared production deficits observed with posterior cortical damage (resulting in aphasia) and subcortical damage (causing Parkinson's disease). Aphasic signers, but not Parkinsonian signers, appropriately synchronized handshape change with movement and produced appropriate pause durations at clause boundaries. However, the aphasic signers produced phonological errors, which violated syllabic well-formedness conditions and made feature substitutions for handshape productions that were not observed with the Parkinsonian signers. The disrupted articulations of the Parkinsonian signers, but not of the aphasic signers, could be predicted from the default specifications of ASL phonology and principles of ease of articulation. Thus, Brentari et al. (1995) concluded that aphasic and Parkinsonian signers show disruptions at distinct levels within ASL phonology: Aphasic signers generally exhibit a breakdown at the phonological level of structure, whereas Parkinsonian signers are impaired in the phonetic implementation of phonological structure.

CONCLUSIONS AND IMPLICATIONS

One overarching finding that emerges from studies of both neurologically intact and brain-injured signers is that the left-cerebral hemisphere is critical for sign language processes, as it is for spoken language. The data from sign language eliminates two competing hypotheses regarding the nature of this specialization. First, sign language does not rely on the generation or perception of fast acoustic transitions, and yet the left hemisphere is dominant for processing sign language to the same degree that it is for spoken language. Second, complex gesture can be dissociated from sign language production, suggesting distinct underlying neural systems. This result also suggests that neither complex motor requirements nor symbolic functions underlie the left-hemispheric specialization for language (although it is possible that there is in fact no nonlinguistic equivalent that can match the high level of motoric complexity of either speech or sign). In addition, the data argue against the hypothesis that the coevolution of language and the neuro–anatomical mechanisms of speech production is what led to the left-hemisphere specialization for language (e.g., Liberman, 1974). Rather, it may be that neural structures within the left hemisphere are particularly well-suited to interpreting and representing linguistic systems, regardless of the biology of language production and perception. The critical question, of course, is *why* are these neural structures well-suited for language, or put another way, what is it about linguistic systems that causes them to be left lateralized? These questions remain unanswered, but the study of signed languages provides a tool by "teasing apart" those aspects of linguistic systems that are fundamental and inherent to the system from those aspects that can be affected by language modality.

Both neural plasticity and rigidity are observed for the neural organization within the left hemisphere for Deaf signers. Neural plasticity is observed for auditory related cortex, which has received little or no auditory input, but nonetheless is engaged in processing the visual input of sign language. More striking, perhaps, is that the same neural structures (e.g., Broca's area, Wernicke's area) are engaged for the production and comprehension of both signed and spoken language. This neural invariance across language modalities points to a biological or developmental bias for these neural structures to mediate language at a more abstract level, divorced from the sensory and motoric systems that perceive and transmit language.

There is currently some controversy regarding the role of the right hemisphere in sign language processing (e.g., Bavelier et al., 1998; Hickok et al., 1998b; Paulesu & Mehler, 1998; Peperkamp & Mehler, 1999). As seen in Fig. 9.4, at least one functional brain imaging study revealed a large amount of right hemisphere activity during sign language comprehension. Whether this degree of right-hemisphere activation is similar to that observed during spoken language processing remains to be seen. For both spoken and sign language comprehension, the right hemisphere appears to be involved in processing some discourse-level functions (e.g., cohesion), facial affect (particularly important for referential shift within ASL), and even some aspects of complex sentence comprehension (Caplan, Hildebrandt, & Makris, 1996; Love et al., 1999). Nonetheless, for sign language, the right hemisphere may play a unique role in the production and comprehension of the topographic functions of signing space, particularly as conveyed by classifier constructions.

Finally, it should be clear that the study of Deaf and hearing signers can provide unique insight into the neurobiological bases for language. By contrasting form and function, generalizations about what determines the neural organization of language can emerge. In addition, because the sign articulators are fully visible, investigation of the neural systems involved in complex motoric processes can be easily studied, and the nature of language as motor behavior can be explored in detail (as in the studies of Parkinsonian signers). The study of signed languages provides an unusual technique for exploring how the brain tolerates or adapts to variation in biology.

SUGGESTIONS FOR FURTHER READING

Corina, D. P. (1998b). The processing of sign language: Evidence from aphasia. In B. Stemmer & H. A. Whitaker (Eds.), *Handbook of neurolinguistics* (pp. 313–329). New York: Academic Press.

Hickok, G., & Bellugi, U. (2001). The signs of aphasia. In R. Sloan Berndt (Ed.), *The handbook of neuropsychology: Vol. 2. Language and aphasia* (pp. 30–51). Amsterdam, The Netherlands: Elsevier.

The reviews by Corina and by Hickok and Bellugi summarize much of the lesion research conducted with Deaf signers within the last 10 years. Each review covers a similar range of studies but from somewhat different perspectives.

Poizner, H., Klima, E. S., & Bellugi, U. (1987). *What the hands reveal about the brain.* Cambridge, MA: MIT Press.

This book provides an in-depth analysis of three LHD signers and three RHD signers and is a classic for the study of sign language and its neural organization.

Epilogue

The study of signed languages still has much to teach us about the nature of human language, cognition, and the brain. The linguistic results thus far reveal substantial similarities between signed and spoken languages, but this is only a starting point. The similarities provide a strong basis for comparison and serve to highlight universal properties of human language. Linguistic investigations are also beginning to uncover clear distinctions between signed and spoken languages, and these distinctions reveal how language modality can affect linguistic preferences (e.g., a preference for nonconcatenative morphology over linear affixation) and grammatical patterns (e.g., systematic distinctions in pronominal reference and verb agreement systems, as described in chap. 2). However, much of the linguistic research has been based on a single signed language: American Sign Language (ASL). Cross-linguistic investigations of signed languages from around the world are crucial to our understanding of both language universals and of modality effects on linguistic structure. Efforts are now underway to develop a typology of signed languages; that is, a classification of signed languages in terms of their shared structural features (e.g., Zeshan, 2000). Such a typology will reveal not only how signed languages may differ systematically from spoken languages, but it will also reveal the nature of structural variation across signed languages.

Furthermore, the sociolinguistic context surrounding signed languages provides a rich resource for understanding language genesis and change, as evidenced by the ongoing investigation of the emergence of Nicaraguan Sign Language (chap. 1). Recently, isolated Deaf communities have been discovered in some remote areas of the world, for example, on a small island south of Japan (Amami Island; Osugi, Supalla, & Webb, 1999) and on the island of Bali (Branson, Miller, Marsaja, & Negara, 1996). Because these communities are relatively small, linguistic research must determine the stage of development of the language, that is, whether it is in the embryonic stage of a home sign system, an emerging pidgin form, or a full sign language (Osugi et al., 1999). Such variation within gestural communicative systems can provide crucial clues to the evolution of language and the nature of the human capacity for language.

Signed languages clearly differ from spoken languages in their ability to manipulate signing space to express both spatial and nonspatial information. Spatial language (talking about space) in signed languages generally involves classifier constructions (chap. 3), but we still know very little about these sign-specific constructions, particularly with regard to their syntactic structure. The comparison of spatial language in signed and spoken languages may also provide insights into the interface between linguistic representations and visuospatial representations (i.e., how we talk about what we see; Jackendoff, 1996). Talmy (in press) recently suggested that for signed languages, the linguistic representation of space systematically differs from that in spoken languages in ways that reflect the structural characteristics of scene parsing in visual perception. For example, spoken languages tend to combine motion path with the ground object ("The mouse went *into the hole*"), whereas signed languages combine path motion with the figure object, just as observed within a visual scene (e.g., the classifier handshape representing the figure object (the mouse) is combined with a movement indicating path; Talmy, in press). Furthermore, nonlocative uses of space may also be quite revealing with regard to how abstract (nonspatial) concepts are mapped to spatial schemas. For example, sign languages appear to obey a basic structural mapping between space and time (e.g., a spatial direction maps to a temporal direction and spatial reference points map to temporal ones; chap. 3). Such studies can help to delineate principles for how space can be co-opted to represent abstract relations and concepts.

Chapter 4 reviewed the current state of the art for psycholinguistic studies of sign language comprehension and production. As with studies of linguistic structure, the psycholinguistic results primarily reveal major similarities between the processing mechanisms involved in comprehending language, whether signed or spoken. However, we know very little about how the visual stream is "parsed" or segmented (e.g., How do signers recognize the difference between transitional and lexical movement online? How do they recognize sign boundaries?). There has also been very little work on syntactic parsing in signed languages, particularly with respect to how grammatical facial expressions are recognized and interpreted in real time. Results from these types of psycholinguistic studies may help us to understand not only the processes involved in sign language comprehension, but they may also shed light on basic issues in high-level visual processing (e.g., providing clues to visual scene parsing and to the recognition of facial expressions). Psycholinguistic studies of sign language production have lagged behind comprehension. We know that signers exhibit "tip-of-the-fingers" effects, slips of the hand, and produce gestures in conjunction with signing. However, there are hints that models of speech production cannot simply be co-opted to explain sign language production. Phonological differences between sign and speech may affect the timing between lexical selection and pronunciation, and the sign language system for self-monitoring may differ from speech because usually signers do not see themselves signing. Future comparative investigations of sign and speech production may help us to understand the cognitive, linguistic, and motoric mechanisms that translate thoughts into linguistic expression.

In chapter 5, we reviewed studies of language acquisition, which showed that Deaf children with Deaf parents acquire ASL in much the same way that hearing children acquire a spoken language, from early babbling to storytelling. We still know very little about Deaf infants' early visual processing of sign language, compared to what we know about hearing infants' early auditory processing of speech. In addition, more research is needed regarding the long and complicated developmental path for achieving mastery of classifier constructions. Given that we are beginning to understand how classifier constructions emerge from gestural home sign systems, research on acquisition may provide insight into the phylogenetic versus ontogenetic development of these complex linguistic structures.

Most deaf children, however, do not acquire ASL from birth because they are born to hearing parents who do not sign. Some of these children may not acquire a primary language until late in childhood because they are not exposed to sign language and their deafness prevents them from successfully acquiring spoken English. Chapter 6 reviewed the effects of late-language acquisition on grammatical knowledge, on language processing, on cognition, and on the neural organization for language. The findings provide strong evidence for a critical or sensitive period for language acquisition during human development. These results also have clear implications for the education of deaf children, suggesting that early exposure to an accessible language (i.e., a signed language) is critical to cognitive, linguistic, and neural development.

Chapters 7 and 8 specifically examined what the study of sign language can tell us about the nature of cognitive systems and their relation to language. Studies of memory for sign and for speech suggest that the architecture of working memory is determined by universal structural properties of language and by specific processing constraints of the auditory and visual sensory modalities. The research reviewed in chapter 8 indicates that linguistic experience can affect certain specific cognitive processes, supporting at least some versions of the linguistic relativity hypothesis. Because signed languages rely on visuospatial cognitive processes, they provide a unique tool for investigating the relation between linguistic and nonlinguistic domains of cognition. Parallel studies are difficult to conduct with spoken language because nonlinguistic auditory processing cannot be studied in the absence of experience with speech. Future research may reveal whether low-level perceptual processing can be affected by sign language experience and the extent and nature of cognitive plasticity (i.e., does the age of sign language acquisition or the length of signing experience impact the observed cognitive enhancement effects?).

Finally, the research outlined in chapter 9 (sign language and the brain) will probably be out of date as this book goes to press. With the accessibility of new brain imaging techniques, there is currently an explosion of studies investigating the neural systems underlying sign language production and comprehension, as well as research that explores the effects of auditory deprivation and/or sign language experience on language-related cortices and cortical regions involved in visuospatial and motion processing. In addition, as we learn more about the brain, new questions emerge that can be investigated by studying signed languages and Deaf people. For example, the recent discovery of *mirror neurons*, which fire both when a monkey produces an action and when it observes another monkey producing a similar action (e.g., Fadiga, Fogassi, Gallese, & Rizzolatti, 2000) has exciting implications for understanding the neurobiological basis for sign language processing. Such neurons could be involved in a "motor theory of sign perception" (analogous to the motor theory of speech perception; Liberman & Mattingly, 1985). As our understanding of sign language processing and the relation between language and cognition grows, it is certain to be complemented by an increased understanding of the neural systems that give rise to linguistic and cognitive functions.

We have come a long way from the myths outlined in chapter 1. Further study of signed languages promises to take us even further in the quest to understand our uniquely human ability to produce and understand language and the cognitive and neural underpinnings of this ability.

APPENDIX A:
Handshapes in American Sign Language

The following is a nonexhaustive list of handshapes that occur in ASL (not all handshapes are contrastive):

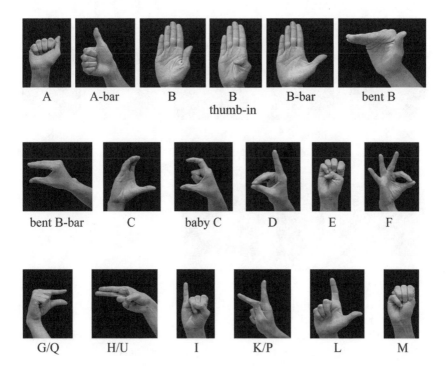

| A | A-bar | B | B thumb-in | B-bar | bent B |

| bent B-bar | C | baby C | D | E | F |

| G/Q | H/U | I | K/P | L | M |

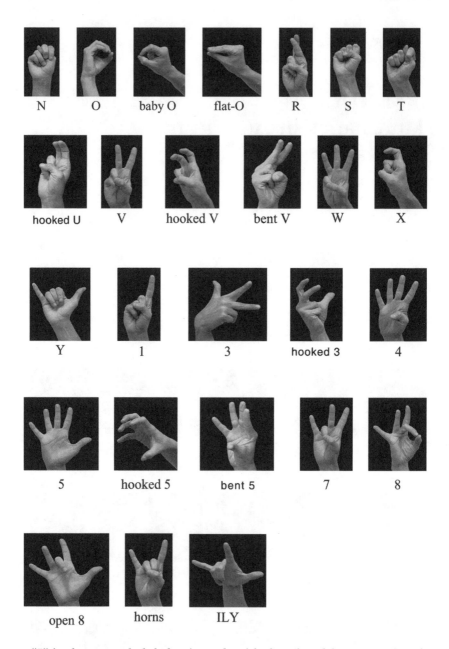

N   O   baby O   flat-O   R   S   T

hooked U   V   hooked V   bent V   W   X

Y   1   3   hooked 3   4

5   hooked 5   bent 5   7   8

open 8   horns   ILY

"J" in the manual alphabet is made with the I handshape, rotating the wrist (see Fig. 2.4 in chap. 2).

"Z" in the manual alphabet is made with the l handshape, which traces a Z-shaped path in the vertical plane in signing space.

APPENDIX B:
Linguistic Distinctions Among Communication Forms in Nicaragua

Linguistic Distinctions Among Communication Forms in Nicaragua*

Home Sign	The Early Peer Group Pidgin	Nicaraguan Sign Language
Signs are idiosyncratic or emblems shared by the culture.	Signs are conventionalized across the community.	Signs are conventionalized across the community.
Large and often symmetrical signs	Large and often symmetrical signs	Use of the two hands is more asymmetric, and signs are articulated within a smaller signing space.
The whole body is involved.	Signs are restricted to limbs, head, and upper torso, but there is little coarticulation between signs.	Signing is more fluid and coarticulation is evident.
Facial expressions only convey affect and caricatures.	Facial expression marks linguistic information (e.g., topics, adverbs), but expressions are linked to single signs and do not spread over later constituents.	Topic marking (a brow raise) and marking for WH questions (an intense nose wrinkle) occur systematically and can spread over more than a single sign.

(Continued)

(Continued)

Home Sign	The Early Peer Group Pidgin	Nicaraguan Sign Language
Often only single gestures are produced.	Pidgin signers are less fluent than NSL signers (measured as signs per minute and number of events recounted in a narrative)	NSL signers take less time to express more information (producing more signs per minute and recounting more events, compared to pidgin signers).
Single gestures depict actions, and participants are often inferred from context, rather than expressed through gesture.	Only one full noun tends to be signed per verb. Pointing before and/or after a verb indicates multiple participants.	More than one noun argument can be expressed per verb. The directional movement of some verbs indicates participant roles (a system of verb agreement is emerging).
Both objects and handling of objects are expressed by showing how the object is manipulated.	Handling classifiers, which represent how an object is manipulated, are equally frequent in the pidgin form and in NSL.	Whole entity classifiers, which represent object class, are more frequent.
	Pidgin signers do not distinguish between handling and whole entity classifiers with respect to agency (i.e., handling classifiers are used even when no agent is involved).	As in many signed languages, handling classifiers imply agency in NSL. When no agent is implied, NSL signers use a whole entity classifier.

*The information in this table is drawn from Kegl, Senghas, and Coppola (1999), Morford and Kegl (2000), and Senghas (1995b).

References

Aarons, D. (1994). *Aspects of the syntax of American Sign Language*. Unpublished doctoral dissertation, Boston University.

Acredolo, L. P., & Goodwyn, S. W. (1988). Symbolic gesturing in normal infants. *Child Development, 59*, 450–466.

Ahlgren, I. (1990). Deictic pronouns in Swedish and Swedish Sign Language. In S. D. Fischer & P. Siple (Eds.), *Theoretical issues in sign language research* (pp. 167–174). Chicago, IL: University of Chicago Press.

Akamatsu, C. T. (1985). Fingerspelling formulae: A word is more or less the sum of its letters. In W. Stokoe & V. Volterra (Eds.), *SLR '83: Proceedings of the Third International Symposium on Sign Language Research* (pp. 126–132). Silver Spring, MD: Linstok Press.

Allan, K. (1977). Classifiers. *Language, 53*(2), 285–311.

Anderson, D., & Reilly, J. S. (1997). The puzzle of negation: How children move from communicative to grammatical negation in ASL. *Applied Psycholinguistics, 18*, 411–429.

Anderson, D., & Reilly, J. S. (1998). PAH! The acquisition of non-manual adverbials in ASL. *Sign Language and Linguistics, 1*(2), 115–142.

Anderson, S. R. (1992). *A-morphous morphology*. Cambridge, England: Cambridge University Press.

Anderson, S. R. (1993). Linguistic expression and its relation to modality. In G. Coulter (Ed.), *Phonetics and phonology: Current issues in ASL phonology* (pp. 273–290). New York: Academic Press.

Ann, J. (1996). On the relation between ease of articulation and frequency of occurrence of handshapes in two sign languages. *Lingua, 98*, 19–41.

Ann, J. (1998). Contact between a sign language and a written language: Character signs in Taiwan Sign Language. In C. Lucas (Ed.), *Pinky extension and eye gaze: Language use in Deaf communities* (pp. 59–99). Washington, DC: Gallaudet University Press.

Aramburo, A. (1989). Sociolinguistic aspects of the black Deaf community. In C. Lucas (Ed.), *The sociolinguistics of the Deaf community* (pp. 103–119). San Diego, CA: Academic Press.

Armstrong, D. F., Stokoe, W. C., & Wilcox, S. E. (1995). *Gesture and the nature of language*. Cambridge, England: Cambridge University Press.

323

Arnold, P., & Murray, C. (1998). Memory for faces and objects by deaf and hearing signers and hearing nonsigners. *Journal of Psycholinguistic Research, 27*(4), 481–497.

Aronoff, M., Meir, I., Padden, C., & Sandler, W. (in press). Classifier complexes and morphology in two signed languages. In K. Emmorey (Ed.), *Perspectives on classifier constructions in sign languages*. Mahwah, NJ: Lawrence Erlbaum Associates.

Aronoff, M., Meir, I., & Sandler, W. (2000). *Universal and particular aspects of sign language morphology*. Unpublished manuscript, SUNY at Stony Brook and University of Haifa.

Astington, J. W., & Jenkins, J. (1999). A longitudinal study of the relation beween language and theory-of-mind development. *Developmental Psychology, 35*(5), 1311–1320.

Atteneave, F. (1957). Physical determinants of the judged complexity of shapes. *Journal of Experimental Psychology, 55*, 221–227.

Baars, B. J., Motley, M. T., & MacKay, D. (1975). Output editing for lexical status from artificially elicited slips of the tongue. *Journal of Verbal Learning and Verbal Behavior, 14*, 382–391.

Baddeley, A. D. (1966). Short-term memory for word sequences as a function of acoustic, semantic and formal similarity. *Quarterly Journal of Experimental Psychology, 18*, 362–365.

Baddeley, A. D. (1986). *Working memory*. Oxford: Clarendon Press.

Baddeley, A. D., & Hitch, G. J. (1974). Working memory. In G. Bower (Ed.), *Recent advances in learning and motivation* (Vol. III, pp. 107–129). New York: Academic Press.

Baddeley, A. D., & Levy, B. S. (1971). Semantic coding and short-term memory. *Journal of Experimental Psychology, 18*, 362–365.

Baddeley, A. D., Lewis, V., & Vallar, G. (1984). Exploring the articulatory loop. *Quarterly Journal of Experimental Psychology, 36A*, 233–252.

Baddeley, A. D., Thomson, N., & Buchanan, M. (1975). Word length and the structure of short-term memory. *Journal of Verbal Learning and Verbal Behavior, 14*, 575–589.

Bahan, B. (1996). *Non-manual realization of agreement in American Sign Language*. Unpublished doctoral dissertation, Boston University.

Bahan, B., & Petitto, L. (1980). *Aspects of rules for character establishment and reference in American Sign Language*. Unpublished manuscript, The Salk Institute for Biological Studies, La Jolla, CA.

Bahan, B., & Supalla, S. (1995). Line segmentation and narrative structure: A study of eyegaze behavior in American Sign Language. In K. Emmorey & J. Reilly (Eds.), *Language, gesture, and space* (pp. 171–191). Mahwah, NJ: Lawrence Erlbaum Associates.

Baker, C. (1977). Regulators and turn-taking in American Sign Language discourse. In L. Friedman (Ed.), *On the other hand: New perspectives on American Sign Language* (pp. 215–236). New York: Academic Press.

Baker, C., & Cokely, D. (1980). *ASL: A teacher's resource text on grammar and culture*. Silver Spring, MD: T. J. Publishers.

Baker, C., & Padden, C. (1978). Focussing on the nonmanual components of American Sign Language. In P. Siple (Ed.), *Understanding language through sign language research* (pp. 27–57). New York: Academic Press.

Baker, M. (1988). *Incorporation: A theory of grammatical function changing*. Chicago, IL: The University of Chicago Press.

Baker-Schenk, C. (1983). *A micro-analysis of the nonmanual components of questions in American Sign Language*. Unpublished doctoral dissertation, University of California, Berkeley.

Balogh, J., Zurif, E., Prather, P., Swinney, D., & Finkel, L. (1998). Gap-filling and end-of-sentence effects in real-time language processing: Implications for modeling sentence comprehension in aphasia. *Brain and Language, 61*(2), 169–182.

Baron-Cohen, S., Leslie, A., & Frith, U. (1985). Does the autistic child have a "theory of mind"? *Cognition, 21*, 37–46.

Basic Sign Communication. (1983). Silver Spring, MD: National Association of the Deaf.

Bates, E., Benigni, L., Bretherton, L., Camaioni, L., & Volterra, V. (1979). *The emergence of symbols: Cognition and communication in infancy*. New York: Academic Press.

Bates, E., McNew, S., MacWhinney, B., Devoscovi, A., & Smith, S. (1982). Functional constraints on sentence processing: A cross-linguistic study. *Cognition, 11*, 245–299.

Battison, R. (1978). *Lexical borrowing in American Sign Language.* Silver Spring, MD: Linstok Press.

Bavelier, D., Corina, D., Jezzard, P., Clark, V., Karni, A., Lalwani, A., Rauschecker, J. P., Braun, A., Turner, R., & Neville, H. (1998). Hemispheric specialization for English and ASL: Left invariance—right variability. *NeuroReport, 9*, 1537–1542.

Bavelier, D., Tomann, A., Brozinsky, C., Mitchell, T., Neville, H., & Liu, G. (2001, March). *Processing of motion velocity in deaf signers.* Poster presented at the Cognitive Neuroscience Society meeting, New York, New York.

Bavelier, D., Tomann, A., Hutton, C., Mitchell, T., Liu, G., Corina, D., & Neville, H. (2000). Visual attention to the periphery is enhanced in congenitally deaf individuals. *Journal of Neuroscience, 20*, U1–U6.

Baynton, D. C. (1996). *Forbidden signs: American culture and the campaign against sign language.* Chicago, IL: The University of Chicago Press.

Bebko, J. M. (1984). Memory and rehearsal characteristics of profoundly deaf children. *Journal of Experimental Child Psychology, 38*, 415–428.

Bebko, J. M., Bell, M. A., Metcalfe-Haggert, A., & McKinnon, E. (1998). Language proficiency and the prediction of spontaneous rehearsal in children who are deaf. *Journal of Experimental Child Psychology, 68*, 51–69.

Bebko, J. M., & McKinnon, E. (1990). The language experience of deaf children: Its relation to spontaneous rehearsal in a memory task. *Child Development, 61*, 1744–1752.

Beeman, M., & Chiarello, C. (Eds.). (1998). *Right hemisphere language comprehension: Perspectives from cognitive neuroscience.* Mahwah, NJ: Lawrence Erlbaum Associates.

Bellugi, U. (1988). The acquisition of a spatial language. In F. Kessel (Ed.), *The development of language and language researchers: Essays in honor of Roger Brown* (pp. 153–185). Hillsdale, NJ: Lawrence Erlbaum Associates.

Bellugi, U. (1990, October). *Spatial language and spatial cognition.* Keynote address presented at the Boston Child Language Conference, Boston, MA.

Bellugi, U., & Fischer, S. (1972). A comparison of sign language and spoken language. *Cognition, 1*, 173–200.

Bellugi, U., & Hickok, G. (1995). Clues to the neurobiology of language. In R. Broadwell (Ed.), *Decade of the brain: Vol. 1. Neuroscience, memory, and language* (pp. 87–107). Washington, DC: Library of Congress.

Bellugi, U., & Klima E. S. (1982). The acquisition of three morphological systems in American Sign Language. *Papers and Reports on Child Language Development, 21*, 1–35. Palo Alto, CA: Stanford University Press.

Bellugi, U., Klima, E. S., & Siple, P. (1975). Remembering in signs. *Cognition, 3*, 93–125.

Bellugi, U., Lillo-Martin, D., O'Grady, L., & van Hoek, K. (1990). The development of spatialized syntactic mechanisms in American Sign Language. In W. Edmondson & F. Karlsson (Eds.), *Fourth International Symposium on Sign Language Research* (pp. 16–25). Hamburg, Germany: Signum-Verlag Press.

Bellugi, U., O'Grady, L., Lillo-Martin, D., O'Grady, M., van Hoek, K., & Corina, D. (1990). Enhancement of spatial cognition in deaf children. In V. Volterra & C. J. Erting (Eds.), *From gesture to language in hearing and deaf children* (pp. 278–298). New York: Springer-Verlag.

Bellugi, U., van Hoek, K., Lillo-Martin, D., & O'Grady, L. (1993). The acquisition of syntax and space in young deaf signers. In D. Bishop & K. Mogford (Eds.), *Language development in exceptional circumstances* (pp. 132–149). Edinburgh: Churchill Livingstone. (Original work published 1988)

Benton, A. L., Hamsher, K., Varney, N. R., & Spreen, O. (1983). *Facial recognition: Stimuli and multiple choice pictures.* New York: Oxford University Press.

Berenz, N., & Ferreria Brito, F. (1987). Pronouns in BCSL and ASL. In W. H. Edmondson & F. Karlsson (Eds.), *SLR '87: Papers from the Fourth International Symposium on Sign Language Research* (pp. 26–36). Hamburg, Germany: Signum Press.

Bergman, B. (1982). *Forskning om Teckenspråk* [Research on sign language]. Stockholm, Sweden: Stockholm University.

Bergman, B., & Wallin, L. (in press). A preliminary analysis of visual mouth segments in Swedish Sign Language. In P. Boyes-Braem & R. Sutton-Spence (Eds.), *The hands are the head of the mouth: The mouth as articulator in sign languages*. Hamburg, Germany: Signum Press.

Bergman, B., & Wallin, L. (2001). The discourse function of noun classifiers in Swedish Sign Language. In V. Dively, M. Metzger, S. Taub, & A. M. Baer (Eds.), *Sign Languages: Discoveries from international research* (pp. 45–61). Washington, DC: Gallaudet University Press.

Bernhardt, B. H., & Stemberger, J. P. (1998). *Handbook of phonological development: From the perspective of constraint-based nonlinear phonology*. San Diego, CA: Academic Press.

Bertenthal, B. I. (1993). Infants' perception of biomechanical motions: Intrinsic image and knowledge-based constraints. In C. Granrud (Ed.), *Visual perception and cognition in infancy* (pp. 175–214). Hillsdale, NJ: Lawrence Erlbaum Associates.

Bertenthal, B. I., Proffitt, D. R., Kramer, S. J., & Spetner, N. B. (1987). Infants' encoding of kinetic displays varying in relative coherence. *Developmental Psychology, 23*, 171–178.

Bettger, J. (1992). *The effects of experience on spatial cognition: Deafness and knowledge of ASL*. Unpublished doctoral dissertation, University of Illinois, Urbana–Champaign.

Bettger, J., Emmorey, K., McCullough, S., & Bellugi, U. (1997). Enhanced facial discrimination: Effects of experience with American Sign Language. *Journal of Deaf Studies and Deaf Education, 2*(4), 223–233.

Bickerton, D. (1981). *The roots of language*. Ann Arbor, MI: Karoma Publishers.

Birdsong, D. (Ed.). (1999). *Second language acquisition and the critical period hypothesis*. Mahwah, NJ: Lawrence Erlbaum Associates.

Blumstein, S. (1998). Phonological aspects of aphasia. In M. T. Sarno (Ed.), *Acquired aphasia* (3rd ed., pp. 157–185). San Diego: Academic Press.

Bonnet, C. (1977). Visual motion detection model: Features and frequency/filters. *Perception, 6*, 491–500.

Bonvillian, J. D., & Folven, R. D. (1987). The onset of signing in young children. In W. H. Edmondson & F. Karlsson (Eds.), *SLR '87: Papers from the Fourth International Symposium on Sign Language Research*. Hamburg, Germany: Signum Press.

Bonvillian, J. D., & Folven, R. D. (1993). Sign language acquisition: Developmental aspects. In M. Marschark & D. Clark (Eds.), *Psychological perspectives on deafness* (pp. 229–265). Hillsdale, NJ: Lawrence Erlbaum Associates.

Bonvillian, J. D., Orlansky, M. D., & Folven, R. D. (1990). Early sign language acquisition: Implications for theories of language acquisition. In V. Volterra & C. J. Erting (Eds.), *From gesture to language in hearing and deaf children* (pp. 219–232). Berlin: Springer-Verlag.

Bonvillian, J. D., Orlansky, M. D., Novack, L. L. (1983). Developmental milestones: Sign language acquisition and motor development. *Child Development, 54*, 1435–1445.

Bonvillian, J., & Siedlecki, T. (1996). Young children's acquisition of the location aspect of American Sign Language signs: Parental report findings. *Journal of Communication Disorders, 29*, 13–35.

Borod, J. C., Koff, E., & Caron, H. S. (1983). Right hemispheric specialization for the expression and appreciation of emotion: A focus on the face. In E. Perecman (Ed.), *Cognitive processing in the right hemisphere*. New York: Academic Press.

Bosworth, R., & Dobkins, K. (1999). Left hemisphere dominance for motion processing in deaf signers. *Psychological Science, 10*(3), 256–262.

Bosworth, R., & Emmorey, K. (1999). *Semantic priming in American Sign Language*. Unpublished manuscript, The Salk Institute for Biological Studies.

Boyes-Braem, P. (1990). Acquisition of the handshape in American Sign Language. In V. Volterra & C. J. Erting (Eds.), *From gesture to language in hearing and deaf children* (pp. 107–127). New York: Springer-Verlag.

Boyes-Braem, P. (1999). Rhythmic temporal patterns in the signing of deaf early and late learners of Swiss German Sign Language. *Language and Speech, 42*(2–3), 177–208.

Boyes-Braem, P. (2001). Functions of the mouthing component in Swiss German Sign Language. In D. Brentari (Ed.), *Foreign vocabulary in sign languages* (pp. 1–48). Mahwah, NJ: Lawrence Erlbaum Associates.

Boyes-Braem, P. (in press). Functions of the mouthings in the signing of deaf early and late learners of Swiss German Sign Language (DSGS). In P. Boyes-Braem & R. Sutton-Spence (Eds.), *The hands are the head of the mouth: The mouth as articulator in sign languages*. Hamburg, Germany: Signum Press.

Boyes-Braem, P., & Sutton-Spence, R. (Eds.). (in press). *The hands are the head of the mouth: The mouth as articulator in sign languages*. Hamburg, Germany: Signum Press.

Braden, J. P. (1994). *Deafness, deprivation, and IQ*. New York: Plenum Press.

Branson, J., Miller, D., Marsaja, I. G., & Negara, I. W. (1996). Everyone here speaks sign language, too: A deaf village in Bali, Indonesia. In C. Lucas (Ed.), *Multicultural aspects of sociolinguistics in deaf communities* (pp. 39–57). Washington, DC: Gallaudet University Press.

Brennan, M. (1990). *Word formation in British Sign Language*. Stockholm, Sweden: University of Stockholm.

Brentari, D. (1990). Licensing in ASL handshape. In C. Lucas (Ed.), *Sign language research: Theoretical issues* (pp. 57–68). Washington, DC: Gallaudet College Press.

Brentari, D. (1995). Sign language phonology: ASL. In J. Goldsmith (Ed.), *The handbook of phonological theory* (pp. 615–639). Oxford, England: Blackwell.

Brentari, D. (1998). *A prosodic model of sign language phonology*. Cambridge, MA: MIT Press.

Brentari, D. (Ed.). (2001). *Foreign vocabulary in sign languages: A cross-linguistic investigation of word formation*. Mahwah, NJ: Lawrence Erlbaum Associates.

Brentari, D., & Benedicto, E. (1999). Verbal classifiers as heads of functional projections: Evidence from American Sign Language. In S. F. Bird, A. Carnie, J. D. Haugen, & P. Norquest (Eds.), *Proceedings of the West Coast Conference on Formal Linguistics* (pp. 69–81). Somerville, MA: Cascadilla Press.

Brentari, D., & Padden, C. (2001). A lexicon of multiple origins: Native and foreign vocabulary in American Sign Language. In D. Brentari (Ed.), *Foreign vocabulary in sign languages: A crosslinguistic investigation of word formation* (pp. 87–119). Mahwah, NJ: Lawrence Erlbaum Associates.

Brentari, D., & Poizner, H. (1994). A phonological analysis of a deaf Parkinsonian signer. *Language and Cognitive Processes, 9*(1), 69–99.

Brentari, D., Poizner, H., & Kegl, J. (1995). Aphasic and Parkinsonian signing: Differences in phonological disruption. *Brain and Language, 48*, 69–105.

Brien, D. (Ed.). (1992). *Dictionary of British Sign Language–English*. London: Faber and Faber.

Brooks, L. R. (1967). The suppression of visualization by reading. *Quarterly Journal of Experimental Psychology, 33A*, 289–299.

Brooks, L. R. (1968). Spatial and verbal components in the act of recall. *Canadian Journal of Psychology, 22*, 349–368.

Brown, A. (1991). A review of the tip-of-the-tongue experience. *Psychological Bulletin, 109*(2), 204–223.

Brown, J. W. (1977). *Mind, brain, and consciousness: The neuropsychology of cognition*. New York: Academic Press.

Brown, P. (1991). *Spatial conceptualization in Tzeltal* (Working paper No. 6). Cognitive Anthropology Research Group, Max Planck Institute for Psycholinguistics.

Brownell, H., Carroll, J. J., Rehak, A., & Wingfield, A. (1992). The use of pronoun anaphora and speaker mood in the interpretation of conversational utterances by right hemisphere brain damaged patients. *Brain and Language, 43,* 121–147.

Brownell, H., Gardner, H., Prather, P., & Martino, G. (1995). Language, communication, and the right hemisphere. In H. Kirshner (Ed.), *Handbook of neurological speech and language disorders* (pp. 325–349). New York: Marcel Dekker.

Bryden, M. P. (1982). *Laterality: Functional asymmetry in the intact brain.* New York: Academic Press.

Butterworth, B., & Beattie, G. (1978). Gesture and silence as indicators of planning in speech. In R. N. Campbell & P. T. Smith (Eds.), *Recent advances in the psychology of language: Formal and experimental approaches* (pp. 347–360). New York: Plenum.

Calder, A. J., Young, A. W., Perrett, D. I., Etcoff, N. L., & Rowland, D. (1996). Categorical perception of morphed facial expressions. *Visual Cognition, 3,* 81–117.

Campbell, R. (1978). Asymmetries in interpreting and expressing a posed facial expression. *Cortex, 14,* 327–342.

Campbell, R., & Dodd, B. (1980). Hearing by eye. *Quarterly Journal of Experimental Psychology, 32,* 85–99.

Campbell, R., Woll, B., Benson, P. J., & Wallace, S. B. (1999). Categorical processing of faces in sign. *Quarterly Journal of Experimental Psychology, 52A,* 62–95.

Capirci, O., Cattani, A., Rossini, P., & Volterra, V. (1998). Teaching sign language to hearing children as a possible factor in cognitive enhancement. *Journal of Deaf Studies and Deaf Education, 3*(2), 135–142.

Capirci, O., Montanari, S., Volterra, V. (1998). Gestures, signs, and words in early language development. In J. M. Iverson & S. Goldin-Meadow (Eds.), *The nature and functions of gesture in children's communication* (pp. 45–60). San Francisco, CA: Jossey-Bass.

Caplan, D., Gow, D., Makris, N. (1995). Analysis of lesions by MRI in stroke patients with acoustic–phonetic processing deficits. *Neurology, 45,* 293–298.

Caplan, D., Hildebrandt, H., & Makris, N. (1996). Location of lesions in stroke patents with deficits in syntactic processing in sentence comprehension. *Brain, 119,* 933–949.

Carroll, J., & Gibson, E. (1986). Infant perception of gestural contrasts: Prerequisites for the acquisition of a visually specified language. *Journal of Child Language, 13,* 31–49.

Caselli, M. C. (1990). Communicative gestures and first words. In V. Volterra & C. Erting (Eds.), *From gesture to language in hearing and deaf children* (pp. 56–67). Berlin, Germany: Springer-Verlag.

Casey, S. (1999, March). *The continuity of agreement: From pre-linguistic action gestures to ASL verbs.* Paper presented at the Second Annual High Desert Student Conference in Linguistics, Albuquerque, NM.

Casey, S. (in press). Relationships between gestures and signed languages: Indicating participants in actions. In A. E. Baker, E. M. van den Bogaerde, & O. Crasborn (Eds.), *Crosslinguistic perspectives on sign language research: Papers from TISLR 7.* Hamburg, Germany: Signum Press.

Chamberlain, C., & Mayberry, R. I. (1994, May). *Do the deaf "see" better? Effects of deafness on visuospatial skills.* Poster presented at TENNET V, Montreal, Quebec.

Chamberlain, C., & Mayberry, R. I. (2000). Theorizing about the relationship between ASL and reading. In C. Chamberlain, J. Morford, & R. I. Mayberry (Eds.), *Language acquisition by eye* (pp. 221–260). Mahwah, NJ: Lawrence Erlbaum Associates.

Chang, F. (1980). Active memory processes in visual sentence comprehension: Clause effects and pronominal reference. *Memory and Cognition, 8,* 58–64.

Chatterjee, S. H., Freyd, J. J., & Shiffrar, M. (1996). Configural processing in the perception of apparent biological motion. *Journal of Experimental Psychology: Human Perception and Performance, 22,* 916–929.

Cheek, A., Cormier, K., & Meier, R. P. (1998, November). *Continuities and discontinuities between manual babbling and early signing.* Paper presented at the Sixth International Conference on Theoretical Issues in Sign Language Research, Washington, DC.

Chiarello, C., Senehi, J., & Nuding, S. (1987). Semantic priming with abstract and concrete words: Differential asymmetry may be postlexical. *Brain and Language, 31,* 43–60.

Chomsky, N. (1965). *Aspects of the theory of syntax.* Cambridge, MA: MIT Press.

Chomsky, N. (1981). *Lectures on government and binding.* Dordrecht: Foris.

Chomsky, N. (1982). *Some concepts and consequences of the theory of government and binding.* Cambridge, MA: MIT Press.

Chomsky, N. (1995). *The minimalist program.* Cambridge, MA: MIT Press.

Chomsky, N., & Halle, M. (1968). *The sound pattern of English.* New York: Harper & Row.

Christenfeld, N. (1994). Options and ums. *Journal of Language & Social Psychology, 13*(2), 192–199.

Cismaru, R., Penhune, V. B., Petitto, L. A., Dorsaint-Pierre, R., Klein, D., & Zatorre, R. J. (1999, October). *Auditory cortex morphometry in the congenitally deaf measured using MRI.* Paper presented at The Society for Neuroscience, Miami, Florida.

Clark, E. (1978). From gesture to word: On the natural history of deixis in language acquisition. In J. S. Bruner & A. Garton (Eds.), *Human growth and development: Wolfson College Lectures 1976.* Oxford, England: Clarendon Press.

Clark, H. (1996). *Using language.* Cambridge, England: Cambridge University Press.

Clark, H., & Gerrig, R. (1990). Quotations as demonstrations. *Language, 66,* 764–805.

Clark, K., Hickok, G., Love, T., Klima, E. S., & Bellugi, U. (1997). Right hemisphere damage aphasia in American Sign Language. *Brain and Language, 60,* 179–180.

Clark, L., & Grosjean, F. (1982). Sign recognition processes in American Sign Language: The effect of context. *Language and Speech, 25*(4), 325–340.

Clark, M. D., Schwanenflugel, P. J., Everhart, V. S., & Bartini, M. (1996). Theory of mind in deaf adults and the organization of verbs of knowing. *Journal of Deaf Studies and Deaf Education, 1,* 179–189.

Clements, G. N. (1985). The geometry of phonological features. *Phonology Yearbook, 2,* 225–252.

Coats, E. J., & Feldman, R. S. (1995). The role of television in the socialization of nonverbal behavioral skills. *Basic and Applied Social Psychology, 17,* 327–341.

Cogen, C. (1977). On three aspects of time expression in American Sign Language. In L. Friedman (Ed.), *On the other hand: New perspectives on American Sign Language* (pp. 197–214). New York: Academic Press.

Cogill, D. (2001). *Classifier predicates, linguistic structures, or templated visual representations?* Manuscript under review.

Collins, A. M., & Loftus, E. (1975). A spreading activation theory of semantic processing. *Psychological Review, 82,* 407–428.

Comrie, B. (1976). *Aspect.* Cambridge, England: Cambridge University Press.

Conlin, K., Mirus, G. R., Mauk, C., & Meier, R. P. (2000). Acquisition of first signs: Place, handshape, and movement. In C. Chamberlain, J. P. Morford, & R. I. Mayberry (Eds.), *Language acquisition by eye* (pp. 51–70). Mahwah, NJ: Lawrence Erlbaum Associates.

Conrad, R. (1970). Short-term memory processes in the deaf. *British Journal of Psychology, 61,* 179–195.

Conrad, R., & Hull, A. (1964). Information, acoustic confusion and memory span. *British Journal of Psychology, 55,* 429–432.

Conrad, R., & Hull, A. (1968). Input modality and the serial position curve in short-term memory. *Psychonomic Science, 10,* 135–136.

Corbett, A., & Chang, F. (1983). Pronoun disambiguation: Accessing potential antecedents. *Memory and Cognition, 11,* 283–294.

Corcoran, D. W. J. (1977). The phenomena of the disembodied eye or is it a matter of personal geography? *Perception, 6,* 247–253.

Corina, D. P. (1989). Recognition of affective and noncanonical linguistic facial expressions in hearing and deaf subjects. *Brain and Cognition, 9,* 227–237.

Corina, D. P. (1990). Reassessing the role of sonority in syllable structure: Evidence from a visual–gestural language. In M. Ziolkowski, M. Noske, & K. Deaton (Eds.), *Chicago Linguistic Society 26: Parasession on the syllable in phonetics and phonology.* Chicago, IL: Chicago Linguistics Society.

Corina, D. P. (1993). To branch or not to branch: Underspecifications in ASL handshape contours. In G. Coulter (Ed.), *Phonetics and phonology: Current issues in ASL phonology* (pp. 63–96). New York: Academic Press.

Corina, D. P. (1998a). Aphasia in users of signed languages. In P. Coppens, Y. Lebrun, & A. Basso (Eds.), *Aphasia in atypical populations* (pp. 261–310). Mahwah, NJ: Lawrence Erlbaum Associates.

Corina, D. P. (1998b). The processing of sign language: Evidence from aphasia. In B. Stemmer & H. A. Whitaker (Eds.), *Handbook of neurolinguistics* (pp. 313–329). New York: Academic Press.

Corina, D. P. (1998c). Studies of neural processing in deaf signers: Toward a neurocognitive model of language processing in the deaf. *Journal of Deaf Studies and Deaf Education, 3*(1), 35–48.

Corina, D. P. (1999a). Neural disorders of language and movement: Evidence from American Sign Language. In L. S. Messing & R. Campbell (Eds.), *Gesture, speech, and sign* (pp. 27–43). New York: Oxford University Press.

Corina, D. P. (1999b). On the nature of left hemisphere specialization for signed language. *Brain and Language, 69,* 230–240.

Corina, D. P. (2000a, February). *Is ASL phonology psychologically real?* Paper presented at the Texas Linguistic Society Meeting: The Effects of Modality on Language and Linguistic Theory, Austin.

Corina, D. P. (2000b). Some observations on paraphasia in American Sign Language. In K. Emmorey & H. Lane (Eds.), *The signs of language revisited: An anthology to honor Ursula Bellugi and Edward Klima* (pp. 493–508). Mahwah, NJ: Lawrence Erlbaum Associates.

Corina, D. P. Bellugi, U., Kritchevsky, M., O'Grady-Batch, L, & Norman, F. (1990, October). *Spatial relations in signed versus spoken language: Clues to right parietal functions.* Paper presented at the Academy of Aphasia, Baltimore, MD.

Corina, D. P., Bellugi, U., & Reilly, J. (1999). Neuropsychological studies of linguistic and affective facial expression in deaf signers. *Language & Speech, 42,* 307–331.

Corina, D. P., & Emmorey, K. (1993, November). *Lexical priming in American Sign Language.* Poster presented at 34th Annual Meeting of the Psychonomics Society, Washington, DC.

Corina, D. P., & Hildebrandt, U. (in press). The psychological reality of phonological structure in ASL. In R. Meier, D. Quinto, & K. Cormier (Eds.), *Modality and structure in signed and spoken languages.* Cambridge, England: Cambridge University Press.

Corina, D. P., Kritchevsky, M., & Bellugi, U. (1996). Visual language processing and unilateral neglect: Evidence from American Sign Language. *Cognitive Neuropsychology, 13*(3), 321–356.

Corina, D. P., McBurney, S. L., Dodrill, C., Hinshaw, K., Brinkley, J., & Ojemann, G. (1999). Functional roles of Broca's area and supramarginal gyrus: Evidence from cortical stimulation mapping in a deaf signer. *NeuroImage, 10,* 570–581.

Corina, D. P., Poizner, H., Bellugi, U., Feinberg, T., Dowd, D., & O'Grady-Batch, L. (1992). Dissociation between linguistic and non-linguistic gestural systems: A case for compositionality. *Brain and Language, 43,* 414–447.

Corina, D. P., San Jose, L., Ackerman, D., Guillemin, A., & Braun, A. (2000, April). *A comparison of neural systems underlying human action and American Sign Language processing.* Poster presented at the Cognitive Neuroscience Society meeting, San Francisco, CA.

Corina, D. P., & Sandler, W. (1993). On the nature of phonological structure in sign language. *Phonology, 10,* 165–207.

Corina, D. P., Vaid, J., & Bellugi, U. (1992). The linguistic basis of left hemisphere specialization. *Science, 253,* 1258–1260.

Cormier, K. Mauk, C., & Repp, A. (1998). Manual babbling in deaf and hearing infants: A longitudinal study. In E. Clark (Ed.), *Proceedings of the Child Language Research Forum, 29* (pp. 55–61). Stanford, CT: CSLI Publications.

Coulter, G. R. (Ed.). (1993). *Phonetics and phonology: Current issues in ASL phonology.* San Diego, CA: Academic Press.

Coulter, G. R., & Anderson, S. R. (1993). Introduction. In G. R. Coulter (Ed.), *Phonetics and phonology: Current issues in ASL phonology* (pp. 1–17). San Diego, CA: Academic Press.

Courtin, C. (2000). The impact of sign language on the cognitive development of deaf children: The case of theories of mind. *Journal of Deaf Studies and Deaf Education, 5*(3), 266–276.

Courtin, C., & Melot, A. (1998). Development of theories of mind in deaf children. In M. Marschark & D. Clark (Eds.), *Psychological perspectives on deafness* (pp. 79–102). Mahwah, NJ: Lawrence Erlbaum Associates.

Crasborne, O. (2000, February). *On the balance between phonological specification and phonetic implementation: Register variation in Sign Language of the Netherlands.* Paper presented at the Texas Linguistic Society Meeting: The Effects of Modality on Language and Linguistic Theory, Austin, TX.

Crawford, E. L., Regier, T., & Huttenlocher, J. (2000). Linguistic and nonlinguistic spatial categorization. *Cognition, 75,* 209–235.

Croft, W. (1988). Agreement vs. case marking and direct objects. In M. Barlow & C. A. Ferguson (Eds.), *Agreement in natural languages: Approaches, theories, descriptions* (pp. 159–179). Stanford, CA: CSLI.

Crowder, R. G. (1967). Prefix effects in immediate memory. *Canadian Journal of Psychology, 21,* 450–461.

Crowder, R. G., & Morton, J. (1969). Precategorical acoustic storage (PAS). *Perception and Psychophysics, 5,* 41–60.

Currie, A.-M. (in press). A cross-linguistic examination of the vocabularies of four signed languages. In R. Meier, D. Quinto, & K. Cormier (Eds.), *Modality and structure in signed and spoken languages.* Cambridge, England: Cambridge University Press.

Curtiss, S. (1977). *Genie: A psycholinguistic study of a modern day "wild child."* New York: Academic Press.

Cutler, A., Hawkins, J., & Gilligan, G. (1985). The suffixing preference: A processing explanation. *Linguistics, 23,* 723–758.

Dahl, H. (1979). *Word frequency & spoken American English.* Connecticut: Verbatim.

Damasio, A., Bellugi, U., Damasio, H., Poizner, H., & Van Gilder, J. (1986). Sign language aphasia during left hemisphere amytal injection. *Nature, 322,* 363–365.

Damasio, A. R., & Damasio, H. (1983). The anatomic basis of pure alexia. *Neurology, 33,* 1573–1583.

Damasio, H., Grabowski, T. J., Tranel, D., Hichwa, R., & Damasio, A. R. (1996). A neural basis for lexical retrieval. *Nature, 380,* 499–505.

Damasio, H., Grabowski, T. J., Tranel, D., Ponto, L. B., Hichwa, R. D., & Damasio, A. R. (2001). Neural correlates of naming actions and of naming spatial relations. *NeuroImage, 13,* 1053–1064.

Davidson, W., Elford, L. W., & Denny, P. (1963). Athapaskan classificatory verbs. In H. Hoijer et al. (Eds.), *Studies in Athapaskan languages* (pp. 30–41). Berkeley: University of California Press.

Day, J. (1979). Visual half-field word recognition as a function of syntactic class and imageability. *Neuropsychologia, 17,* 515–520.

Decety, J., Grèzes, J., Costes, N., Perani, D., Jeannerod, M., Procyk, E., Grassi, F., & Fazio, F. (1997). Brain activity during observation of actions: Influence of action content and subject's strategy. *Brain, 120,* 1763–1777.

Delis, D., Robertson, L. C., & Efron, R. (1986). Hemispheric specialization of memory for visual hierarchical stimuli. *Neuropsychologia, 24*, 205–214.

Dell, G. (1986). A spreading activation theory of retrieval in sentence production. *Psychological Review, 93*, 283–321.

Dell, G. (1988). The retrieval of phonological forms in production: Tests of predictions from a connectionist model. *Journal of Memory and Language, 27*, 124–142.

Dell, G., & Reich, P. A. (1981). Stages in sentence production: An analysis of speech error data. *Journal of Verbal Learning and Verbal Behavior, 20*, 611–629.

DeLoache, J. S. (1987). Rapid change in the symbolic functioning of very young children. *Science, 238*, 1556–1557.

DeLoache, J. S. (1989). Young children's understanding of the correspondence between a scale model and a larger space. *Cognitive Development, 4*, 121–139.

DeLoache, J. S. (1991). Symbolic functioning in very young children: Understanding of pictures and models. *Child Development, 62*, 736–752.

del Viso, S., Igoa, J. M., & Garcia-Albea, J. E. (1991). On the autonomy of phonological encoding: Evidence from slips of the tongue in Spanish. *Journal of Psycholinguistic Research, 20*(3), 161–185.

Demuth, K. (1995). Markedness and the development of prosodic structure. In J. Beckman (Ed.), *Proceedings of NELS 25*, GLSA, University of Massachusetts, Amherst.

de Villiers, J. G., & de Villiers, P. A. (1978). *Language acquisition.* Cambridge, MA: Harvard University Press.

de Villiers, J. G., & de Villiers, P. A. (1999). Linguistic determinism and the understanding of false beliefs. In P. Mitchell & K. Riggs (Eds.), *Children's reasoning and the mind* (pp. 189–226). Psychology Press.

Dively, V. (1998). Conversational repairs in ASL. In C. Lucas (Ed.), *Pinky extension and eye gaze: Language use in Deaf communities* (pp. 137–169). Washington, DC: Gallaudet University Press.

Du Bois, J. (1985). Competing motivations. In J. Haiman (Ed.), *Iconicity in syntax* (pp. 343–365). Amsterdam, The Netherlands: John Benjamins.

Du Bois, J. (1987). The discourse basis of ergativity. *Language, 63*(4), 805–855.

Duncan, S. D. (1972). Some signals and rules for taking speaking turns in conversations. *Journal of Personality and Social Psychology, 23*, 283–292.

Ebbinghaus, H., & Hessmann, J. (1996). Signs and words: Accounting for spoken language elements in German Sign Language. In W. H. Edmondson & R. Wilbur (Eds.), *International review of sign linguistics* (pp. 23–56). Mahwah, NJ: Lawrence Erlbaum Associates.

Eimas, P. (1975). Auditory and phonetic coding of the cues for speech: Discrimination of the [r–l] distinction by young infants. *Perception & Psychophysics, 18*, 341–347.

Ekman, P. (1992). Facial expression of emotion: An old controversy and new findings. In V. Bruce (Ed.), *Processing the facial image* (pp. 63–69). Oxford: Clarendon Press.

Ekman, P., & Friesen, W. (1978). *Facial action coding system.* Palo Alto, CA: Consulting Psychologists Press.

Ellis, N., & Hennelley, R. (1980). A bilingual word-length effect: Implications for intelligence testing and the relative ease of mental calculation in Welsh and English. *British Journal of Psychology, 71*, 43–52.

Elman, J. (1993). Learning and development in neural networks: The importance of starting small. *Cognition, 48*, 71–99.

Emmorey, K. (1990). [Sign frequency effects on reaction time in an ASL lexical decision task]. Unpublished raw data.

Emmorey, K. (1991). Repetition priming with aspect and agreement morphology in American Sign Language. *Journal of Psycholinguistic Research, 20*(5), 365–388.

Emmorey, K. (1993). Processing a dynamic visual-spatial language: Psycholinguistic studies of American Sign Language. *Journal of Psycholinguistic Research, 22*(2), 153–188.

Emmorey, K. (1995). Processing the dynamic visual-spatial morphology of signed languages. In L. B. Feldman (Ed.), *Morphological aspects of language processing: Crosslinguistic Perspectives* (pp. 29–54). Mahwah, NJ: Lawrence Erlbaum Associates.

Emmorey, K. (1996). The confluence of space and language in signed languages. In P. Bloom, M. Peterson, L. Nadel, & M. Garrett (Eds.), *Language and space* (pp. 171–209). Cambridge, MA: MIT Press.

Emmorey, K. (1997a, August). *The neural substrates for spatial cognition and language: Insights from sign language*. Paper presented at the Cognitive Science Society Meeting, Stanford, California.

Emmorey, K. (1997b). Non-antecedent suppression in American Sign Language. *Language and Cognitive Processes, 12*(1), 103–112.

Emmorey, K. (1998, November). *Some consequences of using signing space to represent physical space*. Keynote address at the Theoretical Issues in Sign Language Research meeting, Washington, D.C.

Emmorey, K. (1999). Do signers gesture? In L. Messing & R. Campbell (Eds.), *Gesture, speech, and sign* (pp. 133–159). New York: Oxford University Press.

Emmorey, K. (2000, November). *Analogue vs. categorical expression of spatial relations in American Sign Language and English*. Paper presented at the Psychonomics Society Meeting, New Orleans.

Emmorey, K. (2001). Space on hand: The exploitation of signing space to illustrate abstract thought. In M. Gattis (Ed.), *Spatial schemas and abstract thought* (pp. 147–174). Cambridge, MA: MIT Press.

Emmorey, K. (in press). The effects of modality on spatial language: How signers and speakers talk about space. In R. Meier, D. Quinto, & K. Cormier (Eds.), *Modality and structure in signed and spoken languages*. Cambridge, England: Cambridge University Press.

Emmorey, K., Bellugi, U., Friederici, A., & Horn, P. (1995). Effects of age of acquisition on grammatical sensitivity: Evidence from on-line and off-line tasks. *Applied Psycholinguistics, 16*, 1–23.

Emmorey, K., & Bettger, J. (1995). [Reaction times for Deaf and hearing subjects to discriminate mirror-image nonsense figures]. Unpublished raw data.

Emmorey, K., & Casey, S. (1995). A comparison of spatial language in English and American Sign Language. *Sign Language Studies, 88*, 255–288.

Emmorey, K., & Corina, D. P. (1990a). [Intrahemispheric competition for Deaf signers: Dual task performance for left- versus right-hand finger tapping while watching ASL stories with either extensive or little use of topographic signing space]. Unpublished raw data.

Emmorey, K., & Corina, D. P. (1990b). Lexical recognition in sign language: Effects of phonetic structure and morphology. *Perceptual and Motor Skills, 71*, 1227–1252.

Emmorey, K., & Corina, D. P. (1992, January). *Differential sensitivity to classifier morphology in ASL signers*. Paper presented at the Linguistic Society of America, Philadelphia, PA.

Emmorey, K., & Corina, D. P. (1993). Hemispheric specialization for ASL signs and English words: Differences between imageable and abstract forms. *Neuropsychologia, 31*, 645–653.

Emmorey, K., Corina, D. P., & Bellugi, U. (1995). Differential processing of topographic and referential functions of space. In K. Emmorey & J. Reilly (Eds.), *Language, gesture, and space* (pp. 43–62). Mahwah, NJ: Lawrence Erlbaum Associates.

Emmorey, K., Damasio, H., McCullough, S., Grabowski, T., Ponto, L., Hichwa, R., & Bellugi, U. (2001, March). *Neural systems underlying spatial language in American Sign Language*. Poster presented at the Cognitive Neuroscience Society meeting, New York, New York.

Emmorey, K., Ewan, B., & Grant, R. (1994, January). *A new case of linguistic isolation: Preliminary report*. Paper presented at the Boston University Conference on Language Development, Boston, MA.

Emmorey, K., & Falgier, B. (1999a, January). *Processing continuous and simultaneous reference in ASL*. Poster presented at the Linguistic Society of America Meeting, Los Angeles, CA.

Emmorey, K., & Falgier, B. (1999b). Talking about space with space: Describing environments in ASL. In E. A. Winston (Ed.), *Story telling and conversations: Discourse in deaf communities* (pp. 3–26). Washington, DC: Gallaudet University Press.

Emmorey, K., Falgier, B., & Gernsbacher, M. (1998, November). *Processing ASL vs. reading English: Insights into the nature of suppression mechanisms.* Poster presented at the Theoretical Issues in Sign Language Research meeting, Washington, DC.

Emmorey, K., Grabowski, T., McCullough, S., Damasio, H., & Bellugi, U. (2000, April). *Neural systems underlying lexical retrieval for sign language.* Poster presented at the Cognitive Neuroscience Society meeting, San Francisco, CA.

Emmorey, K., & Herzig, M. (in press). Categorical versus analogue properties of classifier constructions in ASL. In K. Emmorey (Ed.), *Perspectives on classifier constructions in sign languages.* Mahwah, NJ: Lawrence Erlbaum Associates.

Emmorey, K., Klima, E. S., & Hickok, G. (1998). Mental rotation within linguistic and nonlinguistic domains in users of American Sign Language. *Cognition, 68,* 221–246.

Emmorey, K., & Kosslyn, S. (1996). Enhanced image generation abilities in deaf signers: A right hemisphere effect. *Brain and Cognition, 32,* 28–44.

Emmorey, K., Kosslyn, S., & Bellugi, U. (1993). Visual imagery and visual-spatial language: Enhanced imagery abilities in deaf and hearing ASL signers. *Cognition, 46,* 139–181.

Emmorey, K., & Lillo-Martin, D. (1995). Processing spatial anaphora: Referent reactivation with overt and null pronouns in American Sign Language. *Language and Cognitive Processes, 10*(6), 631–664.

Emmorey, K., Norman, F., & O'Grady, L. (1991). The activation of spatial antecedents from overt pronouns in American Sign Language. *Language and Cognitive Processes, 6*(3), 207–228.

Emmorey, K., & Reilly, J. (1998). The development of quotation and reported action: Conveying perspective in ASL. In E. Clark (Ed.), *Proceedings of the Twenty-Ninth Annual Stanford Child Language Research Forum* (pp. 81–90). Stanford, CA: CSLI Publications.

Emmorey, K., & Tversky, B. (2001). *Spatial perspective in ASL.* Manuscript under review.

Emmorey, K., Tversky, B., & Taylor, B. (in press). Using space to describe space: Perspective in speech, sign, and gesture. *Spatial Cognition and Computation.*

Engberg-Pedersen, E. (1993). *Space in Danish Sign Language: The semantics and morphosyntax of the use of space in a visual language.* Hamburg, Germany: Signum-Verlag.

Engberg-Pedersen, E. (1994). Some simultaneous constructions in Danish Sign Language. In M. Brennan & G. Turner (Eds.), *Word-order issues in sign language* (pp. 73–87). Durham, England: ISLA Publications.

Engberg-Pedersen, E. (1995). Point of view expressed through shifters. In K. Emmorey & J. Reilly (Eds.), *Language, gesture, and space* (pp. 133–154). Mahwah, NJ: Lawrence Erlbaum Associates.

Erting, C., Prezioso, C., & O'Grady-Hynes, M. (1990). The interactional context of deaf mother–infant communication. In V. Volterra & C. J. Erting (Eds.), *From gesture to language in hearing and deaf children* (pp. 97–106). New York: Springer-Verlag.

Etcoff, N. L., & Magee, J. J. (1992). Categorical perception of facial expressions. *Cognition, 44,* 227–240.

Fadiga, L., Fogassi, L., Gallese, V., & Rizzolatti, G. (2000). Visuomotor neurons: Ambiguity of the discharge or "motor" perception? *International Journal of Psychophysiology, 35,* 165–177.

Farah, M., Hammond, K., Levine, D., & Calvanio, R. (1988). Visual and spatial mental imagery: Dissociable systems of representation. *Cognitive Psychology, 20,* 439–462.

Farah, M., Wilson, K., Drain, H., & Tanaka, J. (1995). The inverted face inversion effect in prosopagnosia: Evidence for mandatory, face-specific perceptual mechanisms. *Vision Research, 35,* 2089–2093.

Fauconnier, G. (1985). *Mental spaces*. Cambridge, MA: MIT Press.

Fauconnier, G. (1997). *Mappings in thought and mind*. Cambridge, England: Cambridge University Press.

Fernald, A. (1984). The perceptual and affective salience of mothers' speech to infants. In L. Feagans, C. Garvey, & R. Golinkoff (Eds.), *The origins and growth of communication* (pp. 5–29). Norwood, NJ: Ablex.

Fernald, A. (1985). Four-month-old infants prefer to listen to motherese. *Infant Behavior and Development, 8*, 181–195.

Fernald, A., Taeschner, T., Dunn, J., Papousek, M., Boysson-Bardies, B., & Fukui, I. (1989). A cross-linguistic study of prosodic modification in mothers' and fathers' speech to preverbal infants. *Journal of Child Language, 16*, 477–501.

Ferreira Brito, L. (1983, June). *A comparative study of signs for time and space in São Paulo and Urubu-Kaapor Sign Language*. Paper presented at the Third International Symposium on Sign Language Research forum, Rome, Italy.

Feyereisen, P. (1986). Production and comprehension of emotional facial expressions in brain damaged subjects. In R. Bruyer (Ed.), *The neuropsychology of face perception and facial expression* (pp. 221–245). Hillsdale, NJ: Lawrence Erlbaum Associates.

Figueras-Costa, B., & Harris, P. (2001). Theory of mind development in deaf children: A nonverbal test of false-belief understanding. *Journal of Deaf Studies and Deaf Education, 6*, 92–102.

Finney, E., & Dobkins, K. (2001). Visual contrast sensitivity in deaf versus hearing population: Exploring the perceptual consequences of auditory deprivation and experience with a visual language. *Cognitive Brain Research, 11*, 171–183.

Fischer, S. (1973). Two processes of reduplication in American Sign Language. *Foundations of Language, 9*, 469–480.

Fischer, S. (1974). Sign language and linguistic universals. In C. Rohrer & N. Ruwet (Eds.), *Actes du colloque Franco-Allemand de grammaire transformationelle, band II: Etudes de sémantique et autres* (pp. 187–204). Tübingen, Germany: Max Neimery Verlag.

Fischer, S. (1975). Influences on word order change in ASL. In C. Li (Ed.), *Word order and word order change* (pp. 1–25). Austin: University of Texas Press.

Fischer, S. (1982). An orientation to language. In D. Sims, G. Walter, & R. Whitehead (Eds.), *Deafness and communication: Assessment and training* (pp. 9–22). Baltimore, MD: Williams & Wilkins.

Fischer, S., Delhorne, L. A., & Reed, C. M. (1999). Effects of rate of presentation on the reception of American Sign Language. *Journal of Speech, Hearing, and Language Research, 42*(3), 568–582.

Fischer, S., & Osugi, Y. (2000, July). *Thumbs up vs. giving the finger: Indexical classifiers in NS and ASL*. Paper presented at the Theoretical Issues in Sign Language Research meeting, Amsterdam, The Netherlands.

Fitch, R. H., Miller, S., & Tallal, P. (1997). Neurobiology of speech perception. *Annual Review of Neuroscience, 20*, 331–353.

Flege, J. E., Munro, M, & MacKay, I. (1995). Factors affecting degree of perceived foreign accent in a second language. *Journal of the Acoustical Society of American, 97*, 3125–3134.

Fodor, J. A. (1983). *The modularity of mind*. Cambridge, MA: MIT Press.

Forster, K. (1978). Accessing the mental lexicon. In E. Walker (Ed.), *Explorations in the biology of language* (pp. 139–174). Montgomery, VT: Bradford Books.

Fowler, C., Napps, S., & Feldman, L. (1985). Relations among regular and irregular morphologically related words in the lexicon as revealed by repetition priming. *Memory and Cognition, 13*(3), 241–255.

Frauenfelder, U., & Schreuder, R. (1992). Constraining psycholinguistic models of morphological processing and representation: The role of productivity. In G. Booij & J. van

Marle (Eds.), *Yearbook of Morphology 1991* (pp. 165–183). Netherlands: Kluwer Academic Publishers.

Friedman, L. (1975). Space, time, and person reference in American Sign Language. *Language, 51*(4), 940–961.

Frishberg, N. (1975). Arbitrariness and iconicity. *Language, 51*, 696–715.

Frishberg, N. (1983). Dominance relations and discourse structure. In W. Stokoe & V. Volterra (Eds.), *Proceedings of the Third International Symposium on Sign Language Research* (pp. 79–90). Silver Spring, MD: Linstok Press.

Fromkin, V. A. (1971). The non-anomalous nature of anomalous utterances. *Language, 47*, 27–52.

Fromkin, V. A. (1973). Slips of the tongue. *Scientific American, 229*, 109–117.

Furuyama, N. (2000). Gestural interaction between the instructor and the learner in *origami* instruction. In D. McNeill (Ed.), *Language and gesture* (pp. 99–117). Cambridge, England: Cambridge University Press.

Furth, H. G. (1966). *Thinking without language.* New York: Free Press.

Galvan, D. B. (1988). *The acquisition of three morphological subsystems in American Sign Language by deaf children with deaf or hearing parents.* Unpublished doctoral dissertation, University of California, Berkeley.

Gandour, J. (1977). Counterfeit tones in the speech of southern Thai bidialectals. *Lingua, 41*, 125–143.

Garrett, M. (1975). The analysis of sentence production. In G. Bower (Ed.), *Psychology of learning and motivation, Vol. 9.* New York: Academic Press.

Garrett, M. (1988). Processes in language production. In F. J. Newmeyer (Ed.), *Linguistics: The Cambridge survey, III language: Psychological and biological aspects* (pp. 69–96). Cambridge, England: Cambridge University Press.

Garnica, O. (1977). Some prosodic and paralinguistic features of speech to young children. In C. Snow & C. Ferguson (Eds.), *Talking to children: Language input and acquisition* (pp. 3–88). Cambridge, England: Cambridge University Press.

Gathercole, S. (Ed.). (1996). *Models of short-term memory.* Hove, UK: Psychology Press.

Gathercole, S., & Baddeley, A. (1993). *Working memory and language.* Hillsdale, NJ: Lawrence Erlbaum Associates.

Gattis, M. (Ed.). (2001a). Reading pictures: Constraints on mapping conceptual and spatial schemas. In M. Gattis (Ed.), *Spatial schemas and abstract thought* (pp. 223–245). Cambridge, MA: MIT Press.

Gattis, M. (Ed.). (2001b). *Spatial schemas and abstract thought.* Cambridge, MA: MIT Press.

Gee, J., & Kegl, J. (1983). Narrative/story structure, pausing, and American Sign Language. *Discourse Processes, 6*, 243–258.

Gentner, D. (2001). Spatial metaphors in temporal reasoning. In M. Gattis (Ed.), *Spatial schemas and abstract thought* (pp. 203–222). Cambridge, MA: MIT Press.

Gernsbacher, M. (1989). Mechanisms that improve referential access. *Cognition, 32*, 99–156.

Gernsbacher, M. (1990). *Language comprehension as structure building.* Hillsdale, NJ: Lawrence Erlbaum Associates.

Geschwind, N., & Levitsky, W. (1968). Human brain: Left–right asymmetries in temporal speech region. *Science, 161*, 327–340.

Glaser, W. R. (1992). Picture naming. *Cognition, 42*, 61–105.

Goldinger, S. D., Luce, P. A., Pisoni, D. B. (1989). Priming lexical neighbors of spoken words: Effects of competition and inhibition. *Journal of Memory and Language, 28*, 501–518.

Goldin-Meadow, S. (1982). The resilience of recursion: A study of a communication system developed without a conventional language model. In In E. Wanner & L. A. Gleitman (Eds.), *Language acquisition: The state of the art* (pp. 53–77). Cambridge, England: Cambridge University Press.

Goldin-Meadow, S. (1999). The role of gesture in communication and thinking. *Trends in Cognitive Sciences, 3*(11), 419–429.

Goldin-Meadow, S. (in press). *The resilience of language.* Philadelphia, PA: Psychology Press.

Goldin-Meadow, S., & Feldman, H. (1977). The development of language-like communication without a language model. *Science, 197,* 401–403.

Goldin-Meadow, S., & Mylander, C. (1990). Beyond the input given: The child's role in the acquisition of language. *Language, 66*(2), 323–355.

Goldin-Meadow, S., & Mylander, C. (1998). Spontaneous sign systems created by deaf children in two cultures. *Nature, 391,* 279–281.

Goldin-Meadow, S., Mylander, C., & Butcher, C. (1995). The resilience of combinatorial structure at the word level: Morphology in self-styled gesture systems. *Cognition, 56,* 195–262.

Goldsmith, J. (1979). *Autosegmental phonology* (Outstanding dissertations in linguistics). New York: Garland Press. (Original work published 1976)

Goldsmith, J. (1990). *Autosegmental & metrical phonology.* Oxford: Basil Blackwell.

Goldstein, K. (1948). *Language and language disturbances.* New York: Grune and Stratton.

Goldstein, N., & Feldman, R. S. (1996). Knowledge of American Sign Language and the ability of hearing individuals to decode facial expressions of emotion. *Journal of Nonverbal Behavior, 20,* 111–122.

Goldstein, N. E., Sexton, J., & Feldman, R. S. (2000). Encoding of facial expressions of emotion and knowledge of American Sign Language. *Journal of Applied Social Psychology, 30,* 67–76.

Goodglass, H. (1993). *Understanding aphasia.* San Diego, CA: Academic Press.

Goodglass, H., & Kaplan, E. (1983). *The assessment of aphasia and related disorders* (Rev. ed.). Philadelphia, PA: Lea and Febiger.

Greenberg, J. (1966). Some universals of grammar with particular reference to the order of meaningful elements. In J. H. Greenberg (Ed.), *Universals of language* (pp. 73–113). Cambridge, MA: MIT Press.

Grosjean, F. (1980). Spoken word recognition processes and the gating paradigm. *Perception and Psychophysics, 28,* 267–283.

Grosjean, F. (1981). Sign and word recognition: A first comparison. *Sign Language Studies, 32,* 195–219.

Grossi, G., Semenza, C., Corazza, S., & Volterra, V. (1996). Hemispheric specialization for sign language. *Neuropsychologia, 34,* 737–740.

Gumperz, J., & Levinson, S. (Eds.). (1996). *Rethinking linguistic relativity.* Cambridge, England: Cambridge University Press.

Gustason, G., Pfetzing, D., & Zawolkow, E. (1980). *Signing Exact English.* Los Alamitos, CA: Modern Signs Press.

Haglund, M. H., Ojemann, G. A., Lettich, E., Bellugi, U., & Corina, D. (1993). Dissociation of cortical and single unit activity in spoken and signed languages. *Brain and Language, 44,* 19–27.

Hall, C. J. (1992). *Morphology and mind: A unified approach to explanation in linguistics.* London: Routledge.

Hanson, V. L. (1982). Short-term recall by deaf signers of American Sign Language: Implications of encoding strategy for order recall. *Journal of Experimental Psychology, 8,* 572–583.

Hanson, V. L., & Feldman, L. B. (1989). Language specificity in lexical organization: Evidence from deaf signers' lexical organization of American Sign Language and English. *Memory & Cognition, 17*(3), 292–301.

Hanson, V. L., & Feldman, L. B. (1991). What makes signs related? *Sign Language Studies, 70,* 35–46.

Happ, D., Hohenberger, A., & Leuninger, H. (in press). Modality-dependent aspects of sign language production: Evidence from slips of the hand and their repairs in German Sign Language (Deutsche Gebärdensprache DGS). In R. Meier, D. Quinto, & K. Cormier

(Eds.), *Modality and structure in signed and spoken languages*. Cambridge, England: Cambridge University Press.

Harris, M. (1992). *Language experience and early language development: From input to uptake*. Hillsdale, NJ: Lawrence Erlbaum Associates.

Harris, M., Clibbens, J., Chasin, J., & Tibbitts, R. (1989). The social context of early sign language development. *First Language, 9*, 81–97.

Harris, M., Jones, D., Brookes, S., & Grant, J. (1986). Relations between the nonverbal context of maternal speech and rate of language development. *British Journal of Developmental Psychology, 5*, 261–268.

Heilman, K. M., & Van Den Abell, T. (1980). Right hemisphere dominance for attention: The mechanisms underlying hemispheric asymmetries of inattention (neglect). *Neurology, 30*, 327–330.

Heilman, K. M., Watson, R. T., & Valenstein, E. (1997). Neglect: Clinical and anatomic aspects. In T. E. Feinberg & M. J. Farah (Eds.), *Behavioral neurology and neuropsychology* (pp. 309–317). New York: McGraw-Hill.

Henderson, L., Wallis, J., & Knight, D. (1984). Morphemic structure and lexical access. In H. Bouma & D. Bouwhuis (Eds.), *Attention and performance X: Control of language processes* (pp. 211–226). Hillsdale, NJ: Lawrence Erlbaum Associates.

Hickok, G. (1997). [Error types on tests of ASL verb agreement for left- and right-hemisphere damaged signers]. Unpublished raw data.

Hickok, G., Bellugi, U., & Klima, E. (1998a). The basis of the neural organization for language: Evidence from sign language aphasia. *Reviews in the Neurosciences, 8*, 205–222.

Hickok, G., Bellugi, U., & Klima, E. (1998b). What's right about the neural organization of sign language? A perspective on recent neuroimaging results. *Trends in Cognitive Science, 2*, 465–468.

Hickok, G., Kirk, K., & Bellugi, U. (1998). Hemispheric organization of local- and global-level visuospatial processes in deaf signers and its relation to sign language aphasias. *Brain and Language, 65*, 276–286.

Hickok, G., Klima, E. S., & Bellugi, U. (1996). The neurobiology of signed language and its implications for the neural basis of language. *Nature, 381*, 699–702.

Hickok, G., Klima, E. S., Kritchevsky, M., & Bellugi, U. (1995). A case of "sign blindness" following left occipital damage in a deaf signer. *Neuropsychologia, 33*, 1597–1606.

Hickok, G., Kritchevsky, M., Bellugi, U., & Klima, E. S. (1996). The role of the left frontal operculum in sign language aphasia. *Neurocase, 2*, 373–380.

Hickok, G., Poeppel, D., Clark, K., Buxton, R., Rowley, H. A., & Roberts, T. P. L. (1997). Sensory mapping in a congenitally deaf subject: MEG and fMRI studies of cross-modal non-plasticity. *Human Brain Mapping, 5*, 437–444.

Hickok, G., Say, K., Bellugi, U., & Klima, E. S. (1996). The basis of hemispheric asymmetries for language and spatial cognition: Clues from focal brain damage in two deaf native signers. *Aphasiology, 10*, 577–591.

Hickok, G., Wilson, M., Clark, K., Klima, E. S., Kritchevsky, M., & Bellugi, U. (1999). Discourse deficits following right hemisphere damage in deaf signers. *Brain and Language, 66*, 233–248.

Hildebrandt, U., & Corina, D. (2000, February). *Phonological similarity in American Sign Language*. Paper presented at the Texas Linguistic Society Meeting: The Effects of Modality on Language and Linguistic Theory, Austin, Texas.

Hinton, L., Nichols, J., & Ohala, J. (Eds.). (1994). *Sound symbolism*. Cambridge, England: Cambridge University Press.

Hockett, C. (1960). The origin of speech. *Scientific American, 203*, 89–96.

Hoffmeister, R. J. (1978). *The development of demonstrative pronouns, locatives, and personal pronouns in the acquisition of American Sign Language by deaf children of deaf parents*. Unpublished doctoral dissertation, University of Minnesota.

Hoffmeister, R. J. (1987). The acquisition of pronominal anaphora in ASL by deaf children. In B. Lust (Ed.), *Studies in the acquisition of anaphora* (pp. 171–187). Dordrect: D. Reidel.

Holzrichter, A. S., & Meier, R. P. (2000). Child-directed signing in American Sign Language. In C. Chamberlain, J. P. Morford, & R. I. Mayberry (Eds.), *Language acquisition by eye* (pp. 25–40). Mahwah, NJ: Lawrence Erlbaum Associates.

Humphries, T., Padden, C., & O'Rourke, T. J. (1981). *A basic course in American Sign Language*. Silver Spring, MD: T. J. Publishers.

Huttenlocher, P. R. (1994). Synaptogenesis in human cerebral cortex. In G. Dawson & K. Fischer (Eds.), *Human behavior and the developing brain* (pp. 137–152). New York: Guilford.

Ilan, A. B., & Miller, J. (1994). A violation of pure insertion: Mental rotation and choice reaction time. *Journal of Experimental Psychology: Human Perception and Performance, 20,* 520–536.

Ingram, D. (1989). *First language acquisition*. New York: Cambridge University Press.

Itô, J., & Mester, A. (1995). Japanese phonology. In J. Goldsmith (Ed.), *The handbook of phonological theory* (pp. 817–838). Oxford, England: Blackwell.

Jackendoff, R. (1983). *Semantics and cognition*. Cambridge, MA: MIT Press.

Jackendoff, R. (1996). The architecture of the linguistic-spatial interface. In P. Bloom, M. Peterson, L. Nadel, & M. Garrett (Eds.), *Language and space* (pp. 1–30). Cambridge, MA: MIT Press.

Jackendoff, R. (1999). Possible stages in the evolution of the language capacity. *Trends in Cognitive Sciences, 3*(7), 272–279.

Jackson, C. (1989). Language acquisition in two modalities: The role of nonlinguistic cues in linguistic mastery. *Sign Language Studies, 62,* 1–21.

Jakobson, R. (1968). *Child language, aphasia, and phonological universals*. The Hague: Mouton.

Janis, W. (1992). *Morphosyntax of the ASL verb phrase*. Unpublished doctoral dissertation, State University of New York at Buffalo.

Janis, W. (1995). A crosslinguistic perspective on ASL verb agreement. In K. Emmorey & J. Reilly (Eds.), *Language, gesture, and space* (pp. 195–223). Hillsdale, NJ: Lawrence Erlbaum Associates.

Janzen, T. (1999). The grammaticization of topics in American Sign Language. *Studies in Language, 23*(2), 271–306.

Joanette, Y., Goulet, P., & Hannequin. D. (1990). *Right hemisphere and verbal communication*. New York: Springer-Verlag.

Johansson, G. (1973). Visual perception of biological motion and a model for its analysis. *Perception & Psychophysics, 14,* 201–211.

Johnson, J. S., & Newport, E. L. (1989). Critical period effects in second language learning: The influence of maturational state on the acquisition of English as a second language. *Cognitive Psychology, 21,* 60–99.

Jones, D. M., Beaman, P., & Macken, W. J. (1996). The object-oriented episodic record model. In S. Gathercole (Ed.), *Models of short-term memory* (pp. 209–237). Hove, England: Psychology Press.

Jones, D. M., & Macken, W. J. (1993). Irrelevant tones produce an irrelevant speech effect: Implications for phonologically coding in working memory. *Journal of Experimental Psychology: Learning, Memory, and Cognition, 19*(2), 369–381.

Kager, R. (1999). *Optimality Theory*. Cambridge University Press.

Kantor, R. (1980). The acquisition of classifiers in American Sign Language. *Sign Language Studies, 28,* 193–208.

Kegl, J. (1994). The Nicaraguan Sign Language Project: An overview. *Signpost, 7,* 24–31.

Kegl, J., Cohen, H., & Poizner, H. (1999). Articulatory consequences of Parkinson's disease: Perspectives from two modalities. *Brain and Cognition, 40,* 355–386.

Kegl, J., Glimore, R., Leonard, C., Bowers, D., Fennell, E., Roper, S., Trowbridge, P., Poizner, H., & Heilman, K. (1996). Lateralization and intrahemispheric localization studies of a familially left-handed, deaf, epileptic signer of American Sign Language. *Brain and Cognition, 32,* 335–338.

Kegl, J., & Iwata, G. (1989). Lenguaje de Signos Nicaragüense: A pidgin sheds light on the creole? *Proceedings of fourth annual meeting of the Pacific Linguistics Conference* (pp. 266–294). Eugene, OR: University of Oregon.

Kegl, J., & McWhorter, J. (1997). Perspectives on an emerging language. In E. Clark (Ed.), *Proceedings of the Stanford Child Language Research Forum* (pp. 15–36). Palo Alto, CA: CSLI.

Kegl, J., & Poizner, H. (1997). Crosslinguistic/crossmodal syntactic consequences of left-hemisphere damage: Evidence from an aphasic signer and his identical twin. *Aphasiology, 11,* 1–37.

Kegl, J., Senghas, A., & Coppola, M. (1999). Creation through contact: Sign language emergence and sign language change in Nicaragua. In M. DeGraff (Ed.), *Language creation and language change: Creolization, diachrony, and development* (pp. 179–237). Cambridge, MA: MIT Press.

Kegl, J., & Wilbur, R. (1976). When does structure stop and style begin? Syntax, morphology and phonology vs. stylistic variation in American Sign Language. In S. Mufwene & S. Steever (Eds.), *Papers from the 12th meeting of the Chicago Linguistic Society* (pp. 376–396). Chicago, IL: University of Chicago Press.

Keller, J. (in press). Multimodal representations and the linguistic status of mouthings in German Sign Language (DGS). In P. Boyes-Braem & R. Sutton-Spence (Eds.), *The hands are the head of the mouth: The mouth as articulator in sign languages.* Hamburg, Germany: Signum Press.

Kemler-Nelson, D. G., Hirsch-Pasek, K., Jusczyk, P., & Wright-Cassidy, K. (1989). How the prosodic cues in motherese might assist language learning. *Journal of Child Language, 16,* 53–68.

Kendon, A. (1980). Gesticulation and speech: Two aspects of the process of utterance. In M. R. Key (Ed.), *The relationship of verbal and nonverbal communication* (pp. 207–227). The Hague: Mouton.

Kendon, A. (1983). Gesture and speech: How they interact. In J. M. Weimann & R. P. Harrison (Eds.), *Nonverbal interaction* (pp. 12–45). Beverly Hills, CA: Sage.

Kendon, A. (1984). Knowledge of sign language in an Australian aboriginal community. *Journal of Anthropological Research, 40,* 556–576.

Kimura, D. (1993). *Neuromotor mechanisms in human communication.* Oxford: Oxford University Press.

Kimura, D., & Archibald, Y. (1974). Motor functions of the left hemisphere. *Brain, 97,* 337–350.

Kinsbourne, M., & Hicks, R. E. (1978). Mapping cerebral functional space: Competition and collaboration in human performance. In M. Kinsbourne (Ed.), *Asymmetrical function of the brain.* New York: Cambridge University Press.

Klima, E. S., & Bellugi, U. (1979). *The signs of language.* Cambridge, MA: Harvard University Press.

Klima, E. S., Tzeng, O., Fok, A., Bellugi, U., & Corina, D. (1996). *From sign to script: Effects of linguistic experience on perceptual categorization* (Tech. Rep. No. INC-9604). Institute for Neural Computation, University of California, San Diego.

Knapp, H., Beyer, J., San Jose, L., Ackerman, D., Guillemin, A., Braun, A., & Corina, D. (2001, March). *A PET comparison of the neural systems underlying human transitive actions and American Sign Language.* Poster presented at the Cognitive Neuroscience Society meeting, New York.

Koester, L. S., Karkowski, A. M., & Traci, M. A. (1998). How do deaf and hearing mothers regain eye contact when their infants look away? *American Annals of the Deaf, 143,* 5–13.

Kosslyn, S. M. (1980). *Image and mind.* Cambridge, MA: Harvard University Press.

Kosslyn, S. M. (1987). Seeing and imagining in the cerebral hemispheres: A computational approach. *Psychological Review, 94*, 148–175.

Kosslyn, S. M. 1994. *Image and brain: The resolution of the imagery debate*. Cambridge, MA: MIT Press.

Kosslyn, S. M., Brunn, J., Cave, K., & Wallach, R. (1985). Individual differences in mental imagery ability: A computational analysis. *Cognition, 18*, 195–243.

Kosslyn, S. M., Cave, C., Provost, D., & Von Gierke, S. (1988). Sequential processes in image generation. *Cognitive Psychology, 20*, 319–343.

Kosslyn, S. M., Maljkovic, V., Hamilton, S. E., Horwitz, G., & Thompson, W. L. (1995). Two types of image generation: Evidence for left- and right-hemisphere processes. *Neuropsychologia, 33*, 1485–1510.

Krakow, R., & Hanson, V. (1985). Deaf signers and serial recall in the visual modality: Memory for signs, fingerspelling, and print. *Memory and Cognition, 13*, 265–272.

Krauss, R., & Hadar, U. (1999). The role of speech-related arm/hand gestures in word retrieval. In L. Messing & R. Campbell (Eds.), *Gesture, speech, and sign* (pp. 93–116). New York: Oxford University Press.

Krauss, R., Dushay, R. A., Chen, Y., & Rauscher, F. (1995). The communicative value of conversational hand gestures. *Journal of Experimental Social Psychology, 31*, 533–552.

Krauss, R., Morrel-Samuels, P., & Colasante, C. (1991). Do conversational hand gestures communicate? *Journal of Personality and Social Psychology, 61*, 743–54.

Kritchesvsky, M. (1988). The elementary spatial functions of the brain. In J. Stiles-Davis, M. Kritchevsky, & U. Bellugi (Eds.), *Spatial cognition: Brain bases and development* (pp. 111–140). Hillsdale, NJ: Lawrence Erlbaum Associates.

Kubovy, M. (1988). Should we resist the seductiveness of the space:time::vision:audition analogy? *Journal of Experimental Psychology: Human Perception & Performance, 14*, 318–320.

Kucera, H., & Francis, N. (1967). *Computational analysis of present-day American English*. Providence, RI: Brown University Press.

Kuhl, P. (1991). Human adults and human infants show a "perceptual magnet effect" for the prototypes of speech categories, monkeys do not. *Perception and Psychophysics, 50*, 93–107.

Kuhl, P. (1993). Innate predispositions and the effects of experience in speech perception: The native language magnet theory. In B. de Boysson-Bardies, S. de Schonen, P. Jusczyk, P. MacNeilage, & J. Morton (Eds.), *Developmental neurocognition: Speech and face processing in the first year of life* (pp. 259–274). Dordrecht: Kluwer.

Kuhl, P. (1998). The development of speech and language. In T. J. Carew, R. Menzel, & C. J. Shatz (Eds.), *Mechanistic relationships between development and learning* (pp. 53–73). New York: Wiley.

Kuntze, M. (2000). Codeswitching in ASL and written English contact. In K. Emmorey & J. Reilly (Eds.), *Language, gesture, and space* (pp. 287–302). Mahwah, NJ: Lawrence Erlbaum Associates.

Kusché, C. A., Greenberg, M. T., & Garfield, T. S. (1983). Nonverbal intelligence and verbal achievement in deaf adolescents: An examination of heredity and environment. *American Annals of the Deaf, 128*, 458–466.

Lackner, J. R., & Tuller, B. H. (1979). Role of efference monitoring in the detection of self-produced speech errors. In W. E. Cooper & E. C. T. Walker (Eds.), *Sentence processing: Psycholinguistic studies presented to Merrill Garrett*. Hillsdale, NJ: Lawrence Erlbaum Associates.

Ladefoged, P. (1990). The revised International Phonetic Alphabet. *Language, 66*(3), 550–552.

Lakoff, G., & Johnson, M. (1980). *Metaphors we live by*. Chicago, IL: The University of Chicago Press.

Lakoff, G., & Turner, M. (1989). *More than cool reason: A field guide to poetic metaphor*. Chicago, IL: The University of Chicago Press.

Lakoff, R. (1975). *Language and woman's place*. New York: Harper & Row.

Lane, H. (1984). *When the mind hears: A history of the deaf*. New York: Random House.

Lane, H. (1992). *The mask of benevolence*. New York: Knopf.

Lane, H., Boyes-Braem, P., & Bellugi, U. (1976). Preliminaries to a distinctive feature analysis of American Sign Language. *Cognitive Psychology, 8*, 263–289.

Lane, H., Hoffmeister, R., & Bahan, B. (1996). *A journey into the DEAF-WORLD*. San Diego, CA: DawnSignPress.

Lashley, K. (1951). The problem of serial order in behavior. In L. A. Jeffress (Ed.), *Cerebral mechanisms in behavior* (pp. 112–136). New York: Wiley.

Lechelt, E. C. (1975). Temporal numerosity discrimination: Intermodal comparisons revisited. *British Journal of Psychology, 66*, 101–108.

Lee, R. G., Neidle, C., MacLaughlin, D., Bahan, B., & Kegl, J. (1997). Role shift in ASL: A syntactic look at direct speech. In C. Neidle, D. MacLaughlin, & R. G. Lee (Eds.), *Syntactic structure and discourse function: An examination of two constructions in ASL* (pp. 24–45). Boston University (Rep. No. 4), American Sign Language Linguistic Research Project.

Lehmann, C. (1988). On the function of agreement. In M. Barlow & C. A. Ferguson (Eds.), *Agreement in natural language: Approaches, theories, descriptions* (pp. 52–66). Stanford, CA: Center for the Study of Language and Information.

LeMaster, B. (1990). *The maintenance and loss of female and male signs in the Dublin deaf community*. Doctoral dissertation, University of California, Los Angeles.

LeMaster, B. (1997). Sex differences in Irish Sign Language. In J. H. Hill, P. J. Mistry, & L. Campbell (Eds.), *The life of language* (pp. 67–85). Berlin, Germany: Walter de Gruyer.

LeMaster, B., & Dwyer, J. (1991). Knowing and using female and male signs in Dublin. *Sign Language Studies, 73*, 361–396.

Lenneberg, E. (1967). *Biological foundations of language*. New York: Wiley.

Levelt, C. C., Schiller, N. O., & Levelt, W. J. M. (2000). The acquisition of syllable types. *Language Acquisition, 8*, 237–264.

Levelt, W. J. M. (1980). On-line processing constraints on the properties of signed and spoken language. In U. Bellugi & M. Studdert-Kennedy (Eds.), *Signed and spoken language: Biological constraints on form* (pp. 141–160). Weinheim, Germany: Verlag Chemie.

Levelt, W. J. M. (1983). Monitoring and self-repair in speech. *Cognition, 14*, 41–104.

Levelt, W. J. M. (1989). *Speaking: From intention to articulation*. Cambridge, MA: MIT Press.

Levinson, S. (1996). Frames of reference and Molyneux's Question: Crosslinguistic evidence. In P. Bloom, M. Peterson, L. Nadel, & M. Garrett (Eds.), *Language and space* (pp. 109–170). Cambridge, MA: MIT Press.

Li, S. C., & Lewandowsky, S. (1995). Forward and backward recall: Different retrieval processes. *Journal of Experimental Psychology: Learning, Memory, and Cognition, 21*(4), 837–847.

Liben, L. S., & Downs, R. W. (1992). Developing an understanding of graphic representations in children and adults: The case of GEO-graphics. *Cognitive Development, 7*, 331–349.

Liberman, A. (1974). The specialization of the langauge hemisphere. In F. O. Schmitt & F. G. Worden (Eds.), *The neurosciences third study program* (pp. 43–56). Cambridge, MA: MIT Press.

Liberman, A. M. (1996). *Speech: A special code*. Cambridge, MA: MIT Press.

Liberman, A. M., Cooper, F. S., Shankweiler, D. S., & Studdert-Kennedy, M. (1967). Perception of the speech code. *Psychological Review, 74*, 431–461.

Liberman, A. M., & Mattingly, I. G. (1985). The motor theory of speech perception revised. *Cognition, 21*, 1–36.

Liddell, S. (1980). *American Sign Language syntax*. The Hague: Mouton.

Liddell, S. (1984a). THINK and BELIEVE: Sequentiality in American Sign Language. *Language, 60*, 372–392.

Liddell, S. (1984b). Unrealized-inceptive aspect in American Sign Language: Feature insertion in syllabic frames. In *CLS 20*, Vol. 1, *The General Session*. Chicago Linguistic Society: University of Chicago, Chicago, IL.

Liddell, S. (1990). Four functions of a locus: Re-examining the structure of space in ASL. In C. Lucas (Ed.), *Sign language research: Theoretical issues* (pp. 176–198). Washington, DC: Gallaudet University Press.

Liddell, S. (1994). Tokens and surrogates. In I. Ahlgren, B. Bergman, & M. Brennan (Eds.), *Perspectives on sign language structure: Papers from the Fifth International Symposium on Sign Language Research* (Vol. 1, pp. 105–119). The International Sign Language Association, University of Durham, England.

Liddell, S. (1995). Real, surrogate, and token space: Grammatical consequences in ASL. In K. Emmorey & J. Reilly (Eds.), *Language, gesture, and space* (pp. 19–41). Hillsdale, NJ: Lawrence Erlbaum Associates.

Liddell, S. (1998). Grounded blends, gestures, and conceptual shifts. *Cognitive Linguistics, 9*, 283–314.

Liddell, S. (2000a). Blended spaces and deixis in sign language discourse. In D. McNeill (Ed.), *Language and gesture* (pp. 331–357). Cambridge, England: Cambridge University Press.

Liddell, S. (2000b). Indicating verbs and pronouns: Pointing away from agreement. In K. Emmorey & H. Lane (Eds.), *The signs of language revisited: An anthology to honor Ursula Bellugi and Edward Klima* (pp. 303–329). Mahwah, NJ: Lawrence Erlbaum Associates.

Liddell, S., & Johnson, R. (1987, July). An analysis of spatial-locative predicates in American Sign Language. Paper presented at the Fourth International Symposium on Sign Language Research, Lappeenranta, Finland.

Liddell, S., & Johnson, R. (1989). American Sign Language: The phonological base. *Sign Language Studies, 64*, 197–277. (Original work published 1986)

Liddell, S., & Metzger, M. (1998). Gesture in sign language discourse. *Journal of Pragmatics, 30*, 657–697.

Lieberman, P. (1984). *The biology and evolution of language*. Cambridge, MA: Harvard University Press.

Lillo-Martin, D. (1986).Two kinds of null arguments in American Sign Language. *Natural Language and Linguistic Theory, 4*, 415–444.

Lillo-Martin, D. (1991). *Universal grammar and American sign language: Setting the null argument parameters*. Dordrecht, The Netherlands: Kluwer.

Lillo-Martin, D. (1995). The point of view predicate in American Sign Language. In K. Emmorey & J. Reilly (Eds.), *Language, gesture, and space* (pp. 155–170). Hillsdale, NJ: Lawrence Erlbaum Associates.

Lillo-Martin, D. (1999). Modality effects and modularity in language acquisition: The acquisition of American Sign Language. In W. C. Ritchie & T. K. Bhatia (Eds.), *Handbook of child language acquisition* (pp. 531–567). San Diego: Academic Press.

Lillo-Martin, D. (2000a). Early and late in language acquisition: Aspects of the syntax and acquisition of WH questions in American Sign Language. In K. Emmorey & H. Lane (Eds.), *The signs of language revisited: An anthology to honor Ursula Bellugi and Edward Klima* (pp. 401–414). Mahwah, NJ: Lawrence Erlbaum Associates.

Lillo-Martin, D. (2000b, February). *Modality and modularity: Where are the effects?* Paper presented at the Texas Linguistics Society meeting: The Effects of Modality on Language and Linguistic Theory, Austin, TX.

Lillo-Martin, D., Bellugi, U., Struxness, L., & O'Grady, M. (1985). The acquisition of spatially organized syntax. In E. Clark (Ed.), *Papers and Reports on Child Language Development, 24* (pp. 70–78). Palo Alto, CA: Stanford University Press.

Lillo-Martin, D., & Fischer, S. (1992, May). *Overt and covert Wh-constructions*. Paper presented at the Fifth International Symposium on Sign Language Research, Salamanca, Spain.

Lillo-Martin, D., & Klima, E. (1990). Pointing out differences: ASL pronouns in syntactic theory. In S. D. Fischer & P. Siple (Eds.), *Theoretical issues in sign language research* (pp. 191–210). Chicago, IL: University of Chicago Press.

Lillo-Martin, D., Mueller de Quadros, R., & Mathur, G. (1998, November). *Acquisition of verb agreement in ASL and LIBRAS: A cross linguistic study.* Paper presented at Theoretical Issues in Sign Language Research Meeting, Washington, DC.

Linde, C., & Labov, W. (1975). Spatial networks as a site for the study of language and thought. *Language, 51,* 924–939.

Lively, S., Pisoni, D., & Goldinger, S. (1994). Spoken word recognition. In M. A. Gernsbacher (Ed.), *Handbook of psycholinguistics* (pp. 265–301). San Diego, CA: Academic Press.

Loew, R. (1980, October). *Learning American Sign Language as a first language: Roles and reference.* Paper presented at the Third National Symposium on Sign Language Research, Boston, MA.

Loew, R. C. (1984). *Roles and reference in American Sign Language: A developmental perspective.* Unpublished doctoral dissertation, University of Minnesota.

Loew, R. C., Kegl, J. A., & Poizner, H. (1997). Fractionation of the components of role play in a right-hemispheric lesioned signer. *Aphasiology, 11,* 263–281.

Logie, R. H. (1995). *Visuo-spatial working memory.* Mahwah, NJ: Lawrence Erlbaum Associates.

Loke, W. H., & Song, S. (1991). Central and peripheral visual processing in hearing and nonhearing individuals. *Bulletin of the Psychonomic Society, 29,* 437–440.

Love, T., Bellugi, U., Klima, E. S., & Hickok, G. (1999). Left temporal lobe supports sign language comprehension. *Cognitive Neuroscience Society Abstracts, 6,* 96.

Love, T., Hickok, G., Clark, K., Kritchevsky, M., Klima, E. S., & Bellugi, U. (1997). Some similarities in the neural organization of signed and spoken languages. *Cognitive Neuroscience Abstracts, 4,* 107.

Lucas, C. (Ed.). (1989). *The sociolinguistics of the Deaf community.* San Diego, CA: Academic Press.

Lucas, C. (Ed.). (1996). *Multicultural aspects of sociolinguistics in Deaf communities.* Washington, DC: Gallaudet University Press.

Lucas, C., & Valli, C. (1990). Predicates of perceived motion in ASL. In S. D. Fischer & P. Siple (Eds.), *Theoretical issues in sign language research, vol. 1: Linguistics* (pp. 153–166). Chicago, IL: The University of Chicago Press.

Lucas, C., & Valli, C. (1992). *Language contact in the American Deaf community.* New York: Academic Press.

Luce, P. A. (1986). *Neighborhoods of words in the mental lexicon.* Unpublished doctoral dissertation, Indiana University, Bloomington.

Luce, P. A., Pisoni, D. B., & Goldinger, S. D. (1990). Similarity neighborhoods of spoken words. In G. T. M. Altmann (Ed.), *Cognitive models of speech processing: Psycholinguistic and computational perspectives* (pp. 122–147). Cambridge, MA: MIT Press.

Lucy, J. (1992a). *Grammatical categories and cognition: A case study of the linguistic relativity hypothesis.* Cambridge, England: Cambridge University Press.

Lucy, J. (1992b). *Language diversity and thought: A reformulation of the linguistic relativity hypothesis.* Cambridge, England: Cambridge University Press.

MacDonald, M. C. (1986). *Priming during sentence processing: Facilitation of responses to a noun from a coreferential pronoun.* Unpublished doctoral dissertation, University of California, Los Angeles.

MacDonald, M. C., & MacWhinney, B. (1990). Measuring inhibition and facilitation from pronouns. *Journal of Memory and Language, 29*(4), 469–492.

MacFarlane, J. (1998, November). *From affect to grammar: Ritualization of facial affect in sign languages.* Paper presented at Theoretical Issues in Sign Language Research, Washington, DC.

MacLaughlin, D. (1997). *The structure of Determiner Phrases: Evidence from American Sign Language.* Unpublished doctoral dissertation, Boston University.

Maestas y Moores, J. (1980). Early linguistic environment: Interactions of deaf parents with their infants. *Sign Language Studies, 26,* 1–13.

MacSweeney, M., Woll, B., Campbell, R., McGuire, P., Calvert, G., David, A., Williams, S., & Brammer, M. (2001, March). *The effect of hearing status and the use of signing space on the neural bases for BSL processing.* Poster presented at the Cognitive Neuroscience Society meeting, New York.

Mainwaring, S., Tversky, B., & Schiano, D. (1996). *Perspective choice in spatial descriptions* (IRC Technical Report, 1996-06). Palo Alto, CA: Interval Research Corporation.

Mandel, M. (1977). Iconic devices in American Sign Language. In L. Friedman (Ed.), *On the other hand: New perspectives on American Sign Language* (pp. 57–107). New York: Academic Press.

Marentette, P., & Mayberry, R. I. (2000). Principles for an emerging phonological system: A case study of early ASL acquisition. In C. Chamberlain, J. P. Morford, & R. I. Mayberry (Eds.), *Language acquisition by eye* (pp. 71–90). Mahwah, NJ: Lawrence Erlbaum Associates.

Marler, P. (1991). The instinct to learn. In S. Carey & R. Gelman (Eds.), *The epigenesis of mind: Essays in biology and cognition* (pp. 37–66). Hillsdale, NJ: Lawrence Erlbaum Associates.

Marmor, G., & Petitto, L. (1979). Simultaneous communication in the classroom: How well is English grammar represented? *Sign Language Studies, 23,* 99–136.

Marschark, M. (1993). *Psychological development of deaf children.* New York: Oxford University Press.

Marschark, M. (1994). Gesture and sign. *Applied Psycholinguistics, 15,* 209–236.

Marschark, M. (1996, November). *Influences of signed and spoken language on memory span.* Paper presented at the annual meeting of the Psychonomics Society, Chicago, IL.

Marschark, M., Green, V., Hindmarsh, G., & Walker, S. (2000). Understanding theory of mind in deaf children. *Journal of Child Psychology and Psychiatry and Allied Disciplines, 41,* 1067–1073.

Marschark, M., Siple, P., Lillo-Martin, D., Campbell, R., & Everhart, V. S. (1997). *Relations of language and thought: The view from sign language and deaf children.* New York: Oxford University Press.

Marslen-Wilson, W. (1987). Functional parallelism in spoken word recognition. *Cognition, 25,* 71–102.

Marslen-Wilson, W., Tyler, L. K., Waksler, R., & Older, L. (1994). Morphology and meaning in the English mental lexicon. *Psychological Review, 101*(1), 3–33.

Marsh, S., & Emmorey, K. (2000, July). *Tip-of-the-fingers experiences in Deaf signers.* Paper presented at the Theoretical Issues in Sign Language Research meeting, Amsterdam, The Netherlands.

Martin, M. (1979). Hemispheric specialization for local and global processing. *Neuropsychologia, 17,* 33–40.

Masataka, N. (1992). Motherese in a signed language. *Infant Behavior and Development, 15,* 453–460.

Masataka, N. (1995). Absence of mirror-reversal tendency in cutaneous pattern perception and acquisition of a signed language in deaf children. *Journal of Developmental Psychology, 13,* 97–106.

Masataka, N. (1996). Perception of motherese in Japanese Sign Language by 6-month-old deaf infants. *Developmental Psychology, 34,* 241–246.

Masataka, N. (1998). Perception of motherese in Japanese Sign Language by 6-month-old hearing infants. *Developmental Psychology, 32,* 874–879.

Masataka, N. (2000). The role of modality and input in the earliest stage of language acquisition: Studies of Japanese Sign Language. In C. Chamberlain, J. P. Morford, & R. I. Mayberry (Eds.), *Language acquisition by eye* (pp. 3–24). Mahwah, NJ: Lawrence Erlbaum Associates.

Massaro, D. (1987). *Speech perception by ear and eye: A paradigm for psychological inquiry.* Hillsdale, NJ: Lawrence Erlbaum Associates.

Massaro, D. (1998). *Perceiving talking faces: From speech perception to a behavioral principle.* Cambridge, MA: MIT Press.

Mather, S., & Winston, E. A. (1998). Spatial mapping and involvement in ASL storytelling. In C. Lucas (Ed.), *Pinky extension and eye gaze: Language use in Deaf communities* (pp. 183–210). Washington, DC: Gallaudet University Press.

Mathur, G., & Rathmann, C. (in press). Whence modality differences? Under and beyond verb agreement. In R. Meier, D. Quinto, & K. Cormier (Eds.), *Modality and structure in signed and spoken languages.* Cambridge, England: Cambridge University Press.

Mayberry, R. (1992). The cognitive development of deaf children: Recent insights. In F. Boiler & J. Grafman (Eds.), *Handbook of neuropsychology* (pp. 51–68). Elsevier Science Publishers.

Mayberry, R. (1993). First-language acquisition after childhood differs from second-language acquisition: The case of American Sign Language. *Journal of Speech and Hearing Research, 36,* 1258–1270.

Mayberry, R. (1994). The importance of childhood to language acquisition: Insights from American Sign Language. In J. C. Goodman & H. C. Nusbaum (Eds.), *The development of speech perception: The transition from speech sounds to words* (pp. 57–90). Cambridge, MA: MIT Press.

Mayberry, R. (1995). Mental phonology and language comprehension or What does that sign mistake mean? In K. Emmorey & J. Reilly (Eds.), *Language, gesture, and space* (pp. 355–370). Mahwah, NJ: Lawrence Erlbaum Associates.

Mayberry, R., & Eichen, E. (1991). The long-lasting advantage of learning sign language in childhood: Another look at the critical period for language acquisition. *Journal of Memory and Language, 30,* 486–512.

Mayberry, R., & Fischer, S. (1989). Looking through phonological shape to sentence meaning: The bottleneck of non-native sign language processing. *Memory and Cognition, 17,* 740–754.

Mayberry, R., & Waters, G. (1991). Children's memory for sign and fingerspelling in relation to production rate and sign language input. In P. Siple & S. Fischer (Eds.), *Theoretical issues in sign language research* (pp. 211–229). Chicago, IL: University of Chicago Press.

Mayer, M. (1969). *Frog, where are you?* New York: Dial Press.

McBurney, S. (in press). Pronominal reference in signed and spoken language: Are grammatical categories modality-dependent? In R. Meier, D. Quinto, & K. Cormier (Eds.), *Modality and structure in signed and spoken languages.* Cambridge, England: Cambridge University Press.

McCarthy, J. (1981). A prosodic theory of nonconcatenative morphology. *Linguistic Inquiry, 20,* 71–99.

McClelland, J. L., & Elman, J. (1986). The TRACE model of speech perception. *Cognitive Psychology, 18,* 1–86.

McCullough, S., Brentari, D., & Emmorey, K. (2000, January). *Categorical perception in American Sign Language.* Poster presented at the Linguistic Society of America meeting, Chicago, Illinois.

McCullough, S., & Emmorey, K. (1997). Face processing by deaf ASL signers: Evidence for expertise in distinguishing local features. *Journal of Deaf Studies and Deaf Education, 2*(4), 212–222.

McCullough, S., & Emmorey, K., (1999, November). *Perception of emotional and linguistic facial expressions: A categorical perception study with deaf and hearing subjects.* Poster presented at the Psychonomics Society meeting, Los Angeles, CA.

McDonald, B. (1982). *Aspects of the American Sign Language predicate system.* Unpublished doctoral dissertation, University of Buffalo, New York.

McDonald, J., & McGurk, H. (1978). Visual influences on speech perception processes. *Perception and Psychophysics, 91,* 169–190.

McGuire, P., Robertson, D., Thacker, A., David, A. S., Kitson, N., Frackovwiak, R. S. J., & Frith, C. D. (1997). Neural correlates of thinking in sign language. *NeuroReport, 8*(3), 695–697.

McIntire, M. (1977). The acquisition of American Sign Language hand configuration. *Sign Language Studies, 16,* 247–266.

McKee, D. (1987). *An analysis of specialized cognitive functions in deaf and hearing signers.* Unpublished doctoral dissertation, University of Pittsburgh, Pittsburgh, PA.

McKee, D., & Kennedy, G. (2000). Lexical comparison of signs from American, Australian, British, and New Zealand Sign Languages. In K. Emmorey & H. Lane (Eds.), *The signs of language revisited: An anthology to honor Ursula Bellugi and Edward Klima* (pp. 49–76). Mahwah, NJ: Lawrence Erlbaum Associates.

McKeever, W. F., Hoemann, H. W., Florian, V. A., & Van Deventer, A. D. (1976). Evidence of minimal cerebral asymmetries for the processing of English words and American Sign Language stimuli in the congenitally deaf. *Neuropsychologia, 14,* 413–423.

McNeill, D. (1966). Developmental psycholinguistics. In F. Smith & G. A. Miller (Eds.), *The genesis of language: A psycholinguistic approach* (pp. 15–84). Cambridge, MA: MIT Press.

McNeill, D. (1992). *Hand and mind: What gestures reveal about thought.* Chicago, IL: The University of Chicago Press.

Meier, R. P. (1982). *Icons, analogues, and morphemes: The acquisition of verb agreement in ASL.* Unpublished doctoral dissertation, University of California, San Diego.

Meier, R. P. (1987). Elicited imitation of verb agreement in American Sign Language. *Journal of Memory and Language, 26,* 362–376.

Meier, R. P. (1990). Person deixis in American Sign Language. In S. D. Fischer & P. Siple (Eds.), *Theoretical issues in sign language research* (pp. 175–190). Chicago, IL: University of Chicago Press.

Meier, R. P. (1991). Language acquisition by deaf children. *American Scientist, 79,* 60–70.

Meier, R. P. (2000). Shared motoric factors in the acquisition of sign and speech. In K. Emmorey & H. Lane (Eds.), *The signs of language revisited: An anthology to honor Ursula Bellugi and Edward Klima* (pp. 333–357). Mahwah, NJ: Lawrence Erlbaum Associates.

Meier, R. P., Mauk, C., Mirus, G. R., & Conlin, K. E. (1998). Motoric constraints on early sign acquisition. In E. Clark (Ed.), *Proceedings of the Child Language Research Forum* (Vol. 29, pp. 63–72). Stanford, CA: CSLI Press (distributed by Cambridge University Press).

Meier, R. P., & Newport, E. L. (1990). Out of the hands of babes: On a possible sign advantage in language acquisition. *Language, 66,* 1–23.

Meier, R. P., & Willerman, R. (1995). Prelinguistic gesture in deaf and hearing infants. In K. Emmorey & J. Reilly (Eds.), *Language, gesture, and space* (pp. 391–409). Hillsdale, NJ: Lawrence Erlbaum Associates.

Meir, I. (1998). Syntactic-semantic interaction in Israeli Sign Language verbs: The case of backwards verbs. *Sign Language & Linguistics, 1*(1), 3–37.

Meyer, D., & Schvaneveldt, R. (1971). Facilitation in recognizing pairs of words: Evidence of a dependence between retrieval operations. *Journal of Experimental Psychology, 20*(2), 227–234.

Michael, E. B., Keller, T. A., Carpenter, P., & Just, M. A. (1999). An fMRI study of visual and auditory sentence comprehension. *Abstracts of the Psychonomic Society, 4,* 14 (No. 93).

Miller, C. (1994). Simultaneous constructions in Quebec Sign Language. In M. Brennan & G. Turner (Eds.), *Word-order issues in sign language* (pp. 89–112). Durham, England: ISLA Publications.

Miller, G., & Nicely, P. E. (1955). An analysis of perceptual confusions among some English consonants. *Journal of the Acoustical Society of America, 27,* 339–352.

Milner, B. (1971). Interhemispheric differences in the localization of psychological processes in man. *British Medical Bulletin, 27,* 272–277.

Mirus, G., Rathmann, C., & Meier, R. (2001). Proximalization and distalization of sign movement in adult learners. In V. Dively, M. Metzger, S. Taub, & A. M. Baer (Eds.), *Signed languages: Discoveries from international research* (pp. 103–120). Washington, DC: Gallaudet University Press.

Mooney, C. M. (1957). Age in the development of closure ability in children. *Canadian Journal of Psychology, 11,* 219–226.

Morford, J. (1996). Insights into language from the study of gesture: A review of research on the gestural communication of non-signing deaf people. *Language and Communication, 16,* 165–178.

Morford, J. (1998). Gesture when there is no speech model. In J. M. Iverson & S. Goldin-Meadow (Eds.), *The nature and functions of gesture in children's communication* (pp. 101–116). San Francisco, CA: Jossey-Bass.

Morford, J., & Kegl, J. (2000). Gestural precursors to linguistic constructs: How input shapes the form of language. In D. McNeill (Ed.), *Language and gesture* (pp. 358–387). Cambridge, England: Cambridge University Press.

Morgan, G. (1998). *The development of discourse cohesion in British Sign Language.* Unpublished doctoral dissertation, University of Bristol, England.

Morrel-Samuels, P., & Krauss, R. M. (1992). Word familiarity predicts temporal asynchrony of hand gestures and speech. *Journal of Experimental Psychology: Learning, Memory, and Cognition, 18,* 615–622.

Morton, J. (1969). Interaction of information in word recognition. *Psychological Review, 76,* 165–178.

Müller, H. M., King, J. W., & Kutas, M. (1997). Event-related potentials elicited by spoken relative clauses. *Cognitive Brain Research, 5,* 193–203.

Murray, D. (1968). Articulation and acoustic confusability in short-term memory. *Journal of Experimental Psychology, 78,* 679–684.

Natsoulas, T., & Dubanoski, R. A. (1964). Inferring the locus and orientation of the perceiver from responses to stimulation of the skin. *American Journal of Psychology, 77,* 281–285.

Naveh-Benjamin, M., & Ayres, T. (1986). Digit span, reading rate, and linguistic relativity. *The Quarterly Journal of Experimental Psychology, 38A,* 739–751.

Neely, J. H. (1991). Semantic priming effects in visual word recognition: A selective review of current findings and theories. In D. Besner & G. Humphries (Eds.), *Basic processes in reading: Visual word recognition* (pp. 236–264). San Diego, CA: Academic Press.

Neidle, C., Kegl, J., MacLaughlin, D., Bahan, B., & Lee, R. G. (2000). *The syntax of American Sign Language: Functional categories and hierarchical structure.* Cambridge, MA: MIT Press.

Neidle, C., MacLaughlin, D., Lee, R. G., Bahan, B., & Kegl, J. (1998). The right(ward) analysis of WH-movement in ASL. *Language, 74,* 819–831.

Nelson, C. A. (1987). The recognition of facial expression in the first two years of life: Mechanisms of development. *Child Development, 58,* 890–909.

Nespor, M., & Sandler, W. (1999). Prosody in Israeli Sign Language. *Language and Speech, 42*(2–3), 143–176.

Neville, H. J. (1990). Intermodal competition and compensation in development: Evidence from studies of the visual system in congenitally deaf adults. *Annals of the New York Academy of Sciences, 608,* 71–91.

Neville, H. J. (1991a). Neurobiology of cognitive and language processing: Effects of early experience. In K. R. Gibson & A. C. Petersen (Eds.), *Brain maturation and cognitive development: Comparative and cross-cultural perspectives* (pp. 355–380). New York: Aldine de Gruyter Press.

Neville, H. J. (1991b). Whence the specialization of the language hemisphere? In I. G. Mattingly & M. Studdert-Kennedy (Eds.), *Modularity and the motor theory of speech perception* (pp. 269–294). Hillsdale, NJ: Lawrence Erlbaum Associates.

Neville, H. J. (1995). Developmental specificity in neurocognitive development in humans. In M. S. Gazzaniga (Ed.), *The cognitive neurosciences* (pp. 219–321). Cambridge, MA: MIT Press.

Neville, H., Bavelier, D., Corina, D., Rauschecker, J., Karni, A., Lalwani, A., Braun, A., Clark, V., Jezzard, P., & Turner, R. (1998). Cerebral organization for language in deaf and hearing subjects: Biological constraints and effects of experience. *Proceedings of the National Academy of Science, 95,* 922–929.

Neville, H., Coffey, S., Lawson, D., Fischer, A., Emmorey, K., & Bellugi, U. (1997). Neural systems mediating American Sign Language: Effects of sensory experience and age of acquisition. *Brain and Language, 57,* 285–308.

Neville, H., & Lawson, D. (1987a). Attention to central and peripheral visual space in a movement detection task: An event-related potential and behavioral study: I. Normal hearing adults. *Brain Research, 405,* 253–267.

Neville, H., & Lawson, D. (1987b). Attention to central and peripheral visual space in a movement detection task: An event-related potential and behavioral study: II. Congenitally deaf adults. *Brain Research, 405,* 268–283.

Neville, H., & Lawson, D. (1987c). Attention to central and peripheral visual space in a movement detection task: An event-related potential and behavioral study: III. Separate effects of auditory deprivation and acquisition of a visual language. *Brain Research, 405,* 284–294.

Neville, H., Mills, D., & Lawson, D. (1992). Fractionating language: Different neural subsystems with different sensitive periods. *Cerebral Cortex, 2,* 244–258.

Newkirk, D. (1998). On the temporal segmentation of movement in American Sign Language. *Sign Language and Linguistics, 1*(2), 173–211. (Original work published 1981)

Newkirk, D., Klima, E., Pedersen, C. C., & Bellugi, U. (1980). Linguistic evidence from slips of the hand. In V. Fromkin (Ed.), *Errors in linguistic performance: Slips of the tongue, ear, pen, and hand* (pp. 165–198). New York: Academic Press.

Newport, E. L. (1981). Constraints on structure: Evidence from American Sign Language and language learning. In W. A. Collins (Ed.), *Aspects of the development of competence. Minnesota Symposia on Child Psychology* (Vol. 14, pp. 93–124). Hillsdale, NJ: Lawrence Erlbaum Associates.

Newport, E. L. (1982). Task specificity in language learning? Evidence from American Sign Language. In E. Wanner & L. A. Gleitman (Eds.), *Language acquisition: The state of the art* (pp. 450–486). Cambridge, England: Cambridge University Press.

Newport, E. L. (1990). Maturational constraints on language learning. *Cognitive Science, 14,* 11–28.

Newport, E. L. (1991). Contrasting conceptions of the critical period for language. In S. Carey & R. Gelman (Eds.), *The epigenesis of mind: Essays in biology and cognition* (pp. 111–130). Hillsdale, NJ: Lawrence Erlbaum Associates.

Newport, E. L. (1996, September). *Sign language research in the third millennium.* Keynote address presented at the Fifth International Conference on Theoretical Issues in Sign Language Research, Montreal, Canada.

Newport, E. L. (1999). Reduced input in the acquisition of signed languages: Contributions in the study of creolization. In M. DeGraff (Ed.), *Language creation and language change: Creolization, diachrony, and development* (pp. 161–178). Cambridge, MA: MIT Press.

Newport, E. L., Gleitman, H. A., & Gleitman, L. A. (1977). Mother, I'd rather do it myself: Some effects and non-effects of maternal speech style. In C. Snow & C. Ferguson (Eds.), *Talking to children: Language input and acquisition.* Cambridge, England: Cambridge University Press.

Newport, E. L., & Meier, R. P. (1985). The acquisition of American Sign Language. In D. Slobin (Ed.), *The cross-linguistic study of language acquisition* (pp. 881–938). Hillsdale, NJ: Lawrence Erlbaum Associates.

Newport, E. L., & Supalla, T. (1980). The structuring of language: Clues from the acquisition of signed and spoken language. In U. Bellugi & M. Studdert-Kennedy (Eds.), *Signed and spoken language: Biological constraints on linguistic form*. Dahlem Conference. Weinheim, Germany: Verlag Chemie.

Newport, E. L., & Supalla, T. (2000). Sign language research at the Millennium. In K. Emmorey & H. Lane (Eds.), *The signs of language revisited: An anthology to honor Ursula Bellugi and Edward Klima* (pp. 103–114). Mahwah, NJ: Lawrence Erlbaum Associates.

Nishimura, H., Hashikawa, K., Doi, D., Iwaki, T., Watanabe, Y., Kusuoka, H., Nishimura, T., & Kubo, T. (1999). Sign language "heard" in the auditory cortex. *Nature, 397*, 116.

Nowell, E. (1989). Conversational features and gender in ASL. In C. Lucas (Ed.), *The sociolinguistics of the deaf community* (pp. 137–138). San Diego, CA: Academic Press.

O'Connor, N., & Hermelin, B. M. (1973). Short-term memory for the order of pictures and syllables by deaf and hearing children. *Neuropsychology, 11*, 437–442.

Odden, D. (1995). Tone: African languages. In J. Goldsmith (Ed.), *The handbook of phonological theory* (pp. 444–475). Oxford, England: Blackwell.

Okrent, A. (in press). A modality-free notion of gesture and how it can help us with the morpheme vs. gesture question in sign language linguistics (or at least give us some criteria to work with). In R. P. Meier, D. G. Quinto, & K. A. Cormier (Eds.), *Modality and structure in signed and spoken languages*. Cambridge, England: Cambridge University Press.

Oller, K., & Eilers, R. E. (1988). The role of audition in infant babbling. *Child Development, 59*, 441–466.

Oller, K., Wieman, L. A., Doyle, W. J., & Ross, C. (1976). Infant babbling and speech. *Journal of Child Language, 3*, 1–12.

Orlansky, M. D., & Bonvillian, J. D. (1984). The role of iconicity in early sign language acquisition. *Journal of Speech and Hearing Disorders, 49*, 287–292.

Orlansky, M. D., & Bonvillian, J. D. (1985). Sign language acquisition: Language development in children of deaf parents and implications for other populations. *Merrill-Palmer Quarterly, 31*, 127–143.

Osugi, Y., Supalla, T., & Webb, R. (1999). The use of word elicitation to identify distinctive gestural systems on Amami Island. *Sign Language Linguistics, 2*(1), 87–112.

Özyürek, A. (2000). The influence of addressee location on speaker's spatial language and representational gestures of direction. In D. McNeill (Ed.), *Language and gesture* (pp. 64–83). Cambridge, England: Cambridge University Press.

Padden, C. (1983). *Interaction of morphology and syntax in American Sign Language*. Doctoral dissertation, published in 1988 in *Outstanding Dissertations in Linguistics, Series IV*, New York: Garland.

Padden, C. (1986). Verbs and role-shifting in ASL. In C. Padden (Ed.), *Proceedings of the Fourth National Symposium on Sign Language Research and Teaching* (pp. 44–57). Silver Spring, MD: National Association of the Deaf.

Padden, C. (1988). Grammatical theory and signed languages. In F. Newmeyer (Ed.), *Linguistics: The Cambridge survey, Vol. II, linguistic theory: Extensions and implications* (pp. 250–266). Cambridge, England: Cambridge University Press.

Padden, C. (1990). The relation between space and grammar in ASL verb morphology. In C. Lucas (Ed.), *Sign language research: Theoretical issues* (pp. 118–132). Washington, DC: Gallaudet University Press.

Padden, C. (1991). The acquisition of fingerspelling by deaf children. In P. Siple & S. Fischer (Eds.), *Theoretical issues in sign language research* (pp. 191–210). Chicago, IL: University of Chicago Press.

Padden, C. (1993). Early bilingual lives of Deaf children. In I. Parasnis (Ed.), *Cultural and language diversity and the Deaf experience* (pp. 99–116). Cambridge, England: Cambridge University Press.

Padden, C. (1998). The ASL lexicon. *Sign Language & Linguistics, 1*(1), 39–60.

Padden, C., & Humphries, T. (1988). *Deaf in America: Voices from a culture.* Harvard University Press.

Padden, C., & LeMaster, B. (1985). An alphabet on hand: The acquisition of fingerspelling in deaf children. *Sign Language Studies, 47,* 161–172.

Paivio, A., & Csapo, K. (1969). Concrete image and verbal memory codes. *Journal of Experimental Psychology, 80,* 279–285.

Parasnis, I. (1983). Effects of parental deafness and early exposure to manual communication on the cognitive skills, English language skill, and field independence of young deaf adults. *Journal of Speech and Hearing Research, 26,* 588–594.

Parasnis, I., & Samar, V. (1985). Parafoveal attention in congenitally deaf and hearing young adults. *Brain and Cognition, 4,* 313–327.

Parasnis, I., Samar, V., Bettger, J., & Sathe, K. (1996). Does deafness lead to enhancement of visual spatial cognition in children? Negative evidence from deaf nonsigners. *Journal of Deaf Studies and Deaf Education, 1,* 145–152.

Paulesu, B., & Mehler, J. (1998). Right on in sign language. *Nature, 392,* 233–234.

Pederson, E. (1995). Language as context, language as means: Spatial cognition and habitual language use. *Cognitive Linguistics, 6,* 33–62.

Peperkamp, S., & Mehler, J. (1999). Signed and spoken language: A unique underlying system? *Language and Speech, 42,* 333–346.

Perlmutter, D. (1992). Sonority and syllable structure in American Sign Language. *Linguistic Inquiry, 23,* 407–442.

Peterson, C. G., & Siegal, M. (1995). Deafness, conversation, and theory of mind. *Journal of Child Psychology and Psychiatry, 36*(3), 459–474.

Peterson, C. G., & Siegal, M. (1999). Representing inner worlds: Theory of mind in autistic, deaf, and normal hearing children. *Psychological Science, 10*(2), 126–129.

Petitto, L. A. (1987). On the autonomy of language and gesture: Evidence from the acquisition of personal pronouns in American Sign Language. *Cognition, 27,* 1–52.

Petitto, L. A. (1988). "Language" in the prelinguistic child. In F. S. Kessel (Ed.), *The development of language and language researchers: Essays in honor of Roger Brown* (pp. 187–221). Hillsdale, NJ: Lawrence Erlbaum Associates.

Petitto, L. A. (1992). Modularity and constraints in early lexical acquisition: Evidence from children's early language and gesture. In M. Gunnar & H. Maratsos (Eds.), *Minnesota Symposia on Child Psychology, 25* (pp. 25–58). Hillsdale, NJ: Lawrence Erlbaum Associates.

Petitto, L. A. (1993). On the ontogenetic requirements for early language acquisition. In B. de Boysson-Bardies, S. de Schonen, P. Jusczyk, P. MacNeilage, & J. Morton (Eds.), *Developmental neurocognition: Speech and face processing in the first year of life* (pp. 365–383). Dordrecht, Holland: Kluwer Academic Publishers.

Petitto, L. A. (1994). Are sign languages real languages? Evidence from American Sign Language and Langue des Signes Quebecoise. *Signpost, 7,* 1–10.

Petitto, L. A. (1997). In the beginning: On the genetic and environmental factors that make early language acquisition possible. In M. Gopnik (Ed.), *The inheritance and innateness of grammars* (pp. 45–69). Mahwah, NJ: Lawrence Erlbaum Associates.

Petitto, L. A. (2000). On the biological foundations of human language. In K. Emmorey & H. Lane (Eds.), *The signs of language revisited: An anthology to honor Ursula Bellugi and Edward Klima* (pp. 449–474). Mahwah, NJ: Lawrence Erlbaum Associates.

Petitto, L. A., & Marentette, P. F. (1991). Babbling in the manual mode: Evidence for the ontogeny of language. *Science, 251,* 1493–1496.

Petitto, L. A., Zatorre, R. J., Gauna, K., Nikelski, E. J., Dostie, D., & Evans, A. (2000). Speech-like cerebral activity in profoundly deaf people processing signed languages: Implications for the neural basis of human language. *Proceedings of the National Academy of Sciences, 97*(25), 13961–13966.

Petitto, L. A., Zatorre, R. J., Nikelski, E. J., Gauna, K., Dostie, D., & Evans, A. C. (1998). By hand or by tongue: Common cerebral blood flow activation during language processing in signed and spoken languages. *NeuroImage, 7*(4), S193.

Petronio, K., & Lillo-Martin, D. (1997). WH-movement and the position of spec-CP: Evidence from American Sign Language. *Language, 73*(1), 18–57.

Pierrehumbert, J. (1980). *The phonetics and phonology of English intonation.* Unpublished doctoral dissertation, MIT.

Pinxten, R., van Dooren, I., & Harvey, F. (1983). *Anthropology of space: Explorations into the natural philosophy and semantics of the Navajo.* Philadelphia: University of Pennsylvania Press.

Pizzuto, E. (1990). The early development of deixis in American Sign Language: What is the point? In V. Volterra & C. J. Erting (Eds.), *From gesture to language in hearing and deaf children* (pp. 142–161). New York: Springer-Verlag.

Pizzuto, E., & Volterra, V. (2000). Iconicity and transparency in sign languages: A cross-linguistic cross-cultural view. In K. Emmorey & H. Lane (Eds.), *The signs of language revisited: An anthology to honor Ursula Bellugi and Edward Klima* (pp. 261–286). Mahwah, NJ: Lawrence Erlbaum Associates.

Poizner, H. (1981). Visual and "phonetic" coding of movement: Evidence from American Sign Language, *Science, 212,* 691–693.

Poizner, H. (1983). Perception of movement in American Sign Language: Effects of linguistic structure and linguistic experience. *Perception and Psychophysics, 33,* 215–231.

Poizner, H., Battison, R., & Lane, H. (1979). Cerebral asymmetry for American Sign Language: The effects of moving stimuli. *Brain and Language, 7,* 351–362.

Poizner, H., & Bellugi, U. (1984). *Hemispheric specialization for a visual–gestural language.* Paper presented at the International Society for Neuroscience, Houston, TX.

Poizner, H., Bellugi, U., & Lutes-Driscoll, V. (1981). Perception of American Sign Language in dynamic point-light displays. *Journal of Experimental Psychology: Human Perception and Performance, 7,* 430–440.

Poizner, H., Bellugi, U., & Tweney, R. D. (1981). Processing of formational, semantic, and iconic information in American Sign Language. *Journal of Experimental Psychology: Human Perception and Performance, 7,* 1146–1159.

Poizner, H., Brentari, D., Tyrone, M. E., & Kegl, J. (2000). The structure of language as motor behavior: Clues from signers with Parkinson's disease. In K. Emmorey & H. Lane (Eds.), *The signs of language revisited: An anthology to honor Ursula Bellugi and Edward Klima* (pp. 509–532). Mahwah, NJ: Lawrence Erlbaum Associates.

Poizner, H., Fok, A., & Bellugi, U. (1989). The interplay between perception of language and perception of motion. *Language Sciences, 11,* 267–287.

Poizner, H., & Kegl, J. (1992). Neural basis of language and motor behaviour: Perspectives from American Sign Language. *Aphasiology, 6*(3), 219–256.

Poizner, H., & Kegl, J. (1993). Neural disorders of the linguistic use of space and movement. *Annals of the New York Academy of Sciences, 682,* 192–213.

Poizner, H., Klima, E. S., & Bellugi, U. (1987). *What the hands reveal about the brain.* Cambridge, MA: MIT Press.

Poizner, H., & Lane, H. (1978). Discrimination of location in American Sign Language. In P. Siple (Ed.), *Understanding language through sign language research* (pp. 271–287). New York: Academic Press.

Poizner, H., & Lane, H. (1979). Cerebral asymmetry in the perception of American Sign Language. *Brain and Language, 7,* 210–226.

Poizner, H., Newkirk, D., Bellugi, U., & Klima, E. S. (1981). Representation of inflected signs from American Sign Language in short-term memory. *Memory & Cognition, 9,* 121–131.

Poizner, H., & Tallal, P. (1987). Temporal processing in deaf signers. *Brain and Language, 30,* 52–62.

Polich, L. G. (1998). *Social agency and deaf communities: A Nicaraguan case study.* Unpublished doctoral dissertation, University of Texas at Austin.

Poulin, C. (1995). Null arguments and referential shift in American Sign Language. *MIT Working Papers in Linguistics, 23,* 257–271.

Poulin, C., & Miller, C. (1995). On narrative discourse and point of view in Quebec Sign Language. In K. Emmorey & J. Reilly (Eds.), *Language, gesture, and space* (pp. 117–131). Mahwah, NJ: Lawrence Erlbaum Associates.

Posner, M. I., & Petersen, S. E. (1990). The attention system of the human brain. *Annual Review of Neuroscience, 13,* 25–42.

Prinz, P. M., & Prinz, E. A. (1979). Simultaneous acquisition of ASL and spoken English in a hearing child of deaf mother and hearing father: Phase 1—early lexical development. *Sign Language Studies, 25,* 283–296.

Prinz, P. M., & Prinz, E. A. (1983). If only you could hear what I see: Discourse development in sign language. *Discourse Processes, 8,* 1–19.

Provine, K., & Reilly, J. (1992, October). *The expression of affect in signed and spoken stories.* Presentation at the Fourth Annual Meeting of the American Psychological Society, San Diego, CA.

Ramsey, C. (1989). Language planning in deaf education. In C. Lucas (Ed.), *The sociolinguistics of the deaf community* (pp. 137–138). San Diego, CA: Academic Press.

Rauschecker, J. (1995). Compensatory plasticity and sensory substitution in the cerebral cortex, *Trends in Neurosciences, 18,* 36–43.

Rauscher, F., Krauss, R., & Chen, Y. (1996). Gesture, speech, and lexical access: The role of lexical movements in speech production. *Psychological Science, 7,* 226–231.

Reilly, J. S. (2000). Bringing affective expression into the service of language: Acquiring perspective marking in narratives. In K. Emmorey & H. Lane (Eds.), *The signs of language revisited: An anthology to honor Ursula Bellugi and Edward Klima* (pp. 415–434). Mahwah, NJ: Lawrence Erlbaum Associates.

Reilly, J. S., & Bellugi, U. (1996). Competition on the face: Affect and language in ASL motherese. *Journal of Child Language, 23,* 219–236.

Reilly, J. S., & McIntire, M. (1991). WHERE SHOE? The acquisition of conditionals in American Sign Language. *Papers and Reports on Child Language Development, 30,* 104–111.

Reilly, J. S., McIntire, M., & Anderson, D. (1994, January). *Look how's talking! Point of view and character reference in mothers' and children's ASL narratives.* Paper presented at the Boston Child Language Conference, Boston, MA.

Reilly, J. S., McIntire, M., & Bellugi, U. (1990a). The acquisition of conditionals in American Sign Language: Grammaticized facial expressions. *Applied Psycholinguistics, 11*(4), 369–392.

Reilly, J. S., McIntire, M., & Bellugi, U. (1990b). Faces: The relationship between language and affect. In V. Volterra & C. J. Erting (Eds.), *From gesture to language in hearing and deaf children* (pp. 128–141). New York: Springer-Verlag.

Reilly, J. S., McIntire, M., & Bellugi, U. (1991). Baby face: A new perspective on universals in language acquisition. In P. Siple & S. S. Fischer (Eds.), *Theoretical issues in sign language research* (pp. 9–24). Chicago, IL: University of Chicago Press.

Reilly, J. S., McIntire, M., & Seago, H. (1992). Differential expression of emotion in American Sign Language. *Sign Language Studies, 75,* 113–128.

Remmel, E., Bettger, J., & Weinberg, A. (1998, November). *The impact of ASL on theory of mind development.* Poster presented at the Theoretical Issues in Sign Language Research meeting, Washington, DC.

Reynolds, H. N. (1993). Effects of foveal stimulation on peripheral visual processing and laterality in deaf and hearing subjects. *American Journal of Psychology, 106,* 523–540.

Rhys-Jones, S. L., & Ellis, H. D. (2000). Theory of mind: Deaf and hearing children's comprehension of picture stories and judgements of social situations. *Journal of Deaf studies and Deaf Education, 5*(3), 248–261.

Richards, J. T., & Hanson, V. (1985). Visual and production similarity of the handshapes of the American manual alphabet. *Perception and Psychophyscis, 38*(4), 311–319.

Richmond-Welty, E. D., & Siple, P. (1999). Differentiating the use of gaze in bilingual–bimodal language acquisition: A comparison of two sets of twins of deaf parents. *Journal of Child Language, 26*(2), 321–338.

Roelofs, A. (1999). Phonological segments and features as planning units in speech production. *Language and Cognitive Processes, 14*(2), 173–200.

Ross, J. (1967). *Constraints on variables in syntax.* Unpublished doctoral dissertation, MIT.

Roth, J., & Kosslyn, S. M. 1988. Construction of the third dimension in mental imagery. *Cognitive Psychology, 20,* 344–361.

Roy, C. B. (1989). Features of discourse in an American Sign Language lecture. In C. Lucas (Ed.), *The sociolinguistics of the Deaf community* (pp. 231–251). San Diego, CA: Academic Press.

Rubens, A. B., Mahowald, M. W., & Hutton, T. (1976). Asymmetry of the lateral (sylvian) fissures in man. *Neurology, 26,* 620–624.

Russell, P. A., Hosie, J. A., Gray, C. D., Scott, C., & Hunter, N. (1998). The development of theory of mind in deaf children. *Journal of Child Psychology and Psychiatry, 39*(6), 903–910.

Sacks, H., Schegloff, E., & Jefferson, G. (1974). A simplist systematics for the organization of turn-taking in conversation. *Language, 50,* 696–735.

Sanders, G., Wright, H. V., & Ellis, C. (1989). Cerebral lateralization of language in deaf and hearing people. *Brain and Language, 36,* 555–579.

Sandler, W. (1986). The spreading hand autosegment of American Sign Language. *Sign Language Studies, 50,* 1–28.

Sandler, W. (1987). Assimilation and feature hierarchy of American Sign Language. In *CLS 23,* Vol. 2, *Parasession on Autosegmental and Metrical Phonology.* Chicago Linguistic Society: University of Chicago, IL.

Sandler, W. (1989). *Phonological representation of the sign: Linearity and nonlinearity in American Sign Language.* Dordrecht, Holland: Foris Publications.

Sandler, W. (1990). Temporal aspects and ASL phonology. In S. D. Fischer & P. Siple (Eds.), *Theoretical issues in sign language research* (pp. 7–35). Chicago, IL: University of Chicago Press.

Sandler, W. (1993). A sonority cycle in American Sign Language. *Phonology, 10*(2), 243–279.

Sandler, W. (1995). One phonology or two? Sign language and phonological theory. *Glot International, 1*(3), 3–8.

Sandler, W. (1999a). Cliticization and prosodic words in a sign language. In T. A. Hall & U. Kleinhenz (Eds.), *Studies on the phonological word* (pp. 223–254). Amsterdam: John Benjamins.

Sandler, W. (1999b). Prosody in two natural language modalities. *Language and Speech, 42*(2–3), 127–142.

Sandler, W. (1999c). The medium and the message: Prosodic interpretation of linguistic content in Israeli Sign Language. *Sign Language and Linguistics, 2,* 187–215.

Sandler, W., & Lillo-Martin, D. (in press). *Sign language and linguistic universals.* Cambridge, England: Cambridge University Press.

San Jose, L., Corina, D., Ackerman, D., Guillemin, A., & Braun, A. (2000, April). *Positron emission tomography (PET) during American Sign Language (ASL) production.* Poster presented at the Cognitive Neuroscience Society meeting, San Francisco, CA.

Savin, H. B. (1963). Word-frequency effect and errors in the perception of speech. *Journal of Acoustical Society of America, 35*, 200–206.

Schegloff, E., Jefferson, G., & Sacks, H. (1977). The preference for self-correction in the organization of repair in conversation. *Language, 53*, 361–382.

Schein, J. (1989). *At home among strangers*. Washington, DC: Gallaudet University Press.

Schein, J., & Delk, M. (1974). *The deaf population of the United States*. Silver Spring, MD: National Association of the Deaf.

Schein, J., & Stewart, D. (1995). *Language in motion: Exploring the nature of sign*. Washington, DC: Gallaudet University Press.

Schembri, A. (in press). Rethinking the notion of classifier predicates in signed languages. In K. Emmorey (Ed.), *Perspectives on classifier constructions in sign languages*. Mahwah, NJ: Lawrence Erlbaum Associates.

Schermer, T. (1990). *In search of a language: Influences from spoken Dutch on Sign Language of the Netherlands*. Delft: Eburon.

Schermer, T. (in press). The role of mouthings in Sign Language of the Netherlands: Some implications for the production of sign language dictionaries. In P. Boyes-Braem & R. Sutton-Spence (Eds.), *The hands are the head of the mouth: The mouth as articulator in sign languages*. Hamburg, Germany: Signum Press.

Schick, B. (1990a). Classifier predicates in American Sign Language. *International Journal of Sign Linguistics, 1*(1), 15–40.

Schick, B. (1990b). The effects of morphological complexity on phonological simplification in ASL. *Sign Language Studies, 66*, 25–41.

Schick, B. (1990c). The effects of morphosyntactic structure on the acquisition of classifier predicates in ASL. In C. Lucas (Ed.), *Sign language research: Theoretical issues* (pp. 358–371). Washington, DC: Gallaudet University Press.

Schildroth, A. (1976). The relationship of nonverbal intelligence test scores to selected characteristics of hearing impaired students. In C. Williams (Ed.), *Proceedings of the Third Gallaudet Symposium on Research in Deafness: Educational development research programs*. Washington, DC: Gallaudet College Press.

Schlesinger, H. S., & Meadow, K. P. (1972). *Sound and sign: Childhood deafness and mental health*. Berkeley: University of California Press.

Schley, S. (1991). Infant discrimination of gestural classes: Precursors of ASL acquisition. *Sign Language Studies, 72*, 277–296.

Schober, M. F. (1993). Spatial perspective-taking in conversation. *Cognition, 47*, 1–24.

Schwartz, B. (1999). Sparkling at the tip of the tongue: The etiology of tip-of-the-tongue phenomenology. *Psychological Bulletin & Review, 6*(3), 379–393.

Schwartz, C. (1979). *Discrete vs. continuous encoding in American Sign Language and nonlinguistic gestures*. Unpublished manuscript, University of California, San Diego.

Senghas, A. (1994). Nicaragua's lessons for language acquisition. *Signpost, 7*, 32–39.

Senghas, A., (1995a). *Children's contribution to the birth of Nicaraguan Sign Language*. Unpublished doctoral dissertation, MIT.

Senghas, A. (1995b). The development of Nicaraguan Sign Language via the language acquisition process. In D. McLaughlin & S. McEwen (Eds.), *Proceedings of the 19th Annual Boston University Conference on Language Development* (pp. 543–552). Somerville, MA: Cascadilla Press.

Senghas, A. (2000). The development of early spatial morphology in Nicaraguan Sign Language. In S. C. Howell, S. A. Fish, & T. Keith-Lucas (Eds.), *The proceedings of the Boston University Conference on Language Development, 24*, 696–707.

Senghas, A., & Coppola, M. (2001). Children creating language: The emergence of linguistic structure in Nicaraguan Sign Language. *Psychological Science, 12*(4), 323–328.

Senghas, A., Coppola, M., Newport, E. L., & Supalla, T. (1997). Apparent structure in Nicaraguan Sign Language: The emergence of grammatical devices. In E. Hughes, M.

Hughes, & A. Greenhilll (Eds.), *Proceedings of the Boston University Conference on Language Development, 21*. Boston, MA: Cascadilla Press.

Senghas, R., & Kegl, J. (1994). Social considerations in the emergence of Idioma de Signos Nicaragüense. *Signpost, 7*, 24–32.

Shand, M. (1980). *Short-term coding processes in congenitally deaf signers of ASL: Natural language considerations*. Unpublished doctoral dissertation, University of California, San Diego.

Shand, M., & Klima, E. (1981). Nonauditory suffix effects congenitally in deaf signers of American Sign Language. *Journal of Experimental Psychology: Human Learning and Memory, 7*(6), 464–474.

Shepard, R., & Metzler, J. (1971). Mental rotation of three-dimensional objects. *Science, 171*, 701–703.

Shepard-Kegl, J. (1985). *Locative relations in American Sign Language word formation, syntax, and discourse*. Unpublished doctoral dissertation, MIT, Cambridge, MA.

Shiffrar, M., & Freyd, J. J. (1990). Apparent motion of the human body. *Psychological Science, 3*, 96–100.

Shiffrar, M., & Freyd, J. J. (1993). Timing and apparent motion path choice with human body photographs. *Psychological Science, 4*, 379–384.

Shroyer, E., & Shroyer, S. (1984). *Signs across America: A look at regional differences in American Sign Language*. Washington, DC: Gallaudet University Press.

Siedlecki, T., & Bonvillian, J. D. (1993). Location, handshape, and movement: Young children's acquisition of the formational properties of American Sign Language. *Sign Language Studies, 78*, 31–52.

Siedlecki, T., & Bonvillian, J. D. (1997). Young children's acquisition of the handshape aspect of American Sign Language signs: Parental report findings. *Applied Psycholinguistics, 18*, 17–39.

Simpson, G. (1994). Context and the processing of lexically ambiguous words. In M. A. Gernsbacher (Ed.), *Handbook of psycholinguistics* (pp. 359–374). San Diego, CA: Academic Press.

Singleton, J. L. (1989). *Restructuring of language from impoverished input: Evidence for linguistic compensation*. Unpublished doctoral dissertation, University of Illinois at Urbana-Champaign.

Singleton, J. L., & Newport, E. L. (in press). When learners surpass their models: The acquisition of American Sign Language from inconsistent input. *Cognitive Psychology*.

Siple, P. (1978). Visual constraints for sign language communication. *Sign Language Studies, 19*, 97–112.

Siple, P. (2000). Attentional resources and working memory: A new framework for the study of the impact of deafness on cognition. In K. Emmorey & H. Lane (Eds.), *The signs of language revisited: An anthology to honor Ursula Bellugi and Edward Klima* (pp. 115–134). Mahwah, NJ: Lawrence Erlbaum Associates.

Siple, P., & Akamatsu, C. T. (1991). Emergence of American Sign Language in a set of fraternal twins. In P. Siple & S. D. Fischer (Eds.), *Theoretical issues in sign language research* (pp. 25–40). Chicago, IL: University of Chicago Press.

Siple, P., Richmond-Welty, E. D., Howe, J. N., Berwanger, P., & Japser, J. E. (1994, January). *Gaze, joint attention and interaction in twins with deaf parents*. Paper presented at the Boston University Conference on Language Development, Boston, MA.

Sisco, F. H., & Anderson, R. J. (1980). Deaf children's performance on the WISC–R relative to hearing status of parents and child-rearing experiences. *American Annals of the Deaf, 125*, 923–930.

Slobin, D. I. (1973). Cognitive prerequisites for the development of grammar. In C. A. Ferguson & D. I. Slobin (Eds.), *Studies of child language development* (pp. 177–208). New York: Holt, Rinehart, & Winston.

Slobin, D. I. (1991). Learning to think for speaking: Native language, cognition, and rhetorical style. *Pragmatics, 1,* 7–26.

Slobin, D. (1996). From "thought and language" to "thinking for speaking." In J. J. Gumperz & S. C. Levinson (Eds.), *Rethinking linguistic relativity* (pp. 70–96). Cambridge, England: Cambridge University Press.

Slobin, D. I., Hoiting, N., Kuntze, M., Lindert, R., Weinberg, A., Pyers, J., Anthony, M., Biederman, Y., & Thumann, H. (in press). A cognitive/functional perspective on the acquisition of "classifiers." In K. Emmorey (Ed.), *Perspectives on classifier constructions in sign languages.* Mahwah, NJ: Lawrence Erlbaum Associates.

Smith, J. D., Reisberg, D., & Wilson, M. (1992). Subvocalization and auditory imagery: Interactions between the inner ear and the inner voice. In D. Reisberg (Ed.), *Auditory imagery.* Hillsdale, NJ: Lawrence Erlbaum Associates.

Smith, L. B., Quittner, A. L., Osberger, M. J., & Miyamoto, R. (1998). Audition and visual attention: The developmental trajectory in deaf and hearing populations. *Developmental Psychology, 34,* 840–850.

Smith, V. L., & Clark, H. H. (1993). On the course of answering questions. *Journal of Memory and Language, 32,* 25–38.

Smolensky, P. (1996). On the comprehension/production dilemma in child language. *Linguistic Inquiry, 27,* 720–731.

Snow, C. (1972). Mother's speech to children learning language. *Child Development, 43,* 349–365.

Söderfeldt, B., Ingvar, M., Rönnberg, J., Eriksson, L., Serrander, M., & Stone-Elander, S. (1997). Signed and spoken language perception studied by positron emission tomography. *Neurology, 49,* 82–87.

Söderfeldt, B., Rönnberg, J., & Risberg, J. (1994). Regional cerebral blood flow in sign language users. *Brain and Language, 46,* 59–68.

Spencer, P. E., Bodner-Johnson, B., & Gutfreund, M. K. (1992). Interaction with infants with a hearing loss: What can we learn from mothers who are deaf? *Journal of Early Intervention, 16*(1), 64–78.

Stack, K. M. (1999). *Innovation by a child acquiring Signing Exact English II.* Unpublished doctoral dissertation, University of California at Los Angeles.

Stanners, R., Neisser, J., Hernon, W., & Hall, R. (1979). Memory representation for morphologically related words. *Journal of Verbal Learning and Verbal Behavior, 18,* 399–412.

Stein, J. (1984). *The Random House college dictionary.* New York: Random House, Inc.

Steeds, L., Rowe, K., & Dowker, A. (1997). Deaf children's understanding of beliefs and desires. *Journal of Deaf Studies and Deaf Education, 2*(3), 185–195.

Stevens, K., & Blumstein, S. (1981). The search for invariant acoustic correlates of phonetic features. In P. D. Eimas & J. L. Miller (Eds.), *Perspectives on the study of speech* (pp. 1–38), Hillsdale, NJ: Lawrence Erlbaum Associates.

Stivalet, P., Moreno, Y., Richard, J., Barraud, P.-A., & Raphel, C. (1998). Differences in visual search tasks between congenitally deaf and normally hearing adults. *Cognitive Brain Research, 6,* 227–232.

Stokoe, W. (1960). Sign language structure: An outline of the visual communication systems of the American Deaf. *Studies in linguistics, occasional papers 8.* Silver Spring, MD: Linstok Press.

Stokoe, W., Casterline, D., & Croneberg, C. (1965). *A dictionary of American Sign Language on linguistic principles.* Washington, DC: Gallaudet College Press.

Strauss, E., & Moscovitch, M. (1981). Perception of facial expression. *Brain and Language, 13,* 308–322.

Stungis, J. (1981). Identification and discrimination of handshape in American Sign Language. *Perception and Psychophysics, 29*(3), 261–276.

Supalla, S. (1991). Manually coded English: The modality question in signed language development. In P. Siple & S. D. Fischer (Eds.), *Theoretical issues in sign language research* (pp. 85–109). Chicago, IL: University of Chicago Press.

Supalla, T. (1978). Morphology of verbs of motion and location in American Sign Language. In F. Caccamise (Ed.), *American Sign Language in a bilingual, bicultural context: Proceedings of the National Symposium on Sign Language Research and Teaching* (pp. 27–45). Silver Spring, MD: National Association of the Deaf.

Supalla, T. (1982). *Structure and acquisition of verbs of motion and location in American Sign Language*. Unpublished doctoral dissertation, University of California, San Diego.

Supalla, T. (1986). The classifier system in American Sign Language. In C. Craig (Ed.), *Noun classification and categorization*. Amsterdam: John Benjamins North America.

Supalla, T. (1990). Serial verbs of motion in ASL. In S. D. Fischer & P. Siple (Eds.), *Theoretical issues in sign language research* (pp. 127–152). Chicago, IL: University of Chicago Press.

Supalla, T., & Newport, E. (1978). How many seats in a chair? The derivation of nouns and verbs in American Sign Language. In P. Siple (Ed.), *Understanding language through sign language research* (pp. 181–214). New York: Academic Press.

Sutton-Spence, R., & Boyes Braem, P. (in press). Introduction. In P. Boyes-Braem & R. Sutton-Spence (Eds.), *The hands are the head of the mouth: The mouth as articulator in sign languages*. Hamburg: Signum Press.

Sutton-Spence, R., & Day, L. (in press). Mouthings and mouth gestures in British Sign Language (BSL). In P. Boyes-Braem & R. Sutton-Spence (Eds.), *The hands are the head of the mouth: The mouth as articulator in sign languages*. Hamburg: Signum Press.

Sutton-Spence, R., & Woll, B. (1999). *The linguistics of British Sign Language: An introduction*. Cambridge, England: Cambridge University Press.

Talbot, K. F., & Haude, R. H. (1993). The relationship between sign language skill and spatial visualization ability: Mental rotation of three-dimensional objects. *Perceptual and Motor Skills, 77*, 1387–1391.

Tallal, P., Miller, S., & Fitch, R. H. (1993). Neurobiological basis of speech: A case for the preeminence of temporal processing. *Annals of the New York Academy of Sciences, 682*, 27–47.

Talmy, L. (1983). How language structures space. In H. Pick & L. Acredolo (Eds.), *Spatial orientation: Theory, research, and application* (pp. 225–282). New York: Plenum.

Talmy, L. (1996). Fictive motion in language and "ception." In P. Bloom, M. Peterson, L. Nadel, & M. Garrett (Eds.), *Language and space* (pp. 211–276). Cambridge, MA: MIT Press.

Talmy, L. (2000). *Toward a cognitive semantics: Vol. 1. Concept structuring systems*. Cambridge, MA: MIT Press.

Talmy, L. (in press). Spatial structuring in spoken language and its relation to that in sign language. In K. Emmorey (Ed.), *Perspectives on classifier constructions*. Mahwah, NJ: Lawrence Erlbaum Associates.

Tannen, D. (1986). Introducing constructed dialogue in Greek and American conversational and literacy narratives. In F. Coulmas (Ed.), *Reported speech across languages* (pp. 311–332). The Hague: Mouton.

Tannen, D. (1990). *You just don't understand: Women and men in conversation*. New York: Morrow.

Taub, S. (2001). *Language from the body: Iconicity and metaphor in American Sign Language*. Cambridge, England: Cambridge University Press.

Taylor, H. A., & Tversky, B. (1992). Spatial mental models derived from survey and route descriptions. *Journal of Memory and Language, 31*, 261–292.

Taylor, H. A., & Tversky, B. (1996). Perspective in spatial descriptions. *Journal of Memory and Language, 35*(3), 371–391.

Tervoort, B. T. M. (1953). *Structurele analyse van visueel taalgebruik binnen een groep dove kinderen* [Structural analysis of visual language use in a group of deaf children]. Amsterdam: Noord-Hollandsche Uitgevers Maatschappij.

Thelen, E. (1979). Rhythmical stereotypes in normal hearing infants. *Animal Behaviour, 27*, 699–715.

Thelen, E. (1991). Motor aspects of emergent speech: A dynamic approach. In N. A. Krasnegor, D. M. Rumbaugh, R. L. Schiefelbusch, & M. Studdert-Kennedy (Eds.), *Biological and behavioral determinants of language development* (pp. 339–362). Hillsdale, NJ: Lawrence Erlbaum Associates.

Tomasello, M., & Farrar, M. J. (1986). Joint attention and early language. *Child Development, 57*, 1454–1463.

Trask, L. (1993). *A Dictionary of grammatical terms in linguistics.* New York: Routledge.

Tversky, B., Kugelmass, S., & Winter, A. (1991). Cross-cultural and developmental trends in graphic productions. *Cognitive Psychology, 23*, 515–557.

Tyrone, M. E., Kegl, J., & Poizner, H. (1999). Interarticulator co-ordination in Deaf signers with Parkinson's disease. *Neuropsychologia, 37*, 1271–1283.

Ullman, M., Corkin, S., Coppola, M., Hickok, G., Growdon, J. H., Koroshetz, W. J., & Pinker, S. (1997). A neural dissociation within language: Evidence that the mental dictionary is part of declarative memory, and that grammatical rules are processed by the procedural system. *Journal of Cognitive Neuroscience, 9*, 266–276.

Ungerleider, L. G., & Mishkin, M. (1982). Two cortical visual systems. In D. J. Ingle, M. A. Goodale, & R. J. W. Mansfield (Eds.), *Analysis of visual behavior* (pp. 549–589). Cambridge, MA: MIT Press.

Uyechi, L. (1996). *The geometry of visual phonology.* Stanford, CA: CSLI Publications. (Original work published 1994)

Vaid, J., Bellugi, U., & Poizner, H. (1989). Hand dominance for signing: Clues to brain lateralization of language. *Brain and Language, 27*, 949–960.

Vaid, J., & Corina, D. (1989). Visual field asymmetries in numerical size comparisons of digits, words, and signs. *Brain and Language, 36*, 117–126.

Valli, C., & Lucas, C. (1995). *Linguistics of American Sign Language: An introduction* (2nd ed.). Washington, DC: Gallaudet University Press.

Vandenberg, S. G., & Kuse, A. R. (1978). Mental rotations, a group test of three-dimensional spatial visualization. *Perceptual and Motor Skills, 47*, 599–604.

van der Hulst, H. (1993). Units in the analysis of signs. *Phonology, 10*, 209–241.

van der Hulst, H. (1995). The composition of handshapes. In *Working papers in linguistics 23* (pp. 1–17). Department of Linguistics, University of Trondheim, Dragvoll.

van der Hulst, H. (1996). On the other hand. *Lingua, 98*, 121–143.

van der Hulst, H. (in press). Modularity and modality in phonology. In N. Burton-Roberts, P. Carr, & G. Cocherty (Eds.), *Phonological knowledge: Its nature and status.* Oxford University Press.

van Gijn, I., Kita, S., & van der Hulst, H. (in press). How phonetic is the symmetry condition in sign language? In V. J. van Heuven, H. G. van der Hulst, & J. M. van de Weije (Eds.), *Phonetics and phonology: Selected papers of the Fourth HIL Phonology Conference.*

van Hoek, K. (1992). Conceptual spaces and pronominal reference in American Sign Language. *Nordic Journal of Linguistics, 15*, 183–199.

van Hoek, K. (1996). Conceptual locations for reference in American Sign Language. In G. Fauconnier & E. Sweetser (Eds.), *Spaces, worlds, and grammar* (pp. 334–350). Chicago, IL: University of Chicago Press.

van Hoek, K., Bellugi, U., & Fok, A. (1986). *Phonology in Chinese Sign Language.* Unpublished manuscript, The Salk Institute for Biological Studies.

van Hoek, K., O'Grady, L., & Bellugi, U. (1987). Morphological innovation in the acquisition of American Sign Language. In E. Clark (Ed.), *Papers and reports on child language development*. Stanford, CA: CSLI Publications.

van Hoek, K., O'Grady-Batch, L., Norman, F., & Bellugi, U. (1989). *Perspective shift and serial verbs in ASL*. Unpublished manuscript, The Salk Institute.

Vernon, M. (1969). Sociological and psychological factors associated with hearing loss. *Journal of Speech and Hearing Research, 12*, 541–563.

Vogt-Svendsen, M. (1983). Lip movements in Norwegian Sign Language. In J. G. Kyle & B. Woll (Eds.), *Language in sign* (pp. 85–96). London: Croom Helm.

Vogt-Svendsen, M. (in press). A comparison of mouth gestures and mouthings in Norwegian Sign Language (NSL). In P. Boyes-Braem & R. Sutton-Spence (Eds.), *The hands are the head of the mouth: The mouth as articulator in sign languages*. Hamburg, Germany: Signum Press.

Volterra, V., & Caselli, M. (1985). From gestures and vocalizations to signs and words. In W. Stokoe & V. Volterra (Eds.), *SLR '83: Proceedings of the III International Symposium on Sign Language Research* (pp. 1–9). Silver Spring, MD: Linstok Press.

Volterra, V., & Iverson, J. (1995). When do modality factors affect the course of language acquisition. In K. Emmorey & J. Reilly (Eds.), *Language, gesture, and space* (pp. 371–390). Mahwah, NJ: Lawrence Erlbaum Associates.

Wall, L., & Morgan, W. (1994). *Navajo-English dictionary*. New York: Hippocrene Books, Inc. (Original work published 1958)

Wallin, L. (1994). *Polysynthetic signs in Swedish Sign Language* (English summary). Stockholm, Sweden: Stockholm University Press.

Wang, X.-L., Mylander, C., & Goldin-Meadow, S. (1995). The resilience of language: Mother–child interaction and its effect on the gesture systems of Chinese and American deaf children. In K. Emmorey & J. Reilly (Eds.), *Language, gesture, and space* (pp. 411–433). Mahwah, NJ: Lawrence Erlbaum Associates.

Warrington, E. (1984). *Recognition Memory Test*. Windsor, England: NFER-NELSON Publishing Company, Ltd.

Waxman, R. P., & Spencer, P. E. (1997). What mothers do to support infant visual attention: Sensitivities to age and hearing status. *Journal of Deaf Studies and Deaf Education, 2*(2), 104–114.

Weber-Fox, C. M., & Neville, H. J. (1996). Maturational constraints on functional specializations for language processing: ERP and behavioral evidence in bilingual speakers. *Journal of Cognitive Neuroscience, 8*, 231–256.

Weber-Fox, C. M., & Neville, H. J. (1999). Functional neural subsystems are differentially affected by delays in second language immersion: ERP and behavioral evidence in bilinguals. In D. Birdsong (Ed.), *Second language acquisition and the critical period hypothesis* (pp. 23–38). Mahwah, NJ: Lawrence Erlbaum Associates.

Wellman, H. (1990). *The child's theory of mind*. Cambridge, MA: MIT Press.

Werker, J. (1994). Cross-language speech perception: Developmental change does not involve loss. In J. Goodman & H. Nusbaum (Eds.), *The development of speech perception: The transition from speech sounds to spoken words* (pp. 95–120). Cambridge, MA: MIT Press.

Werker, J., & Tees, R. C. (1983). Developmental changes across childhood in the perception of non-native speech sounds. *Canadian Journal of Psychology, 37*, 278–286.

Wilbur, R. B. (1987). *American Sign Language: Linguistic and applied dimensions* (2nd ed.). Boston, MA: College-Hill.

Wilbur, R. B. (1991). Intonation and focus in American Sign Language. In Y. No & M. Libucha (Eds.), *ESCOL-90: Proceedings of the Seventh Eastern States Conference on Linguistics* (pp. 320–331). Columbus: Ohio State University Press.

Wilbur, R. B. (1993). Syllables and segments: Hold the Movements and move the Holds! In G. Coulter (Ed.), *Phonetics and phonology: Current issues in ASL phonology* (pp. 135–168). San Diego, CA: Academic Press.

Wilbur, R. B. (1994). Eyeblinks and ASL phrase structure. *Sign Language Studies, 84*, 221–240.

Wilbur, R. B. (2000). Phonological and prosodic layering of non-manuals in American Sign Language. In K. Emmorey & H. Lane (Eds.), *The signs of language revisited: An anthology to honor Ursula Bellugi and Edward Klima* (pp. 215–243). Mahwah, NJ: Lawrence Erlbaum Associates.

Wilbur, R. B., Bernstein, M. E., & Kantor, R. (1985). The semantic domain of classifiers in American Sign Language. *Sign Language Studies, 46*, 1–38.

Wilcox, P. (1993). *Metaphorical mapping in American Sign Language*. Unpublished doctoral dissertation, University of New Mexico.

Wilcox, P. (2000). *Metaphor in American Sign Language*. Washington, DC: Gallaudet University Press.

Wilcox, S. (1992). *The phonetics of fingerspelling*. Philadelphia: John Benjamins.

Wilson, M. (2001a). The case for sensorimotor coding in working memory. *Psychonomic Bulletin & Review, 8*, 44–57.

Wilson, M. (2001b). The impact of sign language expertise on perceived path of apparent motion. In M. D. Clark & M. Marschark (Eds.), *Context, cognition, and deafness* (pp. 38–48). Washington, DC: Gallaudet University Press.

Wilson, M., Bettger, J., Niculae, I., & Klima, E. (1997). Modality of language shapes working memory: Evidence from digit span and spatial span in ASL signers. *Journal of Deaf Studies and Deaf Education, 2*, 150–160.

Wilson, M., & Emmorey, K. (1997a). A visual-spatial "phonological loop" in working memory: Evidence from American Sign Language. *Memory and Cognition, 25*(3), 313–320.

Wilson, M., & Emmorey, K. (1997b). Working memory for sign language: A window into the architecture of working memory. *Journal of Deaf Studies and Deaf Education, 2*(3), 123–132.

Wilson, M., & Emmorey, K. (1998). A "word length effect" for sign language: Further evidence on the role of language in structuring working memory. *Memory and Cognition, 26*(3), 584–590.

Wilson, M., & Emmorey, K. (2000). When does modality matter? Evidence from ASL on the nature of working memory. In K. Emmorey & H. Lane (Eds.), *The signs of language revisited: An anthology to honor Ursula Bellugi and Edward Klima* (pp. 135–142). Mahwah, NJ: Lawrence Erlbaum Associates.

Wilson, M., & Emmorey, K. (2001). Functional consequences of modality: Spatial coding in working memory for signs. In V. Dively, M. Metzger, S. Taub, & A. M. Baer (Eds.), *Sign languages: Discoveries from international research* (pp. 91–99). Washington, DC: Gallaudet University Press.

Winston, E. A. (1989, July). *Timelines in ASL*. Paper presented at *The Deaf Way*, Washington, DC.

Winston, E. A. (1991). Spatial referencing and cohesion in an American Sign Language text. *Sign Language Studies, 73*, 397–410.

Winston, E. A. (1993). *Spatial mapping in comparative discourse frames in an ASL lecture*. Unpublished doctoral dissertation, Georgetown University, Washington, DC.

Winston, E. A. (1995). Spatial mapping in comparative discourse frames. In K. Emmorey & J. Reilly (Eds.), *Language, gesture, and space* (pp. 87–114). Mahwah, NJ: Lawrence Erlbaum Associates.

Wolff, A. B., Sass, K. J., & Keiden, J. (1994). Case report of an intracarotid amobarbital procedure performed on a deaf patient. *Journal of Clinical Experimental Neuropsychology, 16*, 15–20.

Wolff, A. B., & Thatcher, R. W. (1990). Cortical reorganization in deaf children. *Journal of Clinical and Experimental Neuropsychology, 12*, 209–221.

Woll, B. (in press). The sign that dares to speak its name: Echo phonology in British Sign Language (BSL). In P. Boyes-Braem & R. Sutton-Spence (Eds.), *The hands are the head of the mouth: The mouth as articulator in sign languages*. Hamburg, Germany: Signum Press.

Woll, B., & Sieratzki, J. S. (1998). Echo phonology: Signs of a link between gesture and speech. *Behavioral and Brain Sciences, 21*(4), 531–532.

Woodward, J. (1976). Black southern signing. *Language in Society, 5,* 211–218.

Woodward, J. (1978). Historical basis of American Sign Language. In P. Siple (Ed.), *Understanding language through sign language research* (pp. 333–348). New York: Academic Press.

Woodward, J. (2000). Sign languages and sign language families in Thailand and Viet Nam. In K. Emmorey & H. Lane (Eds.), *The signs of language revisited: An anthology to honor Ursula Bellugi and Edward Klima* (pp. 23–47). Mahwah, NJ: Lawrence Erlbaum Associates.

Yates, F. A. (1966). *The art of memory.* Chicago: Chicago University Press.

Yau, S.-C. (1987). Chinese Sign Language. In J. van Cleve (Ed.), *Gallaudet encyclopedia of deaf people and deafness, Vol. 3.* New York: McGraw-Hill.

Yin, R. K. (1969). Looking at upside-down faces. *Journal of Experimental Psychology, 81,* 141–145.

Yoshinaga-Itano, C., Sedey, A., Coulter, D., & Mehl, A. (1998). Language of early and later-identified children with hearing loss. *American Academy of Pediatrics, 105,* 1161–1171.

Young, A. W., & Ellis, A. (1985). Different methods of lexical access for words presented in the left and right visual hemifields. *Brain and Language, 24,* 326–358.

Young, A. W., Rowland, D., Calder, A. J., Etcoff, N. L., Seth, A., & Perrett, D. (1997). Facial expression megamix: Tests of dimensional and category accounts of emotion recognition. *Cognition, 63,* 271–313.

Zeshan, U. (2000, July). *Sign language typology—the cross linguistic study of sign languages.* Workshop presented at the Theoretical Issues in Sign Language Research meeting, Amsterdam, The Netherlands.

Zimmer, J. (1989). Toward a description of register variation in American Sign Language. In C. Lucas (Ed.), *The sociolinguistics of the Deaf community* (pp. 253–272). San Diego, CA: Academic Press.

Zimmer, J., & Patschke, C. (1990). A class of determiners in ASL. In C. Lucas (Ed.), *Sign language research, theoretical issues* (pp. 201–210). Washington, DC: Gallaudet University Press.

Zwiebel, A. (1987). More on the effects of early manual communication on the cognitive development of deaf children. *American Annals of the Deaf, 132,* 16–20.

Zwitserlood, I. (1996). *Who'll handle the object?* Unpublished master's thesis, Utrecht University, The Netherlands.

Author Index

A

Aarons, D., 44
Ackerman, D., 279, 284
Acredolo, L. P., 173, 189
Ahlgren, I., 183
Akamatsu, C. T., 19, 172, 190, 202
Allan, K., 87, 88
Anderson, D., 48, 49, 51, 183, 184, 185, 200
Anderson, R. J., 219
Anderson, S. R., 14, 23, 42, 62, 134
Ann, J., 22, 175
Anthony, M., 189, 195, 196, 197, 198
Aramburo, A., 9
Archibald, Y., 283
Armstrong, D. F., 161
Arnold, P., 253, 254
Aronoff, M., 58, 133
Astington, J. W., 222
Atteneave, F., 237
Ayres, T., 234

B

Baars, B. J., 158
Baddeley, A. D., 227, 228, 229, 230, 231, 232, 233, 237
Bahan, B., 7, 8, 41, 44, 48, 54, 55, 56, 58, 61, 62, 65, 66, 70, 102, 153, 181
Baker, C., 46, 48, 64, 91, 154
Baker, M., 90
Baker-Schenk, C., 46
Balogh, J., 142

Baron-Cohen, S., 221
Barraud, P.-A., 245
Bartini, M., 221, 222
Bates, E., 173, 182, 211
Battison, R., 19, 30, 36, 38, 86, 277, 291, 308
Bavelier, D., 245, 246, 280, 294, 313
Baynton, D. C., 3
Beaman, P., 237
Beattie, G., 167
Bebko, J. M., 220
Beeman, M., 296
Bell, M. A., 220
Bellugi, U., 14, 17, 18, 24, 39, 46, 69, 105, 118, 119, 120, 122, 131, 139, 140, 141, 157, 158, 159, 169, 180, 181, 184, 185, 186, 187, 188, 192, 194, 199, 201, 202, 213, 215, 220, 224, 225, 228, 229, 230, 234, 239, 246, 247, 248, 249, 251, 252, 258, 259, 260, 261, 263, 264, 265, 266, 267, 272, 273, 275, 276, 277, 278, 279, 280, 282, 283, 284, 285, 286, 287, 288, 289, 290, 291, 292, 293, 294, 295, 296, 297, 298, 299, 300, 301, 302, 303, 305, 306, 307, 308, 313
Benedicto, E., 80
Benigni, L., 173, 182
Benson, P. J., 123
Benton, A. L., 251
Berenz, N., 53
Bergman, B., 39, 88, 133
Bernhardt, B. H., 176

Subject Index